TANGLED BYLINES

TANGLED BYLINES

A Father and Son Cover the Twentieth Century

Clyde H. Farnsworth

UNIVERSITY OF MISSOURI PRESS
Columbia

Copyright © 2017 by
The Curators of the University of Missouri
University of Missouri Press, Columbia, Missouri 65211
Printed and bound in the United States of America
All rights reserved. First printing, 2017.

ISBN: 978-0-8262-2108-7
Library of Congress Catalog Number: 2016960887

∞™ This paper meets the requirements of the
American National Standard for Permanence of Paper
for Printed Library Materials, Z39.48, 1984.

Typefaces: Minion, Frutiger

To Barbara Blaha Farnsworth, my former wife, whose fine bookstore, uphill from the covered bridge over the Housatonic River in West Cornwall, Connecticut, has long been a beacon for a threatened species on the planet, the bibliophile.

Life can be only understood backwards, but it must be lived forward.

—Søren Kierkegaard

History is the shadow cast by the dead. So long as there's light, the shadow will fall.

—Jill Lepore

Contents

Preface   ix

1   Caps and Rockers   3

2   The Crucible   7

3   A Faultless Start   11

4   Cleveland   17

5   Crime and Punishment   30

6   Dad's Whistle   35

7   Ticket to Ride   46

8   Passage to India   62

9   Cathay   67

10   Spin the War   79

11   Airfields of Dreams   83

12   Three Generals and a Generalissimo   92

13   Dolly   99

14   Track of the CAT   108

15   The Fall   113

16   Aftermath   127

17	Fallout	134
18	Reconnections	141
19	South American Way	151
20	Top of the News	162
21	Vienna	166
22	A Son's Story	174
23	Dance of the Apprentices	177
24	England A-Go-Go	182
25	Mission Impossible	192
26	A Death on the Rhine	197
27	One Prague Summer	204
28	Is Paris Worth a Jag?	219
29	Shivaree	226
30	When the Music Stops	233
31	Back to the Future	240
32	Home Again	246
33	Trade Winds	260
34	Merry-Go-Round	266
35	O Canada!	269
36	Oz	278
	Bibliography	287
	Index	289

Preface

A TABLET BY the entrance to the Foreign Correspondents Club of Hong Kong shows Clyde H. Farnsworth, *New York Herald Tribune,* atop a list of club presidents since 1949, when Mao Tse-tung swept to power in China. That's my name, all right, along with the name of the paper I worked for before the *New York Times,* but in 1949 I was a world away in New Haven, Connecticut. My father, who formerly wrote for the Associated Press (AP), Scripps Howard News Service, and the *Chicago Tribune,* never reported for the *Herald Trib,* but he did write briefly for the *Times* as Clyde A. Farnsworth.

The year before Mao's takeover, my father was elected president of the Foreign Correspondents Club of Shanghai. As swaths of northern China fell to the Red blitz, he reported on that civil war while steering the club through harrowing realpolitik. Mao's men, sweeping through Peking in January 1949, arrested Spencer Moosa, an AP colleague, born in Shanghai of Iraqi Jewish parents. Dad led the club's protest after repelling a coup that was led by Vladimir Rogoff of the Russian news agency TASS, who was later identified as a colonel in the KGB and its top operative in China. After a resolution condemning Moosa's detention was approved and published by the Western press, Mao freed Moosa.

As the president, my father also won freedom for two other colleagues, Graham Jenkins of Reuters and George Vine of the *North China Daily News,* who had been arrested by the Nationalist Chinese police for violating censorship by referring to military installations along the Yangtze River at Nanking. Intervening in April 1949 just hours after the two men had been condemned to a firing squad, Dad threatened and cajoled a police colonel to release them; they later said they owed their lives to my father. Days before Shanghai fell, he restarted the club in Hong Kong, where it prospers to this day. Recalling such events, his colleagues feted him at a Hong Kong banquet in 1975.

I didn't know about most of this until much later. Also much later I learned about the aberrant tablet. Irv Molotsky, a *Times* colleague back from Hong Kong, sent me a photo. I couldn't get too excited. It wasn't the first time for such confusion, which might even be considered poetic. Hadn't the poet John Keats made "stout Cortez with eagle eyes" the discoverer of the Pacific? Who now corrects Keats? While working first at the United Press and later at the *Trib*, I often met people who told me how much they valued *my* reporting from China. I explained that it was my dad who had worked in China and that my only Asian experience was dodging mortars in Korea. Later, while we both reported for the *Times*, the confusion was less easily ignored.

My three years at the *Trib* ended with a *Times* offer I couldn't refuse, and London to boot. While I was in London, Dad also linked up with the *Times*. At first I didn't know about the association, which was through Paul Underwood, the *Times*'s central European correspondent and later a professor of journalism at Ohio State University. He and my dad had covered gangland empires together in Ohio during Prohibition. Moving to Warsaw in 1963, Underwood closed the *Times* bureau in Vienna but recommended Dad as a stringer. Foreign Editor Emanuel Freedman went along, picking him up at a fraction of the cost of a full-time correspondent.

I was a rookie in London, and I found out about all this only after Tony Beardsley, the manager of the wire room, handed me a cable from the *Times*'s Foreign Desk addressed to Clyde Farnsworth. It contained questions on a story about an avalanche engulfing a Tyrolean village—scores missing or dead, a tragedy of broad interest. But I'd never even been to Austria. I guessed the intended recipient and told Tony to resend to a second Clyde Farnsworth, then working in Vienna. It took Beardsley a moment to savor the twist. My father soon found an ingenious way to cut future confusion. After toying with various combinations, he wired New York and all *Times* bureaus that henceforth in cable traffic, Clyde A. Farnsworth would be "Clydesworth" on a beefed up *Times* bench.

Identity mix-ups aren't helpful. Pity the poor scholars who are trying to create a second draft of history from our first. Yet many more years elapsed before my father and I began the organized effort to clarify the record of our separate but conjoined lives. That started in 1979, five years before his death.

Like Felix and Oscar in *The Odd Couple*, we were living together, and one night we were having a night out. Years earlier his marriage to my mother had collapsed, and he was now on the outs with Dolly, his second wife. He had invited himself to live with me, and despite my reservations I could not say no. My own marriage was also broken. After a decade and a half in Europe, I had been reassigned to Washington, and one night we two Clyde Farnsworths were chomping on bacon cheeseburgers at a Georgetown eaterie named, appropriately enough, Clyde's.

There was method to that zaniness. Although we were colleagues, linked by blood and name, I didn't know my father well. He'd been absent for much of my youth. More recently we'd worked on stories together in Europe: North Atlantic Treaty Organization (NATO) meetings in Brussels and the Warsaw Pact invasion of Czechoslovakia. But vast swaths of his life were murky, especially after he ditched my mother, who is now dead. She was French, from Orleans, about sixty miles south of Paris, where Joan of Arc won a signal victory in 1429.

By the time of that Georgetown dinner I had long ago turned the page. About Mom's unhappiness I could do nothing. My calculated apathy toward Dad's achievements, initially conceived as filial weaponry against paternal hubris, was absurd. We were professionals. Newsmen suppress feelings to get the story. I was now interested in everything about him, especially what had been tidied over as I was growing up, such as those years in China and a lady named Dolly.

How had he and Dolly met and stayed together for so long? My mother never wavered from the belief that Dolly was part of the Red conspiracy. The real story was even more intriguing. They'd met on New Year's Eve 1942 at a hotel bar in Tehran, where she was a B-girl, hustling drinks. Fleeing Vienna after the Anschluss, she left Europe via Trieste, boarded a steamer to Alexandria (Egypt), and wandered through the Levant, living on her wits and looks and an emerald or two secreted in her bra or golden slipper heel. Soon after meeting my father, she had a visa crisis: the denial of her petition for renewal as a resident alien in Tehran, a particularly dangerous situation at the time. Dad was Prince Charming.

All this was a far piece from the Ashland, Ohio, farm culture he grew up in and from which he always wanted to escape. Newspaper reporting was the key to breaking out. He covered the police beat for papers in Lima and Cleveland, joined the AP in Columbus, and within a year transferred to the cable desk in New York. After the attack on Pearl Harbor, he won a coveted position as a war correspondent and filed from Egypt, Jordan, Iraq, Iran, India, Burma, and China. On the way to Cathay (China), the AP wrote him up in its house organ as a "modern Marco Polo."

My father reported on the air war, once alongside a belly gunner on the first daylight B-29 raid against a Japanese target, the well-defended Anshan steelworks in Manchuria. Much war reporting came from a posting to General Claire Chennault's Fourteenth Air Force in Kunming. Later, for Scripps Howard, his reports on the Chinese civil war appeared with a head shot in its flagship *New York World Telegram* beside such regulars as Eleanor Roosevelt and Robert Ruark.

In my own shortsightedness I had ignored not only the peaks of his reporting life but also the first drafts of some pretty amazing history. To remedy the situation that evening at Clyde's, all I had to do was ask. He wasn't loath to reveal even the most intimate details, and he seemed happy to be pressed. I wanted to learn everything about that time in Iran and later India and China. And because I was fascinated, I assumed others would be, too, so as his story unraveled I urged that he write about his life. He enthusiastically agreed.

But Dad was racing the clock. His health was giving way, through an enlarged, cancerous prostate and a cholecystitis-inflamed gall bladder. He grew tired easily and slept poorly. While he was seeking medical relief, I suggested that he get something down on paper about the China years. Memories can be therapeutic. I worked with him after my duty at the *Times*. We had a decent Remington typewriter (this was well before the digital revolution), plenty of paper, and pleasant living quarters, which looked out over a wooded area off Columbia Pike in Arlington, Virginia, a few miles south of the Pentagon. I thought he would sit down and type out snippets of memory; I expected to come home to raw copy that I would then easily edit.

As a result of either physical or mental inertia, his first output was zilch, and so was the second and the third. Upon my return home each day I found him dozing in an armchair, watching TV, or merely gazing into space. "I tried," he said, "but just couldn't make it come." I changed tactics, figuring it easier for him to dictate. I bought a tape recorder and again set him up. "Talk to the machine," I said. I would later transcribe everything or hire a hungry intern. I urged him to let himself go. Despite the best of intentions, he never recorded more than a sentence or two. He needed another human being. So during my leisure moments I set myself up with a typewriter. I urged him to relax in his favorite chair, and I did what I'd been trained to do: ask questions.

This time the floodgates opened. We sat together scores of evenings as I debriefed him not just on China but on the details of his whole life. After years of playing the violin, I was able to type as fast as he spoke—querying, always querying. Sometimes he got irritated at the degree of precision I demanded, but he always made a valiant effort to answer and occasionally referred to a small pile of notes or letters.

The stories poured out. He shrugged off the ever more cumbersome shackles of the recent past and fled into those fabulously exciting years of his heyday. Despite his failing health, he displayed a retentive memory for quotes, details, names, and even spelling. This was a result, I surmised, of years of groundwork at Ohio newspapers and the AP—and also of a life with minimal alcohol, which set him apart from many of his colleagues, including myself. During my professional years, I was not unknown to take a nip or two—perhaps it was my French blood. Dad, who had been reared by teetotalers in the Bible Belt, was a social drinker—ice cubes all night, except for a couple of binges, mainly in China, which he gleefully told me all about.

Though later ailing after surgery and debilitation, he was amazingly responsive. What he couldn't fill in, I researched myself for context and chronology, such as the deep-running conflicts between General Joseph W. Stilwell and Generalissimo Chiang Kai-shek, the planning behind the B-29 raid at Anshan, or the considerable achievements of General Vladislaw Anders and the Polish Army of the East, whom he encountered in the wadis of northern Iraq in late 1942. The idea of folding two lives into one came from Tom Wallace, a New York literary agent, who helped me give substance to William Wordsworth's "So is it now I am a man; / So be it when I shall grow old, / Or let me die! / The child is father of the man."

TANGLED BYLINES

1

Caps and Rockers

MY FATHER'S FIRST paying job was delivering telegrams for Western Union in Ashland, Ohio. It was 1923. Clyde A. Farnsworth was fifteen years old. One of his cousins, Ralph Matheny, told him about the job. "Nice tips," Ralph said. The cap Dad had to wear was so small that it made him look like a circus monkey, so he tucked it under his arm. The manager was aghast. "You wear the cap!" he ordered. "It's the cap that tells you where to go!" Dad quit on the spot.

From then on, during half a century as a newsman, Dad wore only hats that fit: the fedora of a cocky 1920s police reporter, like Pat O'Brien in *The Front Page*; the US Army officer's cap of an accredited AP correspondent in World War II, dusted off during the Chinese civil war; the green velour Tyrolean hat, worn with a dash of panache by an American correspondent in Cold War Vienna.

Dad landed his first reporting job at age sixteen while he was on spring break with his grandparents in St. Petersburg, Florida. He dearly loved them, but sitting on a rooming house porch, or even dipping his toes in the Gulf of Mexico, didn't quite do it for him, and *The Mill on the Floss*, assigned reading from Ashland High, was a far cry from *Deadwood Dick* and *Riders of the Purple Sage*.

Late one morning, immersed in George Eliot, he heard a sharp crackle and investigated what could have been either the backfire of a car engine or a gunshot. He found people gathered by another porch. An older man living alone seemed jumpier than usual, people said; he had shot himself and was found in his chair, gingerly clutching something wrapped in cloth, which turned out to be a Smith & Wesson. The lawn and porch were blotchy pink.

Dad's grandparents were avid news readers, and Dad knew of one publication not far away, the *St. Petersburg Tourist News*, a glossy, ad-packed weekly tabloid, that was delivered to tourist homes and doctors' waiting rooms. He liked its pictures of smartly dressed young women sipping Cokes. So my father went there to tell the editor what had happened.

J. Clifford McDonald lifted his eyes as the kid walked in. The editor, wearing sleeve garters and a cocked fedora, looked like a riverboat gambler. The kid told him what he had seen and heard. "People said the old man was very nice," my father reported. "If he had troubles, he kept them to himself." McDonald, whose mother had once worked for William Randolph Hearst, took notes on the back of an envelope and sent someone to check. An item appeared in the paper the next day. It wasn't bigger news, McDonald said later, because "no one ever heard of him—and it's not what our readers like to read."

Yet it had other consequences: it launched my father's news career, which spanned half a century in the fraught middle decades of the twentieth century. Thanks to Grandma, a former schoolmistress from southeastern Ohio hill country, Dad had always wanted to be a reporter. At the *Tourist News* he collected bills for the ad and circulation departments, moved to editorial, wrote simple declarative sentences, and eventually made $9.50 a week.

Naturally gregarious, he befriended sources, took notes on the backs of envelopes, and buttered up the chief of police in return for lessons on how to read a police blotter. "The old-fashioned billy has given way to the new-fashioned blackjack at the local police department, following a ruling by Chief of Police George M. Coslick that everything in his jurisdiction must be up to date," one unsigned story read. And so Dad learned a basic rule of the game rarely taught at schools of journalism: make your sources look good, and they'll make you look good. It still plays today, even in the age of Instagram and Twitter.

Later he did triage in sports. The St. Petersburg–Clearwater area was a hot baseball site in the spring of 1926, and sports editor Red McClintock needed a legman. One item the kid helped track was the stake that Yankee Manager Miller Huggins took in local real estate. The house was at Twenty-Third Street and Central Avenue, and Huggins acquired it for an astronomical $40,000—the kind of story, McDonald said later, that readers liked to read. Huggins, who won six pennants and three World Series, died of influenza in 1929.

Friends with the famous, your own words in print—a heady brew, and when spring break was over Dad wanted to continue at the paper, but his grandparents had other ideas. He was growing up too fast, Granddad said, and needed to obey his elders. "Now you just let the boy alone," Grandma said, seeming to better gauge his yearnings. "It'll all work out."

It did, thanks to her diplomacy and shrewdness. Jawing with the principal at the high school near Crescent Lake, she arranged admission for the rest of the year, and McDonald was not averse to giving the kid part-time work for less pay. A dabbler in genealogy, Grandma believed that her grandson would be the first in the family to attend college. His father, Oliver Frank Farnsworth, who had been raised in southeastern Ohio, was an electrician and a carpenter. Building houses solo in spring and summer, he financed winter fishing in Florida. But snowbirding had started even earlier, with Granddad, whose horse-drawn, steam-powered sawmill, created while he was still a young man in the forested hills of southeastern Monroe County, earned him a long life of leisure and travel.

The return to Ashland High from Florida was a coronation. Named editor of both the weekly newspaper, the *Flashlight*, and the 1926 yearbook, Dad also won the top debater prize. After graduation he duly went to college. But his grandparents decided which one: the ultraconvenient, ultrareligious Ashland College, a hop-skip from their house on Grant Street. They also operated a farm in the adjacent village of Nankin.

The college was run by the United Brethren Church, an evangelical Protestant denomination that prepped earnest young men for the ministry. A year was all Dad could stand. Having promised to "try" college, he kept his word, but he rebelled against compulsory chapel and fire-and-brimstone preaching. He loathed wearing the cross on his sleeve. "God is everywhere," he once told me, "in the trees, mountains, a newborn baby, an old man who wears diapers."

Despite his affection for his grandparents, he made a clean break to rekindle his reportorial skills. Bright and malleable, he attached himself successively to two Ohio dailies: *the Lima Morning Star and Republican Gazette* and the *Cleveland News*. He covered strikes, mine disasters, bootleg wars, industrial wars, a botched execution, and the deadliest prison fire in American history.

After a roll in the hay with a teacher from France, my long-suffering mother, he joined the AP as a police reporter in Columbus. The AP made him a war correspondent in the Middle East and Asia. Scripps Howard kept him in Asia and later returned him to the Levant for its anti-imperial awakenings. He also covered Perónism in Latin America and Cold War tensions in Europe. Yet throughout his life, that youthful adventure was always fresh. In a sink-or-swim profession, it was in Florida that Dad learned to swim.

2

The Crucible

MY FATHER'S MOTHER, Myrta McFrederick Farnsworth, died from breast cancer at the age of thirty-five on June 11, 1917—nine weeks after our country entered what President Woodrow Wilson called "the war to end all wars." Dad was nine.

"Oh, my poor motherless children," sobbed Grandma during the funeral at the Church of Christ in Christian Union, also known as the Disciples Church. She bent over the pew where Dad cowered with his three siblings. In her beribboned straw bonnet and ankle-length maroon skirt, she was a hen tending her chicks. It was warm, especially inside the church, and starchy "Sunday clothes" made the kids sticky and itchy. Between hardwood pews and a flower-bedecked altar stood the plain open pine casket before which Oliver Frank, Aunt Lucy, and others lined up for last good-byes.

A year and a half earlier, Dad's family had lost its fifth child, Euphama, from spinal meningitis. Myrta's last resting place was next to Euphama in a wedge-shaped burial ground off the county road to Nankin, beside a low cast-iron fence. When my father took up painting in Vienna, his first subject was his mother's funeral: a raw, sensitive work of muted tints and scumbled contours. It hangs in my waterman's shack in Broomes Island, Maryland.

One of the relatives suggested farming the kids out. Oliver Frank was not opposed, and it made sense to Dad's grandparents, who showered affection on all four children but had eyes chiefly on "Clydie," who was midway between Guy, the baby, and Harry, the oldest, and was two years younger than his sister, Olive. It was like draft baseball, and they liked his stats. He was quieter, more contemplative than the others, quick-witted, and a tireless reader—traits they cherished. When they got him, they shaped him and inevitably spoiled him. It was not the extravagant spoiling that privileged kids now get. He still rose early to do chores. Nobody tied his laces or picked up his kiddie junk. But he could stretch limits—bedtime later and later—even as the grandparents professed to be strict. Lydia (Grandma), was the indulger in chief.

Granddad provided practical lessons like cranking up the Huppmobile roadster and putting new spark plugs into the engine mount; Lydia shaped Dad's inner development. "I worshipped my grandmother," he said, "while my boyish feeling for my grandfather was a mix of fear with respect. He was the only man who could drive me to tears. His comment that my bladder lay too near my tear glands never helped in those crises."

As a former teacher, Lydia knew that gifted children required gentle encouragement, especially after losing a parent. Like tomatoes ripening in her kitchen garden, they demanded supportive stakes. She realized, too, that here was a gift from God of the child she never had. Lydia was the first cousin of Granddad's first wife, Sarah Jane Markley, the birth mother of Oliver Frank, Aunt Lucy (Myrta's sister), and three other children in southeastern Monroe County. Like Myrta, Sarah Jane also died young from breast cancer.

In taking charge as a blood-related stepmother, Lydia let pedagogy lead. A stickler for spelling and grammar, she took over in after-school hours by tutoring in English composition, literature, world history and geography. Years later, with a nostalgic smile, he referred to this as his SSFC, or special school of foreign correspondence. Her nurturing provided the sureness of foot that stood him well in life, nudging him into that prized berth in St. Petersburg, maturing him into a cool and intrepid correspondent whose stories brought the world's wars home to millions and rattled the complacency of a too august bureaucracy in Washington.

"Shake up things," she said, "to make people's lives a little better."

Most of the exotic locales Lydia introduced Dad to from afar he eventually visited and described in thousands of dispatches. So when he helped cover a Christmas Eve service at the Church of the Nativity in Bethlehem in 1942, a plangent time of conflict on four continents, it was her gentle upturned face he saw among those lining up before the basilica's cramped portal. A visit to the Holy Land, and especially that reputed birthplace of Jesus of Nazareth, was part of a tour the grandparents had taken before World War I.

In Wittenberg, Germany, the residents told him about Granddad's namesake, a sixteenth-century scholar named Philipp Melanchthon who lay buried in the Schlosskirche (Castle Church) beside Martin Luther. In the 1500s, Melanchthon was Luther's tutor at the University of Wittenberg, and he and Luther translated the New Testament from Greek to German. Over time, the name Melanchthon, which is Greek for "black earth," was streamlined. The silent *h* was dropped in America, and then the name—given to Granddad—became just plain Lank.

Driving from Berlin to Bonn once while reporting on a divided Germany, Dad spent the night along the Elbe River in Wittenberg. Steeped in the existential struggle of the Cold War, he paid little attention to his surroundings until taking a walk after dinner. Drawn to the old town square, he became aware of a towering figure in scholar's robes peering from a marble plinth toward a line of hills. Reading the inscription Philipp Melanchthon, he gave a start. Lank's parents—farmers Howard and Nancy Cronin Farnsworth of Monroe County—chose the name to honor both their Protestant origins and their hardscrabble land.

Thus, deep in the German heartland a foreign correspondent staggered into the prehistory of his own beginnings. Perhaps it was the small carafe of wine at dinner or the backlight of a gibbous moon, but as he stood there he had an apparition of wiry, often wry, Granddad. Then, as if engulfed by the riverine mists, he also saw his childhood home. As Dad described the magical moment, Lank lay aside the newspaper he was reading and rose from the tufted rocker, his shadow falling across Grandma, who had moved to the piano bench. Her bony fingers flitted across the Baldwin, and both grandparents, in practiced harmony, belted out the amazing number of verses of "Amazing Grace." The boy was encouraged to join, and he too eventually learned all verses.

They then attacked "The Battle Hymn of the Republic," which the boy also memorized, along with musical versions of the Gettysburg Address and Lincoln's second inaugural address. As Grandma segued into the geographical etudes, Lank, repossessing his newspaper and chair, smiled with pride. Lydia thumped a C-major chord and instructed the boy to sing after her in robust obbligato: "British Columbia, Vancouver; Alberta, Edmonton; Saskatchewan, Regina; Manitoba, Winnipeg; Ontario, Toronto; Quebec, Quebec; Nova Scotia, Halifax; Prince Edward Island, Charlottetown; Nova Scotia, Halifax. Only Labrador has no capital."

Lydia improvised other etudes—about the great continents, mountain chains, seas, lakes, and rivers—and the boy never forgot. "In many parts of the planet, people do not even speak English," she told him, a concept that was then hard to fathom. Years later, in glimpsing the same hills and swaths of heaven in Philipp Melanchthon's vision, he realized that as a seasoned reporter he'd already spent more than half of his life in such places.

3

A Faultless Start

AFTER HIGH SCHOOL graduation in June 1927, Dad tried to follow up the Florida job with one in Ashland, at least until college in the fall. He still lived with his grandparents, but Granddad had made it clear that the boy must start paying his way. A softer-hued Grandma insisted that their house was always open.

Alas, there were no reporting, or even clerical, jobs. Other work was available in the booming economy of 1927, but not much to his liking. In laying track for the Erie Railroad, he came up short in brawn, compared with newly immigrated Slovaks. Embedding steel rails was harder than any work on the farm, and after the first week he told himself there must be something better.

He fell back on a 6:00 a.m. to 6:00 p.m. workday, six days a week, at Faultless Rubber Works, a red-brick factory on East 4th Street that was a hop-skip from the railyards. Faultless was the source of Ashland's then undisputed claim as the world's largest producer of condoms and toy balloons. The job wasn't as grueling as laying track, yet in some ways it was worse. In this deafening, stinking place, he handled batches of rubber steaming from the acidic friction of machine grinding. His hands grew calloused, and his lungs burned. Moving from cold steel track to hot slabs of rubber, the teenager developed an enduring compassion for the workers of the world.

Dad's instructor in proletarianism was Charlie Ely, who was a generation older and wiser but never got the break he deserved. He had a habit of propping a booted foot on the edge of the milling pan and shouting above the roar of machinery, "Workers deserve to inherit the earth!"

In those days Charlie and thousands of others were worked up over the Sacco and Vanzetti case. On August 22, 1927, the night Nicola Sacco and Bartolomeo Vanzetti were executed, Charlie was particularly agitated. "All those professors can't be wrong," Charlie shouted into Dad's ear. The reference was to the swell of mostly academic protests against the scheduled execution of the two Italian immigrants who had been accused and convicted of killing a paymaster and a guard during a robbery at a shoe company in South Braintree, Massachusetts. Neither had a criminal record or appeared to be in possession of any of the money, but they were anarchists, and the scheduled execution was marked by worldwide sympathy demonstrations for these immigrants who seemed to have been targeted for their politics. Yet at Faultless, the only notice taken of this possible terrible miscarriage of justice was by Charlie Ely and his impressionable young charge.

Thanks to the grandparents' willingness to cover tuition, Dad matriculated at Ashland College that September. His ambition was to land a newspaper job, and more education couldn't hurt. To earn pocket money he worked part-time with the college publicity department. One task: walking press releases to the *Ashland Times Gazette* a dozen or so blocks away. If the big shots saw enough of him, he figured, they'd consider hiring him. But after the first year, no one had noticed, and he decided he was too big for Ashland, anyway. So with a friend, Filson Roberts, who owned a Red Phantom roadster and whose father ran the custom tailor shop, Dad took off for the closest big city, Toledo.

Nearly the size of Cleveland, Toledo had plenty of skyscrapers, smart shops, and good-looking women in soft chignons, shimmering waves, peacock feathers, and boas. It was mid-1928. He had just turned twenty and was as cocky as they come. Now if he could only get lucky.

The *Toledo News-Bee* accepted him for a two-week trial. The paper was part of the prosperous Scripps Howard newspaper chain, for which Dad later would become a columnist, but for now fate didn't smile. This wasn't St. Petersburg or even Ashland. People were brusque, intent on going about their business, and in the office the the country boy found the lingo hard to understand. When an editor shouted, "Give me a new top, bud," he thought of the toy that spins.

After a couple of weeks an editor drew him aside. "You need more experience, bud! Come back and see us maybe in a year." Someone mentioned an opening in Canton, at the *Canton Repository*. Collecting his things, Dad was so heartbroken that he refused to even take a last look at the city room. Almost as rude a shock was the loss of the Red Phantom roadster he'd been gallivanting in with Fil's bevy of ladies on nighttime sorties by the lake.

Despite the trauma of Toledo, Dad and Fil remained lifelong friends. I ran into Fil years later and came to understand my father's fondness for

him. A jester with a beagle nose and a yen for fast cars, crisp money, and flashy clothes, he had the snappy, cheerful demeanor of a racing tout, but he also made Dad laugh. When the dynamite film *Seabiscuit* came out, Filson seemed to be the spitting image of the William H. Macy character Tick Tock McLaughlin, the wiseacre sportscaster whose corny jokes and outlandish witticisms epitomized the prewar radio era:
 He: What 'cha doing with those scissors?
 She: Cutting time so we can double up.

To check out the *Canton Repository*, Dad bought a rail ticket to what he thought was Canton, Ohio. Instead the clerk sold him a ticket to Kenton, Ohio. The conductor said that the ticket clerk probably understood Kenton because there was no easy way by rail from Toledo to Canton, and Kenton was on the direct line. So Dad ended up in Kenton, a town of eight thousand and the seat of Hardin County in a sea of corn. The nearest town with a newspaper was Lima, twenty miles away. There were no trains to Lima, so he walked and hitchhiked.
 Arriving on Main Street, Dad was drawn to the offices of the *Lima Morning Star and Republican-Gazette,* which was across the street from Gus's Greek Restaurant. Red crepe dangled from one wall of the anteroom near a poster blazoning the coming attraction of Harry Blackstone, the most celebrated magician of the day. Blackstone stood in elegant tails and white gloves coaxing a rabbit from a top hat.
 On other walls were pictures of the Most Wanted Men in America, courtesy of J. Edgar Hoover, and a front page, from the prior May, of Charles Lindbergh, beside his *Spirit of St. Louis* after landing at Le Bourget. As in Florida, Dad was ushered into the newsroom, this time to meet a bushy-haired, bespectacled man with a long aquiline nose and a copy pencil, like a dart, between his thumb and index finger. He was Chalfont Alam, the assistant managing editor. Dad stated his business, emphasizing his experience reporting in Florida and editing the yearbook but omitting the anarchist at Faultless and the unsympathetic editors in Toledo.
 "All we can give you is eighteen dollars a week," Alam said. "We'll call in two weeks." And that was it. In a fortnight the message arrived: "Report for work Sunday!—Alam."

The reporters of this period have long folded into American folklore: A young crusading newsman, hat tilted, hands clutching a candlestick phone, snaps, "Give me the City Desk. I've got a story that'll bust this town wide open!" My father sensed that he was onto something really big when the town seemed to be taking hits from mysterious nocturnal explosions. This was during Prohibition, when hijackings and bloody gang wars were daily occurrences. The booms seemed to represent an eastward drift of Chicagoland. Yet if rival gangs were evening scores, the police seemed to know nothing about it. The cops, he figured, were too scared to react.

Between assignments, Dad wandered into the areas where the booms seemed the loudest, found people professing to be nervous, and worked on a long enterprise piece on nocturnal gang strife. Quickly perusing the article, Alam looked up in brittle astonishment. "Young man, have you never heard of sewer gas?"

"Not so much as to give off such explosions," Dad said, mortified.

Flat-lying towns in Ohio accumulated quantities of natural gas in rock deposits underground, where energy companies later began high-volume, horizontal, hydraulic fracturing, or fracking. In those days gas sometimes escaped, popping manhole covers like popcorn. To Alam the mistake Dad made was a sin of youth and inexperience. But the episode was a warning for the rest of my father's journalistic life not to fantasize. Real news was dramatic enough. No need for fiction. Sewer gas explosions turned into an office joke. At least he kept his job.

As in Florida, Dad started on the police beat, reporting robberies, wife beatings, rapes, suicides, homicides, and other incidents from the blotter. Later he moved to the criminal courts, covering indictments, suits, contracts, and "routine" trials. He worked twelve hours and then had twelve hours off six days a week. It was actually closer to thirteen or fourteen hours on, from a little after noon to around 1:30 a.m., when the presses began to roll. Work was life. Life was work. "Early copy, early copy" was Alam's litany.

Only after the presses stopped did Alam relax, and Dad discovered that his new boss was a collector of rare books. He had first editions of all the Hugh Walpole novels and was also a Chaucer scholar who could be encouraged to recite the prologue of *The Canterbury Tales* in Middle English or the poem *The Parliament of Fowls*. "Chaucer is the father of English poetry, the man who gave us iambic pentameter," Alam proclaimed on such occasions with roseate flourish.

The theatrics usually occurred across the street at "the Greek's." Gus's chili and coffee were nothing special, but from the greasy tables with artificial flowers by the window to the steamy kitchen inside the swinging doors, the place was friendly, predictable, and soothing after the raucous contentions of the newsroom. Even though it was Prohibition, you could always get a drink there simply by calling Gooch Taxi and asking for a milk delivery. The cab brought assorted bottles. The better-grade stuff came from Canada, smuggled by bootleggers, who owned the taxi companies.

During the endless chitchat, one line above all others, sometimes in the broken English of a beaming Gus, wiping fingers on a stained apron, inevitably triggered uproarious acclamation: "The son of a bitch stole my watch."

The play *Front Page* had recently opened on Broadway. Dad and a reporter buddy, Joe Collier, having shelled out for a freshly published version, marveled at the bull's-eye dialogue and hilariously entertaining, yet not-so-farfetched, shenanigans of Chicago newspaper reporting in the 1920s. The play, by Charles MacArthur and Ben Hecht, had a ring of truth about all newspapers. Although the plot, partly about the trumped-up theft of a watch, summed up some of the journalistic high jinks of the day, it also hinted at a bigger truth about the lengths to which humans will go to satisfy their need for a good story.

At the *Star*, however, Dad found the humor less teleological than scatalogical. Typos, the curse of all newspapers, were plentiful, and mostly purposeful, engineered by printers anticipating breaks into hilarity. It was considered funny, for example, that the *r* had been dropped from *shirt*, a slip that occurred so often that Alam ordered the word expunged from the lexicon. "If you must," he said, "sub tunic." Printers, in their fold-up newspaper hats and ink-stained trousers, put every newcomer through at least one initiation, sidling close to ask, sotto voce, "Do you mind if I urinate on you?" The newcomer then saw a dribble at his feet that he later learned was from still-warm linotype matrices.

Heywood Broun, a beefy, gregarious fellow who always seemed to have a shirttail flopping over his belt, came by one day proselytizing for the Newspaper Guild, the journalists' trade union he was forming, and asked Dad and Collier out for coffee at the Greek's. Working conditions were tolerable in Lima, both young men told the older sports writer and columnist from Brooklyn and Harvard—but of course, they added, they wouldn't mind a raise. Without a union, Broun said, there was no way to squeeze an extra nickel in pay, and they knew he was right.

Broun seemed lonely in those days, always on the move, spending nights in cheap hotels around the country while in pursuit of his laudable lifetime goal of better working conditions for journalists. During his proselytizing he wrote a column, "It Seems to Me," which appeared in the same Scripps Howard papers that later published my father. A union didn't exist in Lima in 1928, but in 1933, after joining the *Cleveland News* and recalling not only Broun but Charlie Ely, Dad signed up as a charter member of the guild and supported it forever.

The *Star*'s big boss, Managing Editor P. A. Waters, seemed more actor or politico than news executive. Waters delegated a lot of authority to Alam and rarely intruded in the news process. He wore expensive suits and starched shirts as he wandered about the office with a showman's perpetual smile.

While seeming nonchalant about journalism, Waters turned out to be an accomplished magician. After the paper was put to bed, he sometimes performed sleight-of-hand tricks and once even organized a Houdini-like escape from the kitchen at the Greek's. Grinning, he emerged from behind the swinging doors, chains like snakes dangling from his open palms. In those days before TV, magicians were celebrities, not unlike rap stars of today, and the public flocked to their shows. The accidental death of Harry Houdini two years earlier had been a national tragedy. Blackstone, born Harry Bouton in Chicago, was his heir, and Houdini and Blackstone were the models for Waters.

In 1928 the American Brotherhood of Magicians chose Lima for its convention, and Dad, boasting some dexterity in sleight-of-hand, asked to cover it. He got his wish, and for the week of the convention absorbed more magic than most people in a lifetime. The convention had its serious side, such as reviewing rules of professional conduct, but what attracted the SRO crowds was good magic before the toughest of all audiences, other magicians.

Blackstone, with his Charlie Chaplin–like mustache, frizzy flyaway white hair, and crimson cloak, was the star. During warm-ups with reporters, the master refused to reveal his secrets, which would have breached rule number one of the brotherhood: tight lips. But he did offer pointers on palming coins and concealing cards—tips that reinforced Dad's own status as a parlor amateur.

Dad marveled at Blackstone's canary trick, performed before a rapt audience. A volunteer clasps the cage. In full view the cage collapses. Nothing is seen but a tiny yellow feather trapped in a spotlight floating in gentle arcs to the floor. High art—and not too hard on canaries.

4

Cleveland

MY FATHER HAD visited Cleveland from time to time, mainly for Keith's Palace, the movie and vaudeville house on Euclid Avenue, where he caught his first talkie. The Palace was still there in December 1929, when, after two years at the *Lima Morning Star*, he joined the *Cleveland News*. Presenting a letter from P. A. Waters to Al E. M. Bergener, the editor of the *News*, he was hired on the spot.

Almost two months had elapsed since Black Tuesday, yet nervousness about the stock market hadn't dampened the zeal for Christmas shopping. Under trademark glass and iron roofs downtown, the shops and eateries were full, and spaces for his new Model T were at a premium. Cranes and gantries scratched the sky. The fifty-two-story Terminal Tower, still awaiting dedication, was the butt of hokey jokes. People said things like "Cleveland may be the only city in the world with a tower that's terminal overlooking a lake that's eerie."

Dad made $20.50 a week, 50 percent more than at the *Star*, a princely sum for a rube of twenty-one. Yet professionally he found the going rougher. Cleveland was bigger than Toledo and less communal than Lima. The new boss was more difficult than anyone he'd ever known: unreasonable, unpredictable, incapable of warmth, and whiplike in his harangues. Dad started one story, "Police today were searching for a bandit who stuck up a gas station on the lake front." The boss went apoplectic. "You dumb blockhead! . . . A stickup man *today* held up a gas station. . . . *Today's news today!*"

Besides being cantankerous, Bergener was a sight to behold: pink and rubbery jowls; eyes so bleary that wiping his glasses was the only way to keep the world from fogging up. He shamelessly capitalized on a withered left arm. Once, as Dad's eyes strayed below chin level, he hissed, "Anything amiss there, Mr. Farnsworth?" He smoked a pipe, the plump forefinger on his good hand reloading—forever in and out of the bowl, like a worm in an apple.

Of all his eccentricities, what shocked most was his prudishness. A walking Hays Code, Bergener almost fired a graphic artist for suggesting men and women sleep together. Illustrating a serialized novel, the artist showed a couple embracing in a doorway, and beyond them was a bed. Although the *News* sometimes ran photos of women showing a little thigh, the bed enraged Bergener.

In yet another outburst, as details of a robbery built to a "stop the presses" moment, he lashed out at fellow newcomer, Henry Henson, for mistaking a street name. The error was shouted for all to hear. A paste pot, flung from somewhere inside the city room, landed near Bergener, splattering his shirt. There was absolute silence—the world stopped! Swallowing a grimace, Bergener slowly withdrew a handkerchief, wiped his shirt, and then, as if nothing had happened, shouted: *"Extra! We're going extra!"*

At that moment, despite everything, Dad said, he suddenly loved the old man. For here was the realization that what really counted was not rancor toward any one individual, or personal vindication, but a common struggle to get out a living, breathing newspaper. Gerold Frank, a colleague who distinguished himself as a stylish writer of celebrities' autobiographies ("as told to Gerold Frank"), later identified my father as the pot thrower. Frank was wrong. After all those years, Dad revealed the true culprit: a disgruntled legman named Charlie Humphrey. "But it made no difference," he told me. "Any of us could have done it."

Al Bergener thrived on tension, which at a national level had lifted him to the realm of legend three decades earlier. September 6, 1901: New national telephone hookups were demonstrated at the Pan-American Exposition in Buffalo. A twenty-six-year-old Chicago-based reporter, Bergener was covering William McKinley, who was starting his second term as the twenty-fifth president. Riding high after his popularity in the Spanish-American War and with renewed economic buoyancy, the president worked the crowds in Buffalo's red-brick Temple of Music.

Another young man was also present: Leon Czolgosz, the son of Polish immigrants, a wire-mill worker, and an anarchist. Czolgosz extended a hand wrapped in cloth, as if freshly injured but gripping a 32-caliber Iver Johnson revolver. He shot twice, and the life of another gunned-down chief executive, after Abraham Lincoln and James Garfield, hung in the balance. Eight days later Theodore Roosevelt was sworn in as the twenty-sixth president.

Bergener monopolized the demonstration phone, getting a beat that fast-tracked his career and drew the notice of the Hanna family (coal, steel, and politics). Mark Hanna, a Republican senator from Ohio, had managed both of McKinley's campaigns. His son, Dan Hanna, made Bergener the editor of the *News*.

The Encyclopedia of Cleveland History picks up the Bergener story: "He personally obtained a murder confession from local gangster Leonard 'Kid' Lyons in 1917 and uncovered a bootlegging scandal in the Lakewood police dept. which resulted in a dozen federal indictments during Prohibition. Tracking down fugitive embezzler Geo. J. J. McKay in 1927, Bergener kept him under wraps and milked him for several exclusives before turning him over to police."

Dan Hanna hoped to make the *News*, which was then running neck and neck with Scripps Howard's *Cleveland Press*, the lead afternoon paper. But the *Press* had advantages, including a sharper sense of promotion. Its Soap Box Derby gave prizes to poor kids who coasted the fastest on wheels bolted to a wooden chassis.

The *Press* had another advantage: immigrants, flooding in from southern and eastern Europe, were curious about the old country. The *Press* hired Romanian-born Ted Andrica to visit villages to report on the life left behind. Andrica wrote about geese on muddy roads, births and deaths, and the latest nuptials—personal, descriptive, colorful material. He became a household name in Cleveland, won a Harvard Nieman Fellowship, and held down a special post at the *Press* as nationalities editor. Dad, in later reporting from Eastern Europe for the *Chicago Tribune*, followed the tradition for an even larger ethnic readership.

Dan Hanna's ace in the hole was technology—and the money to buy it. The paper was in a new plant at East 18th Street and Superior—"the beggar who lived in a palace," as *Time* quipped. He introduced rotogravure, or fine-screen photographic reproduction, as well as color printing of the Sunday comics. Color splashed throughout some sections, although the news stayed black-and-white. For all his investment, Hanna demanded high standards of orderliness and decorum. At other news organizations, hats stayed on, rakishly and defiantly, as if in symbolic readiness to quit and move on, but at the *News*, whether your feet were itchy or not, your fedora went into your locker.

Desks were neat, too, trash baskets were everywhere, and there were plenty of shiny brass cuspidors. Charles Dickens, in *American Notes*, deplored chewing tobacco as "offensive and sickening." Nocturnal crews of immigrant cleaning ladies at the *News* scrubbed and polished the spittoons to high luster.

The entire plant at 18th and Superior had the aura of class. The newsroom took up four tennis-court-size areas on the second floor, beside the composing room. The third floor housed photographers and a cafeteria. Hanna installed an elevator. The *Press* had no elevator. Meals were good, and murals by the artists were even better, including a masterpiece by Al Hirschfeld: Ignatz the Mouse ready to bean Krazy Kat.

Heavy plastered Corinthian columns, too hefty to put your arms around, dominated the newsroom, anchoring islands of desks. Although Bergener had a private office, he spent most of his time at the City Desk monitoring coverage. Other archipelagos were Sports, Financial, Religious News, and Real Estate.

Each desk had an upright telephone and a pendant earphone. Reporters positioned the earpieces between the shoulder and the neck, freeing their hands for note taking, typing, and lighting up. Radios picked up police and fire department frequencies. On big stories, the driver of the News Car, often a photographer, rushed plates of emulsions from boxy Speed Graphic cameras to the office lab for processing.

If reporters and photographers took pride in readiness, so too they mobilized for a prank. Valuing the therapeutics of humor, Bergener went along. One escapade with echoes of *The Front Page* was well rehearsed by Dad's arrival.

The News Desk was alerted to something amiss at 9th and Euclid, involving someone important. Everyone knew that Newton D. Baker, the secretary of war under President Wilson, had law offices on Euclid. The desk recruited Dad, who started typing. Another call, also seemingly from 9th and Euclid, described crowds gathered and emergency equipment summoned to lift a streetcar. City Editor Joe Bernstein ordered the new matter to be put ahead, so Dad tore out the old sheet of paper and wrote a new lead. Excitement mounted. The paper would probably go *extra*.

"Wait!" shouted Bernstein. "Someone underneath the trolley!" To Dad: "Better put that ahead!" Photographers Perry Cragg and Eddie Dork rushed outside, hefting their Speed Graphic cameras. Dad juggled another earpiece, torn between typing and taking down more grisly facts. Another call described crews wielding acetylene torches. Still another revealed, "It's Newton D. Baker under the trolley!" Clips were dumped on Dad's desk, and of course no one had more clips than Newton D. Baker. Another call: "They can't get him out! He's pinned! My God! They're cutting off his arm!"

Dad struggled to make sense of it all. He typed, "Newton D. Baker, one of Cleveland's most prominent citizens, fell under a trolley at Euclid and 9th," but then he had to start again: "Newton D. Baker, one of Cleveland's most prominent citizens, lost an arm today in an accident on Euclid and 9th." Bergener took command, offering fresh information: "He's on the stretcher . . . they're taking him away. No, he won't let them! All those bandages . . . he's reaching for something. Christ! He wants the arm! They can't get it away from him!"

"No, he doesn't want the arm," Bernstein corrected. "He wants—he wants the watch! An inscription from President Wilson! Wait! They're reading it: 'To the best secretary of war I ever had.'"

"Make the inscription a sidebar!" shouted Bergener, as the whole office, including Dad, exploded.

Clerks, stationed by a wooden bench beside the City Desk, kept the copy moving from rewrite to editors to linotype machines. Only after an edition closed did Bergener permit the clerks to sit. The bench was on one side of a wooden railing; on the other side was a more public area, where tipsters, press agents, or anyone waited to gab with reporters.

One visitor in 1930 was a tall, dark-haired young woman introduced to Dad by a press agent for the Ringling Brothers Circus, which was about to open in Cleveland. She was a lion tamer, and her name was Maria Rasputin; she was one of four daughters of Grigori Yefimovich Rasputin, the holy man whose ability to heal the hemophiliac son of Czar Nicholas and Czarina Alexandra of Russia earned him influence—and infamy—at the court of St. Petersburg. Maria was born in Siberia, where her mother stayed with her husband throughout his incredible life. Of the four girls, Maria insisted, she was her father's favorite. He saw to her education, and she lived with him in St. Petersburg until his murder weeks before the 1917 Russian Revolution. Fleeing Russia, she learned lion taming in Paris, then found permanent refuge in America after her circus career was cut short by a mauling by a bear. Settling in California, she worked as a machinist, gave Russian lessons, and wrote a memoir.

Payday was every second Monday. Wives gathered by the bench to pick up the pay envelopes. After two weeks the cupboard was bare. The Sunday before the second Monday, my mother recalled, was the cruelest of days. She and the others came early on Monday, usually with toddlers and sewing baskets. Rocking their tots, they gossiped, darned socks, and waited for the heavenly descent of the payroll officer.

With her dark-haired elegance and exotic background, my mother, Marthe Herailh Farnsworth, had colorful ways of expressing herself. The handle of a frying pan was its "tail" (*la queue*). After her brother, Henri, mailed a large box of chocolates from Paris, she brought them with her to the newsroom. "Would you please like *du chocolat*?" she asked everyone. Perhaps she expected polite refusals. But Dad's uncouth colleagues grabbed two or three at a time, and soon that larder too was bare. Bergener didn't much like wives and kids coming in like that. "We're a newspaper, not a nursery," he grumbled. But he didn't stop it. He realized that the biweekly drama was a morale booster in a period when almost everywhere the chips were down.

Early in the evening on Monday, April 21, 1930, the first bulletins of a catastrophic fire at the Ohio State Penitentiary in Columbus clacked across the news tickers. Bergener looked around, his eyes locking on his youngest recruit. He was almost polite. "Big story," he said, "demanding the best!" Dad said that his new French wife had just made dinner. Bergener laughed. Any trouble with Marthe, he said, and he'd talk to her. Dad said that wouldn't be necessary.

Photographer Perry Cragg was already in the Chrysler coupe when the driver screeched to a halt in front of 18th and Superior. At the lakefront Hopkins Airport, the *News*'s Fairchild five-seater airplane was idling. On that night flight to Columbus, the pilot, a veteran of cross-country mail runs, kept the news crew on course, and within ninety minutes they had completed a picture-taking shoot over walls and turrets.

The central block hiccupped smoke. From every hook and ladder brigade in Columbus, hoses pumped into the bowels of the prison. Spotlights caught puffs rising above the battlements and disappearing into the vaults of the gray-black night.

The compound, built a quarter century before the Civil War, was about the size of two football fields. Packed inside was a dense community of forty-three hundred men whom society had done its best to forget. Yet some were already, or would become, quite famous: O. Henry, the short-story writer, was serving time for embezzlement; Sam Sheppard, an osteopathic neurosurgeon, was convicted in 1954 of murdering his wife and was the inspiration for the film and TV series *The Fugitive*. In the spotlights, the graystone was like a festering scab. Yet the main entrance on Spring Street was just blocks away from markets and movie theaters, restaurants and apartment complexes, where life in Ohio's capital carried on.

Outside the portal, National Guardsmen and regular soldiers from Fort Hayes bayonets fixed, formed lines to foil attempts at escape. In the end, one prisoner, rattled by all the commotion, inadvertently strayed outside but quickly turned himself in. Medics and inmate volunteers wrapped bodies in blankets and laid them on stretchers on the cobblestone courtyard. But as the death toll mounted, the medics ran out of stretchers and blankets, and bodies, in scruffy prison garb, were laid in what space could be found on damp prison stone. Water circulated in fetid rivulets. Volunteers dragged the lifeless to drier spots. My father recalled the cry of one prisoner pointing to a still warm corpse: "Go for the living!"

An African American in his early twenties staggered out of a cell block, was felled by smoke, and collapsed with his charge, a Caucasian, still on his back. Medics rushed to attend to both. The rescuer, in a stained T-shirt and tattered trousers, glistened with sweat as he described prisoners in agony. "Man," he said, "we gotta save lives!" The Horticulture Building of the state fairgrounds became a temporary morgue, and the call went out for embalmers. Some bodies could be identified only by their fingerprints. Dozens were unidentified and laid to rest in a mass grave along I-70 west of Columbus.

Dad didn't realize the toll on himself until the next issue of *Colliers* showed Perry Cragg's "zombie" picture of him ankle deep in black waste water. For three days he hadn't changed clothes. Cragg had trouble maneuvering his tripod, plate holders, and other paraphernalia, and for a while my father was his bearer. They'd cooperated before. As Dad lugged equipment, Perry was the second pair of eyes and ears. During each shoot, the photographer kept muttering, "Man's inhumanity . . . " Dad worked well with Perry because Perry never told him what to write and Dad never told Perry what pictures to take. To get the photos into the paper, the *News* maintained a courier service. A messenger sped plates from the airport, and the Fairchild airplane made several round-trips daily. Dad filed from prison offices, dictating from penciled notes.

Perry found a convict he knew slightly, a bright young man named Specks Russell, who was serving time for armed robbery. Perry had covered the trial. Pale and shaking, Specks burst out, sobbing, "It's murder, you know!" Specks, who substituted as Perry's bearer, said that the prisoners, who had been restive for months, were driven to desperate acts by overcrowding.

The fire started high in the west block, which was deep inside and had only distant windows for light and air. Another tragic circumstance was that unlike other prison fires in which mattresses were the main fuel, this resin-treated wood and the other construction materials gave off highly noxious smoke. Mounds of combustible sawdust spread the conflagration, which jumped to wooden rafters in the ceiling and doomed many in the upper tiers. An inquiry later determined that a small group of prisoners started the fire in a botched escape effort.

Most troubling was that the majority of prisoners were locked in their cells, and the guards, who had been ordered to keep the cells locked during disturbances, were tragically slow to unlock them. Scores of men burned to death or were asphyxiated. Some crawled to the toilet bowls of their cells, wet cloths or towels to put over their heads, and desperately, but mostly in vain, attempted to fill their lungs with air.

Warden Preston Thomas testified that he didn't know the extent of the fire and had focused on foiling escapes. Briefly suspended, he kept his job, however, reflecting the still largely Victorian attitudes toward crime and punishment. The count, 323 dead, or 10 percent of the prisoners, made it one of the ghastliest of American tragedies.

Nearly seven months later, around midday on November 5, 1930, the same AP printer reported a coal mine explosion in southern Ohio, which would take the lives of eighty-two men. Not all worked underground. Five were executives of the Sunday Creek Coal Company, the mine operator, and four, ironically, were safety officials on an inspection tour. The number 6 mine was in Millfield, near Athens, 225 miles south of Cleveland. Dad rushed to the scene with photographer Jake Mintz. There were no airports in that hill country, so they drove, with Mintz, the son of a Cleveland cop, at the wheel. They arrived in a little over three hours—this was before interstate highways.

Miners were still trapped below. Corpses were being removed to a funeral home ten minutes away in Millfield; there was a shortage of blankets, and bodies were laid out on the floor. Blackness ringed the miners' eyes. Coal dust layered fingernails, lips, and tongues.

Mintz, recruiting Dad as his tripod bearer, focused not only on the dead but also on poignant scenes of loved ones awaiting miracles outside the main shaft beside tables stocked with coffee and soup. He had precious little time; he piled the Speed Graphic into the coupe and raced back solo, catching the Final edition with a shot of a gathering at the mine entrance. Not all the news was bad: one rescue team found twenty men alive, sealed off in a mine pocket containing oxygen.

The official investigation found that an electric cable had shorted against an underground rail. Although inspectors had previously reported the escape of excessive coal gas, the company had taken only minimal precautions, permitting, for example, open-flame carbide lamps. Under such circumstances, a tragedy was all but inevitable.

Almost next door to the Payne Avenue police station in Cleveland, a rundown mansion had been turned into the biggest, most protected of Cleveland's bordellos. "The best meat loaf and pickled eggs in town," Dad said. "You paid for drinks, but the eats came free, and reporters ran tabs." It was a press club, of sorts, where you sat around in the kitchen talking politics with the women, often even the madam herself, a bright dark-haired woman who fancied politics and devoured newspapers under a Tiffany lamp. Sometimes she recruited Dad and his colleagues as bouncers. A reporter wore a silver badge almost indistinguishable from a Cleveland police officer's, giving both men access and authority. After Dad ejected one particularly obnoxious drunk, the madam asked if he'd like to be her pimp. "You be nice to me, Charlie," she told him, "and I'll dress you up!"

Cleveland isn't even Ohio's capital, but for a few weeks every summer it was the capital of the world of airplanes, to which Bergener assigned a flock of reporters and photographers. Planes were new and exciting, and readers couldn't get enough about them. Although my father never had the money or time to learn to fly, the show instilled in him an admiration bordering on worship for those who did. The National Air Races attracted such movers and shakers as Amelia Earhart, Claire Chennault, Jimmy Doolittle, Charles Lindbergh, Howard Hughes, and Jackie Cochran. Half a million spectators paid to watch.

The event took place at Hopkins Airport beside Lake Erie. Looping around pylons, the planes banked, yawed, and pivoted a few feet off the ground—incredible sound and fury to be witnessed from the packed bleachers. An old Handley-Paige plane from the Royal Air Force, with Wing Commander David Atcherley at the controls, performed an outside loop, then came in for a dead-stick landing. German ace pilot Ernst Udet, an early organizer of the Luftwaffe, showed off mock strafing passes and bombing runs, a sign that beyond all the fun, serious things happened, too.

Air Force Major Claire Lee Chennault used the event to preach a strategy of air power to the few who would listen. It took a war in China to prove the validity of one idea: that bombers, even in formation, were vulnerable to fighter planes. Dad caught up with Chennault after the airman's sharknosed P-40s, dubbed Flying Tigers, dominated the skies of western China, thwarting Japanese bombers.

Dad also rode with the Luftwaffe pilot in a cloth-covered biplane reinforced to withstand the stress of steep dives. The target was a mock village with cardboard houses beside the lake. Pyrotechnical charges were used instead of bombs. Dad described the whole of Lake Erie screaming up at him at the speed of sound. Stuka bombers used the technique to destroy Guernica and the dikes of Holland.

In more tranquil moments, skydivers, hugging sacks of multicolored flour, fell thousands of feet before the breathtaking pop of their parachutes enabled them to descend like gently rocking rainbows. Clowns jumped into open cockpits to taxi around quacking ducks, part of *Hellzapoppin'*-like lunacy on the tarmac. Some spectators dressed sportily in slacks and jodhpurs, others in overalls, proudly displaying grease as an insignia of honor. Women were grease monkeys, too, and it may have been there where the concept of unisex was invented. If grease was a badge of honor, another envied symbol was a pair of goggles. They lodged high on the forehead, to drop at a moment's notice beside the open flaps of a shiny leather headpiece, and the crowds suddenly parted like the waters of the Red Sea.

When Dad interviewed Amelia Earhart, her goggles and headpiece were still in her suitcase. The encounter took place at Cleveland's Union Station. Floyd Bennett Field on Long Island, from which she was supposed to fly, was socked in by fog. It was September 1934. She'd been living in New York since her recent marriage to George P. Putnam, the publisher. She traveled solo, was already a celebrated figure, and was easily identified by Dad on the station platform.

Born in Kansas, Earhart had apple-pie good looks, a freckled nose, and bobbed hair blowing around her square boyish face. She regretted that she had so little time because of a dinner engagement with a prospective sponsor, but then with a winsome smile, she suggested, "Let's do a peripatetic interview." Dad wasn't quite sure what that meant, but any kind was okay with him. They hailed a taxi and conversed during the ride to her hotel. She wanted to talk, and, taking discreet notes, he mostly let her. She was happily married, but she couldn't just be a housewife. Her marriage was a "partnership with dual controls." She was "a driven female," set on goals. Did she want kids? "Someday perhaps." Did she think she would be happier as a man? "Goodness, no! I'm a woman and a flier. The two are not incompatible."

Seven months later, in April 1935, their paths again crossed, in Manhattan. Earhart had earned another trophy, as the first woman to fly alone from Honolulu to California. Dad was on night rewrite at the AP. They met at a reception hosted by the Mexican consul general for a goodwill flight she was to make to Mexico City. From the far side of the room she saw Dad, walked over, smiling warmly, and extended her hand. "I know you from Cleveland," she said. "We had a peripatetic interview!"

The flight to Mexico went without a hitch. But on July 2, 1937, Earhart and her navigator, Frederick J. Noonan, got lost on a flight around the world. Their sixteen-foot Lockheed Electra plane lost contact between New Guinea and Howland Island, and the mystery of what happened lingers to this day.

Until World War II, the closest Dad had ever come to armed conflict was in May 1934 at the Toledo plant of the Electric Auto Lite Company, where Walter Reuther's United Auto Workers (UAW) fought for union recognition. Strikes were mean and bloody, and this one at the lakeside industrial yards was one of the meanest and bloodiest: two were killed and more than two hundred were injured in a monthlong confrontation.

Dad was among the scores of reporters descending on Toledo from around the country; most, like him, were sympathetic to the strikers, who were fighting company thugs hired to break the strike. But it was also hard not to sympathize with the young National Guardsmen called out by Ohio's new Democratic governor, George White, to keep order. Both sides resorted to firearms, but luckily most of the weaponry was more primitive: stones, bottles, clubs, chains, pikes, and even slings. Dad saw workers creating slingshots from inner tubes stretched between street lampposts to pelt lines of police and strikebreakers.

The air was blue-black, polluted by abandoned automobiles, "vomit" gas, and particulates of burning rubber. Dad filed battle reports, as he later did in China and Burma. After municipal workers started a sympathy strike that further paralyzed the city, Auto Lite, which made batteries and was later bought by General Motors, reached an agreement recognizing the UAW as its exclusive bargaining agent. The union also won a 5 percent wage increase, making its workers the highest paid in the world.

In later years, however, the pact led to "sweetheart" bargaining, in which prices rose in lockstep with lucrative wage increases. When the United States could no longer compete with the lower wages of postwar Europe and Asia, the great automotive cities of Toledo and Detroit faltered. But crystal balls were not plentiful in the cruel year of 1934.

During my father's nearly five years at the *Cleveland News*, his relations with Bergener were hitting more lows than highs. Dad admired the editor's technical competence and sense of competitiveness, but he mightily objected to his efforts to rewrite almost every story along the lines of what seemed to be personal taste or conservative politics. As a protégé of the Hannas, architects of Republican political victories, Bergener tended to be supportive of the interests of big business. His explosive reaction to the drawing of the couple with a bed visible in the background also suggested a supercircumspect moral outlook.

The country's long descent into a seemingly bottomless economic pit, which was already generating real suffering, especially in the Farm Belt, pushed young people like my father and mother further and further to the Left. Dad voted for Franklin D. Roosevelt in 1932, but disillusioned by both Democrats and Republicans in 1936, he supported Socialist Party candidate Norman Thomas.

Building for months, Dad's final break with Bergener came mid-September 1934, precipitated by a scuffle on one of the trolleys between the driver and several young male riders. Dad's reporting suggested that the high-handedness of the driver was mostly to blame. Bergener's editing exonerated the driver, and Dad suspected it was because the transit company was an advertiser. Bergener was like a dog with a bone in refusing to let the story go the way it was written. In longhand, Bergener rewrote every sentence, actually cracking the points of pencil after pencil. The last breakage was the proverbial straw.

"For four years I had been dominated by this man," Dad said, "and I simply couldn't take it any longer. He didn't even notice me as I walked up to his desk. He was looking down at the copy, moving his lips with the words he was substituting for mine. I threw my badge on the desk and asked for my pay voucher. He tried to talk me out of it, refused to sign the voucher. He asked me to have lunch first, and then after lunch we'd talk. I did as he asked, but after lunch I was even more determined to quit."

So Dad told him, "You know, Mr. Bergener, everyone out there thinks you're a son of a bitch."

"I know," Bergener replied. "I don't give a damn."

"I buried all those grievances in the four-plus years I've worked for you," Dad said, "but this time I've had enough. I can't take it anymore!"

"It's rough out there," Bergener warned. "Jobs are hard to get. Here at the *News* the door of opportunity is always ajar. Go back, Clyde. Think it over."

"No," Dad said. "I won't."

My mother wasn't happy, which precipitated the first major row between my parents. She accused him of slighting the welfare of the baby (me), because for a time we had no income. Her skills at squirreling away money, honed during World War One in France, saved the day. And luckily, too, he wasn't long in the wilderness.

Morgan Beatty, the AP bureau chief in Cleveland and a mentor during that period, was sympathetic. A hard-drinking, jocular, urbane man, he went on to become a giant of radio news as a commentator for NBC. He wondered how Dad had stuck it out so long. Unfortunately, there was no opening at the AP in Cleveland, but several weeks later Beatty informed him that Ray Cronin Jr., the AP's chief in Columbus, was losing a staffer, and Beatty urged him to apply. Beatty also promised to call Cronin and put in a good word. The Beatty seal of approval was better than that of *Good Housekeeping*. Cronin hired Dad immediately, with an even fatter paycheck: $41 a week, compared to $34.50 at the *News*.

Several months after Dad quit the *News*, Bergener himself left Cleveland to become the paper's Washington correspondent. But Bergener and the increasingly progressive New Deal weren't a good fit, and within a couple of years he retired to Florida. Idling in the sun wasn't his bag, either, however, so in 1937 he returned to Cleveland, first to be a consultant in public relations, then to be a traveling salesman for King Features, selling comic strips such as *Krazy Kat*. He died in 1950 at age seventy-four. At his funeral he was eulogized as a "true son of a bitch."

5

Crime and Punishment

IN THE EARLY evening of October 12, 1933, three men pretending to be Indiana law enforcement officers walked into the red-brick county jailhouse of Lima, Ohio, and requested custody of an inmate arrested for jumping parole in Indiana. His name was John Dillinger. Sheriff Jess Sarber was doing paperwork at a roll-top desk, and his wife was working on a crossword puzzle nearby. Cell keys hung from hooks on the wall.

"Credentials, gentlemen!" Sarber demanded, rising to challenge the intruders. Out came their handguns, and the sheriff was shot twice in the stomach. Later testimony identified the shooter as Harry Pierpont, the number two man in the Dillinger gang. Pierpont and two accomplices freed Dillinger, ordered the fatally wounded sheriff and his wife into the vacated cell, and sped off on a new spree of heists.

Five months later Dillinger was arrested and held in Crown Point, Indiana, to await trial for an earlier homicide. This time he improvised his own getaway. Fashioning a gun from a block of wood blackened with shoe polish, he bluffed his way out, escaping via the police garage in the sheriff's own Ford V-8. The sheriff—Lillian Holley, a rare female law enforcer—never lived it down, and Crown Point became known in the press as Clown Point.

Dillinger's extraordinary run of luck ended on July 22, 1934, when the Federal Bureau of Investigation, tipped off that Dillinger and a girlfriend were at the movies in Chicago, ambushed him under the marquee. Making a break for it, he fell in a hail of bullets—perhaps preferable to what awaited Harry Pierpont, now sentenced to the electric chair for killing Sarber. Dad covered his execution.

Weeks before his October 17 date with "Old Sparky," Pierpont and another condemned gang member, Charles Makley, tried a breakout, using carvings from soap blackened with shoe polish. But that ruse had already been tried. In the shoot-out, Makley was killed and Pierpont was wounded. Treated by prison doctors, Pierpont was finally deemed well enough to be executed, an irony lost on no one.

Electrically powered steel doors opened with a portentous hum when the AP man presented himself at the main Spring Street entrance soon after 11:00 p.m. on October 16, 1934. Guards ushered him into an anteroom behind the warden's office, where a dozen other witnesses and newsmen also gathered.

Preston Thomas, who had kept his job as warden despite the furor over his handling of the fire, greeted visitors. Tall and portly, like Daddy Warbucks in the *Little Orphan Annie* comic strip, he was dressed as if hosting a dinner party, in a dark blue suit, white shirt, and bow tie. After the arrival of all his invitees, the warden donned an overcoat with an astrakhan fur collar, selected an ivory-topped walking stick, led the party into the prison yard, and headed toward a shack attached almost as an afterthought to the southwest corner wall below the trapdoor of the former gallows. A yellow glow showed through two windows below the drainpipe.

As footfalls clacked, the convicts shouted obscenities and banged against steel bars. Prisons are not long on good fellowship, but this was a time when all inmates united in anger over what would happen next. There was no announcement, but the prison population knew, and the inmates expressed their feelings in the only way possible. The bedlam heightened the drama, as if part of an ancient ritual.

Proceeding through the raucous gloom, Warden Thomas led everyone into a ragged semicircle. The heavy-timbered chair rose behind a wooden railing, and the headrest suggested a barber's chair, except for pendant clamps that secured electrodes to a victim's head, arms, knees, and ankles for the lethal rush of voltage. There was also a mask that would spare observers the sight of blood spouting from eyes, ears, mouth, and nostrils. From a room to the side, Harry Pierpont emerged, walking unaided beside a priest. He wore a blue prison suit. His eyes were bloodshot. He had just said good-bye to his parents, Mr. and Mrs. J. G. Pierpont, who owned a farm in Leipsic, Ohio.

Born in Roman Catholic St. Mary's County, Pierpont grew up as the Depression took its toll in the Farm Belt. He was caught up first in petty crime, then as Dillinger's recruit and eventually his number two man. Pierpont's mother said that his troubles began at age twenty-one after a severe head injury. He complained of eye problems, dizziness, and headaches. Today it would be called traumatic brain injury, unleashing a bipolar disorder linked to antisocial behavior.

"You can't witness something like this and be for the death penalty," Dad told me. He described the execution in detail:

> Pierpont slumped into the chair. A priest, who had given benediction, stepped away, and a guard lowered the mask. The same guard moistened electrodes with a salt solution. There was a hush, broken by a loud tap, the warden's cane. It was midnight, and the tap a prearranged signal for another guard to reach inside a wall cabinet to the rear and press a red button. Now a new sound—the shrill of a high frequency generator. Pierpont was jolted, his entire body struggling for release, the chair apparatus rattling, whining, screaming. Some witnesses turned away. A new sound, like the jet of a garden hose, more minutes. The body finally went limp. A doctor stepped up, unbuttoned the shirt. After applying a stethoscope above the waist, he faced the assemblage: "I certify that a sufficient current of electricity has passed through the body of Harry Pierpont to cause his death. Thank you, gentlemen." It was 12:14.

Crime and punishment tangled with eugenics, the belief that the crime rate would fall if society kept "undesirables" from reproducing. Warden Thomas was a believer. Today any genetic reordering would be seen as a gross violation of human rights. Yet in science fiction it still gets batted around. Eugenic wars destroy most of the earth in *Star Trek*. In the video game Grand Theft Auto IV, a corporation called Eugenics Inc. offers genes made to order for new fetuses. Films like *Gattaca* and *The Eugenist* feature genetically engineered superior humans.

In December 1934 Warden Thomas pressed for eugenics before the Ohio legislature. He sought the castration of convicts. "Castration would unsex criminals, yet still leave them able to earn a living," Thomas said, according to Dad's AP account of the testimony. In a visit to Columbus, Assistant Managing Editor Milo Thomson challenged the word *castration*.

"Mr. Farnsworth," Thomson asked, "don't you think *emasculation* might have captured the intent of the bill more precisely?"

Dad replied, "I have a source, sir, the warden himself. I asked him what the purpose of his bill was. His reply: 'to cut off their balls.'"

There was more second-guessing at the AP in Manhattan, where Dad ended up a year later. Again the way was smoothed by Morgan Beatty, who put in a word to Assistant General Manager Marion Kendrick. So by 1935, a dropout in his midtwenties whose grandma had taught him spelling and geography had joined the headquarters of one of the most illustrious news organizations, copping a raise to $60 a week.

Although the AP spanned the globe, Dad was assigned to the nighttime rewriting of local news, and like many before and after him, he found it no fun to be working while others slept—especially with kiddies around. I was four years old at the time. My sister, Suzanne Madeleine, was born on August 12, 1935, and five years later, on August 10, 1940, my brother, Franklin Guy, entered the world.

Yet for the era, Dad was not only making good money but also keeping alive Grandma's dream. Stick it out long enough, he thought, and maybe the cable desk would open up—longer still, and maybe he'd get sent overseas. He was exhilarated, meanwhile, just from being in amazing New York, absorbing the stunning environment and cultural layers. In crossing Madison or Fifth Avenue, he mused about the possibility of seeing the likes of Stephen Vincent Benet, Alexander Woollcott, or Dorothy Parker, all of whom he would recognize from pictures. "I don't care what you write about me," he once said with a twinkle, quoting Parker, "so long as it isn't true."

Dad was an ardent fan of yet another transplanted New Yorker, Edgar Allan Poe, who several decades earlier had lived out his years on Fordham Road in the Bronx. In the drive to Poe's cottage one Sunday afternoon, Dad insisted on reciting "The Bells" and then taught my mother to pronounce *tintinnabulation.*

Local news is said to be boring except to the locals who live it. Yet sometimes it grabs the spotlight, which was the case soon after Dad's transfer when Flemington, New Jersey, was the site of a global attention-grabbing trial: "The greatest story since the Resurrection" quipped another of Dad's heroes, H. L. Mencken.

A German immigrant carpenter, Bruno Richard Hauptmann, was fighting for his life after being accused of kidnapping the baby son of Charles Lindbergh and poet Anne Morrow Lindbergh. The body turned up in 1932 near Hopewell, New Jersey, and in late 1934 Hauptmann was arrested after the authorities traced the ransom money to him. Maintaining his innocence to the last, he was electrocuted on April 3, 1936.

Newspapers occasionally err. Until recently, however, they were loath to admit it. Now they almost revel in corrections, or editor's notes. The AP erred in its report on the Hauptmann verdict the morning of February 13, 1935. Dad wasn't on duty, but he knew something was up when he entered the office later that day to find it "a morgue."

The AP facilities at Flemington lay under the cupola of the courthouse. Under New Jersey law, after a verdict was reached but before it was announced, the jury had to be polled to ensure unanimity. While the polling was underway, nobody could leave or communicate by phone. To beat the competition, the AP chief in Trenton had devised an arrangement to signal from inside.

Botched or misunderstood, his signal suggested conviction with a recommendation of mercy, meaning life imprisonment. The actual verdict was no clemency—the electric chair. The AP ran a correction, making that wintry day bleak. But its unrivaled speed, accuracy, and balance before and after that event meant that the AP need never hang its head in shame.

6

Dad's Whistle

THE WHISTLE, MY bedtime signal, shrilled above the hollers of the kids I was playing with, the chorus of cicadas, and the honks of vehicles enforcing their right of passage. I pretended not to hear. Summer 1940, Mount Vernon, New York: Sounds of clicking from the "A" trolley to the 241st Street Bronx subway line. I'd wangled my way into stickball. It was my turn at bat. I didn't know if Dad could see me, but I could see him, his hands cupped over his eyes to block the setting sun.

I took a practice swing with the sawed-off broomstick, then stepped up to the plate to try to hit the ratty tennis ball to kingdom come. The first pitch I missed, then I whacked the next ball into the arching maple trees for a base hit. Safe at first, I spotted him before a throng of parents.

"Slugger's up past bedtime!" The voice was commanding and nicotine raspy. Our eyes locked. His smile flashed as wide as the grille of a passing Pontiac, and I knew I had an extension.

Dad was sandy-haired with deep blue eyes and a cocky tilt of the head. He also had what my mother, in her lusty French accent, called the *geeft of gahb*, which, as a newcomer to America and a student of melting pots, she said sprang from his Scots-Irish ancestors in Ohio.

He returned to inform her of my dispensation, perhaps in crammed Berlitz French—that is, if Berlitz could translate "stickball"—perhaps *la balle du baton* or *le stickball*. No matter; it wouldn't be a long conversation. Marthe, with her coal black hair, pale luminous skin, and old-world modesty and reserve, avoided French with the non-French, even her own husband. She was in the United States, where one speaks English. For too long she'd endured the mangling of French by Americans, a torment she likened to "La Marseillaise" off-key, or too many riffs by Jack Benny on his "ole Strad."

But, as with rules of French grammar, there were exceptions. It was obligatory to speak French, even with Americans, at the Alliance Francaise, and I recall how pleased she was to find one man who spoke French reasonably well and shared a love for almond-paste cakes of the Sologne. She also spent hours jabbering on the phone to a small circle of French friends. My own knowledge of French owes more to living in France as an adult than learning at her knees. She feared an accent would mar my English; this reflected her growing sensitivity about her own accent, which, despite her years in the United States, never faded.

Had she come here as a little girl, perhaps then she would have had a nirvana of accentless English. But she emigrated in her early twenties. Dad, no easygoing Henry Higgins, was often as impatient with her English as she was with his French, a sign of more intransigent problems later. Initially, people found her accent quaint. But after the novelty wore off, her American friends seemed condescending. She was probably too sensitive, but her inability to master English pronunciation was a sore point all her life. The French travel less well than their wines.

The decision not to force-feed me was after my first trip to France, where she showed me off to the relatives. Upon our return, Dad met us at the French Line pier. I pulled away and ran to him, shouting, "*Voilà papa! Bonjour, papa!*" He backed off, asking, "Who's the little French kid?" She didn't think the joke was funny.

The sun was sinking fast, and soon stickball broke up for the night. Mrs. Roemerman, a neighbor two doors down, the mother of my pal Don, invited everyone over for cookies and lemonade. She rattled a plate of chocolate chip cookies before me. "And so, little Clyde, what does the big Clyde do?"

"He works for the AP," I piped. She seemed puzzled.

"You mean A *and* P?" she asked. "He's in the grocery business?"

"No—the AP! Where you write for newspapers. He's in an office in the city." I puffed out my chest. "I've been there!"

On school holidays I intercepted my father at the train station on his way home from work. I knew the rough arrival time of the New York, New Haven, and Hartford commuter line at the South Columbus Avenue station. From afar I identified Dad's swagger and the rakish tilt of his fedora. Meeting him was the high point of my day. He liked walking almost as much as riding his English racing bike or diving from the high board at the Wilson Woods swimming pool. Still in his early thirties, he kept a fitness routine despite a sixty-hour, six-day workweek. During the tail end of the 1930s, the forty-hour workweek was still only a gleam in Heywood Broun's eye.

After I met Dad at the station, we played guessing games. He tried to guess the dinner menu—often pot roast, or *pot au feu*, Mom's favorite. By this time she was also making American staples like macaroni and cheese, meat loaf and gravy, and apple pie. He quizzed me on what teachers I liked (none), was I getting along better with my kid sister Sue (no), and how the checkers and chess tricks he'd taught me were faring at the playground (I'd yet to meet my match). Then one day he asked if I wanted to tag along to the office. I accompanied him dozens of times, always on Sunday.

An exception was the one Sunday that President Roosevelt said would live in infamy. On December 7, 1941, 353 planes from six Japanese aircraft carriers pummeled Pearl Harbor. What kept me home that day was the *Hopalong Cassidy* double bill at the Embassy Theater, just up from the A&P supermarket. Dad returned late, drained. We sat around the radio. Bulletins crackled as he flicked ashes into a muddy coffee saucer.

The war in Europe was already in progress, and Americans had been divided over what to do. Neighbors with draft-age sons wanted no part of it. World War I's dead and wounded topped 37 million, greater than the population of most countries. My uncles, Paul and Henri, fought at Verdun, one of the war's bloodiest engagements.

But soon all wars would be dwarfed by the attempts to wipe out whole races: fatalities of at least 70 million, mostly civilian. Looking back on the period, many see President Roosevelt as the dominant figure. His New Deal was the force that drove economics and politics, raising aspirations. Yet another fellow also attracted attention: Charles Lindbergh, whose solo transatlantic flight in 1927 made him, for a while, the most celebrated human on earth. Five years later he was again in the news, after the loss of his firstborn.

Hounded by the press, convinced the crime was a product of American moral decay, he and his wife, poet Anne Morrow Lindbergh, fled to Europe. In three years of self-imposed exile, Charles served as a consultant to the Luftwaffe, fell for some National Socialist propaganda, and at one point publicly called Adolf Hitler a "great man." Returning to the United States in 1939, he advocated neutrality. His fame gave him a bully pulpit rivaling Roosevelt's, and after war broke out in Europe, he missed no chance to plead for isolationism.

Mom thought him naive, a dupe of Hitler. But Lindbergh counted in his corner millions of Americans, including George Washington, who in his 1796 farewell address warned against foreign entanglements. Mom was part of a silent minority pushing for American engagement. She hated *les Boches*, a contemptuous term for Germans, calling them bullies and worse. She feared for the safety of her family scattered about in France. It wasn't just personal. For the good of all humanity, she thought, Hitler must be stopped. Her Jewish friends felt the same way, with even more to fear.

While hewing to the AP's longstanding policy of objectivity, Dad let us know, though perhaps only to keep peace at home, that he too favored engagement. It was a longer struggle to convince the public. One aspect people dared only whisper was the jump-start that the war in Europe gave our economy. For the first time in years, employment was rising, both at the AP and at A&P.

Dad warned that if I decided to tag along with him, I'd have to heed his instructions. "Make a nuisance of yourself, that's it—*fini*," he stated firmly. I was as tall as a beanstalk and mature enough to handle the big city, he believed, albeit on a long leash. I agreed. Tagging along was more fun than stickball. An added appeal was that I could skip church. I didn't mind services as much as the itchy wool knickers that were part of Sunday dressing up, even on the hottest days. For tagging along, he permitted casual (nonwool) trousers, or short pants, for which I remain eternally grateful.

My mother voiced no objections to my ecclesiastical truancy. She may have been relieved to get me away from my sister, at least for a day. Sue and I were like France and Germany, constantly at each other's throats. Once during a scuffle we broke a robin's-egg blue enamel vase that had belonged to my doughty great-grandmother, Angele Pouret, who ran a vinegar-making enterprise outside Orleans. Later Sue bashed my teeth into the lid of a piano Mom loved to play, and played so well. If that Ivers & Pond is around somewhere, its rosewood crest probably still bears a cicatrix from my right incisor. Later, with jousting kids of my own, I learned how bickering drives parents bonkers. Now my sister and I can't get enough of each other.

The center of my new world was 50 Rockefeller Plaza, a skyscraper in Rockefeller Center, then a freshly rehabilitated twenty-two-acre section of midtown between Fifth and Sixth Avenues. The AP was a charter leaseholder, having outgrown its older digs on Madison Avenue. Fifty Rock, as the building is called, and its sister towers showcased the latest in technology and design; it hovered over gardens, sculptures, fountains, theaters, museums, restaurants, shops, and even an ice-skating rink. The place still radiates chic and cool, confirming the initial vision.

Dad and I mostly traveled by subway, a longer ride than the New Haven commuter train, but cheaper. The A trolley ran behind our house. In twenty-five minutes we were at 241st Street and White Plains Road, where we grabbed the Lexington Avenue Express. Fifty minutes later we arrived at Grand Central. In those days you rode as far as you wanted for a nickel.

During the long ride from the northeast Bronx, I insisted that we work our way to the lead car, where I played engineer beside the real engineer's locked compartment. Other kids gravitated there as well, and we shoved one another for a good position. The best part of the ride was the long slide into the tunnel after Jackson Avenue under the silt and sand bed of the Harlem River. I worried about those tons of alluvial gunk and water overhead. "Relax!" Dad said, deep in Carl Sandburg's biography of Abraham Lincoln or one of the many sections of the Sunday *New York Times*.

On at least one occasion he drove our old gray Studebaker into the city. Clusters of skyscrapers glistened in the morning haze as we crossed the Harlem River Bridge and swung into downtown Manhattan via Central Park, a site of murders and carjackings. At one red light I asked if he was afraid. He smiled, opened the glove compartment, and reached for something in a cloth—my first sight of the gun a Cleveland police captain had slipped him as a memento. Cops and reporters used to butter each other up. The police had impounded that gun from a local hood, and Dad probably shouldn't have accepted it. "Our secret!" he said. "Don't tell your mother." I never did. I liked secrets. Years later my kid brother came upon that gun in the linen closet. Ever resourceful Frank nearly lost a hand.

Though one of the coolest of men, Dad wasn't averse to packing heat—a bravado he shared with other scribes of the day, some of whom carried guns openly. Growing up in rural Ohio, he accompanied his granddad on hunting and fishing trips. Bearing arms was as natural as picking apples by the oak-timbered barn at the Nankin crossroads.

In a Tegucigalpa marketplace years later he was offered a Beretta M9 for $5—no bullets, just the gun itself, but as an admirer of Berettas for "their fine machining," he couldn't resist, and he slipped it into his rucksack. He was awaiting a visa to enter Argentina and forgot about the gun until his Pan Am flight was about to land in Buenos Aires. He had left the AP by this time, and together with his new employer, Scripps Howard, he was slamming Juan Perón. Any airport incident would have been embarrassing, even job threatening. Where to put the Beretta?

Just before the seat-belt light flashed, he rose, grabbed the knapsack, and headed for the lavatory. Locking the door, he extricated the gun and dropped it into the toilet. He flushed and flushed and flushed again, until two pounds of sleek Italian steel slid on chutes of sweet-scented blue water into those stygian depths. Recounting all this years later, his eyes twinkling, he quipped, "Don't cry for it, Argentina!"

The AP occupied the entire fourth floor at 50 Rock. Exiting the elevator, I became aware of the clacking of teleprinter keys and soon learned that those keys beat out the news of the world. A pervasive pungency, not at all unpleasant, came from the ink, without which those printers could not print. To this day, ink smells restimulate memories of that slice of boyhood at the AP.

By now Dad was on the cable desk, processing the bare bones of news from correspondents around the world. Foreign Editor Glenn Babb noted, "At thirty cents a word the AP doesn't want cable tolls wasted on color and background already on the reference shelves. That's for us to do." The desk shaped the incoming cables into readable news to be transmitted by wire to the hundreds of newspaper and radio station members of the AP.

Although news reporting was a communal effort, the far-off correspondent, not the New York rewrite man, got the byline, which was deemed only fair for the risks he took. It was up to the men at the desk to provide context, check for inconsistencies, and put flesh on the bones. Everything had to be sourced, given a basis for credibility. Today's correspondents no longer truncate. From laptops, tablets, and smartphones, they write as much or as little as necessary to tell the story. But in that yesteryear, the trappings of a story were the gift of the gifted men of the cable desk.

These men had a dress code: unbuttoned vests, uncinched ties, rolled-up shirtsleeves, and Green Hornet eyeshades. Office boys, and even a girl or two, prepared stacks of "books": sheets of flimsy onionskin paper layered with carbon paper. Fed into typewriter rollers, the multiple sheets provided copies for multiple editors.

Dad set me up at an empty desk with a working typewriter, stacks of paper, and chunky black pencils with a string you pulled to expose more lead, and pulling hard enough made the pencil vanish into a heap of curlings. Elsewhere, men were typing away, yanking "books" from rollers and scrawling on them with the thick black pencils. So I figured I'd do the same. Thanks to my home-learned typing, I hunted and pecked. Easily familiar with vampires and werewolves, I spewed out the goings-on as lightning crackled around Vlad's castle on moonless nights in Transylvania.

Since *Superman* comics had just come out, I naturally kept an open mind in case of a drop-in from Krypton. Clark Kent never showed, but the steel-blue-eyed young woman who did appear could have been Lois Lane from the *Daily Planet*. Flora Lewis, a future *New York Times* foreign affairs columnist, was then a clerk. Reminiscing years later, we agreed that our paths first crossed when, fresh out of the Columbia School of Journalism, she was a rare female in the AP newsroom.

I still see Dad, copy pencil slanted off his right ear, tie at half mast, under the torpid propellers of a ceiling fan wafting smoky strings of air. He wrenches a "book" from his typewriter, jabs at it during a second reading, impales a page on a lethal file spike, and shouts "Copy!" A clerk runs it across islands of editors. Last stop: the keyboard and lectern where grizzled teletype operators, stoked with coffee or something stronger, punched out words to hundreds of member papers.

One of Heywood Broun's biggest early battles was over news reading time. The Newspaper Guild insisted it should be on company time. Dad and his mates had to know what was happening in the world, but the AP management held that news reading was leisure and shouldn't count as work. The eventual settlement allowed for reading newspapers on company time—but only during slack periods.

Like Dad, most colleagues had worked at other papers, and even though they were happy with a steady job and solid paycheck, something was missing. They had been big fish in small-town America, and now felt like barely more than guppies in the swirling waters of New York City journalism. There was no more hanging around with cops and mayors and small-time hoods. You worked in a bureaucracy, commuted like a stockbroker, stopped chasing stories, waited for news to come to you. If a bruised ego was the price to pay, you paid it, sensing that your time would come.

A row of clocks on the wall told what time it was around the world. A neighbor once asked Dad what he did all day. "I look at clocks," he said. Teleprinters for incoming cables rimmed the desk, ringing a bell for each take. A cable consisted of little more than a subject and a predicate, such as this one from Louis Lochner in Berlin on June 22, 1941, another infamous day: hitler invades russia stop main push from south and west stop goebbels calls mobilization quote greatest the world has ever seen unquote.

Using old news clips, encyclopedias, Baedeker travel guides, atlases, and any other source available, the cable desk fleshed out background and context, pumping out that era's virtual reality. As what was called a slot man, Dad farmed out the cables, helped rewrite and edit, and controlled what went out on the wire. He would get credit when things went right and was where the buck stopped when they didn't.

He once found himself in a holy mess. The Basques were resisting the dictatorship of Generalissimo Francisco Franco in the Spanish Civil War, and on April 26, 1937, Guernica, the citadel of Basque nationalism, was bombed—symbolizing today, thanks to the Picasso mural, the horrors of war. The AP didn't say so directly but implied that Franco was responsible for the bombing. Reuters said so directly. Roman Catholic bishops, backed by the full prestige of the Vatican, protested that Franco, a Roman Catholic, would never have sanctioned the slaughter of innocent women and children. Dad was reprimanded for letting that implication stand. It turned out that the Luftwaffe's Eagle Squadron, based in the Balearic Islands, had dropped the bombs. Franco had left his dirty work for Hitler.

Though the biggest of the domestic agencies, the AP wasn't the only game in town. Its chief domestic rivals were the United Press (UP) and the International News Service (INS). During my years at the UP, it acquired the INS to form United Press International (UPI). The only change I was aware of was one more reporter, Joe Oppenheimer, on our business news staff of eight under Elmer Walzer. Joe was welcomed with a pair of roller skates. UPI was supposedly so cheap that it wouldn't reimburse taxi or even subway fares. From that legend grew a revelers' institution, the Downhold Club; Skates Athwart was its logo, and its purpose was to host ex-Unipressers at bibulous nostalgia parties. UPI is still around, though only a glimmer of its former self; it is now part of News World Communications, founded by Sun Myung Moon, the leader of the Unification Church (the Moonies).

The foreign rivals of the AP and UPI included Agence Havas of France, Reuters of Britain, the Wolff Agency of Germany, and Domei Tsushinsha (federated news agency) of Japan. Havas was the grandfather. Charles-Louis Havas, a Paris journalist and entrepreneur, started the ball rolling in 1835. Paul Reuter and Bernhard Wolff, both of whom trained at Havas, went off on their own to form the British and German enterprises. During the occupation, the Nazis made Havas a propaganda vehicle. After D-Day it was replaced by Agence France Presse, which remains the main French news agency. DPA, for Deutsche Press Agentur, succeeded the Wolff Agency. In Japan, Domei was reborn as the Kyodo news service.

Reuters soldiers on as Thomson Reuters, absorbed by the operations of the late Canadian media mogul Roy Thomson.

The AP started in 1846 when six New York City papers agreed to share the costs of telegraphed news. As the partnership grew, it became a cooperative financed by fees based on readership. Soon membership in the AP, with an uninterrupted flow of reliable news, was a major competitive advantage. Bigger papers sought to exclude smaller rivals. In a period of giant trusts, news moguls were no different from steel, rubber, or tobacco moguls. Smaller papers, fighting the exclusion, initially made no headway. To survive they formed competing syndicates, from which UP and INS grew. Controversy about "fair" competition raged until 1945, when the US Supreme Court found the AP in violation of the Sherman Antitrust Act. Now, thanks to this ruling, anyone who can afford the fees is free to join.

The AP and other wire services relied on technology that was as revolutionary then as the Internet is today: the telegraph, which a couple of decades before the Civil War converted messages into pulses anywhere that wires went. Before then there were the Pony Express, carrier pigeons, and probably the tom-tom. The teletypewriter followed: pulses activating keys that allowed material to be read instantaneously. Another innovation was the stock ticker, spewing tape coded by punctures and spaces corresponding to securities values. Then someone decided to gather up all that old tape to toss out the window in patriotic parades, and I ended up in one of those parades myself in April 1954—back from Korea, a sergeant, again on the streets of Manhattan, a proud holder of the Bronze Star, delighted to be alive. But like the "pushmi-pullyu" in the *The Story of Dr. Dolittle*, I'm ahead of myself.

When my boyhood interest in the cable desk flagged, I gravitated toward the rec room to play checkers or spend a nickel in the Coke machine. Dad said I could do anything I wanted as long as I didn't pester anyone. If I had problems, I should go only to him. He kept an eye on me when he could, but as insurance he introduced me to one of the clerks, an émigré from the Alpine region of France named Pierre, who later won citizenship as a US Army ski trooper. Pierre shepherded me inside and out. Dad thanked him with invitations to our home on Langdon Avenue for *pot au feu*.

The first time we exited the building, Pierre stopped me, smiled, and pointed up. "Angels!" he exclaimed. I'd almost missed them: five hovering art deco figures in stainless steel, each part of a new communications miracle: phoning, note taking, typing, photographing, and listening to the radio. This was my first of many encounters with Japanese American sculptor Isamu Noguchi's *News*.

Pierre left me to fly solo. I explored oversized lobbies with other reliefs and mosaics; wandered along promenades and sunken gardens; made friends with Atlas, who held the globe up like a hoopster; and marveled at exotic fountains, waltzing skaters, muscular murals, and statues of bare naked ladies. The complex was linked by subterranean concourses. Like a mole, I popped up in one place and then another. Celebrated as a marvel of smart urban renewal in the 1930s, it was a Depression kid's Disneyland. Best of all, it was free. Nothing fired me up more than all those escalators running up and down day and night. Steps disappearing and reappearing were new—and fun!

Since it was Sunday, I was often the only one around, which afforded me more than the usual freedom. I found the fast escalators and the slow ones, took two steps at a time, up or down, and sometimes swooped along the black rubber handrail, like the comic strip character Smilin' Jack pursuing the Mad Arabian. Where treads flattened into combs of smooth steel and suddenly vanished, I balanced myself, counting the clicks, and tried to imagine the complete revolution. I ran up the down escalator and down the up escalator, an early contrarianism that served me well.

I hated public relations spoon-feeding—and the predictable. A corollary: If too many people agree on something, it's probably wrong. Take Prohibition, which turned out so badly it was repealed, or the criminalization of various drugs, which can't help but be revoked. Why should someone dying painfully of cancer be denied the relief that marijuana or other drugs provide? I understand the need for rules, but at times journalists must break them—slipping under police tape to report a grisly event, digesting confidential documents to spill allegations of malfeasance, or seeking to redress the balance for the greater good, even though the way forward is ill-defined and probably best left that way!

Sometimes Dad joined me. He tried to explain the gilded statue beside the rink. "Prometheus," he said, "stole fire for mankind, then was bound to a rock as an eagle nibbled his liver." I turned back to the bare naked ladies. Sometimes he shelled out for a concert or a film at Music Hall, a new world around the corner with the Rockettes wheeling to the Wurlitzer. When the lights faded and the curtains lifted, we entered the noirish domain of *The Maltese Falcon* or *The Thirty-nine Steps*.

More often I haunted the cheaper Museum of Science and Industry, where phones played back what you said to them, and steel marbles bounced around seemingly forever. After perpetual motion, it was perpetual news at the Newsreel Theater: girls in dirndls tossing flower petals at goose-stepping soldiers; tanks on cobblestone streets and frozen tundra; carcasses of bombed buildings; Princesses Elizabeth and Margaret Rose waving from the rubble of St. Paul's. That's when it started coming together about Prometheus.

Tagging along with Dad ended in early November 1942, when Dad joined the ranks of AP war correspondents. By this time he had shifted at Berlitz from crash-course French to crash-course Russian. He was to replace Henry J. Cassidy in Moscow. A second man in Moscow, Eddie Gilmour, who had married a Russian, was staying put.

Mom, Sue, and I, and by now our cuddly brother, Frank, all bid him a tearful good-bye. The parting took place on a chill and drizzly November evening after we all had dinner together at the Champlain, Mom's favorite restaurant on West 46th Street. A taxi later took us the dozen blocks to Penn Station.

Dad trailed the porter along the red carpet of the Silver Meteor for Miami. He gripped a stylishly thin Hermes typewriter. A musette bag for medical supplies, also new, hung from his trench coat. From the sliding door of the bullet car, he waved—like Alan Ladd bidding adieu to Veronica Lake in *This Gun for Hire*. Mom tried to smile. She'd been quiet the whole evening. I knew she was unhappy. Later she told me that she knew he'd never come back. Since she sometimes made pronouncements that didn't materialize, I took it with a grain of salt. But this time she was right. Never again did they see each other as husband and wife.

While their relationship deteriorated, for me the die was cast. I took to newspapering as easily as Michael Douglas, the son of Kirk, took to acting, or Chris Wallace, the son of Mike, took to TV news. Reporting was bred in the bones. Fifty Rock pumped so much ink into my veins I had no choice—and no regrets.

7

Ticket to Ride

THE SIGN IN the cockpit of the twin-engine C-87 inspired little confidence: **IF WE FAIL TO FIND ASCENSION, OUR WIVES WILL GET A PENSION.**

In 1942 there were no easy routes across the North Atlantic. Dad flew from Miami to San Juan, Puerto Rico, across the equator to Belém, Brazil, in the Amazon delta, then southeast along the Brazilian coast to Natal. From there it was an eight-hour jump to Ascension Island in the South Atlantic and a similar hop to Accra, Ghana, on the west coast of Africa.

The pilot negotiated the uneven Ascension runway, and the passengers and crew found a mess tent with flapjacks, soybean sausages, and coffee. Dad traveled with another freshly minted correspondent, George Tucker, a product of Virginia military schools, whose judgment of locales was based on the martinis they served up. Ascension was "the pits."

Tucker and my father saw the world through different prisms. Straight-backed and mustachioed, like Smilin' Jack, Tucker was all pucker and starch. Dad, curious about anything and everything, was more willing to bend with the wind. The two made it to Accra, then across the upper half of Africa to Khartoum, Sudan, with a jag north to Cairo. They arrived three weeks after the pivotal battle of El Alamain, a heavily contested Egyptian seaport 150 miles northwest of Cairo.

Field Marshall Erwin Rommel was so close to victory, or so the story went, that he had already booked his accommodations at the Shepheard Hotel, a glorious relic to Cairo's imperial past that was burned to the ground by anti-British mobs in 1952. Yet in 1942, despite the war, the place was still like something out of *The Arabian Nights.* Houseboys wore purple and red uniforms with tarbooshes and copious pantaloons that tightened around the ankles. Potted palms and tropical plants rose toward frescoed ceilings. Antique elevators creaked up and down ten floors. The walnut-paneled lobby buzzed mostly with the astringent nasals of Oxbridge. The filigreed exterior of the hotel—Moorish arches, bulbous domes, and Juliet balconies—blended with a walled-in garden. The doorman, in a flowing burnoose, procured cabs. If you agreed, he held out his hand for the tip, adding, "I'll find a boy to get you one."

Although Rommel didn't quite make Shepheard's, both AP men did. The hotel was off-limits to enlisted men, but Dad and Tucker wore uniforms with the two silver bars of army captains, the honorary rank of accredited correspondents. As they stepped out of their taxi, two Australian grunts, recognizable by their jaunty hats with upturned brims, were passing and gave exaggerated bows. "Gabardine swine!" Dad heard one mutter. "That's where they wins the fuckin' war!"

After checking in, Dad and Tucker adjourned to meet Anatole, the central European bartender, and Tucker graded the martinis, straight up with a twist, "A-plus." Tucker moved west to join Field Marshal Bernard Montgomery's campaign against Rommel's now retreating Afrika Korps in the Libyan desert. My father trekked east, filing features from Jordan, Palestine, Syria, Iraq, and Iran.

Dad was to enter Russia along its southern frontier at Ashgabat, Turkmenistan, then make his way fifteen hundred miles north by rail and truck to Moscow. But in a screw-up that completely altered his life, the Soviets rejected his visa application. Unwittingly, he'd applied before AP journalist Henry Cassidy had physically exited Russia. Under an AP-TASS reciprocity agreement, the AP could put two men in the Soviet Union, and TASS, in turn, could put two men in the United States. The Russians, sticking meticulously to the accord, said *nyet* to a third visa while two American correspondents were already inside Russia.

Further dooming Dad's mission to Moscow was the Soviet refusal to grant a visa to anyone once rejected. Little could be done. Americans increasingly met such officiousness, and worse, in their dealings with the prickly Stalin regime—which, with the battle of Stalingrad still raging, had a lot more than journalistic protocols on its mind.

When AP General Manager Kent Cooper learned of the imbroglio, he ordered Dad to link up with the American Tenth Air Force to cover its possible intervention in the Caucasus. Roosevelt and Stalin had worked out a plan: if the Nazis weren't stopped at Stalingrad, US airpower would deploy inside Russia against Hitler's Panzers. Joseph Stalin already greatly depended on American military supplies, via Iran and the Russian city of Murmansk. Yet unwilling to signal to his populace any dependence on the West, Stalin ordered massive relabeling, with Chrysler tanks and even underwear and socks marked Russian-made.

In preparing for Russia, Dad picked up a blue-gray balaclava, the knitted headgear with nose and eye openings used in the Crimean War. Although he never made it to Russia, he kept that piece of cloth for years. It was ideal, he said, for shining shoes. He bought it in Cairo at Cicurel's, a Jewish-owned department store destroyed in the same nationalist fury that leveled Shepheard's.

While waiting to enter Russia, he wasn't idle. Features he wrote from wherever he happened to be at the moment recorded the life of the times. The *Mount Vernon Daily Argus* picked up several of his articles. Neighbors stopped me to say they'd seen "interesting stuff" by my father. Here's his description of wartime Cairo:

> As in ages past, the mingling currents of the Christian and Moslem worlds funneled through the streets. The fezzed and robed driver of an American-made taxi could have been carrying a visiting British India officer to a luncheon engagement with a Fighting French official just back from Equatorial Africa. The prosperous Egyptian merchant taking his thick Turkish-style coffee and morning smoke at a sidewalk table might have laid down his hookah to give street directions to a visiting American.

Wealth and poverty streamed together. "Filthy children forage swiftly along the sidewalks for cigarette butts, flies buzz with awful persistence and settle on the infected eye of a baby riding the shoulder of its veiled mother. A limousine drawing to the curb disgorges a European prince or an Oriental nabob."

He described a bemedaled, one-armed Free French soldier, Leon Bouvier, eighteen years old, who drove a Bren-gun carrier in a convoy transporting munitions into the battle of Bir Hakheim. When the convoy drew hostile fire, Bouvier ran for cover. A truck bearing fuses exploded, throwing Bouvier into the air, ripping his clothes, and tearing off most of his right arm and left thumb. A medic with a Scottish patrol pumped him with morphine and tried to get him into a field hospital. But in the midst of what was then a powerful German offensive, field hospitals were being dismantled, and Bouvier didn't get proper attention until seven days later upon reaching Alexandria. With an empty sleeve and a slew of medals, he told Dad, "I always wanted to be a hero. I have been kissed by five generals."

* * * * *

Cairo Bureau Chief Ed Kennedy lived and worked at the AP office on the twelfth floor of the Immobilia Building, a five-minute walk from Shepheard's. Brooklyn-born, Kennedy was a flamboyant figure with habits his colleagues found disconcerting. He was rude and self-centered, and he upended the conventions of almost any era by working all day in pajamas and a bathrobe. Yet the man was an AP legend and had probably earned the right to do exactly as he pleased. He had covered Field Marshal Montgomery's campaign the year before, including the capture of the Libyan port of Tobruk from the Italian Army, and was still living off one incredible incident.

Wearing his captain's bars, Kennedy suddenly found himself on the fast-changing desert battlefield separated from British forces and within hailing distance of a large Italian unit. Yet far from showing hostility, the Italians were waving frantically at him, trying to make him understand something. It turned out they wanted an Allied officer, any Allied officer, to accept their surrender. Kennedy obliged, leading his legion of Italian fighters through the lines of amazed British troops. It was a sensational coup and one of the AP's proudest moments.

Yet the same reporter also got the AP into a pack of trouble. As the war ended in Europe, Kennedy and sixteen other correspondents witnessed the German surrender on May 7, 1945, at General Dwight D. Eisenhower's headquarters in Reims. Mopping up in the east, the Soviets accepted the surrender in Berlin thirty-six hours later. Both President Harry Truman and Prime Minister Winston Churchill agreed to delay the announcement to show solidarity with Stalin. But hearing a snippet of the news on German radio, Kennedy broke the embargo. He said he thought the embargo had already been broken.

Although Kennedy was a temporary journalistic hero, the military took its revenge, "disaccrediting" him from future cooperation. As the furor mounted, the AP, not immune to government pressure, fired him—not its proudest moment. Later, implicitly acknowledging that it had been too harsh, the AP found him a new job, with a paper in California, the *Monterey Peninsula Herald*.

Kennedy maintained, with some justification, that the embargo was political censorship. "It's downright criminal to withhold such news from millions of people who have been in the war," he wrote. My father wondered how anyone could expect the containment of news of such magnitude. But other reporters who stuck by the accord never forgave Kennedy for robbing them of what would have perhaps been the biggest story of their lives.

From Cairo, Dad moved to Transjordan (now Jordan) at the end of 1942 to report on the Arab Legion, the crack desert force of twenty thousand men who helped the British keep order in their protectorates. He stopped in the Holy Land, not from any deeply religious feelings but to honor his devout grandparents. Jerusalem meant an overnight train ride across the Suez Canal on a swing bridge extending from, then folding back into, a bank of the canal. A new travel companion joined him, Paul Lee, assigned to write up the Christmas midnight Mass at the Church of the Nativity. Dad rode with Lee in a taxi the eight miles from Jerusalem to Bethlehem and later made the following observation:

> A mass any time in that church would be a powerful experience. During a war that seemed to pit the good angels against the bad ones, it overwhelmed. The utter simplicity of the altar and the rounded stones of the nave worn down by the shuffle of pilgrims over the ages helped suspend belief in practical wartime reality. Yet if there is a God and if He engineered a celestial event here 2,000 years ago, was there any doubt whose side he'd be on today?

As one man contemplated such universals, the other took notes for a story destined to be one of the most widely read ever. The two later bid adieu, and Dad caught a ride to Amman on a British flatbed signals truck. "I laid out a bedroll thinking I might sleep," he said, "but stars splashing across the sky had other ideas. I gazed upward all night, half forgetting about the bumps and the cold."

Upon arriving in Amman, he looked up Michael Foote, the British high commissioner for Transjordan, then an autonomous state in the framework of the mandate from the League of Nations to govern Palestine. After the Ottoman Empire collapsed at the end of World War I, Britain filled the vacuum left by the departing Turks until 1946, when Transjordan became sovereign. The name was changed to Jordan in 1949.

Foote, a past editor of Lord Beaverbrook's *London Evening Standard*, was a tall, handsome fellow, later head of the Labour Party. He knew everyone worth knowing in Amman and promptly introduced Dad to General Sir John Bagot Glubb, the Arab Legion commander. Glubb joined the force in 1930, when it was little more than an unruly Bedouin band, and shaped it into the most effective fighting unit in the Middle East, respected not only for its marksmanship but also for its way with the *khanjar*, a curved knife that opened a belly as handily as a can of bully beef. A soldier from Lancashire, wounded three times in World War I, Glubb crushed a German-inspired revolt in Iraq in 1941 and routed the Vichy French in Syria. He spoke fluent Arabic, wore Arab garb, and rode both a camel and a horse. His men called him Glubb Pasha, an honorific handed down by the Turks.

That chill day in 1942 in Amman, Glubb and his schoolmistress wife, Muriel, invited Dad for Christmas dinner. Their home was a terraced, flat-roofed house with a splendid view on an Amman hillside. Various military officers, diplomats, and wives were also present for traditional roast beef, Yorkshire pudding, and plum pudding flamed with brandy.

While attacking dessert, Dad heard the skirl of bagpipes. Glubb pulled the drapes aside to show a band of Bedouin pipers in tartans and plaids, trained by pipers from the Scottish Guard, playing a slow march on the terrace. With Britain—and thus Scotland—fighting for survival, and all civilization up for grabs, Dad, who was never averse to emotional outbursts, said he was close to tears at that moment. He certainly was in the retelling.

The next day Glubb organized a tour of the bivouac area of the Legion's First Desert Mechanized Regiment on a gray dusty plain. Dad arrived as the muezzin called devout Muslims to afternoon prayers. Rectangular furrows marked the places where the soldiers, drawn from Bedouin tribes of the desert, knelt down and bowed toward Mecca. Lithe as tigers, each man sported an abundant beard or mustache. The men also wore red and white shawl-like *hattas* (kaffiyehs) with tasseled edges over an olive-drab adaptation of the Bedouin robe, drawn tight at the waist with a rope from which dangled sidearms and a menacing *khanjar*. Dad met a regimental cook who was scooping out the ashes of an old fire and preparing to lay a new fire on which to roast the evening sheep. The animal stood by, unconcernedly eating tufts of wiry grass.

Besides writing features on Glubb and the Arab Legion, Dad profiled Transjordan's leader, Emir Abdullah ibn Hussein (who became King Abdullah I in 1946). His palace was next door to the Philadelphia House Hotel, where Dad was staying. The name derived not from the American metropolis but from the ancient Greek word for "city of brotherly love." The Greeks so loved the word that at least ten other Philadelphias showed up on the maps of their empire.

Abdullah was not in residence. But thanks to Foote's intervention and a chauffeured Humber touring car, they found Abdullah at his more temperate winter quarters on the banks of the Jordan. Descending to the lusher valley near the Dead Sea, they passed the black goat-hair tents of the local herdsmen and villages of stone houses. Foote explained that the population of the Arab world was roughly divisible between "houses of hair" and "houses of stone." Pressing for unity, Abdullah resided in his riverside "house of hair," or tent, part of the year and his "house of stone," or palace, the rest.

Abdullah and his brother Faisal (who became the king of Iraq in 1921) had bristled under Turkish rule and worked closely with T. E. Lawrence (Lawrence of Arabia) to inspire the Arab revolt against the Ottoman Empire in 1916. They had been encouraged by their father, Hussein ibn Ali, the Sharif of Mecca, a direct descendant of the prophet Mohammed through Fatima, the prophet's daughter, and Hassan, her eldest son.

Foote brought a dog-eared copy of *Seven Pillars of Wisdom*, Lawrence's account of the Arab uprising and the British role in it. He opened to the description of Abdullah: "short, strong, fair-skinned, with a carefully trimmed brown beard, masking his round smooth face and short lips. In manner he was open, or affected openness, and was charming on acquaintance. He stood not on ceremony, but jested with all comers in most easy fashion; yet when we fell into serious talk, the veil of humor seemed to fade away. He then chose his words and argued shrewdly."

At one point, Abdullah seemed to grate on Lawrence: "His casual attractive fits of arbitrariness now seemed feeble tyranny disguised as whims; his friendliness became caprice; his good humor love of pleasure. The leaven of insincerity worked through all the fibers of his being."

Foote cautioned Dad against taking Lawrence too literally. The emir was very much his own man, Foote said, who liked to think things out for himself. The emir was also deeply religious, prayed dutifully, and lived in complete abstinence of alcohol. Like many of his tribesmen, he was an active hunter, especially fond of hawking. Foote also instructed Dad on the manners expected by Arab royalty of their guests: (1) no smoking, (2) never expose the sole of your shoes, and (3) sit with knees "virginally clamped."

From the Humber, white tents appeared on the horizon. As they drew closer, the emir's banner fluttered over a weary-looking Bedouin sentry. Aides ushered them through a series of interconnected tents laid with multiple thicknesses of oriental rugs into one space with particularly ornate furniture. Three or four servants hovered.

A short, bow-legged man, with luminous, mesmerizing eyes rose from a brocade-upholstered chair to welcome them. He was warmly dressed, despite the mild temperature of the valley. An ankle-length robe of soft camel's hair covered a tight-fitting vest of scarlet wool over a blue shirt. A golden dagger peeked from a scabbard. Black congress gaiters encased his surprisingly small feet. On his head was the traditional red and white *hatta* with a black silk cord. His face was bronzed, and he still maintained the carefully trimmed beard that had once impressed Lawrence.

Abdullah asked them to sit on chairs placed next to his. Servants brought them thimble-size cups of sweet coffee. While still making small talk, Abdullah drew out a thin gold watch, then apologized for having to leave for midday prayers. Upon his return, he urged them to stay for lunch, and they followed him into the dining tent. Servants brought china basins of water and fresh towels with which to wash their hands. Drying his fingers, Abdullah described a trick of his favorite falcon. It would settle on the horns of a gazelle and flap its wings to steer the prey within rifle range. As he talked about the crafty bird, he seemed to be studying Dad, as if weighing what to say when the conversation turned to more timely subjects.

Lunch—sliced roast chicken and boiled wheat, slabs of mutton, fried potatoes, and a rice course—began without ceremony and ended with tiny fried cakes, suggestive of doughnuts, and platters of fruit. As soon as a plate emptied, a silent waiter appeared at one's elbow with another heaping platter. Midway through the meal, Abdullah broached the subject of a Jewish homeland in Palestine. He called Jews "people of the book" (the Bible is recognized by Islam) and said they were entitled to a settlement area and "wide powers of local autonomy" within a federal structure. "Arabs have no intention of persecuting, still less of driving out, the Jews who have made their homes in Palestine," he said. "On the contrary, it is only just that in areas of Jewish settlement they be given wide powers of local autonomy and, somehow in accord with their numbers, just representation in a federal center."

How much less blood might have been spilled in the Middle East had moderates like Abdullah, sometimes called the "lone wolf" of the Arab world, stayed in charge! Arab politics required that he use his Arab Legion against Israel in the 1948 War of Independence. But he later sought a settlement based on the federalism outlined to my father in those closing days of 1942, a courageous position in light of the permanent war sought by extremists.

On July 20, 1951, upon entering the Mosque of Omar in Jerusalem, this unusual leader, then king of Jordan, was shot and killed by a twenty-one-year-old fanatic. Unharmed was Abdullah's fifteen-year-old grandson Hussein, who accompanied him. Hussein's father, Talal, succeeded Abdullah as king, but about a year later mental illness forced Talal to abdicate. In 1953, at age seventeen, Hussein was crowned the new king of Jordan.

Although most analysts predicted that he too would meet an assassin, Hussein, after dissolving ties with Britain, fought off the efforts of the Palestine Liberation Organization to take over Jordan, took meaningful steps toward a constitutional democracy, and kept the kingdom intact for the next half century. He died on February 7, 1999, from non-Hodgkins lymphoma and was succeeded by his son, now King Abdullah II, who, from most accounts, continues an enlightened leadership. But Abdullah II is very much his own man in his own time. A science fiction fan, he took a bit part while still the crown prince in a *Star Trek Voyager* episode, and as king he planned a *Star Trek* theme park in the port of Aqaba. A Jordanian publicity release said that the park "will deliver a variety of multi-sensory 23rd-century experiences."

From Amman, Dad journeyed eastward to interview Faisal II, the seven-year-old king of Iraq, and to write about Polish soldiers suddenly released from gulags who were filtering into northern Iraq to form units to fight the Wehrmacht. First he had to get to Baghdad. He rode north to Damascus on the Hejaz Railway, the narrow-gauge line built by the Ottoman Turks to carry the faithful to holy sites on the Arabian peninsula. Its tracks were sabotaged during Peter O'Toole's guerrilla war in the fabulous David Lean film *Lawrence of Arabia*.

From Damascus it was due east to Baghdad across hundreds of miles of the Badiet-esh-Sham, or the Syrian desert, a stretch of frying-pan heat refracted by endless black lava beds. For this leg of the journey he transferred to the oddest vehicle he'd ever ridden in, and certainly the most fun: a trailer mounted on gigantic balloon tires and pulled by a tractor. He called it a moon buggy, and it offered the epitome of that era's luxury: air-conditioning, generated by the tractor's battery; mixed drinks with ice cubes from a small refrigerator; box lunches distributed by a uniformed steward; and soft reclining seats. Since most of the voyage took place at night, he caught up on his sleep. By noon the next day, he had crossed the Euphrates River and was in Baghdad. Two Syrian brothers developed the amazing service, but unfortunately it never returned a profit, and not long after Dad's trip the enterprise went belly-up.

Thanks to a letter of introduction from Abdullah to the Iraqi royal household, he next met the young King Faisal II of Iraq (the grandson of King Faisal I and the grandnephew of Jordan's King Abdullah), whose room in the palace was fitted out in a kind of prehistoric Playskool environment. The newest toys by his side included a three-foot model of a General Ulysses S. Grant tank brought from Cairo by his uncle and regent, Abd al-Ilah, and a model of a Hurricane fighter plane. A schoolmaster—the king's tutor in English, French and arithmetic—said the plane had been a gift from the Royal Air Force on Faisal's seventh birthday.

Faisal was dressed as if in an English boarding school: white shirt, red plaid tie, gray flannel shorts and jacket, and gray woolen socks. (He later attended London's Harrow School with his first cousin, Hussein of Jordan.) He suffered from asthma, and a handkerchief dangled from his side pocket. Faisal was seated. As my father introduced himself, the boy rose, adopting a practiced regal bearing, his head tilted and his thick black hair pomaded high. He advanced as adult royalty might, hands outstretched.

"How do you do," he enunciated precisely. Dad shook his hand warmly, noticing that his kneecaps were bruised from scampering on the floor. He told of his own son (me), almost the same age, in the Minnie S. Graham School in Mount Vernon. "I hope he has nice toys," the boy said. Dad later found a model of the same Hurricane fighter to send me, which I treasured for years.

Faisal, the nominal ruler of 3.5 million Iraqis, succeeded to the throne in 1939 upon the death of his father, Ghazi, in a car accident. Although he apparently wanted for nothing, he also stirred Dad's sympathy. Like the princes whom William Shakespeare's Richard III dispatched to the tower, he seemed expendable.

Eleven years later, in 1953, Faisal II ruled in own right. But floods hit Iraq, and he was blamed. More bad luck, or bad advice, included his choice of a prime minister, who insisted on strong ties with Britain. Israel's 1956 Sinai Campaign, coordinated with Britain and France, further destabilized the regime. Two years later, during a coup on Bastille Day, July 14, 1958, Faisal, twenty-three, and most of his family were gunned down in their Baghdad palace courtyard. Instability followed. The Ba'ath Party, modeled after the authoritarian Communist and Nazi Parties, took power, paving the way for the brutal dictatorship of Saddam Hussein, which lasted decades.

Soon after filing his story on the boy king, Dad found troops on maneuvers in northern Iraq who represented the Polish Army of the East, a ragtag cohort freshly freed from gulags that kept the nationhood of Poland alive in its darkest days. That story went back to the August 1939 Hitler-Stalin pact that carved up Poland. Most of the Polish soldiers who surrendered to the Soviets at that time ended up in labor camps. Under Stalin's orders, many of their officers were executed, including twenty-two thousand in the Katyn Forest near Smolensk. The apparent motive was to crush nationhood.

But in June 1941, two years after their pact, Hitler turned on Stalin, grabbing all of Poland and invading Russia. Stalin never foresaw the double-cross, and for a while he refused to believe it. In desperation he accepted a plan from Churchill to free most of the Poles still in his gulags as reinforcements against Hitler. So an incarcerated general, escaping Stalin's murder by a fluke, was extracted from Lubianka, the notorious KGB prison next door to the Kremlin, and given carte blanche to round up an army. His name was Vladislaw Anders, a former cavalry officer who had been captured in East Prussia twenty months earlier. This was the man the AP was now prepared to interview in northern Iraq.

The Poles were already in training camps in Iraq, Iran, and Palestine, preparing to fight in North Africa and Italy. They will forever be linked to the seizure of a monastery the Germans converted into an almost impregnable fortress atop Monte Cassino, about eighty miles southeast of Rome. After a seven-day siege in May 1944, its capture opened the way for the Allies to take Rome.

In Baghdad in December 1942, Dad was in cable contact with Anders. They arranged to meet near the Kurdish town of Khanakan in the Mosul oil patch about a hundred miles north. A clean-shaven young tanker in a requisitioned Tatra automobile picked him up at his Baghdad hotel. Somehow, because of mishaps conceded on the Pole's part, they didn't start until late in the day. My father described what happened:

> It was getting dark, and the tanker didn't know his way. The hard-crusted earth, grooved by wadis, was inhospitable and offered few distinguishing

features. We continued at a snail's pace, headlights dimming, signs of a failing battery or generator. The lights got so weak we could barely see. He stopped, pulled up the hood, fiddled inside. I wasn't sure what this would do for the battery. He worked minutes without tools and wasn't much of a mechanic.

He suddenly slammed the hood and just stood there in the darkness. He muttered something in Polish, then broke down and literally sobbed. It was a terrible moment. I got out of the car and approached him, wearing what I hoped was a comforting smile. He looked up and said in English so softly I could barely hear, 'I have brought disgrace to the whole Polish Army of the East."

"Nonsense," I said. "You just got lost."

I asked him to get back into the car and let me drive. Meekly he obeyed. The battery had just juice enough for the engine to turn over. I kept the lights off. Moonlight was enough to see by. My companion stared silently into the dusk. Luckily we soon ran into a Polish motorized patrol, and I followed it into the compound. We surprised a badly shaven, sleepy guard, who, upon seeing my uniformed companion, waved us forward. The night-duty officer welcomed me, got me something from the mess tent, and showed me to a bedroll on the hard-baked earth. Another chilly night in the Middle East under the stars.

Anders saw my father the following morning in his headquarters tent, warmed by a crackling wood fire. His long, thin, aristocratic nose overhung a close-cropped bristle of mustache as he spoke of "thousands" of Poles coming out of Russia: "Every day and week, while we were forming in Russia, men came to join us." He never spoke ill of Stalin. He made no mention of Katyn—he probably didn't even know of it. Unwilling to jeopardize any further exodus, he said, Poland above all wanted good relations with Russia. "We want to be treated as an ally," he explained.

Though handpicked by Stalin for that unusual army, Anders never considered going back to Poland after the war. A Soviet-backed regime had grabbed power by then, and most of the surviving Polish fighters, probably realizing they'd be reimprisoned or even shot on their return, made new lives in the West. Settling in England, Anders became the doyen of the Polish émigré community. He was married to the actress Irena Anders and died in England in 1970. In accordance with his wishes, he was buried among his comrades in the Polish War Cemetery at Monte Cassino.

From Baghdad Dad journeyed northeast to Tehran via a spur of the Trans-Iranian Railway, which penetrated the mountainous border region through countless tunnels. Sikh warriors under British command and Kyrgyz (or Kirghiz) tribesmen under Soviet command secured the right-of-way against any Nazi sabotage. After an overnight ride, morning brought an amazing sight. Against the backdrop of snow-capped peaks, Sikh guards in white garments like clinging underpants made their toilette along the rail bed. Each wore a steel bracelet on his right wrist and carried a small ceremonial dagger at his waist. With their turbans off as they combed their long black hair, the men looked like the bearded ladies at Ohio carnivals. Caught unaware, they may have looked comical to an outsider, but nothing was funny about their fighting skills and courage.

During one tense period after the train had been forced to halt at the far end of a tunnel, Dad inspected the cause of the stoppage, which turned out to be the derailment of a forward flatcar. Workmen struggled to right the car, which carried armored vehicles, weaponry, and explosives, all destined for Russia. Plainly visible were signs: danger, no smoking, black powder.

A burly Kyrgyz guard with a Tommy gun squatted on the track no more than twenty feet from the derailed flatcar. Removing a tin cigarette box from his pocket, he lit up. A Sikh guard, with holstered sidearm and ceremonial dagger, rushed up, snapped the cigarette away, and squashed it with his heel. The Kyrgyz snarled and pointed his gun at the Sikh. The Sikh blithely walked away.

The relationship of those two couldn't have been any more strained than the powers they represented. Rivals in southwest Asia for the past century, Britain and Russia were allies now only because of a common enemy. The Red Army had seized the north of Iran, the British fleet had seized the south, and dismemberment was a real possibility. Roosevelt did not want Iran to be a Nazi puppet, but neither did he favor Iran's partition into British and Soviet spheres. The British and Soviet presence had forced the abdication of the first shah, Reza Khan Pahlevi, an army officer who had come to power in the 1920s and seemed too close to Hitler for comfort. Roosevelt engineered his replacement by his son, Mohammed Reza Pahlevi, which started a storied intimacy between Washington and Tehran that lasted until the presidency of Jimmy Carter.

The center of US influence was the Persian Gulf Service Command, a thirty-thousand-man army of longshoremen who unloaded the Liberty ships that made it across seas infested with U-boats to speed supplies to Russia. Thanks in part to those arms and materiel, the Wehrmacht was stopped in Stalingrad in February 1943.

Tehran was an enigmatic, brooding place on the last day of 1942, when Dad arrived at the central station—a drafty, sprawling neoclassical structure completed by the shah's father three years earlier. Clearly visible to the north were the icy domes of the Alborz Mountains, once known for sheltering murderous black-robed mullahs high on hashish and opium.

The mountains seemed to shut out the world and influence the social structure. The northern districts that rose to the Alborz foothills enjoyed fresher air and cleaner streets. Here lived the more privileged, including the shah in his walled-in, heavily guarded Niarvan Palace. Melted snow provided fresh water, flowing downhill through ancient tunnels that dated back to the shahs of the ninth century. Along the side streets, the gutters flushed the city, depositing garbage and other refuse into the less favored southern districts.

Iranians, though always polite, were suspicious of the influx of US military personnel, and the Americans themselves had little desire to mix. Persian was hard to learn, and the soldiers looked upon Iranians with ignorance, suspicion, and derision. Separation was carried to such limits, Dad said, that military health bulletins warned against eating the country's wonderful pistachios. Army messes offered nothing faintly Persian. Only daring culinary explorers ventured into the many wine gardens or restaurants. Uninhibited, Dad favored an aromatic eatery near the rail station that featured a delicious rice and mutton curry.

Iran was so important to the Allied war effort that the AP constantly demanded new features. One was about freely available opium. Teahouses offered gooey balls of the stuff, smoked in clay pipes and held against a charcoal ember or an open flame. As the ball bubbled, smoke funneled through the stem, so that while some clientele enjoyed tea and biscuits, others were getting stoned.

Dad reported on farmers harvesting opium by using a clawlike tool to lacerate the pod of the flower and draw out the raw gum. A wider market existed than the teahouses, especially for the opium derivative heroin. But substance abuse wasn't yet a problem in the United States or the overseas military. Of most concern in early 1943 was venereal disease (VD). Dad broached that issue in a venture south to Khorramshahr, the headquarters of the Persian Gulf Service Command. An attractive port and railhead with boulevards studded with date, palm, and fig trees, that town had now become the base for a raucous stevedore battalion unloading ten-thousand-ton Liberty ships lucky enough to fend off the U-boats. But at that moment, sick leaves in the battalion had risen precipitously. The reason: gonorrhea.

The threat was deemed such that the Red Army might not be able to hold its position, and Russia, and the war itself, could be lost—at least that's what Captain Jerry Sadler told his men. Sadler, a taut Texan, had just taken command of the port battalion. His first action was to ban all passes and furloughs until the VD rate subsided. "You won't get off this base until your plumbing's fixed," he told an assembly of longshoremen. "I'll take care of you better than you're taking care of yourselves, but then you gotta take care of me."

Thanks to Sadler's exhortations and the good work of army medics, the clap crisis came under control. Tonnages into Russia rose again, and Sadler became a major, then a lieutenant colonel. He was an officer who loved barbershop quartets, chewed Copenhagen tobacco, and provided what he called the finest mess in all Persia, which included ham hocks, grits, and barbecued ribs. Before the war Sadler had been active in Texas politics. He later served in the state legislature and ran unsuccessfully for governor.

Dad also ran into US Navy personnel, including sailors on shore leave playing softball on a baked mudflat at Bandar Shapour, the port beside Khorramshahr. Gunner's Mate Third Class Alphonse Palaski from the USS *Vance*, a destroyer escort, was "starring at field and plate," said the AP dispatch.

Decades later I got a letter from Palaski's daughter, Elaine Amoriggi of Smithfield, Rhode Island, enclosing the full AP story from "somewhere in Iran." She wrote me blindly: "I hope if you are his son you enjoy reading the article and maybe pass it on to your family. He captured what the men in WWII went through in such tough times on a ship." I quote an edited paragraph as yet another example of the war's reach: "Americans are buckling down here to the toughest overland war-transport job in the world, beset by some of the world's worst weather and health conditions. The Persian Gulf region in May, June, and July vies with Death Valley for the distinction of being the world's hottest spot. . . . This heat, from which nighttime brings little relief, saps man's strength. . . . Even the fleeting touch of skin to metal is enough to blister."

Beyond the pockets of wartime American influence, Iran was desperately poor. Nowhere was this more in evidence than at the School for Productive Children at Isfahan, a center for Persian carpets south of Tehran. The site of the school was an alley reeking of feces and garbage. Outside the sooty stone premises were skeins of wool draped like wigs over empty oil drums. Inside, kids sat tying knots with fingers that, Dad wrote, "fluttered like butterfly wings."

A carpet in the making resembled a harp. Nine- to twelve-year-olds fingered the strands as a supervisor snipped the projecting ends. Dad wrote that these kids were at it twelve hours a day, seven days a week, yet they were luckier than the kids who were permanently maimed to ply the beggars' trade.

8

Passage to India

"AND HERE, SAHIB, he is parting her hair with his lingam," said Mahmoud, the Muslim guide in an obvious tone of disapproval. Dad was standing in the Temple of Love in Benares, India, the holy city of Hinduism on the upper Ganges River. In the quiet of the temple, the sex of the crude wooden carving did not jump out as though from the back alleys of Calcutta, Delhi, and Bombay.

The trip to Benares was part of an exploratory venture north while Dad settled in at the AP bureau in Delhi. The carvings in the Temple of Love were historical curiosities, faintly amusing in their celebration of sex organs. Having found a spot under the eaves and elevating a leg to support a new Zeiss Super Ikonta, Dad changed his film. A scream suddenly pierced the hallowed precincts.

The Hindu caretaker ran up, shaking his fists. Mahmoud looked embarrassed. "You've got your foot on the *yoni*, Sahib," Mahmoud told Dad. Without fully understanding, Dad withdrew. "I'll give him a few extra *annas* [coins]," Mahmoud said to my father. "If I did not know this man, you would be in great trouble. We should move on." What looked like abstract stonework to support a stray foot was actually an ancient collection of symbolic pudenda. He had stepped on the glorification of the female elements of creation.

Sex was not only a religious preoccupation of the Hindus—whose beliefs fuse gods, animal spirits, and the senses—it was also a voucher for commercial exploitation. Brothels were legendary, as was the profusion of porno stalls, where, for instance, Dr. Aziz in E. M. Forster's *A Passage to India* browsed before entering the Marabar Caves. In those years of the Raj (British Crown rule in India), when so many Britons were fleeing Victorian morality, Hindu merchants had discovered pornography's lucre.

In Delhi Dad joined another AP legend, Preston Grover, the manager for India, who was from Farmington, Utah. Assigned to continental Europe as World War II broke out, Grover had been touring a factory in the Lowlands when the RAF bombed it. He walked away without a scratch. Later he was on a Royal Navy patrol boat sunk by Nazi dive bombers and managed to swim to safety. I myself met this lucky, plucky fellow in the early 1970s during his retirement years in Paris. He was square-jawed and bore a likeness to the actor Robert Taylor. When Dad was in town, I invited Grover to my apartment, and the two old scribes, relaxed and loquacious after excellent Burgundy, relived their swirls of memories.

Inevitably they talked of yet another member of the Delhi bureau of 1943: a young, bright, well-educated Hindu named Radakrishnan. Unwittingly, Dad had made yet another faux pas with an invitation to the young man to lunch. They were in the starchy dining room of Wenger's Flats, an apartment hotel near Delhi's center, in the same building as the AP office four stories up. The restaurant, a symbol of Britain's imperial presence, was popular for its fare and ambiance. A giant cloth curtain, or *punkah*, hung across the ceiling. Regularly agitated by a servant, or *punkah wallah*, it fanned the diners and kept flies at bay.

The guests descended a grand staircase meant for lords in sashes and medals and ladies in tiaras and gowns. As Dad descended, a gecko appeared from nowhere. Thanks to a misstep, it decamped tailless, which the barefoot staff, from their looks of horror, clearly regarded as a bad omen.

Radakrishnan was prompt, wearing his finest *dhoti*, an elaborate white loincloth that drapes Hindu men to their ankles. Several British military officers cast jaundiced glances, along with the native staff. Radakrishnan ordered soup, salad, and a meatless curry, and he handled the utensils unfamiliarly, as if more used to eating with his fingers. Apart from a comment that his mother refused to eat celery because it cried in pain audible to her ears, he spoke little. Ohio boyhood reminiscences sparked little interest. Weeks later, after he and Dad had gotten to know each other better, Radakrishnan confided that Dad's invitation had put him in an impossible position. The AP reporter in him could not say no, but the rest of him was full of cultural taboos in this eatery of the Raj.

A similar gulf existed when the new correspondent met the leader of the independence movement, Mohandas K. Gandhi. In those days the revered Mahatma was preaching self-sufficiency. My father hoped for some elaboration, but of course he realized that practically anything the man said was news.

He found Gandhi in a wooden shack in an alley barely wide enough for a taxi. The grizzled seventy-three-year-old, with fuzzy gray hair fringing his baldness, received Dad cross-legged on a *charpoy*, a traditional woven bed. But as Dad introduced himself, the face turned blank. Gandhi seemed to be sucking something hard in a practically toothless mouth. An attendant rushed up excitedly to say that this was one of the Mahatma's "silent days."

The Mahatma rationed his talk, along with food and energy. Grover, or someone else, must have known and forgotten to warn Dad. Though miffed at the mix-up, Dad could only look at the man with greater respect. The presence stared into space, wearing a simple pair of bent rimless glasses, which in a few years would transform the sunlight of a roiling subcontinent into raging fire.

Upon a brief return to India in late 1945, Dad recalled seeing thousands of Gandhi's rebellious countrymen shouting to their British overlords, "Quit India!" One protest started on Calcutta's Chowringhee Road. He saw mobs methodically overturn British military vehicles and set paper fires to ignite vapors and gas. The explosions ripped along "like rows of fiery dominoes."

Dad also recalled a train ride in 1945 from Bombay to Calcutta. He was in a compartment with British army officers, including a stiffly mustachioed brigadier and a young viceroy commissioned officer (VCO), an Indian national who owed his rank to the British viceroy of India. Lunchtime was at hand, and a bearer—in white jodhpurs, barefoot, and with his turban jauntily cocked—brought a tray of whiskey and soda. Talk was spirited, but suddenly feeling hunger pangs, Dad asked, "When do they quit serving lunch?"

The Indian looked up puzzled. Dad repeated, "Quit—stop," gesturing with his hands. The brigadier intervened. "You're using an Americanism our friend here doesn't understand. Definitely not the King's English, you know. In acceptable English, *quit* means 'change,' as in get out of a place."

The VCO flashed a toothy smile. "As in 'Quit India'?" he asked. Britain finally did, two years later.

Dad himself quit India in the spring of 1943 upon drawing China in the AP's lottery. Grover pulled him aside to announce that J. Reilly O'Sullivan, embedded with the Fourteenth Air Force in Kunming, was returning to

New York. "The job's yours!" he said. It was a magical moment for Dad. He told Grover about covering the Cleveland Air Races, about meeting Amelia Earhart, and of his love of fliers and flying.

But Grover gave him one last assignment in India: Allied operations on the Burma Road, which was now in Japanese hands. Those seven hundred miles, once linking northeast India to southwest China, were a jumping-off point for jungle fighters. From Delhi, Dad hopped a transport to Assam and linked up with a two-seater L-5 plane dubbed the Flying Jeep, which was used as an artillery spotter and which found a jungle strip almost into Burma itself. He then flagged a British armored personnel carrier headed east on reconnaissance. Rattling ever deeper into enemy territory, the major in charge noted with British calmness, "If we draw fire, we'll ditch and *appreciate* [assess] from there."

Their destination was a camp of Chindits—British and Gurkha fighters who took the name of the dragon statues around Burmese temples; today, after several film treatments, they are better known as Wingate's Raiders. They were just back from blowing up bridges, ammo depots, and rail lines behind Japanese lines. Dad met their leader, Orde Wingate, an India-born British officer, Christian fundamentalist, and early supporter of Zionism, who was among the more controversial and charismatic wartime figures. Churchill invited General Wingate to a summit the following August (1943), where he lectured on guerrilla tactics to the Allied chiefs of staff. Now in a spot where Assam folds into Burma, Wingate met the AP. Dad described the occasion as follows: "The recon vehicle broke into a clearing. A group ahead, in fatigue caps festooned with fishhooks, looked like anglers beside a Scottish stream—except for their varied states of undress and chain smoking. They had just returned from blowing up a communications center across the Chindwin River, five days distant, and were running redhot cigarette butts over swollen leaches."

Wingate, who had a black beard and an eagle nose, had just celebrated his fortieth birthday on the jungle trail. He was born into a military family that traced its roots to William the Conqueror. But nothing about him signified either such lineage or the rank of brigadier general. Nor could he be mistaken for just one of the men.

"The hooked staff always with him made him look like an Old Testament prophet," Dad recalled. "He spoke like a prophet, too, leaving little doubt he considered himself a divine instrument for the destruction of Japan's presence in Burma. The Japanese were destined to taste the bread of adversity and the waters of affliction."

Wingate's raiders severed a key rail link between Myitkyina and Katha and later helped create jungle strongholds that facilitated the retaking of Burma and the retreat of all enemy forces from the Asian mainland. One of his most potent ideas was to clear enough space for gliders. Their stealth and capacity to transport troops, equipment, and even mules led to ever larger jungle strips, then later to the permanent jungle bases that hastened Japan's retreat.

Wingate was especially proud of ongoing efforts to clear a patch codenamed Piccadilly, a hundred miles behind Japanese lines. To mark the alliance with the United States, he dubbed another site Broadway. Jackie Coogan, a former child film star whom Dad later interviewed in Kunming, was among the guerrillas at Broadway. Coogan, who piloted a glider into Broadway, told Dad, "Those Burmese natives were surprised to see us over their paddy fields, but you should have seen their faces when out hopped a team of terrified mules!"

C-47s towed gliders at the end of a nylon line. But it was hard to make out anything below and to keep the tow lines from severing. If you survived a landing beneath that green mantle, the hike out invited leeches, Japanese patrols, and myriad other hazards. Yet stealth worked. The Japanese didn't learn of the enemy in their midst until too late. Although Wingate saw his theories confirmed, he died before Japan's surrender. About a year later, on March 24, 1944, a B-25 with Wingate and nine others crashed with no survivors. All ten lie in Arlington National Cemetery.

The itinerary to China paralleled Marco Polo's spice route, the Silk Road. Unlike the plucky Venetian merchants who had to contend with such hazards as foul Himalayan weather, broken axles, and brigands, Dad linked up with the Air Transport Command in Assam, then boarded a twin-engine Douglas C-47 Skytrain that was carting supplies into Free Nationalist China across the roof of the world.

Yet that seven-hundred-mile passage, which American soldiers promptly dubbed the Hump, was probably just as treacherous. Pilots, including Ted Stevens, a future senator from Alaska, coped with Japanese Zeros, perilous ice, gale-whipped rocks, lethal windshifts, moiling monsoons. One thousand people failed to make it, and the wreckage from those valiant misadventures is still being found to this day.

9

Cathay

IT WAS APRIL 1943 when the sun set on my father in China for the first time. Half a world from AP headquarters, the C-47 taxied at Wujiaba beside the Blue Lake of Kunming. In the lea of those icy Himalayan reaches, he stepped into semitropical softness, the sun cavorting behind ice cream cone–like peaks and jocular wind-sculpted formations of forests turned to stone.

Dad secured his pile of belongings and went for a walk. From the cluster of dun-colored hangars and Quonset huts, he headed for lofty pines along the water's edge. An old woman was ahead on a footpath leading to ancient grave mounds. She wore leggings and walked strangely, as if on tiptoe. He stepped up his pace and guessed that her unusual wobble was from the binding of her feet as a child.

"*Hao pu hao*," he said, bowing, bravely using a phrase-book greeting. She returned the bow. Although her face was like parchment, he wondered about the gentlemen who might have looked upon her in her younger days, drawn by her delicate sway and the soft roll of her hips. Missionaries largely stopped the cruel practice of tying a girl's feet back against themselves to arouse the male libido. He was struck by the sorrowful image of this woman falling between the cracks, working painfully all these years with her elegantly misshapen feet.

The lake was never far away. Beyond tawny fields of mustard, fishermen worked the skiffs. Web-footed, chokered cormorants disgorged their catch into buckets after diligent poking. A boy leading a mob of ducks approached Dad. The boy held up a bamboo pole with a feather at its tip and dangled it ahead of the lead duck. The boy pressed a thumb upward in greeting, shouting: "*Ding how* [very good]!" Dad smiled. Yes, everything was very good.

The road traversed ancient paddies. An army truck with bombs rattling in its bed returned him to the present. The driver, a corporal from Rhode

Island, grinned, said the bombs were disarmed, and offered a ride back to the base.

J. Reilly O'Sullivan, from Kansas City, looked like Jiggs in the *Jiggs and Maggie* comic strip. Before returning to the United States, he was made a comrade in arms in the Nationalists' famed Seventy-Eighth Division—the first time, said Commanding General Ho Ying-chen in the formal ceremony, that any foreigner had been so honored. J. Reilly introduced Dad to preppy young men and women from the Office of Strategic Services (OSS). Kunming was a base for clandestine activities in Indochina, including the distribution of mimeographed anti-Japanese propaganda.

Since bikes were plentiful and it was dinnertime, everyone was about to ride off to an Annamite restaurant on Qingyun Street. (Dad and I had been avid cyclists on paths beside the Hutchinson River Parkway.) Dad recalled the following:

> Everywhere the city throbbed with pedicabs, rickshaws, pickpockets, street vendors, beggars. Carts, tipping with fruits, vegetables and dry goods, lined the curbs. Kunming was at the crossroads of old trading routes for spices, tin, and opium, and also a holiday resort for the French in Indo-China escaping the heat. At its south gate, a customs shack still collected duties on goods entering the city. After dinner of rice, snails, bamboo shoots, and the local beer, we took a more circuitous route back, winding along cobblestone lanes lined with one- and two-story mud-and-stone houses. Soon the wind bore up the odor of excrement. Sullen men (women too—impossible to tell) loaded night soil from privies into barges on the cargo canal for delivery to farms around the Blue Lake.

The party headed toward a marble pagoda, built, someone said, to honor a chaste widow. They passed the four-story graystone Fourteenth Air Force building adjacent to Bill's Nightclub. A billboard beckoned to striptease inside. Dad left that for the younger set and ascended toward the pagoda to feast his eyes on the concupiscent night folding around a lissome city.

Until the end of the war, Kunming was where Dad often hung his hat—and also a much coveted Ike jacket. The jacket, which tightened smartly at the hips, was the fashion hit of the day, popularized by Dwight Eisenhower. That particular jacket was part of an exchange with an army *Stars and Stripes* reporter named Andy Rooney, later the author of homespun, often curmudgeonly, philosophy and humor on the CBS show *60 Minutes*. Having filed on the war in Europe, Rooney arrived in Kunming in the spring of 1944 to check out Asia. His memoir, *My War*, described the swap with my father.

"Everyone wanted an Eisenhower jacket even though they were only a rumor in China," Rooney wrote, and "Clyde Farnsworth, for all his sophisticated worldliness, desperately wanted one." Dad, in turn, owned a pair of Carl Zeiss binoculars that Rooney coveted. "We talked about a swap one night at dinner, and afterward Clyde tried on my Eisenhower jacket. We were not really the same size or shape, but my jacket seemed to fit him, and we agreed on the exchange. I always thought I got the best of the bargain."

I did, too. Later Dad gained weight, making the jacket a hard fit. But I'll bet Rooney got good use of those binoculars, if only for bird-watching in Central Park. Rooney also lauded Dad's greater knowledge of the dining scene in Kunming, where few restaurants met any sanitary standards. The rules, which Rooney and other colleagues religiously adopted, included having vats of boiling water brought to the table for the visible rinsing of all utensils and the serving of all food bubbling hot.

"None of us ever got what was then known to GIs, even in China, as 'Delhi-belly,'" Rooney wrote in his memoir. "Under Clyde's gastronomic direction we ate well and stayed well."

Dad commuted by air between Kunming and the wartime capital of Chungking four hundred miles away at the western end of the Yangtze gorges. Here he joined dozens of colleagues at the press hostel, run by the Nationalist government both to house foreign reporters and to keep tabs on them.

A rectangle of mud-and-wattle huts, the hostel overlooked the confluence of the Chialing and Yangtze Rivers. To enhance the natural beauty, Minister of Information Hollington K. Tong, American educated (University of Missouri and Columbia University) and a former editor of the *Peking Daily*, arranged for lawns, gardens, and even a luxuriant banana tree for shade on the many hot days. Yet not even such a well-connected operative could control packs of brazen rats. Some colleagues fended them off with baseball bats. Dad filed on a battle in bed after one of the beasts gorged on his bottle of glue. All wartime stories had to be cleard by censors. In this case, a censor read the piece with amusement, stamped approval, and delivered this lecture: "You foreigners make such a big thing of our rats, but we see them differently. Now that you have seen our rats up close, did you notice how bright their eyes are, how sleek their fur? Our rats are healthy rats. We have a saying that in good times we feed the rats because in bad times they feed us."

Thanks to Dad's suggestion for better showers—welding old fuel drums together to make a larger receptacle for heating and storing water—the new AP man was elected to the management committee. His term started around the time the hostel was looking for a second cook, which introduced him to what was known as "friend business," or "squeeze."

The number one cook had just taken a lesser post and recommended a friend for the old one. Both went before the mess committee to discuss the terms of hire. When the friend asked for a sum considerably more than number one would get, Dad asked number one how he could tolerate his friend making so much more.

"Because I now do the shopping!" he said. Number one controlled the fund for food purchases, and following an age-old tradition, would *squeeze* a hidden fee from each market outlay. The committee tolerated the long-practiced scam. Otherwise, the scribes might have had to make their own meals.

The houseboys had a racket, too, but the committee put its foot down this time. Lightbulbs were burning out with unusual frequency. The houseboys usually tapped the funds set aside for new bulbs and the fare to go downtown to buy them. But by now the houseboys were replacing bad bulbs with good ones from other rooms and pocketing the funds. The panel decreed the smashing of all dead bulbs and a member's presence to monitor each act of destruction.

The censor's hut was outside the hostel grounds near a telegraph office, and both were open twenty-four hours a day. Censorship in wartime was a fact of life, and stories could back up for hours awaiting the oval clearance chop. Late one night Dad rushed to the hut and found it locked. Having learned of a Japanese breakthrough in an offensive in western China, he wanted to rush out an exclusive, but to do so he had to rouse Jimmy Wei, a deputy of Tong's, to unlock the place. Together they came upon the spectacle of the censor sprawled out dead drunk. Dad recalled Wei's cry of despair: "And how do they ever expect us to become a great country, Mr. Farnsworth?" Tong later created a school for censors to increase their number and professionalism and broaden their knowledge of English.

A cultivated diplomat who was later the ambassador to Washington from the Republic of China, Tong, despite his American education, probably never quite got used to some of the more disconcerting habits of his largely American wartime clientele. Frankie Cancellare, a photographer for Acme Pictures and a Brooklynite crony of Dad's, developed a fit of xenophobic anger one evening.

"I'm tired of fuckin' China," he roared to no one in particular, "tired of the Chinese, tired of this Kuomintang chickenshit. I want to do something for George Washington!"

"Go chop down a cherry tree, Frankie!" someone shouted.

Frankie stood up, bleary-eyed, his short stocky frame a bit unsteady. "Fuckin' A! I'll chop down their goddamned banana tree!"

Where he found the ax no one was sure. But there he was on that manicured lawn slashing away so aggressively that no one dared to stop him. "I wanna see their faces when they wake up to see their precious banana tree face down in that flower bed!" he growled.

When the ever civilized Dr. Tong inspected the damage the next morning, it was up to the new AP man to concoct a rationale. Cancellare had been an arborist before taking up photography, Dad told Tong, and he believed that the tree in question had been stricken by a blight that would endanger all the trees of China. Tong, too polite to press further, inquired whether Dad had enjoyed his shower that morning.

Less given to bellicose fulminations was another colleague, Brooks Atkinson, the drama critic of the *New York Times*, who after the attack on Pearl Harbor took leave from Broadway to cover the war in China. A lean, sinewy, crusty New Englander, Atkinson described one evening how he had won a wager with a Broadway crony and triumphed over *New York Times* stylistic vigilance. He had bet $20 that he could get *tuches*, the Yiddish word for *derriere*, in print in the *Times*, which shunned words that might offend a family readership. His review of a short-lived musical made reference to a "tap and tokas [sic] number," but to get around the possible objections, he exploited the *Times*'s pride in its sophisticated typography by instructing the copy editor to place a cedilla beneath the *k*. Although a cedilla under a *k* is utterly meaningless, the copy editor dared not counter such apparently unimpeachable authority; the word appeared, unpronounceable but acceptable, and Atkinson won his bet.

With typical generosity, Atkinson helped Dad publish a novelette in *Liberty* magazine in 1944: the fictionalized account of a downed American flier who bailed out near the border between Japanese-occupied and Free China, and was rescued by lepers at the Colony of Forever Peaceful Hill, established by Christian missionaries. A Japanese detachment pursued the flier and his rescuers. The lepers protected the flier, precipitating a confrontation with the Japanese commander, who lost face before his men, which gave the flier a chance to escape. Dad offered the story as bedtime reading. Atkinson couldn't put it down, so he sent it to New York agent Leah Salisbury, who placed it with *Liberty*, which ran it in two installments and paid the princely sum of $1,000.

Dad worked closely with Spencer Moosa, the resident AP correspondent, a gentle, humorous man whose lean frame and tonsured baldness fringed with gray made him look like a medieval scholar. Born in Shanghai of Jewish parents who had emigrated from Baghdad, he held a British passport, spoke the English of a well-born Indian, and more than got by in Arabic and Chinese.

The AP office was in the northwest corner of the press hostel compound. Moosa and his wife, Nina, a White Russian countess, resided in adjoining quarters. She gave the place class: chintz curtains beside an icon of St. George slaying the dragon, shelves filled with cups of fresh flowers, and the collected works of Anton Chekhov and Alexander Pushkin. The room contained three desks: one for Spencer, one for his Chinese assistant, and one for visiting VIPs, such as Dad from Kunming or Preston Grover from Delhi. A map of the Yangtze gorges dominated one wall.

Moosa worked his Chinese assistant hard, so it was a high-turnover job, focused on the "mosquito press"—news sheets from towns in the Japanese-occupied Yangtze Valley. Hand-set on transportable flatbed presses and delivered irregularly by underground courier, these sheets were valued because of the light they shed on life in the war zone: descriptions of air raid damage, accounts of food shortages, and indications of troop movements. Like mosquitoes, the papers had to be fleeting, to avoid Japanese detection and deadly punishment. Moosa adapted their content to the AP's daily war report, with attribution and additional sourcing.

One story noted that caskets were piling up beside local village railroad stations, causing a health hazard. The rural Chinese traditionally sought burial in their home villages, so families went to great lengths to get the bodies of their loved ones returned. This was not easy in wartime, and the extent of the delays became a barometer of the regional toll of the war.

Moosa capitalized on the death jitters to deal with a serious office annoyance. Crossed wires at the Chungking telephone exchange triggered maddening wrong numbers. The calls tapered off only after Moosa identified himself in Chinese as the proprietor of a shop where coffins were made.

His creativity came into play again, this time as a rather cruel, though not completely unjustified, practical joke. A colleague named Violet Fisher, a handsome, blue-eyed Briton under contract to supply features for the Beaverbrook press in London, used the office as her second home, freely monopolizing files, desks, and other facilities and pumping Moosa, or anyone around, on news tidbits. "Spensah," she'd shout, "can I see your blacks [carbon copies] on Chiang Ching-kuo?" Her overbearingness matched her thoughtlessness. Never did she put things away. After her visits, the office was "like Georgia after Sherman," quipped *New York Times* photographer George Alexanderson, who dubbed her "Violent Fisher."

Finally, the gentle, soft-spoken Moosa could take it no longer. He composed a telegram to her, signing it "the Beaver," the well-known nom de plume of Lord Beaverbrook. Moosa gave the telegram seemingly authentic stamps and smudges. The text complained that she was not sending usable copy and was missing important stories. The day after its receipt, a crestfallen Violet entered the office, all sparkle gone. She asked for nothing. Moosa still wasn't satisfied and mercilessly sent a follow-up, demanding that she follow the reporting example of her rival, Stuart Gelder, the Chungking correspondent of the *Manchester Guardian*. Moosa shared his joke with too many people. Violet found out, never forgot, and never forgave. But in the end Moosa won: she stopped pestering.

It was a twisting, two-mile descent from the press hostel to the commercial center of Chungking. Rickshaw operators relished the course. Striking a balance between their weight and their passengers', they were like flying squirrels, straw-sandaled feet skimming the surface.

Not all hostel residents used just run-of-the-mill rickshaws. Joe Alsop, the future *New York Herald Tribune* columnist, then an aide to Chennault and a man of some private means, had a custom-built rickshaw with leather upholstery, brass fittings, and scaled-down, gleaming brass carriage lamps—a Rolls Royce of rickshaws.

Alsop, Moosa, Atkinson, Dad, and everyone else used at least the common variety. Downtown, besides the scattered offices of the wartime government, there were hives of merchants, and the streets were a mess. Oranges, lemons, pomelos and other fruit towered on rickety barrows as the merchants jostled for favored positions. Carbide torches gave off garlicky odors in the frequent rain. The displays of the Szechuan farmers probably exceeded anything yet seen from California or Florida. People ate wantonly, carelessly tossing peels and pits. Eventually, however, with consummate efficiency, every last peel was collected, boiled in a vat, and recycled as marmalade or jelly, for sale in the same markets.

As a wartime hub of commerce and manufacturing, Chungking maintained a wartime film industry. China's Hollywood had been Shanghai until the Japanese seizure of the coast in 1937, when filmmakers, and anyone else who could, fled the thirteen-hundred miles up the Yangtze River. Directors, actors, cameramen, and writers all worked from jerry-built studios, making feature films and propaganda shorts. The talent included such reigning queens as Butterfly Wu (*Scattered Blossoms in the Tears of Rain*) and Li Lihua (*Flower Girl*), who, like Alsop, used custom rickshaws.

Up the long hill they came in their wartime finery, for press conferences, interviews, and photo shoots. Even when not seeking publicity, this special royalty hung around the hostel, lunching in the dining room, playing killer mah-jongg with Nina Moosa or Mrs. Tommy Chow, the wife of the Reuters chief, adding luster and glamor to a beleaguered city and to the press itself.

In November 1943, the Japanese forced a crossing of the Yangtze above the great lake of Tung Ting in south-central Hunan Province. Their objective was Changteh, a walled town of fifty thousand beyond the north shore, and eventually the larger urban complex of Changsha, the provincial capital. Their goal was control of the "rice bowl," so named because the region fed half of China.

After fierce resistance, Changteh fell. But within days the Chinese counterattacked and, supported by the Fourteenth Air Force, won it back. The Chinese said they inflicted "heavy" casualties, and in December 1943 they ran a press tour to back up the claim and counter criticism of not doing enough in the war effort. Dad hated junkets, but he joined this one because he didn't want to get scooped.

The party included Israel Epstein of the UP, Vadim Sinelnikov of TASS, Guenther Stein of the *Manchester Guardian*, Harrison Forman of the *Times* of London and Brooks Atkinson of the *New York Times*. It also included Allied military attachés and assorted Nationalist minders. They all stayed overnight in Changsha, an attractive city still unscathed by the war. Dad recalled narrow streets and shop signs in gilt calligraphy that denoted the wealth of its merchants. Mao Tse-tung, the son of a prosperous grain dealer, had been born seventy miles away, in the village of Shaoshan, but Changsha was where he was schooled and launched his political career.

From Changsha, the party edged north by riverboat into the contested lake region, staying overnight in Taoyuan, near Changteh, where the fighting was fiercest. To demonstrate a signal victory, the Nationalists recruited gravediggers to exhume freshly buried Japanese soldiers. Amid much shouting, the diggers laid out the corpses in parallel trenches. After a photo shoot, everyone retreated to a Belgian missionary's residence for a surreal tea party of bonbons and petit fours.

That night they stayed in the empty dorm of the riverside Taoyuan girls' junior high school, where the Kuomintang hosts threw a banquet in the gymnasium. Shaoshing—a nutty-flavored Chinese rice wine, served warm and deemed essential after the day's horrors—flowed smoothly. Christmas carols, led by Atkinson, were sung in a raspy, buzzed harmony, and the Nationalist hosts enthusiastically applauded each rendition. At last everyone repaired to bed upstairs, but since these were minibeds for schoolgirls, most opted for blankets on the floor.

At dawn came a reminder that war doesn't take a Christmas holiday. The school came under attack by three Zeros. Hung over and trying to belt up, the distraught members of the press rushed into the courtyard; the more lithe and nimble of them found refuge in willows and reeds by the riverfront. When Dad emerged, one Zero seemed to be diving straight at him. He hit the ground and covered his head. Yards away the earth spewed. Shrapnel grazed the shoulder of a nearby Australian military attaché; it was amazing that this was the only casualty.

Despite that grizzly interlude, the Chinese guides had still more to show. Opening a sealed cellar, they uncovered captured land mines, grenades, artillery shells, and other explosives, which, had the Zeros' aim been a little better, could have blown the illustrious group into the South China Sea. Ashen-faced, Rankin Roberts, a US army press officer, warned that a riverboat to Changsha risked another attack. The safest return was by foot along a hundred miles of paddy paths. For those unused to walking, the hosts offered ponies, rickshaws, and sedan chairs.

Dad hoofed it for a while beside Harrison Forman, a highly articulate companion who expressed relief that they weren't returning via Changteh. Forman described an incident two years earlier while he was stringing for the *New York Times*. According to Forman's published dispatch, Dr. Robert Lim of the Chinese Red Cross had confirmed a macabre experiment. On November 4, 1941, a Japanese plane circled Changteh's walls, dropping not bombs but foodstuffs and clothing, seemingly a humanitarian gesture. Within a week, however, six Changteh residents had come down with symptoms of bubonic plague: black tongues, dark spots on the skin, and swollen glands. All six died, according to Forman's March 1, 1942, report.

Dad faced a more immediate crisis: his Brazilian-made mosquito boots were falling apart. Flapping soles, bound with medical adhesive tape, left blisters, causing such discomfort that he persuaded himself to use one of those sedan chairs, borne by four sinewy men with a relief detail of two trotting behind. Dad described it as follows:

> I was comfortable enough, but only after overcoming second thoughts of having four little men, any two of whom I could practically carry, trot along hour after hour levering my 180 pounds and the weight of the chair on their bony shoulders. They didn't seem to mind. I was giving them work. Behind those curtains, coddled by a soft inner light, I was suddenly back in the days of the dynasties. The only sounds—hard breathing of the men outside and the squeak of bamboo poles against lashings. '*Dinghao* [very good!],' I said every time we stopped. And we stopped often, at intersections of lanes, where merchants offered noodle and soup dishes, duck, and pig barbecues. The smells were great, and everyone ate.

Without further incident the party returned to Changsha, where Marshal Hsueh Yueh, the governor-general of Hunan, tossed a banquet in their honor. The marshal, a little man seemingly engulfed by his boots, was reputed to be one of the great Nationalist field commanders. In September 1939, having successfully defended Changsha, he earned the nickname Little Tiger—perhaps an exception that proved the rule because the Hunanese, like Texans, reveled in bigness. Everything seemed big: chopsticks, bowls, and even scrapers for a furred tongue.

That banquet was in yet another girls' junior high school. Almost hidden by a screen behind the host and his family was a beefy gentleman in a cotton-wadded suit, a Mauser pistol coddled on his lap: Little Tiger's chief of security and taster. Dad joined Epstein of the UP, Forman of the London *Times*, and Stein of the *Guardian*. A one-eyed, crimson-faced brigadier general came over, introduced himself in passable English, and, weaving slightly, flung a gauntlet: whoever chugged the most Shaoshing was the better man. Dad, albeit a light drinker, was "elected" to represent the Western press, and he foolishly accepted.

The pale liquid was poured from a teapot into earthenware rice bowls. Bowl after bowl the two men swigged. They toasted Allied solidarity, defeat of the common foe, and the long lives of Generalissimo Chiang Kai-shek, President Franklin D. Roosevelt, Prime Minister Winston Churchill, and French leader Charles de Gaulle. The wine was heady. When one bowl was emptied, it was turned upside down to await the refill for yet another toast.

Dad let the press down with an unconditional surrender!

Everyone adjourned to a Chinese opera in the auditorium. Taking his seat, Dad heard a loud gonging, saw a blurring of colors, and hastily made for the exit. Forman, his antennae up, helped him back to his room, where a charcoal brazier glowed. That sudden warmth, the smell of acrid smoke, and the endless Shaoshing proved explosive. The coals, like Mount Vesuvius, ignited lava and ashes into the above and beyond. Somehow, with Forman's help, Dad made it into bed.

If one sedan chair rescued the AP, another nearly became an international embarrassment. It was May 1944, and Dad was covering the visit to China by Vice President Henry Wallace. On a side trip up the Min River in western Szechuan, Wallace was inspecting an irrigation project. His host was Col. J. L. Huang, the head of Madam Chiang Kai-shek's New Life Movement, which cobbled elements of Confucianism and Christianity. Huang arranged for the party to walk a mile upriver to a Taoist temple, where all admired the view, sipped green tea, and munched watermelon seeds. For the return, sedan chairs were available.

Wallace, a fitness enthusiast, refused to be lifted and persuaded Huang to join in a switch in which they would together act as coolies to bear a member of the international press. Frankie Cancellare had earlier overheard Wallace plotting and informed Dad. Several news colleagues had already departed on sedan chairs, and Dad's crew followed behind. Wallace and Huang fast approached, aiming to trade places with two of Dad's bearers. Forewarned, photographers were rushing to memorialize the event.

What a photo op—the vice president of the United States and his Chinese host bearing an AP reporter! For kicks, Dad said, he had half a mind to go along, until he noted the miserable look on Huang's face. Feeling Huang's chagrin more than his own, he demanded to be put down.

Wallace was crestfallen. A great publicity shot had just been missed!

10

Spin the War

BISECTING BURMA ON a jagged north-south line is the wide, deep, bountiful Salween River, which rises in the Himalayas, flows through precipitous gorges to alluvial plains in the south, and waters half the rice crop of Southeast Asia. In early 1944 Nationalist Chinese troops controlled the territory east of the river, and the Japanese Imperial Army controlled the area west of it.

General Joseph W. Stilwell, the commander of the American forces in China, Burma and India, tried to get Chiang Kai-shek to attack across the river. He believed that if the Japanese were pressed by Chiang, they could be driven out of Burma and all of Southeast Asia. But Chiang, confronting a renewed Japanese offensive in western China, figured he was already spread too thin, and he also agonized over Mao, who was holed up in north-central China. Chiang had no doubt that once this war was over he would face an inevitable showdown with the Reds. The Chiang-Mao rivalry went back to 1927, when Chiang executed prominent communists in what was known as the Shanghai Massacre. Chiang consolidated power under a new government in Nanking. Mercy would not abound once the tables were turned.

Chiang finally ordered that Salween offensive, thanks to wire reports by Dad and a United Press colleague, Al Ravenholt, another American farm kid turned Asia hand. Born in Milltown, Wisconsin, Ravenholt worked his way across the Pacific Ocean as a cook on a Swedish freighter, spent months trucking medical supplies into the Chinese interior with the International Red Cross, and then joined UP.

The two agency reporters had been invited to the US military command in Kunming to be briefed by Brigadier General Frank Dorn, Stilwell's deputy. In early 1942, Stilwell, Dorn, and a small contingent of American and Chinese troops retreated from Burma into Assam, barely ahead of the

Japanese, and vowed to win Burma back. But it couldn't happen without Chiang's help.

Under the terms of that backgrounder, Dorn was not identified. He was "a source close to the Chinese-American command." Similar anonymous sourcing exists to this day. If governments make news and news organizations are to disseminate that news, the press still probably has little choice but to go along. That source questioned the fitness of the Nationalists to wage an offensive against the Japanese, one of the most highly sensitive issues in the wartime alliance. Dorn said it outright: "The Chinese are suffering a morale problem and cannot be counted on as a firm ally against the Japanese."

A crafty officer with an anthropological bent, Dorn had served in the Philippines before the war and completed a study of the Negrito language, which is spoken by the aboriginal peoples on the peripheral islands. He now focused on the linguistics of Chiang's pride. Yet under that backgrounder there could be no hints that an American officer ever uttered such words. It was with shock that Chiang's Chungking command saw the agency reports from Kunming, guessed the source, and decided it had to prove the source wrong.

On April 11, 1944, the Nationalist army crossed the Salween. Together with forays by Allied jungle fighters, the move eventually squeezed the Japanese out of Southeast Asia. That Chiang gave no official notice to his ally of the impending attack, Dad said, was his way of venting spleen.

The Chinese point advanced westward along a turf of spungy jungle hills. After twenty miles, roughly following an old caravan route famous for rubies and jade, they hit resistance, the citadel of Teng-chung, now heavily fortified by the Japanese. Various American elements, including tactical units of the Fourteenth Air Force and medical teams, were primed for support as Y-Force advisers (*Y* for Yunnan, the province bordering Burma).

Several days after the initial crossing, Dad caught an L-5 Flying Jeep from Kunming to a freshly cleared jungle strip near the citadel. A *laoping*, or common soldier, wearing baggy fatigues and an all-purpose smile, guided him to the approaches. Among jacaranda and pyinkado trees, vultures pecking at a dead monkey seemed unperturbed by the chatter of close-up fire.

Dad described the scene as an incredible throwback to earlier pages of war. Secured by ropes and netting or clinging to weaving bamboo ladders, Chinese soldiers climbed walls that seemed as wide as they were high, perhaps thirty feet. Others, with crude hammers, pounded spikes into stone to wind more ropes for handholds. Still others used battering rams against the massive wooden gates. Inside, the Japanese defenders fired down point-blank from fortified parapets, themselves targets of Chinese snipers. The defenders used mortars, adjusting the elevation so the rounds would drop just a few feet outside the walls.

It was dangerous not only for any poor fighters but for harebrained spectators as well, and Dad soon ducked back into the relative safety of the heavy jungle foliage. He later came upon another clearing where Chinese reserve soldiers were gathered for a mess call. Each *laoping* carried a stockinglike cloth looped over his shoulder with the day's rice ration, which was tossed into the common pot. In lining up, men kept a watchful eye on their fellows to ensure a rough equity in the distribution of the hash of the freshly snared jungle birds that supplemented the rice. The birds had been chopped into a chewy mash and fried. He tasted it, found it too powerfully seasoned (even for him), explored the jungle again, and came upon a hillside burial site with a partial view of the citadel.

Stopping for his own K rations, which he had wisely packed earlier, he struck up a conversation with an American Y-Force adviser who said they were about to witness a spectacular show, the high-noon bombing of the citadel by the Fourteenth Air Force. Shark-toothed P-40s arrived on schedule, along with higher-altitude B-25s. The P-40s peeled off to drop 250-pound bombs inside the walls, then returned for strafing runs. The B-25s loosed ethereal escalators of arcing 500-pound bombs.

The adviser said that the wounded were being tended to at a nearby village. "Follow the puddles of blood!" he told Dad. On a path around the rice paddies, Dad indeed found dark splotches pointing the way to a village, which was deserted except for the dead and the wounded and a team of Y-Force Americans. One wore a surgeon's mask and captain's bars and greeted him, "Welcome to the asshole of the world!"

The surgeon, who hailed from Kentucky, had worked in industrial medicine at DuPont. His assistant, a sergeant, added, "Believe it or not, we're it for the whole Chinese army!" The operating room was a courtyard, and the operating table was a door extracted from a hut and fitted with a rubber sheet. Water buffalo sloshed nearby in lilied shallows, their ropy tails waving off the flies.

A *laoping* with multiple perforations lay on the table. His intestines had been pulled out through an incision in his abdomen and were piled on top of his body. Tracking the patient's pulse and respiration as best he could, the doctor fingered the guts inch by inch, trying to sew up the perforations. Dad watched as the patient's perspiration and breathing intensified, as if the fellow were running a race up a steep hill. Then silence.

The darkness of the jungle was almost total. The doctor, flashlight in hand, made the rounds of the huts where the wounded lay. At each doorway he counted heads, sometimes entering to check a pulse. Dad shared a granary with other members of the medical team. They lodged over a pair of water buffalo. He heard soporific rhythms as the beasts rubbed their ridged horns against the wooden rafters, then shamelessly slipped off into deep sleep.

Next morning the team cranked up again. Another *laoping* lay on the table. The sergeant peeled away bloody bandages covering his face and neck. Shattered bone and teeth studded a coagulating river of blood. "Hey, captain," the sergeant shouted, "when you get a minute, look at this—and we're all out of silver wire!"

11

Airfields of Dreams

NEAR WHERE CHINA elbows Tibet, the US Army Corps of Engineers and thousands of Chinese peasants built airfields for B-29 Superfortresses rushed off Boeing assembly lines in Wichita, Kansas. From the spring of 1943 through the summer of 1944, Chengdu, the capital of the western Szechuan Province, was the forward base from which to strike Japan for the first time since Lieutenant Colonel James Doolittle's carrier-based raid on April 18, 1942. Eastern Siberia would have been a lot closer, but Stalin said *nyet*.

Besides a megatonnage of aviation fuel lugged over the Hump, the treacherous air passage into Free China, each Superfortress required specially reinforced runways of at least a mile in length. Yet China had few bulldozers, tractors, or back-end loaders. Its strength was manpower, and so those airfields were mostly built by hand. Later on, as the western Pacific Islands fell one by one to amphibious assaults, Chengdu was replaced as a US base by the Marianas: Guam and Tinian. Two atomic bombs later, the war ended. But in 1943, all eyes were on the peasants of Chengdu.

Dad described whole villages extracting boulders from riverbeds and moving them with carts, sledges, and oxen to crushing and paving sites. As many as 750,000 people participated. The racket from their hammers and axes was like a sky full of click beetles. It couldn't have been much different in the building of the Great Wall or the pyramids of Egypt. Yet even as these peasants labored, they showed high spirits, smiling up at their new GI friends, sensing a common purpose, tossing *V* for victory signs with gnarled, dirt-caked fingers. In less than a year, four airfields with eighty-five-hundred-foot runways and six smaller fields for fighter planes were built, along with barracks, mess halls, roads, and storage pits, all under the operational command of the Twentieth Air Force.

In August 1944, Operation Matterhorn, the code-name for the strategic bombing of Japan, came under Major General Curtis LeMay, at age thirty-eight the youngest two-star general in the US Air Force. Having caught the eye of Air Force Chief of Staff Henry (Hap) Arnold, LeMay was transferred after commanding a B-17 air division in the Eighth Air Force in Europe. Dad met him in Chengdu in late August 1944. LeMay had just led a Superfortress squadron in from eastern India after hitting enemy rail installations near Bangkok.

"How was the flak?" Dad asked in the briefing room.

"Piss poor!" LeMay spat out, chomping his signature cigar butt.

The AP wrote around the salty language, calling the flak (antiaircraft fire) "very poor" and adding, "LeMay left no doubt how poor it was." Two decades later, during the Vietnam War, LeMay resorted to even starker bluntness, warning the North Vietnamese to "draw in their horns, or we're gonna bomb them back to the Stone Age."

B-29s from Chengdu hit Japan on June 16, 1944. In a night raid they targeted naval repair facilities and a steel mill at Yawata on northern Kyushu. Dad reunited with an old buddy from the *Cleveland News*, William T. Shenkel, now a rising star at *Newsweek*. Having covered the Fifth Army advances in Italy, Shenkel arrived in Chengdu expressly for the air campaign against Japan. He flew a superfortress dubbed the Limber Dugan over Yawata. But against that plane at that moment in history, Japan's defenses weren't quite so "piss poor." Pummeled by antiaircraft, the Limber Dugan crashed. Shenkel and the eleven-man crew perished.

Dad told me, "We barely had time to dwell on such things. Everyone knew he could be next. Empty chairs in the mess hall were the only reminders of the missing. Soon these were filled by other young men."

Six weeks later, on July 26, 1944, it was his turn to ride the tiger. The target was the Showa Steel Works at Anshan, Manchuria. It wasn't Japan, but it was no piece of cake, either, since it was the first daylight B-29 raid against a Japanese target. Showa furnaces made a third of the coke for Japan's steel industry.

Dad attended the sunrise briefing inside a new hangar of bamboo and lashings. Eight hundred men stood around—the flight crews of seventy-two Superfortresses, including Dad's Monsoon over Anshan. An intelligence officer showed slide projections of Japanese fighters. Men fidgeted. Cigarette smoke drifted around silvered cones of light.

The AP story included an unintentional breach of censorship derived from that briefing, which almost cost Dad's accreditation. The degree to which military censorship was then enforced stands in sharp contrast to more recent exercises of press freedom, such as Wikileaks or the Pentagon Papers, and it will probably take forever to find the happy medium between the public's right to know and the sanctity of the jealously guarded secrets of national defense. Winding up the briefing, the intelligence officer said, "In case any of you guys gets his ass shot off over the target but can still make it to your alternate, you know what to do!"

"Egg in your borscht!" came a voice from the back, followed by snickers.

Monkeyshines from the Catskills, Dad thought, and incorporated the assumed GI wisecrackery into his account. Alas, when the intelligence officer, Colonel Jesse Williams, a former functionary at Texaco, read the clippings, he lost his cool. He accused Dad and the AP of a serious breach of security.

"Egg in your borscht" was not just a wisecrack. Under a secret protocol between Roosevelt and Stalin, it was code for safe harbor for disabled American aircraft. Stalin vetoed US bases in Russia, but he assented to letting crippled American planes land in Siberia, provided it got no publicity. Moscow could have used the AP story to revoke the accord. Denied such landing rights, more American airmen might have perished. It was a very serious charge. Dad demonstrated that the story had cleared through the regular channels. Only an informed reader would ever notice, and the breach was inadvertent. Colonel Williams eventually backed down, but he rode Dad hard for weeks.

Because monsoon rains had mired the Chengdu strips, Brigadier General LaVerne G. Saunders, the leader of the Anshan raid, delayed takeoff for three days. Finally, in the predawn of July 29, 1944, the engines of seventy-two Superfortresses roared to life, a din like the rubbing together of all the fortune sticks of fate. Dad climbed into Monsoon over Anshan through a belly hatch. Inside were bare ribs, sheet metal, tubing, wires, and rivets, all state-of-the-art from Wichita. Outside was the first light over craggy Szechuan hills.

Pilot Bill Kingsbury was in his seat, his earphones tuned to voice channels for takeoff. Copilot Earl F. Brown made the introductions: flight engineer John J. Holecek; radio operator Harold L. Eckstrom; bombardier Donald W. Barton; radar specialist Frederic Wolkoff; navigator Hillard L. Perry; gunners Clarence R. Hazelton, George D. Smith, Anthony J. Yosco, and Kenneth H. Bransdorf.

For trim, or balance, Kingsbury asked Dad to ride near the rear radar blister, or nodule. After full throttle, Kingsbury released the brakes and they were off, rattling and thumping, fuel tanks sloshing, and eight five-hundred-pound bombs stowed in the bay. Wolkoff lifted the belly hatch for a gander. "Put it back!" Dad shouted. "If we don't look, those damned hills go away!"

Rainwater snapped up as prop wash (a current of water created by the propeller) and lashed the underbelly. The straining plane lifted, but not fast enough to miss a treetop that knocked out a radar blister. They were luckier than a neighbor on the right, however. Two of its four propellers were feathered and had no thrust at all. When the pilot tried to return to base, he collided with a crag. Dad witnessed the fireball. There was more trouble as they approached the Yellow Sea. Foamite successfully doused the smoke from a short circuit in the control panel.

At the coast they were alone. Single-engine planes, more vulnerable to Japanese fighters, had the option of going for less well-defended targets. Kingsbury called Dad to the flight deck and asked him to make the decision.

Dad took not a second to ponder. "I want my ticket punched for the full ride," he said. Not only did he want the story; he also counted on super pictures with a new Zeiss Ikonta camera from the post exchange. "Okay," Kingsbury said, ordering battle stations. "We go for it!" Left unsaid was what all this revealed about the power of the press.

Within a half hour they were twenty-five thousand feet above the target. Already two ground fires were visible, marking the drop zone. Dark and light puffs below signaled enemy antiaircraft fire. Kingsbury warned on the intercom that Zeros had scrambled. Gunners rattled off protective bursts. Monsoon over Anshan headed straight for the red eye of the blast furnace. For thirty seconds, bombardier Barton, now commanding, was locked on course. Puffs rocked the heaving, rattling, throbbing aluminum frame. Dad, madly snapping pictures, held his breath.

"Bombs away!" Barton shouted. Kingsbury again took over and went into evasive action, weaving, rolling, practically looping the leviathan, to pass the danger zone unscathed. But an hour into the return, one of the gunners reported that a release mechanism had jammed. Two live bombs were stuck in the bay. Barton unjammed it. They now had to pick a new target before returning. Kingsbury found a Japanese airfield near Loyang in the Yellow River basin and drew desultory fire. A Zero scrambled thousands of feet below. There was no real threat. The two bombs cratered the intersection of two runways, a perfect strike.

Thirteen hours after takeoff, Dad was back at Chengdu. Gunner Yosco jumped from the hatch, spread-eagled, and kissed the runway. Dad, excited about his pictures, rushed to the base photo shop and watched his negatives appear sharply in one of the basins. However, during the wash process, a technician accidentally turned on the hot water. Holding the negatives to the light a few minutes later, Dad saw those thirty seconds over Anshan dissolve before his very eyes in a breakdown of the emulsion. His precious images were a washout, but not the remembrances.

Late in 1944 Japanese troops overran eleven major American airfields and six satellite strips in south and west China. Elements of Chennault's strained Fourteenth Air Force sporadically struck the advancing Japanese columns, but because the defensive ground forces were inadequate, the sites were abandoned after the removal or destruction of anything of use.

Dad joined a demolition team at Kweilin to report firsthand on this underreported facet of the war. Japan's military was breaking through the Allied defenses in western China, threatening to link up with the enemy in Burma and Indochina to create an impregnable fortress in the heartland of Asia. As it turned out, the Japanese were spread out even more thinly than the Allies, and they cracked first. But in the fall of 1944, as those airfields fell one by one, Asia seemed up for grabs. The base at Kunming, and even the capital of Chungking, were vulnerable.

Flying into Kweilin from Kunming in another L-5 plane, he saw the enemy's mechanized units and infantry columns advancing south along the roadbed of the Hunan-Kwansi Railway, just ahead of the main Japanese force. Gerry McAllister, the accompanying public affairs officer, estimated that they had a couple of hours at most.

Otherwise, the scene was a perfect watercolor: rice paddies and water buffalo kissed by the sun and surrounded by cone mountains. But during the landing, potholes stuffed with bombs, fuses, detonators, and primer cord returned them to grim reality. Because of the immediacy of the threat, Brigadier General Casey Vincent, the base commander, conscripted them into his demolition teams as part of the efforts to deny anything of use to the enemy. Scorched earth was new work for the AP, but Dad undertook it with patriotic gusto.

In the mess hall were stacks of canned peaches. With newly requisitioned 45-caliber Colts, the men plugged them dead in their tracks, making a once-in-a-lifetime spectacle of geysering peach syrup spraying the walls and ceiling. Chinese looters had depleted the gasoline stocks, so the pyro-tyros made bonfires of wastepaper and wood. As the conflagration spread, Dad and McAllister were again drafted, now as jeep drivers for demolition teams setting fuses around the base.

Mission accomplished, they churned up the red-clay roads, fleeing south just ahead of enemy spearhead brigades toward another air base at Liuchow, which was also slated for demolition. Soon after reaching higher elevations, they heard bellowing detonations. The sky turned pink and orange. Although Liuchow was just fifty miles away, detours to avoid Japanese patrols took most of the night.

Stepping into a shower later, Dad saw water swirling blood-red into the drain. He assumed he'd been hit, but he felt okay. And then it suddenly dawned on him that this was merely a laterite runoff from every inch of his aching body.

One of Chennault's medium bombers, a twin-engined B-25, returned from a mission over the Yangtze River valley crippled by ground fire that knocked out its hydraulic system. With brakes failing, it came to rest in a paddy field. During the landing a wing tank exploded, setting the fuselage afire. The crew members jumped out, except for the waist gunner, who was pinned by a wing butt ripping into the fuselage. His buddies tried to free him, but the flames spread fast. Colonel John A. Dunning, the wing commander, arrived with base fire trucks and organized one last effort to free the delirious gunner, who was being incinerated. Dunning unholstered his Colt 45 and killed the gunner.

The AP witnessed none of this. It all came out in the court-martial in Kunming. One American had killed another, and no matter what the circumstances, military justice demanded a reckoning. Wing Commander Dunning was charged with manslaughter under Article 32 of the Uniform Code of Military Justice. Dunning's air force defense lawyer pointed out that no bullets were ever found in the burned-out wreckage, which meant that the cause of death was uncertain. The trial still went through its painful process. In the absence of conclusive proof, the presiding officer ruled that a reasonable doubt existed that the gunner was killed by Dunning's gun, and he dismissed the charge.

Dad found out about all this after overhearing a celebration of the ruling in the Kunming officers' mess. After being filled in by one of the men, he decided it was one hell of a story, starkly showing the grisly choices often faced in war. He filed the story, but the local military censor refused to clear it, apparently believing that it would give succor to the enemy. Dad protested that the news would get out anyway, and it was far better that the facts be accurately presented than the public read a corrupted version.

That argument cut no weight locally, but Dad had the right of appeal. The story was encoded and sent off to an Office of War Information (OWI) tribunal in Washington. Rarely were local censors overruled, but he felt strongly enough to take his chances. The censorship had nothing to do with military security and everything to do with the blinders on injustice that sometimes exist under military law. If the appeals tribunal agreed with the local censors, the story was dead. But on the off chance of disagreement, the story would be forwarded to the AP for immediate use. Dad won, and the story appeared nationwide.

A twist shows how reporters may be personally affected by their reportage. Dunning returned to active duty and was given command of a Chinese-American composite wing at Liangshan, another one of the threatened forward airbases. Dad, visiting Liangshan weeks later, had no idea that Dunning was the commanding officer. The two met, and upon hearing the name of the reporter, the colonel turned truculent. Though anonymous in the article, Dunning had been identified closely enough for his wife, who devoured everything about the Fourteenth Air Force, to enclose the clip in a letter, asking, "Was that you, John?"

Dunning upbraided Dad for writing it. "What purpose did it serve? I wanted to tell her about this in my own way, after the war, and not have her read about it in some goddamned newspaper!" It was unfortunate that the colonel's privacy was invaded, Dad replied, but he insisted the incident was legitimate news. "No matter what the circumstances, the shooting of one American by another must never be a private act," Dad said, which made the colonel even steamier.

"I trust you as a pilot," Dad said, holding his ground. "Why don't you trust me as a newsman?" Calmer, Dunning asked what the purpose of the visit was. Dad explained his interest in the Japanese offensive and said he hoped to accompany an aerial reconnaissance mission and then write about it.

"Oh, that's easily arranged," Dunning said, suddenly amiable, and they set a time to meet after lunch. The reporter had visions of an uneventful jaunt in another L-5 and never expected to see Dunning again. But at the appointed hour the colonel was on the tarmac, noting almost pleasantly that he himself would serve as the guide.

The plane was no lazy L-5 this time, but instead a dual-control P-40 Warhawk, fast as a bullet. Dunning told him to jump in and handed him a helmet. Buckling up, Dad struggled with defective chin straps as Dunning gunned up the horsepower, and they roared into the wild blue yonder. Thanks to g-force, centrifugal pull, and a lot of other things, those defective straps continued slapping his face until he finally wrestled the helmet onto his knees. And the flight proved to be no simple recon mission. Dunning joined two other Tigers, all loaded with jellied gasoline canisters and thousands of rounds of ammo. They napalmed and strafed Japanese positions while dodging heavy ground fire. Eyes teary, head pounding, and lungs exploding, Dad felt the heat of the flaming pines before they zoomed into a cloud bank.

Back at Liangshan, the colonel was laughing. "Enjoy the ride?" he asked.

Major Horace S. Carswell Jr., who played football at Texas Christian University in Fort Worth, was part of the Fourteenth Air Force's night bomber group that targeted shipping in the South China Sea. Using top-secret radar and night-vision scopes, Carswell piloted a four-engine B-24 Liberator bomber the night of October 26, 1944, when he and a crew of ten picked up blips from a dozen Japanese vessels headed toward Hong Kong.

In the first pass they dropped six five-hundred-pound bombs on a destroyer without drawing fire. In the second pass they scored two direct hits on a tanker, but enemy shells crippled the hydraulic system, punctured a gas tank, knocked out two engines, wounded the copilot (Second Lieutenant James L. O'Neal), and shredded the chute of the bombardier (First Lieutenant Walter A. Hillier).

Losing altitude fast, they were almost at sea level before Carswell, a former flight instructor at Randolph Field, Texas, regained control. He could have crash-landed on the coast, which would have meant the possible capture of the crew and technology, including a top-secret night-vision scope linked to the Norden bombsight. Or he could have coaxed the plane over coastal mountains as high as four thousand feet to return to Liuchow, two hundred miles north. He ordered the crew to dump the nonessentials.

Using the old roller-coaster trick from flying school, he lifted the nose until the plane nearly stalled, regained speed and momentum, and repeated the cycle to thirty-five-hundred feet, when a third engine sputtered. "No one thought it possible to get one of those planes up from sea level on only two engines," navigator Charles A. Ulery said in the later reconstruction.

Carswell ordered the crew to jump, and with the exception of the bombardier and injured copilot, they did. Staff Sergeant Carlton H. Schnepf, an assistant engineer, said the jumpers hit the ground seconds after their parachutes opened. Schnepf, the last out, later offered this view: "Number two sputtered again. Then I jumped. The plane crashed about five hundred feet away. It burned all night. I couldn't get near the fire."

Of the eight jumpers, two didn't make it: copilot James H. Rinker and gunner Kaemper Steinman. Thanks to "blood chits"—flags sewn on the back of flight jackets identifying the wearers in the service of Free China—the remaining six found their way back.

Although censorship barred any reference to radar and underground railroads, the AP's reports on the mission helped win Carswell and the crew national recognition. Then on February 27, 1946, two-year-old Robert Ede Carswell, his mother at his side, had a Congressional Medal of Honor pinned to his shirt. Later, Griffiss Air Force Base at Fort Worth was renamed Carswell Air Force Base.

On the details of the Carswell story, Dad collaborated with Jack Randolph, a correspondent with the Office of War Information. OWI walked a narrow line between security and legitimate news, assisted by one of that day's most respected newsmen, Elmer Davis, formerly of CBS News, whom Roosevelt tapped as OWI chief. Davis believed that Americans must be "truthfully informed" within the dictates of security, and Randolph was a handpicked Davis lieutenant.

Randolph came to China because, he told Dad, "I got tired of sitting on my ass all day in Washington!" He also loved airplanes. He once observed that the closest thing to perfection he'd ever seen in this world was "an Immelmann turn performed by a stunt flier named Claire Chennault," which put the two on the same wavelength. Dad and Randolph interviewed the survivors from that downed Liberator bomber and had no qualms spreading the word of American heroism.

12

Three Generals and a Generalissimo

DAD SAW A lot of General Claire Chennault, who'd been fighting the air war against Japan since 1937, when Chennault resigned from the US Army Air Corps to accept an offer from Madame Chiang Kai-shek to build China's air force. Having gobbled up Manchuria, Japan was about to strike China proper. Madam Chiang and her husband, the generalissimo, were desperate. Roosevelt, even then agonizing over Japan's aggressiveness, closely followed the interplay, and it was not hard for the president to decide to help Chennault help China.

Washington provided new highly maneuverable P-40s, a giant improvement over the dumpy Fiat biplanes then in use, but it also encouraged the formation of the American Volunteer Group to support Chiang in the air war. After unsung artists painted tiger sharks on the noses of P-40s, those Flying Tigers joined a new legion of world heroes. After the attack on Pearl Harbor, Roosevelt ordered Chennault back into active duty, and by the time Dad arrived in Kunming, sixteen months later, Chennault was wearing a second star as the commander of the Fourteenth Air Force and a key player in evolving US policy in China.

Though a generation older than Dad, Chennault still had the reflexes of a young boy. Once, as the newsman and the general sipped Cokes in Kunming, a fly alighted on Chennault's bottle. Faster than the eye could see, the older man crushed it and, with a boyish grin, let it drop to the floor. "Plenty of practice," he said, "from when flies buzzed the Dr. Pepper bottles in Baton Rouge," where he grew up.

In Kunming, Chennault lived at the edge of the airfield with a dachshund named Joe, which he took to hunt widgeons around Blue Lake. Joe earned his keep. Those ducks went into pies that Chennault's Chinese cook prepared Louisiana style—that is, with plenty of Tabasco, or "Louisiana ketchup." Another Joe, press aide Joe Alsop, who rode that fancy rickshaw in Chungking, went to great lengths, including use of the diplomatic pouch, to ensure that the Tabasco supply never ran dry. Unashamedly, Alsop was not averse to using family pull. Through his mother, Corinne, both Presidents Franklin and Teddy Roosevelt were distant cousins.

Despite Chennault's strong likes and dislikes for food and other things, he was a square shooter with his men. He demanded high performance on the job. Off-duty rules were lax. Of Cajun blood, he even encouraged the viticultural activities of a flock of French monks who cultivated a drinkable cabernet from terraced hills beyond the lake. Those wines, almost all of what remained of France's erstwhile imperial reach in China, added a certain joie de vivre.

Nor was female companionship wanting. Gonorrhea took a lesser toll than at Khorramshahr. Chennault authorized that women from Kweilin and other towns to be flown in. But medics cleared them first. If sex was going to happen, he wanted it to be healthy sex. During one visit to Kunming, Joe Stilwell, technically Chennault's boss, learned of the goings-on and blew his stack, ordering them shut down. Dad overheard Chennault's crude protest: "And how do you expect a man to fight a war," Chennault shouted, "if he can't get a piece of ass?"

The son of a cotton farmer, Chennault was born in Commerce, Texas. As a kid, he toiled in cotton and pepper fields around Waterproof, Louisiana, but he also hit the books, managing to put himself through a year at Louisiana State University before enlisting in the army. In his late teens he learned to fly in what was then the Air Service of the Army Signal Corps. Stilwell, the son of a doctor, grew up in Yonkers, New York, with all the privileges of the American bourgeoisie. He was preparing for Yale when he won an appointment to West Point through a relative who had known President McKinley.

The personal lives of the two generals were also at polar extremes. Chennault had long ago split with his wife, Nell, whom he'd dated in high school, and he maintained several liaisons fairly openly until his second marriage in 1947 to Anna Chan, a reporter for the China News Service, thirty-two years his junior. Stilwell, on the other hand, was ever faithful to his wife, Winifred, in Carmel, California, and wrote to her daily. The two men were also different kinds of fighters: Chennault an unconventional, hard-driving, white-knuckle flier; Stilwell an acid-tongued, fiercely proud, intellectual foot soldier.

Stilwell's nerve center was Chungking, between the press hostel and the headquarters complex of Generalissimo Chiang Kai-shek's government. Despite the strain between Chiang and Stilwell, the Wellesley-educated Madam Chiang, ever the charmer, always made a fuss over Stilwell, much as she did over Chennault. When Stilwell was called away, without fail she went to the airport to greet him on his return. She invited him to receptions. When photographers were present, she drew close to him to project the much-vaunted warmth of Chinese-American friendship.

All the play-acting made Stilwell uncomfortable. An old infantry officer whose acid tongue earned him the nickname Vinegar Joe, he was trying to fight a war, not engage in cocktail party chitchat with people he didn't like. He preferred to be with Americans, usually staff officers or even reporters, with whom he let his hair down, peppering his speech with epithets that were usually directed at Chiang or his Nationalists. "Don't let the bastards grind you down," he'd say, adding the Latin original, "*Illegitimati non carborundum.*" And then with another pointed reference to Chiang, he opined, "The higher a monkey climbs, the more you see its ass!"

The Chinese put Stilwell up at an elegant colonial-style residence called Chialing House, named after one of the two rivers that join at Chungking. To accommodate his passion for the movies, a lower floor was fitted with a screen and projector. Like Chennault with Tabasco, the Stilwell film craving was requited by diplomatic pouch. Dad once joined Stilwell and staff for a dinner that was followed by one of the newest Hollywood films. Barely touching dessert, Stilwell rushed to the screening, plopping in a favorite rattan chair. "What's the movie tonight?" he asked the noncom fiddling with the projector.

"*You Were Never Lovelier,* General," the noncom replied, affecting a high pitched voice.

"I know that!" Stilwell shot back, to the snickers he always played for. It was just like him, Dad said. If he could make a joke, he would. Soon he was fidgeting like any twelve-year-old, complaining about all the "love stuff." It was a 1942 romp starring Rita Hayworth and Fred Astaire, set in Buenos Aires. Stilwell didn't like it. He prized action, not dancing. He liked westerns as well as gangster and war movies. In this case, Dad recalled, he politely stayed seated to the end. When Chennault later saw the movie, he said he liked looking at Rita Hayworth.

The contrasts between the two generals also came out in policy differences.

Chennault wanted a limited air offensive against Japan in China using forward bases east and north of Kunming. Stilwell's eyes were on the retaking of Burma. Roosevelt sided with Chennault. The air strategy proved effective and less costly.

A bigger rift occurred over dealing with Chiang Kai-shek, one of the big five World War II leaders. As the brother-in-law of Sun Yat-sen, the founder of the Republic of China in 1912, Chiang was an instigator of the Revolution of 1911. He consolidated power into the Kuomintang, or Nationalist Party, and now tried to hold off his two sworn enemies, Japanese imperialists and Chinese Communists.

Both Americans went back years with Chiang. Stilwell knew him in the mid-1930s, but they never hit it off. Stilwell prided himself as an old China hand and even learned Mandarin. Dad speculated that Stilwell's linguistic knowledge, far from aiding mutual understanding, may actually have put him and Chiang on the wrong foot. Intent on showing his linguistic mastery, Stilwell shooed away interpreters in his meetings with Chiang and insisted on speaking Mandarin. But Chiang, favoring a dialect from his home province of Chekiang in the southeast, wasn't that familiar with Mandarin. Stilwell's arrogance as a linguist may have led to misunderstandings.

A more fundamental difference was Stilwell's generally sympathetic view of Mao Tse-tung as a rough-hewn agrarian reformer. Stilwell believed that Mao and Chiang could be made to work together, so that after this long war American soldiers could finally get home to their wives and sweethearts. But Mao and Chiang had fought each other even longer. They were mongoose and cobra, and no soft talk could ever defuse their congenital hatred of each other.

Favoring the broad-brimmed campaign hat of the prewar army, Stilwell retained what Chennault called a "treaty-port" attitude toward the Chinese. Translation: Despite years of civilization, the Chinese still needed outsiders to instruct them. To no surprise, such arrogance made Chiang's fur fly. Stilwell spread demeaning stories, calling Chiang "petty," "corrupt," "the lily-livered Chink," and "the peanut." Chiang was indeed small in stature by American standards, but at five foot six he was big by Chinese standards. Dad once asked Stilwell what China most needed to carry on the war, and the general replied, "The cutting off of one hundred well-selected heads, with you-know-who first on the chopping block!"

The differences came into relief during the Japanese offensive in western China in 1944. Chiang sought to pull his troops from Burma to meet the threat. Stilwell believed that the quickest way to end the war was to pour troops into Burma. Yet Japan's offensive menaced air bases and the wartime capital itself. Chiang faced not only the newly aggressive Japanese Army but also Mao himself, who was threatening to break out of a protected enclave in north central China and rewage civil war. Dad said that Stilwell underestimated both Chiang's Japanese *and* Chinese adversaries.

Another basic conflict was over what Stilwell believed was the institutionalized corruption in the Chinese Army, which he blamed on the Nationalist leadership. Examples were legion. It was common for unit commanders to pay more than the market price for rice and cabbage and to split the difference with the merchant. Some signed payrolls for phantom soldiers and pocketed the money.

Chiang, whose personal life was austere and irreproachable, tried to root out corruption, but the army, like the country, had autonomous zones run by warlords. To Dad, it was like holding Roosevelt responsible for the black market activities of American troops in Naples or political machines in Kansas City.

It also missed the point that China was not yet a nation of laws and institutions where corruption was clearly defined. What Americans called corruption could be seen as the network of obligations you learned to accept as part of everyday living. Not giving a job to a cousin, or not skimming proceeds to help a friend, was considered a failure to meet overriding human obligations.

Beyond this, Chiang, though once a revolutionary, now seemed to incarnate the old order. The Reds cleverly presented themselves as democratic reformers anxious both to root out old ways of corruption and defeat the Japanese. They didn't keep caged cicadas, hoard gold, worship their ancestors, dawdle over lidded teacups, spoil their children, nibble watermelon seeds, smoke opium, or dally with singsong girls while the masses remained illiterate, overworked, and underfed.

So again it was a war of spin. Some Americans had met the Red leaders and sent back glowing reports of hearty, genial men seemingly hell-bent on improving the well-being of their countrymen. There was Mao himself, the imposing leader from Hunan, a little puffy in his drab cotton-quilted uniform, but purportedly sincere and well-meaning—also such top aides as Chu Teh (Pepsodent smile), Chou En-lai (onyx eyes), and Lin Piao (granite face).

Among the more celebrated reporters charmed by the Reds were Edgar Snow, a former correspondent for the *Saturday Evening Post,* and Agnes

Smedley, the author of *China's Red Army Marches* and *Battle Hymn of China* and once the mistress of Richard Sorge, who was later convicted as a Soviet spy. Smedley called Chiang "that feudal bastard." To Snow, Mao was "Lincolnesque."

Men on Stilwell's staff, such as John Paton Davies and John Stewart Service, State Department sinologists on loan to the army, joined the pro-Mao chorus, speaking of the inevitability of replacing Chiang with the "democratic and progressive" Communists. During the truce Mao sent representatives to Chungking to woo the Western correspondents. His most skilled practitioner was Chou En-lai, later the foreign minister, who played the foreign press, Dad said, as if bowing "Moon Reflected on Second Spring" on his erhu (two-stringed violin).

The highly cultivated Chou had traveled the world, unlike Mao, who rarely stepped outside China. At mellow lunches and dinners with the foreign press in Chungking, Chou offered a message of sweet harmony. He magnified the Red contribution to the war effort, emphasized corruption in the Kuomintang, spoke of the importance of agrarian reform, and offered tours to interview Mao himself. To Dad, Chou was the velvet-smooth yet steel-hard propagandist who did more than anyone to tilt progressive Americans to the communist cause.

Here is an account of one of those repasts: "We offered numerous toasts to joint efforts in the war. At the end of the meal, Chou asked me whether I thought American aid to China was lining the pockets of Chiang and his Kuomintang warlords. I said I had no real evidence it was. I described machine politics in America and said if he ever wanted to see corruption, he should visit Kansas City."

Through control of Lend-Lease supplies, Stilwell, ever more anxious to get this war over with and go home, actually toyed with an idea from Davies and Service to arm Mao. When Chiang heard about this, he was livid. Convinced that any such arms would be used more against the Nationalists than the Japanese, he finally made it clear to Washington that he could no longer work with Stilwell. On October 19, 1944, Roosevelt, desperately ill and with a lot else on his mind, including an election campaign in which he was running for an unprecedented fourth term, ordered Stilwell home.

His successor was a far less controversial figure with far lighter baggage: General Albert C. Wedemeyer, the American deputy to Lord Louis Mountbatten, the commander of the Southeast Asia Command. Whereas Stilwell had been imperious, Wedemeyer was reasonable and conciliatory.

Whereas Stilwell showed contempt for "the peanut," Wedemeyer evinced respect for a wartime ally and his larger-than-life accomplishments. Whereas Stilwell had been intrigued by the idea of arming the Chinese Communist Army; Wedemeyer was aghast. Dad and Wedemeyer tended to see things through a similar lens, and the two enjoyed a cordial relationship, underscored by Wedemeyer's decision to pin a China-Burma-India Theater ribbon on him in a ceremony in Chungking in 1945.

13

Dolly

DAD NEVER QUITE got enough of China. He saw it not only in those tragic years of world war but also in the doomed struggle of Chiang Kai-shek. Recognized as a seasoned China hand, Dad was elected president of the Foreign Correspondents Club of China in 1948 and covered the Nationalist flameout while trying to rehabilitate a destitute press organization. On top of it all, he contended with no end of flare-ups from my mother.

By then he'd quit the AP and was writing for Scripps Howard. Upon Mao's takeover in 1949, Dad exited Shanghai to restart the club in Hong Kong, where it continues to this day. Even with that Red tide rising, he remained abroad, working in Asia and then Europe, lining up employers, which post-AP and Scripps Howard included the *Chicago Tribune*, *Time* magazine, NBC, and the *New York Times*. It hadn't been easy. In 1945, months after the war's end, he was down and out in Shanghai, the result of sudden prudery at the AP over his relationship with a refugee from Hitler's Europe, Paula Prcic-Dittrich, also known as Dolly. She was the reason he never came home.

Dolly, he confided to me years later, was the sort of exotic, bewitching female he had always hankered for. Had three kids and constant money worries maybe lessened Marthe Herailh's allure? As the second of my two wives, the poet Elisavietta Ritchie, put it to me, "Love is seldom simple, though loving is."

I met Dolly, and she was indeed breathtaking. Her face was round, like a porcelain saucer, and her lips were ruby red, often in a moue. Her cheekbones were high, smooth, and daubed with celestial pink; her hair was the black of a sultry night, and her eyes were flickering blue like fiery coal. She favored wide, floppy hats in pastels that accented the paleness of her skin. She spiked a concierge's knowledge of half a dozen languages with earthy Serbo-Croatian. A favorite spike: *Bog je prvo sebi bradu stvorio* (Everybody looks first after themselves).

The news of the relationship was a shock to us all in Mount Vernon. I hated my father for putting us through such pain and suffering and material deprivation. Sue and I helped our mother cope as best we could, but the wound was impossible to cauterize. Even my kid brother, Frank, at three, knew something was up. Later I came to accept the whole Dolly story as part of the fuller Clyde Addison Farnsworth. Now, in tranquility, I can certainly agree that it made him more interesting. "Don't judge the old man," he told me when we spoke of these things years later, and I not only accepted him but also came to grudgingly respect Dolly.

It was an enduring union, like a good swatch of twilled fabric. Despite wear and tear, they stayed together for more than three decades. How will I ever forget the image of Dolly in a silky Chinese gown, peeking out demurely from behind her Ming, Qing, or whatever sunflower fan and lacquered paper parasol? From his hospital room in Arlington, Virginia, Dad dictated the positioning of that photo, and it must have been the last thing captured by those retinas before all systems crashed from metastasized prostate cancer in 1984.

Dolly was born in Vienna; her Jewish father, Jakob Berman, was a doctor in Hapsburg government service delivering free medical treatment at the reaches of the Austro-Hungarian Empire. Her mother, Zora Prcic, was an Eastern Orthodox Bosnian Serb, whom the good doctor met, impregnated, and perhaps even loved, in the village of Bosanska Gradiska on the Sava River between Sarajevo and Zagreb.

Dr. Berman did all the right things. He made arrangements for Dollica's birth in October 1916 at Vienna Allgemeines Krankenhaus (Vienna General Hospital). It was the middle of a world war, but as a civil servant he had enough influence to place her with foster parents, a childless couple named Dittrich who gave her a home and a civilizing education. They enrolled her in a Catholic girls' elementary school in Vienna's eighth district and later in a high school, the Real Gymnasium, on Hasnerstrasse in the sixteenth district. Dolly's favorite subjects were piano, sewing, and cooking.

Herr Dittrich operated a shop that sold *stumpfen*, or millinery foundations. She visited and was encouraged to try the newest offerings. Gazing at herself from every luscious angle in the floor-to-ceiling mirrors, she had trouble pulling herself away. When boys noticed, the Dittrichs and Berman made arrangements for her to spend summers in Bosnia. The headgear—shawl, hood, or kerchief—was less alluring than Herr Dittrich's feathery hats, but the village offered other pursuits. One of Zora's brothers ran a cafe where Dolly picked up the killer chess she played all her life, humbling me and countless others who thought they knew the game. I still see her hovering like a tropical bird, a smirk on those ruby lips, dragging off to its doom some wretched enemy knight or bishop.

Thanks to those summers and her Viennese foster parents, Dolly's youth was relatively happy—until the ominous stirrings of National Socialism. Her story is that of the many who couldn't qualify for the new order. Most perished in the camps. Luckier ones escaped with diamonds and gold pieces stashed in their soles. Some, like Dolly, took flight and lived on their wits and looks.

Dr. Berman fled to Bern, Switzerland, during the Anschluss of 1938, the Nazi-engineered political union of Germany and Austria. He died before world war erupted a second time in a generation. Dolly fled via Trieste, finagled a steamer ticket down the Adriatic into the Mediterranean, and pushed steadily eastward away from a continent gone mad. She holed up in Beirut, Aleppo, Damascus, and Baghdad, overstaying and hastily moving on until reaching Tehran, where she met a man with a meal ticket. It happened on New Year's Eve 1942 at the bar of the Ferdowsi Hotel, not unlike Rick's Café in *Casablanca*, where people from everywhere hung out and told fascinating stories, and no one could go home. She was the number one B-girl, which meant the top hustler of drinks—mostly smuggled Armenian "bubbly"—and had the right to tell anyone to buzz off.

That evening she wore golden slippers and a self-made evening gown from scraps of taffeta and lace picked up at the local bazaar. Someone introduced a red leatherette crank-up phonograph and out came the big band sounds of Tommy Dorsey and Xavier Cugat. An American warrant officer pretended to be in the ring in Cordoba, and people yelled "Olé, olé!" Dad asked her to dance, and she accepted, but only after she had done the rumba on the thirty-foot bar, kicking off her slippers and shaking to the roar of the legion of admirers. He was the lonely, good-looking stranger, who also happened to carry the carte blanche of an accredited war correspondent. He checked the action as the red leatherette phonograph wheezed all the old familiar tunes.

Photos of Dad show a resemblance to the actor Alan Ladd. But Ladd didn't talk much. Dad was a fantastic talker, yet that evening he let her do the talking. He fell in love first with her story. She deserved to be saved, and he wanted to save her. He would have saved everyone in that bar if he could. She asked him a few weeks later to accompany her to the police station to assist in the renewal of her identity card legalizing her stay in Tehran. She had a passport from the Triune Kingdom of Serbs, Croats, and Slovenes, the precursor to Yugoslavia formed after the collapse of the Hapsburg Empire. But in 1943 Yugoslavia was under Nazi occupation, and the passport had long expired.

The station was scuzzy, like the fetid hold of a freighter in the tropics. Cockroaches whizzed across the floor unfazed or perhaps even encouraged by the unending lines. Everyone seemed to tell the same story: the need for a haven from the war. Everywhere the gates had shut.

People pressed slowly toward the few clerks who sat on high stools behind barred windows that stayed open only part of the day. If you didn't make it one day, you came earlier the next. The presence of an Allied uniform helped Dolly get the interview as a first step to the renewal of her papers. With excruciating diligence, the clerk took down her particulars, then asked how long she intended to stay. "Of course, I don't know!" she exploded in Persian, mixed with salty Serbo-Croatian. "You tell me how long the war will last!" Notice came in three weeks that she would not be extended and was subject to immediate deportation.

Maybe this was her strategy. Stratagems were part of her considerable skills. But Hitler was not playacting. Dolly was trying to survive as best she could. At any rate, Dad predictably asked her if she wanted to hitch her wagon to his. By helping, he rationalized, he was doing good. He didn't consider the long-term consequences. The war didn't allow such luxury. Life was cheap, to be enjoyed to the fullest in the eternal present. He was in his midthirties and supremely confident of his skills. She was eight years younger, and he felt good about her.

He worked out the protocols to fill empty space on the Air Transport Command flights, first to Delhi, then over the Hump to Kunming. It was not complicated: flights ran all the time, and his connections to the greatest army and grandest news agency in the world did no harm. He and Dolly made no secret of their cohabitation. His colleagues accepted them and imposed no moral standards.

In Kunming he set her up in a cheap boardinghouse. Sometimes they were together, sometimes not. She made her own friends, including other Jewish refugees, who were also thankful to be alive. He bought her a Singer sewing machine, and as he went about the business of reporting the war, she organized a parallel life as a couturier, making gowns and millinery for Chinese and European clients who became her friends. Within that wartime expatriate community, Dolly was a hit. But after the atomic bombs at Hiroshima and Nagasaki in August 1945, the war was over. People went home, and the codes of wartime *carpe diem* were quietly rescinded. In returning to the prewar status quo, the AP was no exception. Dad rejoined India manager Preston Grover in Delhi. Because of his earlier Iranian experience, Dad was drafted to cover the threatened Soviet annexation of Azerbaijan, which had the State Department in a tizzy and was a sign of the coming Cold War.

But another cold war was also brewing, over Dolly. The adversary wasn't so much Preston Grover, whom my father liked as a colleague and friend. It was Kent Cooper, the testy, often fractious AP general manager who, my father said, "loved to micromanage his correspondents' lives." Cooper tried to slam a well-shod foot on the extramarital affair. Such cavorting may have been okay in Kunming under wartime conditions, but not in peacetime Delhi. Cooper ordered Grover to order Dad to ditch Dolly. Cooper was also partly responding to tearful missives from my mother wondering why in God's name her husband hadn't come home. She told me she was writing the letters. At fourteen, I didn't encourage her, nor did I discourage her. Yet the crisis in Delhi was postponed because of the absence of one of the parties. Dolly returned to Europe to check on how her own mother had fared and also to renew her now well-expired Triune Kingdom passport. Dad worked out transportation, and she was gone for half a year.

Upon her return to Delhi, Dolly recounted something monstrous. It was no relief that stories like this in that early postwar period were almost commonplace. Zora Prcic, her relatives, and practically all others in that village of Bosanska Gradiska had been gunned down in the war's final days by the Nazi-backed Ustashi. The river Sava, one survivor told her, "ran red with blood."

Dad never abandoned Dolly. Especially under such circumstances, he could not. In January 1946, he and Grover, who was acting as proxy for Cooper, had it out. Grover said the AP did not appreciate his unconventional lifestyle and that upon his return from Azerbaijan he might want to return to 50 Rock and visit with his wife and three children.

Dad was furious. He had no intention of returning like a whipped dog to New York and resuming the nine-to-five commuter existence that had ruled him in an earlier decade. He said that by all accounts he did his job reasonably well and that, damn it, his private life was his own affair. He left the office in a huff. Grover followed up with a letter telling him he must resign at once.

It was a shock. The AP had been good to him, providing a steady paycheck, lifting him from Ohio into the glitter of Manhattan, and then sending him to some of the most alien and fascinating places on the globe. It gave him the chance to tell the stories he loved to tell. He had much to thank the AP for. Yet now he was angry, angrier than he had ever been. This behavior was outrageous. His employer was not his moral guardian. Dolly was not some transient prostitute. He had obligations in Mount Vernon; he recognized them and would discharge them. But he would not be bound by the strictures of hypocritical whited sepulchers in Delhi or New York.

Fortunately, he had other prospects. During the period in Kunming covering the Fourteenth Air Force, he and Claire Chennault had become close, and the general at one point confided his hope of starting a civilian cargo airline in China after the war. Would Clyde ever consider moving over to public relations, ne asked?

Dad had a newsman's scorn for that benighted profession. A favorite joke: The difference between a rat and squirrel? PR. But after the blow-up, he fired off a letter to Chennault explaining his situation and asking if the PR job just might still be open. It was—not quite yet, Chennault wrote back, but in a few months it would be ready, and he should stay in touch. With that letter as slapdash insurance, he and Dolly plunked meager savings into passage on a ten-thousand-ton Liberty ship from Calcutta to Shanghai. A love boat to China seemed ideal for sorting out their lives.

One typhoon and six weeks later, in early March 1946, they saw Shanghai for the first time, aboard a lighter that dodged sampans and junks of all sizes, shapes, and colors to bring them to that incredible dockside, otherwise known as the Bund. Before them were the stately columns of the Customs House, the battlements of the Bank of China, the gnome's hat of the Cathay Hotel, and other pieces in the jigsaw of financial and trading houses, hotels, and department stores. The structures were around twenty stories, and separated the city's watery face from its duller backside, which stretched miles on the Yangtze plain. Although battles had been fought on the approaches, Shanghai came through the war largely unscathed.

And so in that year of 1946, Shanghai was a throbbing, at times shocking, mix of beauty and squalor—a place of unrestrained capitalism, unbridled sleaze, and an incredible gap between rich and poor. Six million Chinese were now joined by refugees and officials from Europe and Russia and a cross-section of other nationals, including the US military. The place reverberated with a raw, electric energy. Until the Bamboo Curtain, Shanghai was surely the happy-go-lucky, good-time-Charlie, get-rich-quick, no-holds-barred capital of the world.

Rickshaws and three-wheeled pedicabs fought for trade. Dad and Dolly hired two pedicabs—one just for their luggage, which included a valise filled with her exotic hats. They rode through bedlam to the Foreign Correspondents Club at Broadway Mansions, a seventeen-story red-brick tower overlooking Soochow Creek, Garden Bridge, and Hongkew. Built in the early 1930s, it mostly accommodated American military advisers, with the top four floors reserved for the foreign press. Dolly and Dad's room on the thirteenth floor looked out over Garden Bridge. The boats below were like circus-clown cars spewing people. At street level you caught more than a whiff of primitive sanitary conditions, but from on high it was all very romantic. In the setting sun, boats bobbed like rose petals on shimmering water.

Thirteen proved lucky. A letter awaited: the job was firm. Dad was to be the public affairs officer and official photographer. As a reporter, he had sometimes taken news pictures, having absorbed pointers from such pros as the *New York Times*'s George Alexanderson, the *Cleveland News*'s Perry Cragg, and Acme Photos's Frankie Cancellare. Pay from the new airline, to be called the Civil Air Transport (CAT), was a princely $10,000 a year plus expenses, 20 percent more than the AP had paid. The bad news was that snags delayed employment by six months. Having blown most of their savings on that slow boat, Dad and Dolly could no longer afford the pricey Broadway Mansions. Downward mobility led them to the Metropole Hotel, also off the Bund, and then to the even seedier Burlington Hotel at 1225 Bubbling Well Road. A well indeed bubbled there until the 1920s, when it was plugged, leaving only a quaint name.

Burlington rules included no cooking, which didn't trouble Dolly, who set up a hotplate in the bathroom, and they lived almost exclusively on bean curd, stir-fried vegetables, and boiled rice. Bill Newton, the Scripps Howard Asia correspondent and yet another crony from Ohio, happened by for dinner. After the meal, Newton rose and asked with a mischievous grin, "May I use your kitchen?"

Although life was low on the hog, Dad drew a high perk: the right to a navy jeep from CAT motor pool at Hungjao Airport. Streets, especially those off the main boulevards, were still the domain of pedestrians. People spilled into them from packed shanties, creating virtual room extensions in the public spaces. Laundry arched across narrow passageways, fluttering like pennants. Curbs were used almost exclusively for cooking meals. Yammering crowds blended with the Klaxons of vehicles, the clacks of mah-jongg tiles, the frying sounds of live firecrackers, and the ungodly gonging of Chinese opera in the vicinity. An obbligato of dance tunes— "Hey There," "Tenderly," and "Slow Boat to China"—wafted from the roof garden of the Park Hotel above the racecourse on Nanking Road.

In driving, the number one rule was to blow your horn—eventually people moved. You had to take care that your fender didn't nudge a gesturing finger or a tender backside. In a tight space a crowd could turn against you. Dad was struck by indications everywhere of how cheap life was. Every morning, trucks with open bays stopped to pick up corpses of the homeless. An even more harrowing sight was the ejection of a female pedicab passenger during a swift turn in the face of an oncoming green bus. Even though she was crushed, the traffic never stopped.

Besides being an extension of the home, the streets were one big market, everyone buying or selling: silk fabrics, surplus war materiel, bric-a-brac, and food. At one stand a woman was filleting eels using a knife honed from bone. Dad watched her lift the lid of her hamper and saw an ossified *danse macabre* as eel skeletons, their heads attached, rattled their lives away. A more common sight was twine looped around a piece of fat pork.

Dad learned about gestures, words, and even the games people played. Someone in a heated discussion might point to anyone's nose, a symbol of foulness, or screech the equivalent of "Turtle egg!" Female turtles were rumored to sleep with snakes. People threw fingers at each other, betting on the total number of fingers exposed. The Chinese were, and still are, the world's biggest gamblers. People lived near their place of work and sometimes in it. A noodle shop was a bedroom for almost as many people as there were noodles in a pot. Flour by day dusted bedding by night.

A short distance from the markets were the former British and French concessions, remnants of the old treaty port days. Even after the Japanese occupation, the concessions retained much of their original flavor: colonial mansions, plane tree–shaded parks, and, especially in the French concession, a plenitude of eateries near the main drag of Marshall Joffre Street, in Pidgin, Joffie Lu. To the north, between Garden Bridge and the North Station, was Hongkew, the former American concession, where

Japan settled twenty thousand Jewish refugees from Nazi-occupied Europe. Japan rejected Hitler's demands for a Final Solution. In the Shanghai ghetto, Jews retained religious, educational, and cultural autonomy, but put up with curfews and suffered severe food shortages.

Many denizens later went to America. Some made it big, including W. Michael Blumenthal, a business executive, who under President Jimmy Carter was the sixty-fourth secretary of the treasury, and Pete Silberman, the national news editor of the *Washington Post*.

Yet another was a Vienna-born musician named Peppi Paunzen. In the 1930s the Paunzen family—Peppi, his brother Harry, their mother, and an aunt—saw the writing on the wall. Peppi sold a business wholesaling goose liver before fleeing. Like Dolly, the Paunzens exited via Trieste but had the means to book all the way to Shanghai. When the valuables hidden in their in heels gave out, they lived off the piano-playing of Peppi, an alumnus of the Vienna Academy of Music who had an impeccable ear.

Dad and Dolly first met Peppi on Bubbling Well Road. American show tunes were emanating from a raunchy sailors' bar. Investigating, they found a bony, seedily dressed Western gentleman tickling the ivories while dragging on a cigarette butt. They lit up, too, and hit it off right away. By this time Dad was well installed at CAT public relations; picking up more on Peppi's background, he groomed him as the official CAT photographer. The twin functions of information officer and photographer were getting too much for Dad to handle alone. He figured that if Peppi survived the war and still played the piano as well as he did, he had wits enough to take good pictures. Chennault went along, and Peppi didn't disappoint.

Sounding more Catskills than CAT, Peppi once offered this thumbnail sketch of his life: "I was born in Vienna at a very early age when I was quite young of two parents. I began playing piano for short beers at age five and took up photography to enhance my nervous disposition."

14

Track of the CAT

THE CIVIL AIR Transport story went back to General Chennault's partnership with Whiting Willauer, a Harvard-trained former Justice Department lawyer who worked out the legalities for US military airmen to fly in China before World War II. They joined what was known as the American Volunteer Group, a legal entity that allowed the retention of citizenship and military status. After the attack on Pearl Harbor, the group folded neatly into the Fourteenth Air Force. After the war, Willauer used similar skills to negotiate a $2 million start-up loan with the Chinese National Relief and Rehabilitation Agency, then part of the United Nations. The money bought CAT's first planes, 15 C-46s and four C-47s, which were then in storage in Hawaii and Manila and went for $5,000 each—little more than a new car at the time.

Everyone agreed on the compelling need for the airline. After years of war, towns and villages were piles of rubble. Famine threatened. Yet food, farm tools, breeding stock, medical supplies, and building materials were piling up at coastal warehouses awaiting distribution. Valuables rotted or were stolen. It would take time to rebuild roads and railroads. Chennault, Willauer, and their friends in Washington saw the carrier as the key to China's economic rebirth. Former Flying Tigers began hauling food, seeds, medicine, relief supplies, and even luxuries. In January 1947 CAT moved its first goods; ten months later it was moving a million tons a month, and seventeen months later it was moving 4 million a month. Melons were in Shanghai less than twenty-four hours after being picked in northwest Kansu. Breeding rams of Australian strains found their way into the grasslands of northwest China.

Dad was the chief contact for the press and served as the editor of the *CAT Bulletin*, a monthly newsletter. He rode with those breeding rams for an early picture story. On that C-46 flight from Canton to Lanchow, rams and people made it without a hitch. On the return, the plane hit freezing fog. Ice coated the propellers and formed on the wings in the thickness of an arm. Both engines belched smoke, and the plane started weaving. To avoid a disastrous spin, pilot Bob Rousselot backfired hot exhaust. "Miraculously," said Dad, who often said he didn't believe in miracles, "the sun came out, and the ice peeled."

Later he asked Chennault about the lack of defroster boots on those early planes. Chennault said Washington's bureaucrats didn't believe that icing occurs in China. "China to them is a warm country," Chennault said. "But ice will form over hell if you fly high enough." On another flight, a C-47 out of Lanchow, they ran into zero visibility soon after takeoff. Rushing to the flight deck, Chennault, while hovering, shouted at the pilot, "Mountains here are higher than what's on your altimeter."

"Not according to the route maps," the pilot replied.

"Fuck the route maps!" Chennault fired back. "Half the maps of China are wrong for flying." The wings and propellers were already icing, forcing a return to Lanchow, which probably saved their lives.

Anna Chan, a China News Agency reporter whose father was a Nationalist diplomat in San Francisco, joined the press circles around the Fourteenth Air Force in Kunming in 1944. Chennault saw her at such gatherings and was amused, then bemused, by the woman, who looked to him like a demure maiden. She wore her hair in the traditional two tight pigtails and always seemed to dress in a tailored sack of blue cotton. She was twenty, and he was fifty-four. Later she sought interviews, to which he readily agreed, and these interviews tended to become longer and more and more exclusive.

Dad's closeness to Chennault once forced him into the embarrassing situation of accidental voyeur. He, Chennault, and Anna were driving together in southern China. Two rooms remained at an inn—the only guesthouse for miles. The two men took the twin beds in one room, and Anna took the bed in the second room. The next morning, while Dad was still asleep, Chennault, a chain-smoker, started clearing bronchial phlegm. As if that were a prearranged signal, Dad suddenly heard the swoosh of silken slippers and caught the fleeting glimpse of a negligee. Like a dutiful daughter, Anna had heard the activity and was carrying a glass of boiled water for the bicarbonate she knew the general favored. Merrily, she tinkled a spoon against the glass, and through it all, my father said, "she was daughter no longer."

On December 21, 1947, Chennault and Anna were married at the general's home at Holly Heath on Hungjao Road in suburban Shanghai. With a Speed Graphic camera, which came with the job and he later ceded to Peppi, Dad was the official photographer. The reception had one hilarious moment. Arrangements had been made for the "Wedding March" from the opera *Lohengrin* to be on the phonograph when Anna made her entrance. Whoever prepped the phonograph goofed and out blasted "Turkey in the Straw."

Chennault, who had been in China almost continually since 1937, had divorced his first wife, Nell, the mother of their eight children. With Anna he ended up fathering two more.

Financial hazards loomed during other moments of the new airline, leading Chennault—and Dad—to do some "buckraking." Whether for political, philanthropic, or just plain business reasons, in Hollywood, Washington, or in China, lesson number one of fundraising was, and still is, throw a banquet.

In April 1947 in Canton, CAT's base, Chennault invited a list of rich local merchants to dinner in the biggest hall and put his PR man in charge. The main course was suckling pig, which, to Dad, was the epitome of Chinese cookery. The skin had to be the right crispness: crunchy, firm, and brittle yet slightly chewy. If it was too chewy, CAT would lose face. If the banquet failed, so too would the enterprise. A successful banquet would make the flowers bloom.

Dad retained the best caterer in Canton, who arrived early on the appointed day with workers bearing baskets and boxes of food and utensils, including shovels for digging barbecue pits. The invited guests numbered one hundred, ten to a table, each table beside a pig of around a hundred pounds slowly turning on a spit over aromatic wood. Roasted over the open fire, the skin, presliced into postage-stamp morsels, would be easily removable. Each diner would tweeze with chopsticks, then dip into a dish of granulated sugar for a taste sensation. If the roasting went awry, with the skin sticking to the carcass, the banquet, and thus the whole enterprise, would fail.

The moment of truth arrived, and the boldest of the tweezers tweezed and tasted. Silence! Silence of the pigs! Slowly smiles beamed accompanied by nods of approval. A smattering of claps then exploded into thunderous applause.

CAT started with a big advantage: probably no foreigner, and certainly no American, had a better reputation among the Chinese than General Claire L. Chennault. Everyone knew he had saved China. Ample testament to this was provided as he set out on his first return trip to the United States at the war's end. So many people turned out at the airport at Kunming to wish him well that his car couldn't clear the gates. The solution was very practical and very Chinese: the car was lifted as if in a mosh pit and passed across innumerable sets of hands to the boarding ramp.

Although the communist regime was no fan of Chennault's, even it too eventually recognized his signal wartime achievements. In recent years the Beijing government has built several memorials. One, beside the preserved Fourteenth Air Force headquarters in Kunming, features an impressive Chennault statue. An old Flying Tigers strip in Hunan offers mock-ups of warplanes and other memorabilia. In Kweilin, at the very airport Dad, Gerry McAllister, and demolition teams incinerated, visitors now find a Flying Tigers Heritage Park.

With a fat CAT paycheck, Dad started sending Mom some money, which took some of the sting out of the letters from Mount Vernon. It was still an impossible situation. World War II was over, and he was expected back. Yet because of Dolly he couldn't return. One answer was to invite his family in Mount Vernon to China. He made the proposal by letter, hoping at least temporarily to take the heat off. The idea was that she would drag Sue, Frank, and me to Canton. We'd go by ship and attend school there. He'd find a house, he told her, and we'd probably live a fairly comfortable temporary expat existence. He'd have to be in Shanghai mostly, because of "job imperatives." What he never said was that he'd be in Shanghai with Dolly.

Although my mother objected to such a split existence, she jumped at the trip, and in her next letter she enthusiastically reported her contacts with the American President Steamship Line, which ran the main Pacific passenger service. Alas, it turned out that Dad had acted without Dolly's knowledge. When she found out, she went ballistic. The arrangement would never work, she howled. Instead of making things better, it would make things worse, and she was certainly right. She said he was nuts, a pipe dreamer, and a lot of other less polite things in Serbo-Croatian.

Most cutting was her talk about her own future. He was always thinking of Marthe, she bawled, but what about Dolly and her future? She had given him good years, too. Was he to abandon her? No, she shouted, as angry as she'd ever been, he would not abandon her—if Marthe came over, Dolly would abandon him. He must divorce his wife or lose his mistress. It was an ultimatum—perhaps elements of her killer chess. His king was in check, and she went for checkmate.

He realized that divorce was inevitable. But he also knew this was not the time or place for that conversation. Yet to defuse the immediate crisis, he wired my mother not to come. There'd been a change in plans. He cited uncertainties over CAT's future and the political situation in China. "It is bad enough for me to be stranded on the far side of the world without risking the stranding of my entire family," he wrote with perfect sincerity. By return mail, she spoke of her "keen disappointment that this merciless separation has to continue."

At this point, he believed there was nothing more he could do. He was comforted somewhat by the thought that set against the searing drama of civil war, such predicaments seemed almost insignificant. Unlike millions in China, the Mount Vernonites slept in warm, clean beds at night and didn't go hungry. He accepted the financial responsibilities for his family, but he also knew that in the final resort he could not give up Dolly.

15

The Fall

THOUGH WELL OFF in public relations, Dad always itched to return to newspaper reporting. Burnishing images was okay, but nothing beat the pulsing highs of hard news. So in mid-1947, when fellow Ohioan Bill Newton of Scripps Howard asked him to be the China stringer, he eagerly accepted. The CAT airline was a ticket to remote places and a way to back up Newton. The two worked so well together that in early 1948, upon his own reassignment to Europe, Newton suggested Dad as his replacement.

What an electric moment! Since Dad's tangle with Kent Cooper, any return to full-time journalism had been only a pipe dream. Now it was within his grasp. But to avoid a future crash, he himself raised the issue of Dolly. Might the Scripps Howard brass have inhibitions similar to AP's? Newton said his own marriage had collapsed and that the only thing Scripps Howard demanded from private life was stability. Newton made the recommendation, and within days Editor in Chief Walker Stone formally invited Dad to join Scripps Howard as an Asia correspondent. He was accepted for his ability and experience. His personal life was his own.

Scripps Howard sought interpretative news stories for papers as diverse as the *Rocky Mountain News*, the *New York World Telegram*, the *Cleveland Press*, and the *Memphis Press Scimitar*. It was exciting to have his stories appear again in Cleveland, where Dad had worked for four years and had his first child. And now he had inherited a fantastic story that had enormous implications for the second half of the century. Mao's sweep was a tragedy unfolding: yet another example of the power-hungry sucking the blood of the innocent, this time millions of unwary Chinese.

Few in America still believed that Mao's men were agrarian reformers. From the transfers of arms stashes and other actions, it was clear that Stalin was in cahoots. Washington had the power to stop the tragedy. But unlike in Europe, where President Truman took a firm stand, he missed the boat in China, which became all too clear in Korea and Vietnam and inside the Bamboo Curtain itself.

The joy of being able to write news again was mixed with sadness about leaving CAT. The airline was doing well, and its employees were fired up. He loved Chennault, who, he hoped, would not misunderstand. They had a long chat. Now just forty, Dad explained the importance of newspaper reporting to him. Chennault heard him out and gave his blessing. They had been through much. Dad saw him as a father figure. "If you ever want to come back," Chennault said, a smile parting those iron jaws, "there is always a place for you in my organization."

At a going-away party, Dad couldn't hold back the tears. Throughout their days in the Far East, they remained the closest of friends. Peppi Paunzen stayed on as the CAT photographer; he loved the work, and the pilots and crews loved him. He made them laugh. Chennault took Dad's suggestion of Ed Souder Jr., the NBC hand in Chungking, as his replacement, and Souder and Peppi collaborated well. Soon Dad and Dolly extricated themselves from the seedy Burlington Hotel. They stayed at what wags called the CAT House, a mansion on Lu Boulevard reserved for Flying Tigers lodging, and then eventually returned to Broadway Mansions and even got their old room back overlooking Soochow Creek.

The following year, on July 12, 1949, tragedy struck. A KLM Lockheed Constellation airliner crashed in a monsoon squall on its approach to Bombay, killing all forty-five people aboard, including Bill Newton, who was returning to Europe after a reporting trip to the Dutch East Indies just before its birth as independent Indonesia. For Dad it was the loss of a brother. They had come out of the same crucible. A consolation was that Bill Newton died with his boots on. Among his personal effects, later received by his family in Columbus, Ohio, were these lines from a poem by John Galsworthy taped to a piece of cardboard:

> For who would live so petty and unblest
> That dare not tilt at something ere he die;
> Rather than, screened by safe majority,
> Preserve his little life to little end,
> And never raise a rebel cry!

On China policy, Dad and Scripps Howard raised that rebel cry. They tore into both the former Roosevelt and the current Truman administrations for simplemindedness and worse. China was being "sold down the river," editorials thundered, and the United States was walking blindly into a disaster. Before, Dad had simply watched. Now he had carte blanche to add to the mix. If Americans knew what was happening, what the stakes were, there might still be time to fix it.

Through NATO, the United States built military security for Europe that allowed institutions to rebuild, businesses to prosper, and people to get back to work. Yet instead of strengthening China's security to foster parallel developments, Washington undercut it. Dad reported at length on the secret protocols in the Yalta Conference agreement of February 1945, through which FDR let Stalin establish imperialistic spheres of influence to tilt the civil war battlefield in Mao's favor.

China was too far away to matter much to Churchill. FDR was ill, his condition unhelped by exhaustion after the long flight from Washington, and he was easy prey for the wily Joe Stalin. Two months later FDR was dead. Not until the late 1940s, thanks to Scripps Howard, did the world learn what had been given away.

Hoping that the Soviet Union would enter the war in Asia, Roosevelt, according to the then still secret pact, sanctioned one more imperialistic carving up of China: specifically, the internationalization of the Manchurian port of Dairen with safeguards for the "preeminent interests" of the Soviets; restoration of Port Arthur as a Soviet naval base; joint Soviet-Chinese operation of the Chinese Eastern Railway and the South Manchurian Railway on the understanding that the "preeminent interests" of the Soviet Union would be safeguarded; Soviet possession of Outer Mongolia, southern Sakhalin, and the nearby islands of Kunashiri, Etorofu, Skikotan, and Habomai; and Soviet possession of the Kurile Islands.

In return, Stalin committed troops against Japan within three months of the German surrender. Those troops deployed on August 8, 1945, two days after the bombing of Hiroshima and one day before the bombing of Nagasaki. The Soviets crossed into Manchuria and remained there until the following spring. They seized food stocks; dismantled cement plants, steelworks, and other assets; and sent back what they could to the USSR. Edwin W. Pauley, who later investigated for Truman, said that the Soviets made away with more than $2 billion of "war booty," a large sum even in those days, and that the resulting destabilization led to the communist takeover.

In addition, the Soviets captured stores of weaponry from the fleeing 500,000-man Japanese Kwantung Army, which had occupied Manchuria since 1931. That stash—including 500,000 rifles, 2,700 artillery pieces, and

138,000 machine guns—went straight into the hands of Mao's Moscow-trained military chief, Lin Piao, which sealed the takeover. As the Soviets exited, Pauley reported, 105 additional Manchurian cities and towns went to the Reds.

The Truman administration tried to induce Mao and Chiang to cooperate. When this didn't work, Truman embargoed all military aid to Chiang, effective July 1946. By then Lin Piao controlled the captured Japanese weaponry and was training reserves. Twenty-one months later Truman rescinded the embargo. But conditions had already turned against Chiang on the ground.

So while communism weakened in Western Europe, where it was largely seen as an alternative form of absolute despotism, Mao's Soviet-reinforced army and fantastic propaganda, serviced mostly by well-meaning but ill-informed progressives in the West, drove the conquest in China. It was an especially impressive feat because communism was at such odds with the Confucianism that had guided China for centuries, with its cultivation of virtue and emphasis on humaneness and filial piety.

Among the handful of concerned Americans, Claire Chennault, who saw all this happening from CAT's eagle eye, was aghast. In a scathing analysis that Dad helped prepare for the Scripps Howard newspapers, the general asserted, "Russia used her invasion of Manchuria to lay the foundations of a Communist regime where no Communists had been before."

Another worrier was John K. Singlaub, an intelligence officer in Mukden and, in 1977, the chief of staff of the US forces in Korea. That was the year President Jimmy Carter decided to withdraw American ground forces from the Korean peninsula, creating such a furor that the order was immediately rescinded; four decades later the US forces remain. General Singlaub publicly criticized the Carter initiative and was summarily relieved of command.

I myself never met Singlaub, but here's what he told my *New York Times* colleague Shirley Christian, then the paper's defense correspondent, in a 1985 interview: "I saw firsthand what happened when the United States withdrew support for Chiang. The units there ran out of ammunition. The US government decided to stop sending repair parts for their airplanes, [and] their vehicles, [and] refused to allow them to buy ammunition to fire from their American howitzers. That demoralization started the whole fall of China to the Communists."

In 1947 Truman, concerned about the flak his administration was taking on China and desperately anxious to win both the public relations battle and the 1948 election, appointed Albert Wedemeyer as his special China envoy. By now everyone knew that the man who succeeded Stilwell in 1944 was more hard-nosed about the Chinese Communists. Truman hoped to get cover from Wedemeyer, but he didn't. In a report prepared for the president, Wedemeyer called it as he saw it. What saved Truman was the decision to muzzle the general until after the election, and good soldier Wedemeyer obeyed. These days, leakers and whistleblowers, bloggers and tweeters would have done their stuff. But that early postwar era was a different world.

The 1948 election came and went. Truman narrowly beat his Republican contender, Thomas E. Dewey, and the Wedemeyer Report then saw the light of day as a government white paper. It debunked the myth that the Chinese Communists were agrarian reformers who would brace the country with necessary rigors. "The bulk of the Chinese are not disposed to Communism and they are not concerned with ideologies," Wedemeyer wrote. "They desire food, shelter and the opportunity to live in peace." He also declared that any communist takeover in the heartland of Asia constituted disaster for the United States and the free world.

But by 1949 it was too late. Cities were falling right and left. And the Wedemeyer Report became just another part of the superheated debate over who lost China—an argument that raged into the 1950s and beyond. World War II had ended, and the administration, though drawing the line on aggression in Europe, balked in Asia. As Wedemeyer and other critics so predicted, the communist victory in Asia turned out to be a disaster for America, presaging the loss of both blood and treasure from the stalemate in Korea and the long drawn-out and dolorous quagmire in Indochina. Mao then joined Stalin and Hitler as the globe's greatest killers.

Paul Johnson, a British historian, called Mao's legacy a series of experiments on hundreds of millions of people. "After forty years of ferocious civil conflict in which millions had died," he wrote, "none of Sun Yat Sen's original aims, which included Parliamentary democracy, freedom of the press and habeas corpus had been secured, and time was back where it had started with a despot—albeit a much more confident and oppressive one."

Among the victims, oddly, was Dad's old traveling companion, Israel Epstein of United Press, who spent five years in Quincheng, a maximum security prison northwest of Beijing, much of it in solitary confinement. One more refugee from Hitler's Europe, Epstein had been among Mao's chief apologists. After the 1949 takeover, he chose to live in China and was rewarded with special citizenship and privileges. But during those horrifying years of reeducation and murder known as the Cultural Revolution, no one, not even a loyal friend, was safe.

Mukden is an industrial city in southern Manchuria that the Nationalists managed to hang on to throughout most of 1948. My father revisited it in February that year and reported about life under siege in a series for Scripps Howard:

> It was a grisly twist of fate that Communist armies were doing to Mukden what the Nazis only a few years earlier had perpetrated at Leningrad. This is a city under siege, a city of despair. The more than 1 million inhabitants live only 12 hours a day. Between 6 PM and 6 AM, heat and light are cut off. Rifle fire echoes in darkness and people listen at their shutters to the distant thump and rattle of mortars and machine guns. There is no fuel, although 120,000 tons of bituminous coal sit in the stockpiles in Fushun only 20 miles away. Fushun is linked by rail to Mukden, but there are few rail cars. The people of Fushun scavenge hundreds of tons of coal each day from open-pit mines, and bags of such coal have found their way to the city at black market prices.

The siege lasted until October 1948, pinning down thousands of Nationalist troops. Astutely, Lin Piao let the city fall, as Dad wrote, "like overripe fruit." As the fighting spread, Dad also reported that people were voting the only way possible: with their feet. The world was getting used to that also in places like Berlin, Korea, and Vietnam.

Tens of thousands of Chinese took to the roads and rails, pushing overloaded conveyances as they balanced shoulder-pole baskets of personal belongings, fought for handholds on the outside of railcars, and waited hours and even days for a train going anywhere, as long as it was away from the fighting. Wily opponents sabotaged bridges, roads, and railroads to block access by defending troops.

One of the wiliest was Lin Piao's deputy, Liu Po-cheng, an alumnus of Moscow's Frunze Military Academy who was known as the "one-eyed dragon" because he had only one good eye. His signal achievement was the destruction of tracks and bridges on the Lunghai Railway, a critical link parallel to the Yellow River. In early 1949 Dad was on the Lunghai plain where Liu had just struck. Tracks were upturned as far as the eye could see. Dad was embedded with a Nationalist division under General Wang Fu, a diminutive, urbane, hearty fellow whose mission was none other than the destruction of the crafty Liu. But from what seemed apparent to Dad, hell might freeze over first.

Wang was driven to a commandeered farmhouse in a sputtering Ford, a jerry can tied to the hood as an improvised radiator. As maps were unfurled, a field telephone linked Wang to his base, and cooks were dispatched to scout out fowl in the villages for dinner. On this occasion a hand-brushed message gave Wang raw intelligence about the whereabouts of Liu. Wang plotted the distance on a map, measuring with his knuckles. "I just happen to have a ten-*li* (three-mile) fist," he declared. With a clenched fist representing the miles, Wang proclaimed Liu to be twelve hours away. Pointing to his nose and using such salty imprecations as "little turtle egg," Wang swore he'd find Liu "dead or alive."

But alas, it was already late afternoon. Wang still had to bathe in the portable metal bathtub towed by his command car. A fire of dried weeds heated water to a gentle warmth. Afterward Wang dressed with all his medals for dinner in a requisitioned farmhouse. Outside, in improvised fortifications, sleepy sentries smoked, imbibed, and dozed.

The dinner with guests and staff included concubines in long silken gowns. Halfway through the meal an orderly brought out a beat-up phonograph and cranked it up to play Viennese waltzes from a private collection.

His infatuation with *drei viertel takt* (three-four time) stemmed from his prewar years as a member of a military mission in Vienna. After dinner Wang was the first on his feet, encouraging the guests to join. Thus, the scraping bow, the sweeping curtsy, and the kissing of a hand were assiduously revived in northern China in the latter days of the civil war.

Liu Po-cheng was always a bridge too far—that is, until April 1, 1949, when in a moment of *his* choosing, Liu overwhelmed Wang and all the Nationalist defenses around the then capital of Nanking. Wang retreated, and the following month all those assets, including his ten-*li* fist, had to defend Shanghai. On a warm night in May, as the city was about to fall, Wang billeted his troops at the wharf of a Shanghai shipping company. He appropriated the billiards room for his quarters, accompanied by that beat-up phonograph and his concubines. He spread pillows on the billiards table and lay with his ladies. Just before dawn he unholstered his service pistol and blew his brains out.

In the months before Shanghai fell, the foreign press numbered about a score of reporters, half Americans. Since the hostel days in Chungking, the club had reorganized as the Foreign Correspondents Club of China, with a bar, a restaurant, and accommodations atop Broadway Mansions, not unlike the National Press Club today in the National Press Building in Washington. In the summer of 1948, as Mao consolidated in northern China, Don Starr, the *Chicago Tribune*'s Far East correspondent, was president. But planning a marriage and a return to Chicago, he sounded out Dad to succeed him. Dad agreed reluctantly and was easily elected.

Thanks to their girlfriends, the two men had both a professional and a personal relationship. Starr's fiancée, Mathilde, also from Vienna, was close to Dolly. The two had met in Kunming, where Mathilde spent the war years married to a Chinese optometrist named Shu-shih. She cooked on charcoal, boiled water for drinking, picked up basic Chinese, and got along badly with her mother-in-law. Once the war was over, she hastily divorced the good doctor and fled to Shanghai, again bumping into Dolly and, through Dad, meeting Don Starr.

With all his preoccupations, including the need to report on the civil war, Starr had let the club pretty much run itself. Inevitably, it hemorrhaged money and ached for professional management. Through Peppi, now CAT's ace photographer, and others from the Hongkew Jewish community, Dad heard about Kurt Wolf, a former apprentice at Vienna's Imperial Hotel, who seemed ideal for general manager. Wolf took a firm hand in the kitchen, and the food quality so perked up that for a period Broadway Mansions was deemed Shanghai's premier place for dining. And the bottom line improved.

Also through the Hongkew network came the Joachim brothers, a violinist and cellist whom Dad hired away from a dive on Hengshan Road in the French Quarter to play classical and popular music for dinner and dancing. The brothers brought along a Filipino drummer named Sandy to beef up the rhythm and blues. For maître d' came Liao, a cook and bottle washer from Dad's Chungking hostel days who had helped educate Dad on kitchen scams. The finances further improved.

Li, the barman, found a magnificent piece of teak for a cheap price. He and Dad went off to inspect it, with Dad trying to teach him Rudyard Kipling's poem "Mandalay": "Elephants a-piling teak / In a sludgy, squdgy creek." Workmen installed the teak and an impressive wall mirror, and an even bigger profit center emerged. Yet no matter how bracing the melodies and the martinis, the clouds were getting darker. Having captured Mukden, Mao dashed across the Great Wall to collar Tientsin and Peking, both without a fight. On January 22, 1949, he entered Peking, his freshly designated capital, in a captured American jeep.

To report all this, the AP sent Dad's old pal Spencer Moosa, whom Mao's men roughed up and put under house arrest. Dad convened an emergency meeting to condemn the arrest as a gross violation of freedom of the press and wired the resolution to news outlets and Mao's headquarters. A cabal, whom Dad labeled "friends of Mao," led by the TASS man, Vladimir Rogoff, worked to rescind the resolution. But Mao, perhaps realizing he'd overstepped in also making war on the AP, at least at that time, suddenly freed Moosa.

Despite the political gulf, Dad and Rogoff enjoyed a congenial personal relationship. A couple of months earlier Rogoff had invited Dad to dinner at a seafood restaurant in the French Quarter. The TASS man was beefy, broad-shouldered, and a little shorter than Dad's six feet. As they were about to sit down, the Russian said, as if in some undeclared contest, "You may be taller than I am, Mr. Farnsworth, but I am a tall man when I sit down."

Indeed he was. He held his barrel torso erect in the chair despite having downed several vodkas. It turned out that he was particularly interested in Dad's connections with Chennault, convinced apparently of both men's ties to American intelligence. Dad learned little about Rogoff but had a pleasant time anyway reminiscing with him about life as a reporter. The Russian was yet another who found that Dad loved to talk.

The restaurant's specialty was a kind of shellfish no larger than a fingernail called "watermelon seeds of the sea." Rogoff sucked each one clean of flesh and broth and laid the empty shells out in a pattern suggesting a house by rolling waves.

"I would like to retire to a house by the sea," the Russian said wistfully, adding, "May I give you a piece of friendly advice, Mr. Farnsworth?" Dad smiled warily. "When the People's Republic of China comes to power, do not hang around, or you may never be able to retire to your house by the sea." Dad was amused, even touched. He wasn't surprised to read years later in the published papers of the Soviet military intelligence defector Oleg Penkovsky that this same Rogoff was a colonel in the KGB and its top agent in China.

To the north and west, as cities and towns yielded to the Red legions, Shanghai came under enormous pressure from both the tsunami of refugees and hyperinflation. Chinese money was literally hauled around in wheelbarrows. Amid incidents of violence, foreign nationals were advised to leave. For a story on their exodus, Dad rode out to Longhwa Airport with James Moody, the director of the International Red Cross in China, who was sending his sons Jimmy and Michael back to America. As the boys argued over which toys to take and who would get the window seat, Dad wrote the following in the *New York World Telegram,* then a clarion in the Scripps Howard chain:

> Chinese Michaels and Jimmys were scrambling for perches on the roofs of railway cars, trudging the endless roads, swarming into the cities to beg and shiver in their rags. Chinese Michaels and Jimmys take to the road with sacks of rice to carry for their parents—if they are lucky enough to have food and parents. More often they have only chopsticks and bowls of tin cans in which to gather gifts of rice or backdoor slops and the garbage of city restaurants.

In an amazing coincidence years later, I ran into Jimmy at a dinner party in Washington that my wife, poet Elisavietta Ritchie, cohosted with a friend from the World Bank, Rebecca Chamberlain-Creanga. I recalled the name Jimmy Moody, and the age was about right, so I inquired if he was the same Jimmy described in Dad's story that I'd clipped years earlier.

Imagine my surprise when he said yes and asked how on earth I knew. Both fathers had passed away, as had his younger brother Michael. Having grown up in China and Greece, Jimmy followed his dad's footsteps in humanitarian assistance, taught economics at the University of Wisconsin, served ten years as a Democratic congressman from Wisconsin, and became one of those odd creatures one occasionally meets in Washington: a friend.

Despite draconian controls, there were food riots and looting throughout China. The increasingly jumpy Nationalist authorities imposed martial law, a strict curfew, and censorship so rigid that publication of practically any military information led to summary execution. Two press club members almost tragically put the decrees to the test. Graham Jenkins of Reuters reported where the Communist troops had crossed the Yangtze. George Vine of the *North China Daily News* published related data on military concentrations along the Nanking-Shanghai front.

When the two were arrested in mid-April 1949, they protested that they knew nothing of the decrees, which had been published only in Chinese.

The arresting officer, a police colonel named Yeh, served under General Mao Sen, the Shanghai police commissioner, known as "bloody Mao." Yeh had orders to get rid of fifth columnists, black marketers, and currency racketeers. Posters with grisly post–firing squad photos at every corner showed that Yeh meant business.

Vine managed to phone his German-born wife, Ellen, and begged her to seek help from the British consul or anyone at the press club. She called the consulate. The consul was at a dinner party. Asked to wait till morning, Ellen screeched that by then it could be too late. She found Dad at the press club. He had the phone number of police headquarters in his notebook, and he learned that Vine and Jenkins were indeed there, had confessed their guilt, and were awaiting the assembly of a firing squad. With his curfew pass and several blankets, he drove to a house on Avenue Edward VII, its backyard surrounded by high stone walls, a site already notorious for frequent executions. He demanded to see Colonel Yeh, sending in his card as the president of the correspondents' club.

Yeh, a swarthy man with fierce, flashing black eyes, met him in a dimly lit, sparsely furnished room on the ground floor. The prisoners were in the attic, a slit of a window affording the sight of what they called "execution garden," bounded by a wall chipped by shells. Yeh refused access upstairs, but he did accept the blankets.

"He laughed frighteningly when I asked for their freedom," Dad said, "but he didn't throw me out, which I assumed meant he was willing to listen to some form of supplication." Years in China had left Dad in no doubt that he'd have to do this the Chinese way, which meant humbling himself, accepting the men's guilt as his own, kneeling as an act of contrition, and throwing himself on Yeh's mercy. He also knew it important not to give up or leave. The chances were slim that they would execute the two Britons while he was still on the premises. He spent a night and a day in that horrid place, much of the time on his knees.

"These are filial sons," he told Yeh just before the policeman relented, "the sole support of their widowed mothers in England. Mr. Vine is married to a wonderful girl who wanted to make a new life in China. Yes, they have committed grievous offenses, but it was unintentional, and surely they have learned their lesson. Let me restore them to their families. If not, you will not be helping China or yourself. You will instead bring down the combined wrath of the Scripps Howard Newspaper Alliance and His Majesty's government."

The colonel asked him to bring Ellen Vine to the headquarters. Dad knew it would be pressing his luck to leave before getting a firm commitment, so he called Kurt Wolf at the club and asked him to bring Ellen. The following morning Colonel Yeh released Vine and Jenkins to Ellen and Dad, and they took the two shaken men back to Broadway Mansions. Years later in an account of the episode in *The Fall of Shanghai*, British author-journalist Noel Barber wrote that Vine and Jenkins "owed their lives to Farnsworth."

Shanghai consisted of people who were prepared to welcome the Reds, others who backed the Nationalists, and a broad apolitical middle that was just hoping for stability. Communism's supporters, spreading the word that life would get better after "liberation," gained the upper hand, especially that spring when the People's Liberation Army massed at the outskirts of town. In the turmoil leading to May 27, 1949, when the city succumbed without a fight, some capitalized on the situation by extorting money from any foreigners who were still around.

The club shared the building of Broadway Mansions with a US military advisory group. On May 14 the advisers, mostly Marines, got orders to leave. As landing craft embarked from the Bund wharf to navy vessels in deep water, the houseboys of Broadway Mansions, realizing they were now jobless, turned sullen and then hostile. A group barged into the club lobby and started stacking tables, chairs, and other furniture. Other personnel dared not intervene. When Dad asked the chief steward to tell them to stop, the steward cowered. "*Bu fangbien, bu fangbien*" (it is not convenient), he muttered. In a commanding tone my father ordered, "*Stop it! Halt!*"

The group's leader, a man whom Dad had never seen before, said the furniture was now the property of "the people." The man spoke for the new Broadway Mansions Collective and demanded that the club negotiate the use of its own furniture and provide severance pay for all the workers. He was a strapping, unpleasant-looking fellow with rotting stumps for teeth and limbs like smokehouse hams. When Dad said he was not prepared to negotiate, the fellow picked up a chair and ripped it apart like a stewing chicken. Whacking a leg near Dad, he muttered incomprehensibly. When Dad said in Mandarin that the man wasn't too friendly, he raged apoplectically. He never touched Dad, but the choice seemed to be to either appease or call back the Marines.

Dad told him that directors could authorize outlays for furniture, but they were not responsible for any obligations of the US military. Another whack—even closer! Shaken, Dad added that if this new collective could secure the premises, the board might agree to modest compensation. The fellow demanded an offer in writing. Dad obliged, stamping a sheet with the pocket seal he always carried (and later gave me), which had his name in Chinese chirography.

That seal turned the enemy into a friend, who with a big smile now insisted that they throw a banquet to celebrate the accord. Several anxious club members had nervously gathered, and since there were enough for a quorum, the recommendation was fast approved. Kurt Wolf had stores of rice and chicken, and with loyal hands he got the feast underway. Li brought out Chivas and Napoleon brandy from the teak bar.

Outside Broadway Mansions, everything was in furious commotion and locomotion. Arteries pulsed with millions of souls. Dad's CAT ties gave him near godlike status. The airline ran a service to Canton, Taiwan, and Hong Kong, a ride he had power to give that could be life itself. He felt the greatest responsibility toward the people identified with the club. Several planes filled with employees and their dependents, among them kitchen-scam instructor Liao, who ended up in Kerrville, Texas, where he ran a restaurant called China Dollar.

Another lucky fellow was a twelve-year-old waif whom some Marines had adopted at the US Navy barracks in the dock area around Woosung. The Marines gave him food, chewing gum, and a bunk and taught him GI English. They called him Harvey, after the phantom rabbit in the Mary Chase play. "A lot of Wongs in the neighborhood," an officer explained. Harvey's only clothes were oversized olive-drab fatigues and a too-large white toque emblazoned with USMC in gold letters. The boy learned to salute smartly, shouting at the top of his lungs, "*Semper fidelis*" ("Always faithful," the US Marine Corps motto). As the detachment pulled out, its officers begged Dad do something for Harvey, and he did, arranging a flight, with Dolly, to safer Canton.

Dad's greatest disappointment was a rejection of all offers of assistance by a close Chinese friend, Bennett Yuan, a Nationalist information officer, who, reflecting the highest Confucian values, was in fact trapped by them. The son of a judge in Nanking, Bennett attended a missionary college and married into a prominent Kuomintang family. His wife had no brothers and was the older daughter, so under Confucian tradition, upon the death of her father Bennett became the head of the family. His wife's mother had recently moved from Nanking to Kunming to Shanghai, and she absolutely refused to move again. Filial duty required the head of the family to remain with her, so Bennett and Dad said good-bye at Longhwa. In the coming bloodbath, Bennett was undoubtedly one of the first to be executed.

As the tarmac faded on the flight to Hong Kong later that day, sadness tugged at Dad's heart, not only for the loss of his friend but also for the passing of this chapter of his life. China had been home for nearly seven years. He loved the country, spoke its language, visited all its provinces and major cities, ate what the Chinese ate, drove its roads, flew over its mountains, braved its storms, rode its mules and rickshaws and sedan chairs, and walked when he had no choice. He knew there was no return. He was quitting an extraordinary, diverse, exotic, contradictory place whose people seemed capricious and inward-looking yet were also very practical and self-sustaining. They deserved better than what seemed to be in store.

Despite his personal ups and downs, the years had been good for Dad professionally. He was a twice-weekly columnist with thumb-size headshot photo in scores of US newspapers. Judging from the incoming cables, the editors were happy. And what he wrote mattered. He was cited in Washington, even read into the Congressional Record as part of the rancorous debate over "the loss of China." He was said to be part of the "China lobby," which amused him to no end. Lobbies are usually tied to big money, which he never had and never sought.

16

Aftermath

DAD HAD A mission. The board of the Foreign Correspondents Club had authorized reserve funds, much restored during his stewardship, to create a successor club in the British colony of Hong Kong. Upon arriving at Kai Tak Airport, he phoned fellow club member Bill O'Neill of Reuters, who had already bailed out. O'Neill put him in touch with an estate agent, and the three went for a ride. After twenty-five minutes of switchbacks above the Star Ferry, they hit the jackpot at 41A Conduit Road: what the English call a great house, a Downton Abbey kind of place, with a porticoed entrance, a long driveway, lawns, too many rooms to count, and a grand view of the harbor. As a home it was sheer extravagance; as a journalists' club it was ideal. There was space for news tickers, a bar, a restaurant, a library, rooms and suites, and even a pool table. A Greek shipping magnate owned it and would rent it for a sum within reason.

Dad couldn't get over the view: the stunning backdrop of opalescent Kowloon Bay, with planes in an almost continuous stream peeling over Stonecutters Island to alight on the Kai Tak runway. To the north and west were rugged hills of the Chinese mainland. The place proved so popular it was two decades before the club moved again. Hollywood loved it, too. In *Love Is a Many-Splendored Thing*, a 1955 film, the building metamorphosed into a hospital where William Holden watches Jennifer Jones tend the war wounded. She plays a doctor who falls for a correspondent (Holden) who is killed in Korea.

The place later succumbed to a frenzy of development and was torn down to make room for a posh high-rise apartment building. The club moved to the penthouse of an anonymous skyscraper and eventually to its present site, a renovated cold-storage warehouse on Ice House Street, an easy walk from the ferry. The current quarters lack the old one's grandeur, which is preserved in photos and an artist's rendering beside the central staircase. Although Dad never returned to China, he did get as far as Hong

Kong in 1975 when the club honored him at a special banquet. He also had a joyful reunion with Marine mascot Harvey Wong, who lived the American dream: he prospered as a shipping magnate.

Despite the fall of Shanghai, there was still scattered resistance to the Communists' juggernaut. Canton surrendered in October 1949, but the Nationalists still controlled much of the interior, including Kwangsi, Kweichow, Szechuan, and Sian Provinces. Chiang Kai-shek sought to rally his forces from Chungking, but it was a war too late, and he faced a growing number of defections by his officers and the provincial leaders.

Chungking fell on November 30, and the Nationalist leadership moved west to Chengdu, where peasants once pummeled rocks into B-29 runways. Again Chiang found little support. On December 7, the Yuan, or executive council, voted to transfer the capital of the Republic of China to Taipei. On December 10, just before Chengdu fell, Chiang, with his son Chiang Ching-kuo, flew from an old B-29 runway to Taipei. Neither of them ever set foot on the mainland again.

On December 16, during a rare trip abroad, Mao Tse-tung was in Moscow to give his personal thanks to Stalin for helping to deliver China. "For many years the Soviet people and the Soviet government have repeatedly given aid to the cause of the liberation of the Chinese people," Mao said in an unusual public acknowledgment of the assistance. No longer was there even the pretense that Chinese communism was a domestic agrarian reform movement. Stalin, celebrating his seventy-first birthday, ordered the Soviet press to print every word. He controlled more than half the world, a greater swath than anyone in history, and was used to accolades.

Yet Mao was no mere subject. Two pontiffs ruled world communism, and tensions were already stirring. Apparently to undercut his new rival, Stalin kept Mao waiting for five weeks in frigid Moscow, until January 22, 1950, before granting a second audience.

A conversation with the Soviet ambassador to China in 1958, unearthed years later from Chinese archives, left little doubt about Mao's feelings. "I got so angry I once pounded the table," Mao said, according to *New York Times* reporter Tim Weiner, who quoted from those archives in a story in December 1995. Mao's ire signaled trouble and anticipated the Soviet-Chinese split in 1959.

Chiang, meanwhile, avoided the public and the press throughout most of 1949. But in mid-December Dad flew to Taipei on the promise of an interview, and within days he was received in a newly renovated office near New Park, a quarter taken over by the Kuomintang after Japan's defeat in 1945.

The office had a large desk, a life-size portrait of Dr. Sun Yat-sen, the founder of the Republic of China, a flag of the republic, and a tastefully decorated Christmas tree. Dad had seen Chiang before, mostly on horseback during ceremonial occasions on the mainland, but this was their first one-to-one meeting.

He expected a gaunt, depressed figure crushed by the long struggle. Instead a seemingly unruffled fellow of sixty-two greeted him with a defiant smile. Dad said Chiang was like one of those toy soldiers that you knock over and it springs back, daring to be knocked over again and again. Chiang sprang from behind his desk, his movements spare and precise, and shook the journalist's hand. Slight of build, he was dressed in a creased uniform revealing not an ounce of fat. His face was like smooth copperplate beneath coal-black hair. Only the eyes, tinged with the filigree of an insomniac, betrayed the strains of the past months.

Dad sat at a low table, where tea was served. Some of Chiang's composure dissipated as he described the "deplorable conditions" on the mainland and pointed to the incompatibility between communist ideology and traditional Chinese values. He promised to go back across the hundred-mile-wide Straits of Quemoy with a force to restore Nationalist rule. The US Navy's Seventh Fleet had other ideas. Under Truman's orders, it policed the straits, keeping both sides apart, and except for sporadic raids and artillery duels, Mao and Chiang went their separate ways. Under Mao, the Great Proletarian Cultural Revolution turned China into a charnel house. Under Chiang, and later his son, Chiang Ching-kuo, Taiwan enfranchised its people and encouraged entrepreneurialism. The Taiwanese dug pots of gold instead of graves.

In more recent years, though still a one-party state, the People's Republic of China has joined the club of Asian Tigers, the highly free-market and developed economies of Singapore, South Korea, and Taiwan. For example, China has offered bargains to consumers through the purchasing department of Walmart. Should the two Chinas ever federate, the world would face opportunities and challenges with a tiger on steroids.

The last American diplomat to leave China was Angus Ward, the Canadian-born consul general at Mukden. It was not an easy exit. Arrested in

October 1948 upon the capture of that city, he was released after fourteen months in an unheated cell, where he had lived mostly on bread and water. The US State Department took a docile, acquiescent position, apparently still hoping to charm Mao into diplomatic ties; this stand infuriated many, including members of Congress, Dad, and Scripps Howard editorial writers. Stories about Ward's captivity and editorials about America's "humiliation" kept the waters roiled. It's unclear why Mao acted so swiftly with Moosa but so tardily with Ward—perhaps it was a sign of his greater respect for the press than the Department of State.

When Ward was finally freed in December 1949, more than four years after World War II had ended, the globe seemed to be teetering toward another catastrophe. Eastern Europe was incarcerated. Bookies wagered how long Soviet tanks would take to reach Calais. Stalin tested a hydrogen bomb. Within months North Korean tanks crossed the Thirty-Eighth Parallel.

Reporters in the Far East had orders from their home offices to find Ward at all costs and get his story. State Department officials, under Secretary of State Dean Acheson, were of no use. Although Ward, a seasoned Foreign Service officer, was one of their own and had been subjected to inhumane treatment in the line of duty, the pinstripes apparently considered any reporting about this unseemly. Hoping the story would just go away, Acheson did everything possible to bury it. Through luck and perseverance, Dad got the coveted interview, and the story refused to die.

All he had to go on was a Radio Peking report that Ward was being taken by rail from Mukden to Taku Bar, the anchorage for Tientsin. In Hong Kong, Dad booked passage on a twenty-thousand-ton Victory ship headed up the Chinese coast and eventually to Kobe, Japan. His colleagues in Tokyo, now his competitors, had boarded a freighter from Yokohama, also bound for Taku Bar. Dad arrived ahead of the competition. Ward was there, too, but was incommunicado and heading for Yokohama-Tokyo on the same vessel that would be returning with the competing, Japan-based reporters. Dad tried to book passage as well but was summarily refused. He didn't savor having to explain to his editors how he'd just lost out on one of the biggest news stories of the year.

There was still a chance. His freighter was due in Kobe twenty-four hours earlier than his rivals would arrive in Tokyo. He traveled the 250-mile distance by high-speed train, stopping at Number One Shimbun

Alley, the Tokyo press club, to reconfirm Ward's itinerary. He reached the docks as Ward's vessel arrived.

A diplomatic car whisked Ward away—no statement. Ward had stuck to his cabin, except for walks on deck with two leashed white Siberian cats, part of his entourage at the consulate; they had been liberated with him but had probably been treated a lot better. He refused to talk to any of the Tokyo-based reporters and was whisked off, with cats, to a US Army guesthouse at Camp Drake, the American military base outside Tokyo. The other reporters gave up on the story, but Dad, keeping his own counsel, decided it just might be worth a try in the more tranquil Drake surroundings. Using his military accreditation, he gained entry and staked out the residence.

After several hours Ward emerged, pulled energetically by the two long-legged, leashed Siberians, which looked a lot healthier than their master. Though sporting a freshly trimmed Vandyke, Ward wore an overcoat that, Dad said, couldn't mask the hollow concentration-camp look that the early postwar world was already too familiar with.

As Dad unzipped a shouldered wire recorder and stepped forward, Ward sized him up, shook his head, and in a surprisingly robust voice said, "Nothing doing! No interviews!" Though Canadian-born, he spoke with a Scottish burr. Despite the brush-off, he didn't turn away, an ambivalence that offered Dad some hope. Ward had already been debriefed by intelligence pros, but it couldn't have lasted long. Our spies had little interest in his impressions of Red China from a train window or a prison cell, and maybe the man really did want to talk.

"No interview," Dad repeated, trying to put him at ease. "I won't even use this!" He dramatically put the machine back into its case. "Just say what happened in your own words." Ward seemed to pay attention as Dad described the vigorous news campaign that had surely contributed to his release. "To keep the record straight," he went on, never taking his eyes off Ward, "I'll get an official stenographer, and you tell the world in your own words what you've endured."

Silence. The cats were silent, too, straining at the leash.

"I guess it would be all right," Ward finally said.

It was the one-to-one Dad had hoped for, but the promise of a government stenographer made it seem like official business. Despite all Ward had endured, he didn't want to appear disloyal. A quiet, contemplative, scholarly man, he had been put off by the journalistic pack. Not only was he a diplomat, he was also a linguist and a scholar. He picked up Russian from his Russian mother, married a Finnish woman, and knew several Chinese dialects; since 1927 he had been working on a dictionary of the Mongolian language.

The stenographer, borrowed from a Drake headquarters battalion, took it all down in a ninety-minute outpouring. The fifty-five-year-old diplomat spoke of his "hellish treatment": the deprivation of food, freezing cold, lack of warm clothing, brutality of the guards, trumped-up charges of espionage, and other abuse by his Chinese captors. Upon his release, they made him pay $7,000 for a train ticket for the four hundred miles from Mukden to Tientsin!

Returning to Number One Shimbun Alley, Dad worked through dawn's early light on a series of articles recounting the horrific experience. They were a sensation—and also an embarrassment to Acheson and the entire Truman administration, which once again had to defend its China policies. Although the presidential election was two years away, the seizure of China by seeming barbarians, with what seemed like a wink and a nod from the grandees of Washington, predictably triggered fireworks and led to the eight-year takeover by Eisenhower Republicans in 1952.

Mao's victory saw Claire Chennault and his partner Whiting Willauer try to make a go of running an air transport business outside China that linked Taipei, Hong Kong, Haiphong, Manila, and Tokyo. Profits were small and layoffs inevitable. In Washington the newly established Central Intelligence Agency watched with growing interest. With China shut off, the demand for intelligence rocketed, and the Civil Air Transport airline, which knew China intimately, was a prized asset. If necessary, its pilots could find remote airstrips, contact pockets of resistance, and transport agents. It was dangerous work yet doable. The spy agency offered to subsidize the airline, with an option to buy. President Truman approved the deal in March 1950, and by July, just after war had broken out in Korea, the option was exercised. On top of secret missions inside Red China, CAT contracted with the air force to move materiel and personnel between Japan and the new Korean war zone.

CAT flew a total of fifteen thousand missions for the government, including ones ferrying me—Corporal Farnsworth, later Sergeant—to and from Tokyo for rest and recuperation in February 1953. Down from Korea's central highlands, I rode in an army truck to Chunchon, then boarded a

CAT C-47 for Tetchikawa, Tokyo's military airport. Five days later, after a little R&R, I faced the return to Heartbreak Ridge.

Rita, a singer in one of the clubs, sought to improve her English. Her father had served in World War II as an army doctor in the Philippines. She and her grandmother barely survived the 1945 firebombing organized by General Curtis LeMay. "Everything [was destroyed]," she said. A blizzard paralyzed Tokyo, similar to one during the firebombing that blocked the fire trucks. Warmed by sukiyaki in a restaurant off the Ginza (a popular shopping area of Tokyo), we stirred the *nabemono* (hot pot) and drank saki. She cried when my five days were up, and I did, too.

17

Fallout

GENERAL DOUGLAS MACARTHUR, the World War II Pacific commander and the father of postwar Japan, occupied the fifteenth-floor penthouse suite in Tokyo's Daichi Life Insurance Building, which afforded a splendid view of the Imperial Palace down to the stonework in the emperor's moat. One day in mid-March 1950, the sun seemed to wrap MacArthur in a halo by that window as Dad arrived for his scheduled interview. The reporter tried not to stare at the dyed-black hair matting the creeping baldness. He took a coffee and sat, as directed, opposite MacArthur's higher wing chair.

"It cannot be emphasized enough that we are going to pay the consequences of the fall of China for years to come," MacArthur said, adding, "Japan now must be a bastion of freedom in the Orient." Though splitting with the Truman administration on China, he had its full support on Japan. He had created democratic institutions and jump-started the economy. Having liquidated the cartels that ran so much of prewar industrial life, he incorporated American-type watchdogs over financial, antitrust, and other sectors. "Once accepting the ways of democracy," MacArthur said, "the Japanese will never give them up."

Dad was skeptical. "My impression of the Oriental masses," he responded, "is that their political vision reaches only to the rim of their rice bowl." The general returned a look of sharp disapproval. "That is a very animalistic concept. The Japanese will never let this way of life go!"

Years have shown MacArthur right. The Japanese have not given up on democracy and, with almost no natural resources, have been clever enough to turn defeat in war, including the carnage from firebombing and two atomic bombs, into one of the highest living standards in the world. Yet as their governments rise and fall with periodic elections, the depths of democratic commitment may be open to question. The country continues to be ruled by an elite power group. Factions change, yet the same kinds of people hold on indefinitely.

Scripps Howard was MacArthur's last appointment of the day. As Dad exited, several salutes from an honor guard lining the hallway died in the making as the spit-and-polish guard saw only a crumpled civilian ambling toward the elevator. That guard—in snow-white helmet liners, white gloves, blue fourragères, matching kerchiefs, and lustrous combat boots with not a lace out of place—was a sample of the splendor that MacArthur wrapped himself in as the proconsul. At ground level the phalanx stretched as far the eye could see to a chauffeured black Crown Imperial limousine in the plaza. Within minutes MacArthur emerged, in emblematic Ray-Ban sunglassess and braided cap, and each position snapped to attention, the guards smartly clicking their heels. It was a ceremony fit for an emperor.

Japan annexed Korea in 1910 and ruled it until 1945, when Soviet troops, mopping up in Manchuria, crossed into Korea and installed a communist regime in the upper half of the peninsula under Moscow-trained Kim Il-Sung. American troops occupied the lower half. In 1948, under a demilitarization agreement with Stalin, the US Army's Twenty-Fourth Infantry and First Cavalry Divisions returned to Japan. But the Soviet military stuck around to train North Koreans in everything from burp guns to T-34 tanks, and within a few years the North was more than a match for the South.

On January 12, 1950, Secretary Acheson, in a speech before the National Press Club, omitted South Korea from a defense perimeter that could count on American support. On June 25 that year, North Korean armor barreled across the Thirty-Eighth Parallel. All of Korea was threatened, and Washington now realized that millions more humans were about to live not too happily under communism. Republicans again yelled bloody murder, joined by some Democrats. President Truman, desperately trying to rectify the situation, ordered the two army divisions back into the fray.

By a fluke, Truman even enlisted the United Nations. The Russians, who could have vetoed defensive moves by the Security Council, had walked out that January, allowing an American resolution for the collective defense of Korea to go forward. In the end, sixteen UN members dispatched battalion-size units, or greater, alongside the United States and South Korea.

In the early days of the Korean War, the First Cavalry and the Twenty-Fourth Infantry were unready. GIs in Japan had gotten used to warm beds, available women, good chow, and movies every night. Months had passed since they had even lifted an M-1 or a carbine. Then overnight they were called on to stop what Stalin had just made into the toughest small army in the world.

North Korean units decimated forward elements of the Twenty-Fourth and what existed of the South Korean Army, and pushed the defenders back to the southern port city of Pusan. Later that summer and in the early fall, the defenders rallied and pushed deep into North Korea, close to the border with China. On November 1, 1950, four months after the war had started, Chinese troops intervened. Human waves overwhelmed Allied lines. Two years of heavy fighting ensued before a new equilibrium was found along the Thirty-Eighth Parallel. In thirty-seven months, Seoul changed hands four times.

During the first week of July 1950, Dad flew into Taijon, a dusty, shell-pocked town a hundred miles south of Seoul. He broke into tears seeing those kids from Middle America in full retreat, bootless at times, ragged, and smeared with grime and blood. Clerks and mess units, usually at the rear, faced an enemy that was everywhere and nowhere: Borodino, Caporetto, Cannae of Punic War (II). As the GIs straggled into Taejon, they barely had time to don fresh socks and T-shirts before being pressed again into that ever fraying line.

A schoolhouse on the town square served as headquarters for General William F. Dean, who had orders to buy time. South of Taejon was the Naktung River, Taegu, Pusan, and the South China Sea. Dean personally led an antitank team to target Soviet T-34s with bazookas. He was captured, held in intolerable conditions, released after three years, and awarded the Congressional Medal of Honor.

Dad succumbed to dysentery. Halazone tablets, with the smell and taste of chlorine, were supposed to prevent that kind of thing—another example of what didn't work that calamitous summer of 1950. He flew out of Taejon hours before it fell. The ride to Tokyo on a C-47 hospital plane was the setting for a heartfelt article on the efforts to save one GI:

> A lone nurse, Lieutenant Virginia Pecan from Brooklyn, was in charge of 20 men on stretchers. . . . A badly off GI, getting blood and plasma on the ride out, was last to board. . . . A great pad of bandages lay over and below

the right shoulder, and a blood-smeared GI blanket covered the rest of him. Clenched between his teeth was a plastic tube to depress his tongue and assist breathing. Lt. Pecan was on her knees with an air syringe to clear the pink froth. The plane taxied down the runway past the still burning wreckage of a less fortunate C-47. . . . As the plane climbed, Lt. Pecan hung another bottle over her newest charge—600 centimeters of refrigerated, anti-coagulant, universal type whole blood. Her hands seemed small and efficient. She was just over five feet tall and weighed about 100 pounds. Close-cropped reddish curls sought escape from her flight cap.

The roll of her patient's grimy, tousled head seemed in protest of some nightmarish horror. For the next few minutes her hunched and beaten figure hovered. . . . She sent S/Sgt Harold Miller to the rear for an oxygen kit. After he broke it out, she cupped the rubber mask over the patient's mouth and nose. Miller adjusted the flow. She held the mask with one hand. With the other she roved from forehead, to heart, to abdomen. Oxygen hissed. "More!" Her eyes screamed. Her hands rubbed his upper chest until tears laved her cheeks.

Upon the outbreak of war, Truman appointed MacArthur to command the UN forces. At age seventy, the general still had fire in the belly and Sun Tzu on the brain—*The Art of War*, written 2,500 years earlier, laid out strategic planning. "Take advantage of your enemy's unreadiness," Sun wrote. "Make your way by unexpected routes and attack unguarded spots." Such principles MacArthur used to great effect in his 1944–1945 New Guinea campaign and again in September 1950 for an amphibious landing at Inchon.

After the debacle at Taijon, Allied troops held at Pusan and finally pushed back. Inchon hastened the liberation of Seoul and pried open the north. But Mao and Stalin refused to abandon Kim. Six weeks after Inchon, half a million Chinese troops swept across the Yalu, making a long winter for yet more Americans in the wrong place at the wrong time. An African American schoolmate of mine, Harry Sanders, who was great at stickball, was among the fallen.

Tumult in the Far East led to Dad's temporary reassignment to the United Nations in New York, where the war in Korea and tensions in the Formosa Straits dominated the agenda. The United Nations had not yet moved to Manhattan and was still at Flushing Meadow in Queens, a site Dad knew well from the 1938–1939 World's Fair. As a favor to the UN public affairs office, he took a break from reporting to give the actor Rex Harrison, who was as winning in person as in his portrayals on stage and screen, a tour of the place. They were almost exactly the same age, both born in March 1908. Harrison was less interested in such coincidences than in the tales of a reporter's life in the Far East. He offered an aisle ticket to the play he was appearing in with his wife, Lili Palmer, with an invitation to Sardi's Restaurant later to continue the conversation. "Oh, just a little thing," Harrison said lightly about the play. "*Bell, Book and Candle*, about witchcraft. You might enjoy it." Tickets went at scalpers' prices.

Dad never made it. Editors were trying to reach him. It was October 12, 1950, Columbus Day, and he suddenly learned that he was about to explore more of Grandma's new lands. The president had decided to meet MacArthur at an unnamed site, and Dad was to cover it. He hustled to make arrangements on the press plane, a Boeing Stratocruiser—wheels up at 6:00 a.m. at Andrews Air Force Base. Charlie Ross, Truman's press secretary, worked the clearances.

Checking out of the Statler, Dad rushed across to Penn Station for the next express to Washington, booked a room at the Mayflower Hotel, and took a dawn cab ride on Suitland Parkway to Andrews Air Force Base. He was delighted to see some old buddies—including, as his seatmate, Frankie Cancellare, the fellow with a thing against Chungking banana trees. To no one's surprise, the first stop was Independence, Missouri, where Truman chatted up the hometown folk and led reporters on a merry walkabout. The next stop was Hawaii, where a hula-skirted woman hooped a lei over his head as he cheerfully waved to well-wishers.

The reporters had no idea of the destination, but so far it was fun. Only when they were once again over blue water did Ross reveal that they were going to Wake Island, an atoll fiercely contested in the war, home to gooney birds and weathermen. A "compromise," Ross noted. MacArthur and the president each had to go halfway to meet the other.

They couldn't have been more different: the general with an imperial bearing, whose military and nation-building exploits lent him heroic stature; and the plain, diminutive small-town former haberdasher with rumpled suits, who played poker and piano and was not averse to telling people, including generals and reporters, exactly what he thought of them.

MacArthur arrived first and rode out in a sedan chair to greet the president. The two were driven in a black Chevy to a nearby Quonset hut, where they conferred for two hours. They strolled at the water's edge, then retired to the patio of a beach house where their aides joined them, and all enjoyed an island dinner bathed in glorious sunset. Ross and other officials were free and easy with such trivia but imposed a blackout on substance. The president was saving that for a press conference in Washington, and his loyal acolytes leaked nothing. For want of anything better, Dad went to bed.

The president slept on Air Force One. No one divulged where MacArthur slept, and it seemed worth probing. The morning after, Dad explored a part of the island with residential huts set aside for service personnel. He met a housewife in shorts and a halter top who complained that she was still coping with bottles and ashtrays from the MacArthur entourage. He went back and got Frankie Cancellare, and they returned to the woman with a plan in mind.

She led them to the master bedroom, and Frankie asked her to write on the wall with her lipstick exactly what he dictated. The photo of her on her knees on the unmade bed, clutching the lipstick and showing cleavage, appeared in hundreds of papers beneath Frankie's words: MacArthur slept here.

Dad attended the press conference in Washington. Unaccredited to the White House, he was barred from asking a question. Andy Tully, the Scripps Howard White House reporter, asked one for him: Did Formosa (Taiwan) come up in the talks with MacArthur? Tully got a confusing answer. As the conference ended, Dad rushed over to Charlie Ross to say he didn't understand the response on Formosa. Ross stiffened, looked past Dad, and uttered, "I thought the president made himself perfectly clear."

Dad felt a presence by his left elbow and turned to see the diminutive Truman, who had suddenly appeared. "And what was it, young man, you didn't understand?" Truman asked edgily.

"Frankly, Mr. President, I didn't understand whether you and General MacArthur discussed Formosa." Truman bristled. "General MacArthur and I discussed the whole situation in the Far East. I didn't discuss the Formosa question because there is no Formosa question. I settled that six months ago."

"Thank you, Mr. President," Dad said, quietly elated. He exited to write a story that received a banner headline in all Scripps Howard newspapers. Before the meeting on Wake Island, MacArthur and other military leaders had been urging material assistance to Formosa. Truman's statement that the matter was already resolved signaled that the request was denied; this was the brunt of Dad's piece and a subject of huge interest at the time.

Truman's reference was to a statement the previous April: "The United States government will not provide military aid or advice to the Chinese forces on Formosa."

So at Wake Island, Truman and MacArthur agreed to disagree on Formosa. But within weeks the Chinese swarmed into Korea. As that war now entered a more perilous phase, an even more serious rift developed. MacArthur insisted on punishing Mao, but Truman, fearing a wider conflict, again put the brakes on his commander. MacArthur asked specifically to bomb the Yalu River bridges, which Chinese troops were using to cross into North Korea. He also sought to "unleash" Chiang, who offered to raid the mainland and contribute troops to fight alongside the UN forces. Truman denied both requests. MacArthur fretted that he was being forced to fight with his hands behind his back, and he called the conditions imposed on him "one of the strangest anomalies known to military history."

Dad, some of the press, and many on Capitol Hill, chiefly Republicans, were sympathetic. It seemed incomprehensible that it would be off-limits to bar waves of Chinese infantry from gathering for pitched battles against outmanned GIs. Also, aggressive deployment of Chinese Nationalist forces against mainland China might force the Communists to defend their homeland, reducing their capacity to further destabilize Korea.

Yet others saw in MacArthur a loose cannon and feared the consequences of a wider war, which could involve not only China but also the Soviet Union and conceivably trigger World War III, complete with nuclear weapons. The gulf between the general and the president widened so much that within six months of the Wake Island meeting, MacArthur, who had served the United States through two world wars, was fired.

Many commentators concluded that Truman needed a scapegoat. Truman's supporters enjoyed the spectacle of the pompous old soldier being brought down a peg and insisted that the president employed thoroughly justified restraint in light of the incendiary global conditions. Yet if Truman had thoughts about a second term, the "fall of China" and rising American casualties in Korea doomed that. Although Truman is revered today for his grit as the little guy who "gave 'em hell," a Gallup poll taken in November 1951 showed that only 23 percent of Americans thought that he was doing a good job—one of the lowest ratings ever for a sitting president, even below Richard Nixon at the nadir of Watergate.

18

Reconnections

FROM A. B. Davis High School in Mount Vernon, I went to Yale as a scholarship student and was also a cocky presence at one of the residential colleges, Trumbull. Out of the blue in my junior year, Dad waylaid me under the dimly lit faux-medieval archway. He had just returned from Wake Island, and I from a dinner of "shit on a shingle," aka chipped beef on toast.

"Farnsworth," he barked. It had been eight years since we'd said goodbye at Penn Station, but that voice, gravelly from years of cigarette smoking, was unforgettable. He was in shadows, looming like Orson Welles beyond the street lamps in *The Third Man*. I moved from instantaneous shock to unbridled joy and rushed into his arms. We'd been in desultory contact over the years, and thanks to the now steady work at Scripps Howard, he footed some of my college tab. A crowd of the curious gathered, and he asked if there was someplace we could talk. I invited him to my room, up one flight, overlooking passage to Elm Street.

He declined the ratty, ultra-deep armchair I'd acquired for $1 from someone down the hall, but he did take a hard wooden desk chair. The only thing he drank was water. As I procured a couple of plastic glasses, he expressed wonder at my choice of wall art: several magazine photos of June Allyson, a song and dance princess I adored who was raised in the north Bronx, not far from Langdon Avenue, where I had grown up; and the reproduction of an old man with a bulbously gnarled nose beside a youth, by Domenico Ghirlandaio (1449–1494), a mentor of Michelangelo. The ugliness of the nose accented the affecting sublimity between the old man and a youth, perhaps a loving grandson. June Allyson was the idealized girl next door.

Friends dropped by a little later to share impressions of books and philosophy. After introductions and a bit of conversation, he invited one and all to Mory's, where he'd never been before and hadn't been since.

Although it never came up, the idea obviously tickled him that as a product of the school of hard knocks, he was now holding forth on global affairs in this sanctum of the gilded aristocracy, which had turned out, for example, the immaculately misguided Dean Acheson.

We attacked rarebits and drank ale as he fielded questions about the Far East and everything else. Peter Fornacca, Bill Hegener, Larry Hemmerling, Art Rosen, Tony Gallombardo, John Cromwell and others were a rapt audience. Hemmerling, a history major, said it was the high point of his academic year.

Dad slept at the Taft Hotel, and the next day he asked me to accompany him by train to Mount Vernon. My sister Sue was a sophomore at Davis High. We waited for her classes to end and caught her gabbing with her friends, then the three of us caught the A trolley to Langdon Avenue.

The reunion was agonizing. I knew Mom's feelings, having heard them for the past eight years. I now knew Dad's. It was a circle that couldn't be squared. I refuse to go over the arguments. He wanted a divorce that she wouldn't give. He tried to soften her with a shiny new Chevy convertible, and she took the car but didn't give in on the divorce. She now knew about Dolly. She didn't know the ropes in her adopted country, but her gut said that whatever was happening wasn't right.

She had carved a niche for herself as a substitute teacher of French at Davis High, which had somewhat restored her self-esteem. When the calls came, which were often because the regular teacher was too frail for rugged Mount Vernon winters, her whole demeanor changed. She chose her best dark suit and pumps; then, before a mirror in the chill bathroom, she smartly applied lipstick and rouge to engage the day. Sometimes she asked me to help pull together an old-fashioned whalebone corset so the clasps would meet. Once her toilette was complete, she was transformed—chic, bright, and witty, and if there was anything that made me a supporter of women's liberation long before that term was invented, it was those mornings when she prepped to sally forth into a savage world.

She had taken on complete responsibility for us in our most formative years, which Dad sloughed off and then belatedly tried to make amends for. When he returned, we were mostly grown up. Frank was eleven, Sue was fifteen, and I was a big shot of nineteen, forced into proxy fatherhood, which my siblings hated me for and which I hated more.

But by 1950 I had moved on, leaving Mom more or less to fend for herself. She must have felt abandoned. There wasn't much I could do about that except feel guilty, which I did, and later I tried to make up for it. Life wasn't fair, she said. I agreed. It was around 1950 that she told both my sister and me about the second newsman she'd dated in Cleveland. So stung was she by Dad that she had to show her wiles as a femme fatale—if only to her loving kids.

At any rate, it was mind-blowing to speculate that we could have also sprung from William F. McDermott, the legendary drama critic of the *Cleveland Plain Dealer,* beloved by most theater folk, a little older than Dad and divorced. Having just met the dashing police reporter from the *Cleveland News,* Marthe politely fended off the older man, but they remained friends. McDermott too was a war correspondent: Spain, 1937, and the Italian front in World War II. During her unhappy years, she rued her decision not to dump Dad for "Weel-i-am." She told us of other admirers, including Salvador Dali, who made a play for her on one Atlantic crossing in 1934 aboard the *Champlain.* She described him as "bizarre" with his thin upcurled wax mustache, but she added that she found him "*amusant.*"

Eventually Dad got a no-fault divorce in Juarez, and he and Dolly were married in a simple ceremony in Rome in January 1951. He promised Mom financial support, which in later years, after he broke with Scripps Howard, was erratic at best, and she was unable to enforce it without costly lawyers. Yet with funds from me, including Korea combat pay, and from Sue, who took a clerical job in New Rochelle soon after high school, Mom got by.

By this time, too, Dad's job again was changing. His editors sought younger blood in the Far East, where the story had turned into savage struggles over promontories with names like Pork Chop Hill, Old Baldy, and Heartbreak Ridge. Scripps Howard Editor in Chief Walker Stone recalled Dad's AP dispatches from the Middle East a decade earlier and encouraged him to revisit. After years of colonialism, the upheaval was galvanizing.

As an added inducement, Stone said Dad could install himself anywhere within reason and commute. Dad suggested Rome, and Stone said, sure, why not? Since quitting China, Dad and Dolly had camped in Hong Kong. But to Dolly, Rome was superior—still reasonably priced and less than two hours by air to anyplace in the region. It was also a giant step closer to what she really wanted: Vienna. They chose a bed-and-breakfast on the Via della Mercede, a short walk to the Forum, and as in Mount

Vernon, Kunming, Chungking, Shanghai, and Hong Kong, Dad commuted. The news centered on Egypt and Iran, both convulsed by waves of anticolonialism, nationalism, and xenophobia.

In May 1951, Egypt seemed to choose Dad. Pressure was mounting against King Farouk and his reformist prime minister Mustafa Nahas Pasha, who, in trying to better social conditions, alienated the military. The writing was on the wall for the ancien regime, but Shepheard's was still the grand hotel of 1942, physically little changed, its public rooms of the same faded elegance, recalling pith helmets and crinoline, the doorman in a flowing burnoose, summoning his stable of "boys" to hail a taxi. Anatole's double ran the bar, and his martinis were just as popular. Instead of Allied staff cars, Farouk's red Cadillac and cream-colored Rolls Royce alternated in reserved spaces beside the verandah.

Yet on Sharia Ibrahim Pasha and the lesser streets not far from Shepheard's, conditions were more unsettled. Dad described malformed children with flies that were "like mascara around their eyes." He wrote of a new surliness and hostility toward Westerners. There had been "incidents": cars overturned, rocks tossed at the British embassy, and anti-Western graffiti. Westerners were advised not to travel alone. Then in January 1952 Shepheard's was burned to the ground by what Ernie Hill, a *Chicago Daily News* colleague, called the "snarling mobs of Ibrahim Pasha." The protests were against both the colonial presence and the venality of Farouk. The mobs also razed Circurel's, a Jewish-owned department store, where Dad had bought his shoe-shining balaclava.

Within five months a military coup toppled Farouk. It was only a minor inconvenience; having stashed away public funds in Swiss banks, Farouk spent the rest of his life at fancy watering holes, mostly eating. At three hundred pounds, he was known as a stomach with a head. An eatery in Rome was where this faded symbol of the ancien regime breathed his last after a massive heart attack in 1965.

At the time Shepheard's burned in early 1952, Dad was in Tehran. The Egypt story competed with a dispute between Iran and the British-controlled Anglo-Iranian Oil Company over the profits from oil. In a standoff between Britain and elected leader Mohammed Mossadegh, Truman dispatched W. Averell Harriman, the heir to a railway fortune and a former ambassador to Moscow, to mediate. But not even such a seasoned negotiator could bridge the gap.

Shortly before the showdown in which the British-owned oil company was nationalized, Harriman invited a handful of English-speaking correspondents to the breathtaking villa his mediation team took over in north Tehran in the foothills of the Alborz Mountains. But it turned out to be a social occasion in which Harriman held forth on everything under the sun except the issue at hand. He spoke of his friendship with Roosevelt and seemed to regard Stalin highly: "Only a man as tough as Stalin could have held the Soviet Union together." Foreign Minister Vyacheslav Molotov was a man with a "great sense of humor," and KGB Chief Lavrenti Beria had "cold iron eyes." The cameos were interesting, the surroundings spectacular, the drinks excellent, and the finger food, including Caspian caviar, sumptuous. Harriman had been around reporters long enough to know that like Farouk, they loved to eat.

Thoroughly relaxed and looking sharp in his Saville Row pinstripe suit, this grandee, of the same swatch as Dean Acheson, seemed to be inviting features on himself and his remarkable life amidst the movers and shakers. But, as Dad noted, newsmen were not adoring biographers. Each was under time pressure to write about the Iranian crisis, and the home offices were never satisfied. Dad grew fidgety. Ed Clark from the UP and others exhibited malaise. At the end of a long reflection by Harriman on Roosevelt and his unerring wisdom, Dad asked him whether he had anything to say on the mediation efforts in Iran. "Absolutely nothing," Harriman replied stiffly, as if such a direct question were an affront.

"In that case, Mr. Ambassador," Dad said, pushing back his chair as he rose, "I'm leaving now." Walkouts were popular—the Soviets had shown the way at the United Nations. Several of Dad's colleagues followed him out. It was an extreme yet understandable reaction. Harriman was obviously a fascinating fellow, not least because he had money and influential friends. But enthralling chaps are of little interest to news stiffs without the catnip of news.

Within days came the nationalization, the threat on which Harriman was too discreet to comment, followed by an alliance of Mossadegh with Moscow, which had already fielded troops in Azerbaijan. These would have been interesting subjects for Harriman to broach, but he steered clear of anything newsworthy.

Mossadegh, apparently no communist himself and not even a particularly devout Muslim, was a stem-winding orator, hypnotizing crowds with emotional speeches. Dolly, who once joined Dad to revisit her still booming Ferdowsi bar, called him "a tear shedder." Tears literally cascaded down his bony cheeks as he fired up the cheering throngs against Western capitalism. Although a popularly elected leader, he drew support from the vocal, white-shirted members of the newly energized Tudeh (Iranian Communist Party) who overturned cars, scrawled graffiti against the old regime, and terrorized conservative elements of the population. Such demonstrations led both Britain and the United States to fret openly about yet another communist takeover.

Years later, thanks to disclosures by the *New York Times*, it became known that the CIA, along with Britain's MI5, bankrolled the opposition to Mossadegh, giving the shah an advantage in the showdown, which took place in August 1953. One operative was Kermit Roosevelt, the grandson of Theodore and a cousin of Franklin, a buttoned-up fellow I met in Washington, DC, in late 1979. Predictably, the Teddy side of the clan supported Republicans and the FDR side supported Democrats, and Kim in 1979 signaled he was no admirer of President Jimmy Carter.

Carter declined to bolster the shah during the Islamic Revolution early in 1979, just before the Grand Ayatollah Ruhollah Khomeini seized power. A few days later, Islamist cohorts took over the US embassy, and during the 444-day hostage crisis, Carter stumbled. Over the prior quarter century, Kim Roosevelt noted the evening we met, the shah had been a strong ally of both the United States and Israel and also a progressive ruler—for example, he was one of the few regional leaders (besides those in Israel) to promote education and other rights for women. But the Shah also created a secret police division, SAVAK (Organization of Intelligence and National Secruity), second to none in cruelty. Its formation was assisted by both the CIA and Mossad.

Kim's CIA caper of 1953, still secret in 1979, was code-named Operation Ajax after a Greek warrior who, in a fit of insanity, according to Sophocles, attacked a flock of sheep he believed to be Spartan warriors. When he came to his senses, Ajax realized his error and killed himself. The target of the CIA's Ajax caper was Mossadegh, who under the shah was convicted of treason in 1953. After three years in prison, Mossadegh spent the rest of his days under house arrest and died in 1967.

If Iran and Egypt weren't big enough stories, Dad also eyed southeastern Europe. Yugoslavia's leader, Josef Broz Tito, had already broken with Stalin, and one of the issues was how far he would go to engage with the West. Dolly more than paid her way, translating from the local press and, thanks to her ease with German and French as well as Serbo-Croatian, interpreted during conversations with non-English-speaking officials. She was particularly helpful in June 1952 in an encounter between Tito and Lord Mountbatten, the last British viceroy of India.

That odd couple met at Tito's cliffside retreat at Brioni, overlooking the blue-green Adriatic. Both Tito and Mountbatten were stiff in starched, beribboned uniforms. Yet it was hard to imagine two men less alike: the short, stocky, no-holds-barred guerrilla fighter breaking out of Stalin's Cominform (Communist Information Bureau), and the ramrod-stiff uncle of the queen of England, then commanding the Mediterranean fleet. But their body language also suggested at least one common trait: flaming egos.

Yugoslavia, Egypt, and Iran—Dad needed a cold shower to know where he was. He now had second thoughts about Rome; closer to the action would be preferable. Beirut leapt to mind, then still a miracle of coexistence between Muslims and Christians. Dolly said it was the only city in the Middle East where she could be happy. With home office approval, they bid Rome *arrivederci* and took a modest apartment on the palm-studded Beirut Corniche.

Then Dad did what he had wanted to do for some time: bought a car. Thanks to those reviled colonials, Middle Eastern roads were as good as Ohio's, and he could drive to work: Cairo, 350 miles; Ankara, 440 miles; Aleppo, 180 miles; and Damascus, 50 miles. Even Tehran, at 1,200 miles, was doable. Dolly rode shotgun. He bought a Buick Roadmaster, which he compared to Jake LaMotta, the Bronx-born middleweight of the day, aka Raging Bull. Both could take punishment. Dolly read road signs and interpreted when necessary. It was a region she knew well after the Anschluss.

Although Beirut was no hardship, Dolly never let up in her campaign to return to Vienna, where she still had friends and foster parents and where even those terrible wounds of war were healing. She begged Dad to get an assignment in Vienna, and as always, he tried to appease her. But editors had other ideas.

In mid-1953, prospects were zero in Europe, and younger hotshots were drifting into the Middle East. Yet another part of the world ached for coverage: Latin America. The hard nationalism of Argentina's Juan Domingo Perón was turning that entire continent toward a new kind of National Socialism, of which Americans, his editors felt, should be made more aware. They urged that he go there for a few months, then they'd all reassess.

It was another invitation too good to refuse. He loved a terra incognita and felt a reflow of the same energy that initially propelled him into the Middle East and Asia: Grandma Lydia's presence. He was being paid to explore yet another part of the world where people didn't speak English.

Dolly was not happy. She wanted no part of this crazy adventure. She wanted to settle down, make strudel, play a little Mozart, attend the Vienna State Opera, and, if she chose, design dresses for friends. They packed up in Beirut, sold what they could (including the Roadmaster), and went their separate ways, splitting at the airport. Dolly flew to Vienna to be with her foster parents, with whom she had renewed contact after her mother's death, and Dad flew half a world away to Buenos Aires.

Buenos Aires, it turned out, was in one of its recurrent convulsions of worker demonstrations for the caudillo, and after a brief period of settling in, Dad again proved a quick study, delivering several well-received columns on the precariousness of daily living with men on horseback. The city itself he found rather attractive, with its broad boulevards, chic shopping districts, engaging eateries, and lavish helpings of both impromptu and institutionalized gaiety. Everything was great except the regime, which stomped on human rights and individual freedom. Intolerance and strong-arm tactics seemed built into the caudillo's appeal. Inflation was yet another problem. Though richly endowed, the country was being bankrupted by its love of idleness and good times.

Dad made another discovery: after a few weeks without Dolly, he had little joy in reporting any of this. They communicated sporadically, and finally she agreed to join him, not in Buenos Aires (no way she could face those goose-stepping brownshirts on the Plaza de Mayo) but in Montevideo, Uruguay, across the oceanic Rio de la Plata from Buenos Aires. As in Rome and Beirut, they set up residence.

Despite the silvery sheen of that water, fortune didn't shine. Dolly suffered a breakdown, caused by unmanageable instability and aggravated by restless thoughts of the wartime murder of her mother. Dad found a psychiatrist who recommended an immediate return to Vienna. So after long and costly travel, Dolly recuperated for seven weeks at a clinic in the Vienna Woods. Dad now had to absorb Dolly's ever mounting bills in addition to his support of the family in Mount Vernon. I had graduated from college, but Sue and Frank were still in school. I figured it was best to join the army, a beau geste, preferable to finding what could only be part-time work as a potential draftee. I had to get away from a curdling domestic situation, and the army might even send me to France. The only other option was graduate school—and a student deferment—but I didn't have the gall to ask for support. Both parents made it clear that it was now my turn to give.

European Command (EUCOM) wasn't in the cards. After sixteen weeks of basic training at Fort Dix, New Jersey, I drew Far East Command (FECOM) and a long, storm-whipped crossing from Seattle to Yokohama aboard the USS *General R. L. Howze*, named after a World War I leader. Thanks to a last name that started with a letter in the first half of the alphabet, I got orders to train for a month as a medic in Japan before being assigned to Korea. Medics were dropping like flies, and the army suddenly needed a lot more. I "graduated" and was whisked to the front.

In response to pained shouts—"Medic! Medic!"—I climbed out of my frozen foxhole and readjusted my aid bag, which contained all the things I'd been drilled on at "medical school," from morphine tubes and tourniquets to Ace bandages and APC tablets. Gulping dyspepsia, I went to work. Later, I stopped thinking about what shrieked overhead. If it was time, it was time!

I drew the first platoon of Item Company in the 179th Regiment of the 45th Division. We patched up many young men, giving the worst of the wounded the second most important thing in our power after life itself: a ticket home. After our stay at Heartbreak Ridge, we moved to another forsaken place called Christmas Hill, named after a Chinese attack the prior Christmas. In looking back on it now, I am proudest not of my Bronze Star but of a comment from one of the Koreans supplementing our unit, whom we called Katusas; one day, out of the blue, he smiled up at me and said, "You number one medic, Doc!"

Years later, like everyone, I saw *M*A*S*H*, both the movie and the TV series. It was diverting, exhilarating, and compelling entertainment. My only regret was that I never got far enough behind the lines to meet a Hot Lips Houlihan. I remember the words of my fellow medic, Brooklyn-born Burt Eckstein, a Purple Heart veteran from King Company: "What a great comfort it is for troops on the line to know there are so many in the rear ready to support them!"

I was transferred when Captain Richard Lillge picked my name from the regimental records. He said I was the only enlisted man in the unit with a college degree. He probably saved my life. That transfer got me off the hill, off patrols, and into the safety of a headquarters detachment—still within artillery range, but beyond trench warfare and the infernal cascades of incoming mortars. The new job was to write and edit a mimeographed single-sheet newspaper. I reported on firefights, patrols, and anything newsworthy about the 179th Regiment, code-named Pagan.

I was not at all happy about the choice I had to make. I'd built up strong attachments in the platoon. Although it may sound disingenuous, I really was distressed to leave my buddies. We had come through a lot together! I'll never forget opening cans of K rations and, when we were lucky, passing around a fifth while shooting the shit around a pot-bellied stove. The first days I was never far from Item Company, trying to assuage my guilt. It didn't work. The buddies saw through me. They were polite but now distant. Having crossed over—even though, as I constantly pleaded, it was not on my initiative—I was no longer one of them.

With the new job came fewer hazards and my own jeep. For any foot soldier, wheels were sweet liberation. The need was legitimate: to get to regimental units that were now my news beat, spread out miles apart, up and down those infernal, muddy, potholed, land-mined hills. Back at regimental headquarters, I wrote dispatches from notes, typed out the stencils, and printed the mimeographed sheets. I managed editorial, production, and circulation, and I can vouch that this paper was avidly read by all it served. The job had proved to be a little too much for my predecessor, who transferred to chaplain's assistant, but I loved it. The name of the paper, *Pagan Poop*, shows the evolution of language in a few short years. *Poop* used to mean information; now it's what breaks from the sterns of ships and babies.

I was so proud of what I was doing that I actually took time to inform Dad by letter and enclosed two dispatches: one about a patrol that took heavy casualties in a trench infiltration, and the other about searchlights projecting across no-man's land to illumine enemy movements. Both were avidly read by everyone in the regiment, illustrating another axiom of journalism: All news is local.

19

South American Way

THE STORY IN Latin America got bigger. Dr. Milton Eisenhower, the president's brother and favorite policy adviser, was to tour the area and plant the seeds for what would become John F. Kennedy's Alliance for Progress. Dad set the scene by describing the conditions of the workers and peasants and the various proposals for American support.

One stopover was the Palace Hotel in Guatemala City, during a long weekend devoted to a religious festival. He dallied at a sidewalk café, listening to the dirge of trumpets as a procession shuffled on cobblestones behind a soaring crucifix. It was a warm evening, like summers in Ashland, Ohio, and as he sipped a Coke a fly dive-bombed. He didn't try grabbing it in flight as Chennault would do, but the general's feat evoked a smile. A quarter of his life had been abroad. He was as well-traveled as anyone on earth. The urge to get away from small-town America was now well spent. He was more Flying Dutchman than Marco Polo. He loved the tang of newspaper reporting, but did it have to be so damned peripatetic?

The procession of mainly young people triggered memories of Ashland. Newspaper work takes the man out of the small town, but it never takes the small town out of the man. Young bucks were tapping out a Latin beat, and he wondered whether anything in Guatemala City was comparable to the Mecca, for instance, or the Arcade, Ashland's spittoon-studded poolrooms, where youths in overalls and kerchiefs hung out and where he was forbidden to set foot. The fellas in Guatemala mostly wore tight black suits, but he figured they weren't all that different. Everywhere they mamboed to the same beat.

Young women, not far off, in floral dresses and shawls, twittered like jungle birds. One by one they fluttered into the street, where the long procession followed a crucifix hoisted by a white-garbed acolyte. Soon it was quiet again, and the flies renewed their dive-bombing. A young man approached and asked for a match. Dad offered a Zippo lighter and encouraged him to sit. He accepted a Coke and asked whether Dad was North American. Dad admired the tact. It was the height of rudeness to ask obvious gringos whether they were from the United States. He found a much-folded letter from me in Korea, dated June 29, 1953, and read it aloud. I recalled writing it—my first letter to him from the army. From platoon medic, I had just been made editor of the paper, and I gave him that news. I enclosed copies of the paper.

"Miss letters from you," my letter began. He felt chastened and told the youth he would write back that very night. The last time we'd seen each other was during a drive from Washington, DC, to Fort Dix in New Jersey in November 1952, before I shipped out from Seattle. He told the youth that maybe I was destined to become a journalist, too. Would that please him? the youth asked. "It's the old man's ticket to immortality," Dad replied.

After the youth left, he really did write a letter to me, which I looked at again years later and understood how difficult it must have been. He said his most valuable service to me would be to edit my stories and offer pointers. "I know from experience that an editor's knife can be sharp and unpleasant," he wrote, "even if the one wielding it is a loving father." He criticized passive verbs and clichés and reconstructed paragraphs to sharpen style and highlight action. He gave me the following advice:

> In the simple editing (not the rewrite) I have tried to keep away from the copyreader's well-known pitfall. That is (and I have had many editors and copyreaders) the inclination to edit another man's story into language which the copyreader himself would have used merely for the reason that he would have used that language. I have had copyreaders do over stories of mine so that they read not better, but only as if the copyreader had written them. This I have tried to avoid in the editing job.
>
> The environment of this story is of course something that in your medium needs not to be pictured. But even there I think it needs at least a little descriptive touch. Pine-studded ridgeline. Naked rocks. Rain-washed gravel. I don't know. My imagination is left searching. A concluding note: A story needs to answer most of the reasonable questions that it inspires in the reader, even subconsciously. If a story doesn't do that, in some sort of compromise with the space it is to earn, it is not satisfying. The best way of

satisfying this need is to ask yourself the questions. They will come to you if you back off and reflect.

If you can stand your old man's bitchiness (really it's something else), you will continue to send me your work and let me give it the works.

I didn't respond. I felt let down, hurt. I was expecting praise, also something more personal, insights into his life, perhaps regrets that he'd put his family through so much stress. He said he was a "loving father." Nothing in that missive made me believe it.

He wound up that Latin American assignment, as prearranged, in October 1953. For both him and his editors, it turned out to be more glint in the eye than enduring passion, and at a lunch in Washington he made yet another pitch for a European posting. Sometime after the first martini they tempered their refusal with an alternative: return to the Far East to cover the reconstruction of both Japan and Korea. A truce had ended the Korean War, and both South Korea and Japan were rebuilding like mad, starting down the economic path to Asian Tigerhood.

As Dad recounted the conversation, it sounded like a terrific offer. He would write about practically anything he wanted. He had the experience and the expertise, and the income would keep flowing. Alas, he told them, the only way he could accept such a new arrangement was to split with Dolly, who after her breakdown was intent on remaining near treatment in Vienna.

Declining the second martini after having hardly touched the first, he figured he had no choice but to tender his resignation, which they regretfully accepted. Walker Stone, who drove him across the Potomac to Washington National Airport for the flight to Europe, begged him to reconsider. He repeated what he'd already said: between his job and Dolly, he had to choose Dolly. Strangely, he felt elated. He would rejoin his wife on the last major continent he had yet to explore. He had all his marbles, relative youth, and confidence. Something would work out.

What he immediately thought of was fiction. Ever since the acclaimed *Liberty* magazine novelette he'd written in 1944, *The Colony of Forever Peaceful Hill*, about a downed pilot in wartime China, storytelling was seen as a fallback. He could do it anywhere, he liked to say, as long as he had paper, a typewriter, and a carton of Chesterfields. He had ideas galore: derring-do or romance in China, jungle action in Burma, abominable snowmen in the Himalayas, hugger-mugger in Guatemala, and a bildungsroman in Ohio. A New York agent, Bertha Klausner, whose office was across the street from Grand Central Station, had encouraged him for years.

With severance, back pay, and reveries about reporters who'd made it big in the literary world—Mark Twain, Jack London, Ernest Hemingway—he bought a spacious top-floor walk-up apartment in a six-story building at 2 Hohenstaufengasse in central Vienna. One problem was the bomb-damaged ceiling. That first winter he and Dolly affixed a tarpaulin to the roof, fired a wood stove, and camped on the premises.

Alas, bestsellers are not made overnight, and soon they were again scraping bottom. He decided to borrow from family and friends. People could always say no. Some did, except for close family: his own dad, who'd remarried; his younger brother, Guy, employed at a radio station in Missoula, Montana; his sister, Olive, a dental technician in Ashland; and me. I had no real money, but that spring, freshly mustered from the army and hired by UP, I did have meager savings, most of which were given to Mom. In a supplicating letter he reminded me that he had partly financed my education. I didn't bother to tell him I'd won scholarships and taken out loans, or that a dunning letter from Yale had arrived just as I was prepping for yet another patrol. I told the treasurer, in a reply that may still be cooling somewhere in New Haven, that Uncle Sam had given me other stuff to do besides paying off a goddamned student loan!

Mom said I'd be crazy to give Dad a cent. Give her the money instead, she pleaded. She was bleeding financially. I was out of the nest, but she still had my teenage sister and brother, who needed support. I did what I could. Fortunately, Dad came to realize that his family couldn't bail him out forever. We weren't Rockefellers, and he wasn't Hemingway. He had to start paying people back.

(*Above*) Jim Haizlip after landing at the National Air Races in Cleveland to win the Bendix Trophy, 1932. Clyde A. Farnsworth is the reporter on the right in sunglasses.

(*Right*) Clyde A. Farnsworth with his son, Clyde H. Farnsworth, in Columbus, Ohio, 1934.

(*Above*) Clyde A. Farnsworth (left) speaking to Captain Jerry Sadler in Khorramshahr, Iran, 1943.

(*Below*) The press gets a smile from Ambassador Joseph E. Davies, the special representative of President Roosevelt, upon his arrival at an undisclosed airport in Persia en route to Moscow, 1943. In the background, left to right, are Harold B. Miner, the second secretary of the American Legation; and C. Vaughan Ferguson, the third secretary of the American Legation. In the foreground, left to right, are Ambassador Davies; Clyde A. Farnsworth, an Associated Press war correspondent; and Oskar Guth, a United Press correspondent.

(*Above*) Clyde A. Farnsworth, freshly arrived in Kunming, China, 1943.

(*Below*) Clyde A. Farnsworth (center), of the Associated Press, and Albert Ravenholt (left), of the United Press, meet with an unidentified Nationalist Chinese general (right) 1944.

(*Above*) Representatives of US news agencies and magazines meet with General Claire Lee Chennault, the commander of the Fourteenth Air Force's Flying Tigers, and discuss the Chinese war situation with him, 1944. Left to right: Harold R. Isaacs, *Newsweek*; Anna Lee Jacoby, *Time*; Albert Ravenholt, United Press; Clyde A. Farnsworth, Associated Press; Brigadier General Edgar E. Glenn, the chief of staff; Major General Claire Lee Chennault; and Theodore H. White, Time-Life. Joe, General Chennault's dachshund, looks on.

(*Below*) Clyde A. Farnsworth (right) with Major General Claire Lee Chennault at Kunming, 1944.

(*Left*) Dolly, 1945.

(*Right*) Clyde H. Farnsworth before his discharge, 1954.

(*Right*) Clyde H. Farnsworth before descending two thousand feet into a coal mine in Lallaing in northeastern France, the land of Emile Zola's *Germinal*, . Courtesy of New York Times Pictures, 1974.

(*Below*) People at work in the Paris Bureau on rue Caumartin, 1971. Left to right: accountant Charles Cauvet, bureau secretary Natasha Chassagne, reporter John Hess, and author Clyde H. Farnsworth. Courtesy of New York Times Pictures.

(*Above*) Clyde H. Farnsworth (left) with Ed O'Toole in a 1962 edition of *Times Talk*. Courtesy of New York Times Pictures.

(*Below*) *New York Times* colleagues Robert D. Hershey Jr. (left), Richard E. Mooney (center), and Clyde H. Farnsworth (right) at the Newseum in Washington, DC, 2012.

20

Top of the News

CALL IT LUCK of the Irish. Again an old friend came through. Jack Howard, the son of Roy, one of the Scripps Howard founders, phoned from the United States in mid-1955 to talk about broadcasting. Jack, long an admirer of Dad's work from Asia, managed the chain's broadcasting properties, and one of these, WCPO in Cincinnati, was looking for a newscaster. Dad's gravelly voice was just right for the job, Howard said. "People will listen to you, Clyde. You command authority."

Trained to put words together for the average reader, Dad looked forward to doing the same for the average listener. On top of this exciting new challenge, he could return to his Ohio roots. This time Dolly didn't protest too much. The United States, which had just saved the world in World War II, didn't turn her off the way Argentina did. She needed no one to tell her the seriousness of their financial affliction.

Dad knew from his reporting days in Ohio that Cincinnati was not only a clean and attractive city, it also smacked of central Europe. The largely German-descended natives supported gaily lit outdoor restaurants, beer halls, and wine gardens—not all that different from Vienna. And like the Danube, the Ohio River had popular walks and parks. (To Marlon Brando in *Apocalypse Now,* those parks offered "the touch of heaven.") Summers were hot and humid, but no worse than summers in Shanghai or Hong Kong. Vienna was hot, too, and Ohio had American air-conditioning. It was an experiment; they'd try to make it work. If not, they still had Vienna. Dolly had had the roof repaired, furnished the place with their Chinese bric-a-brac, and then rented the apartment out, adding schillings to the pot.

WCPO was both a TV and radio station, the latter offering news and popular music out of the second-floor premises of the *Cincinnati Post.* Like the citizenry, the paper and the station leaned conservative. Dad shared a soundproof booth at the head of the stairs with Jack Fogarty, the senior newscaster. Lean, puckish, and unflappable, Fogarty, a ten-year veteran of the station, was highly professional. No matter what the story, his voice imparted the appropriate modicum of approval, disapproval, amusement, and bemusement. The listeners loved him, and Dad valued his obiter dicta, such as Fogarty's First Law of Radiodynamics: "Never pause to correct a verbal slip. Go on talking as if nothing's happened. The listener will think he's misunderstood."

Dad's early broadcasts fell into a monotone. Fogarty urged more attention-grabbing intonation. He advised practice with lilt and animation before the bathroom mirror, citing Demosthenes—"Small opportunities are often the beginning of great enterprises"—but stopped short of pebbles in the mouth. Fogarty and Dad prepared their own material, rewriting for radio news what came over the wires or from their own newsroom, broadcasting five-minute news breaks every hour on the hour, with thirty-second updates on the half-hour. If a big story broke, they interrupted radio and even TV broadcasts.

Fogarty, with the blessing of station chief Mort Watters, gave Dad a show of his own from 7:00 to 8:00 p.m. in which he developed the news in imaginative ways. *Top of the News*, Dad called it. He invited local politicians and other mucky-mucks for lively unscripted discussions. He had the freedom to range beyond the city limits for features. When a nineteen-year-old went on a rampage killing ten people in Nebraska and Wyoming, Dad phoned the father, who attributed the lethal behavior to an incident when his son was struck on the head by flying lumber. During a visit of Queen Elizabeth II to New York, he found she was staying at the Waldorf Towers, reached her equerry, and encouraged the man to explain how managing a troop of horses had evolved into attending the queen.

While *Top of the News* gathered acclaim, Dad promoted still another show—this time with astronomers, physicists, and even science fiction writers, on the future of space travel. The format would have allowed diversification into other sciences, such as nuclear physics, geology, and anthropology. Years before National Public Radio's *Science Times*, he believed that the radio public was ready for science. But not in the 1950s. Thanks, but no thanks, the brass said. It may be no accident that one of Dad's grandsons, Warren Hammond (the son of my sister, Suzanne), wrote computer codes, taught advanced software, and distinguished himself in science fiction. His prize-winning trilogy (*Kop*, *Ex-Kop*, and *Kop-Killer*) is about life on a planet turned into a penal colony and Earth's supplier of cocaine.

Even without science news, the shows made Dad a local media personality. He cut a stately figure in Cincinnati's pedestrian traffic, often brandishing an elegant horn-handled walking stick and velour Bavarian burgomeister's hat. If recognized, he invariably tipped his hat, European style, to the delight of the passersby.

Though avoiding another mental collapse, Dolly was again a fish out of water. She felt none of the same attractions as Dad and was just plain bored. This wasn't Vienna—not even close. She had no interest in the Reds, whatever they were (the baseball team, just before Dad's arrival and at the height of the Communist scare, changed its name from Reds to Redlegs to avoid any inference). Nor did she care about the city's renowned flapjacks, or beef hoagie patties. But this time there was no breakdown—no ultimatum. She simply quietly disclosed one evening that her foster parents, the Dittrichs, were again ailing and that she should be by their side.

There was no way Dad could fight her flight, and at this point he didn't want to. He was proud of having reestablished himself and was actually enjoying life as a minicelebrity. He'd set up a network of good friends, especially in the more bohemian district across the river in Covington, Kentucky; he attended gallery openings and was often called on to speak on global affairs.

Dad's means were now sufficient to support both Dolly and the family in Mount Vernon, and he was resolved to stick it out for as long as possible, with or without Dolly. He toyed with broadening into television broadcasting, and in a moment of euphoria he asked the station if it would fund a few weeks of TV broadcasting school in Chicago. As he said years later, moments of reaching for the moon are often damned. WCPO had just discovered what was called Color Radio, with jingles, weather, news headlines, promos, rock wop, and doo wop. "Less talk, more pop" was Fogarty's pithy summary of the new direction. Not only did the station not need a second TV broadcaster, it didn't even need a second radio newscaster. He got the ax. "Nothing personal," manager Mort Watters said. "Ratings are down."

Dad took the news philosophically. It was February 1958. He had been there for four good years and had given the station his best shot. It worked for a while, then it didn't. Though disappointed, he was ready to move on. He had paid off his debt and sporadically tested the fiction market.

He would miss some friends, especially Fogarty, but the conclusion was inescapable: Cincinnati and he no longer fit. Perhaps an even more telling factor was that he missed Dolly.

21

Vienna

WHEN DAD RETURNED to Vienna in the spring of 1958, the Ringstrasse, coffeehouses, streetcars, and public spaces all had a familiar, welcoming look, and Dolly seemed to be everywhere, especially in the buxom priestesses of Artemis holding up the facades of buildings with their flavescent locks of stone. At 2 Hohenstaufengasse in the first district, the women were even more *zaftig* (pleasantly plump) than he remembered. The six stories of honey-colored sandstone contained two apartments: his on the top floor and that of the *hausbesorgerin*, or concierge, on the ground floor. In between were the offices, open only a few hours on weekdays, of the Lower Austrian provincial government, including its unemployment bureau.

The building now had an elevator, limited to two people and going up only—an inconvenience more than made up for by the roominess of the top-floor apartment, which included two sunny bedrooms, a large study, and a living room where Dolly kept her Yamaha piano and a sewing room with a new Singer. Scrolls from Mongolia graced the hallway: hunters with arched bows on fleet-footed steeds, herons swooping over craggy buttes. A shaft in winter collected pirouetting snowflakes, as Dolly, visible just beyond the window pane, made apple strudel in a twin-oven kitchen.

Dad created his own work space with an oversized desk and areas for spreading out papers and documents. A reclining swivel armchair was ideal for writing or rocking himself to sleep. Within arm's reach were atlases, gazetteers, clippings from old newspapers, and works on China and the Iron Curtain by Walter Laqueur, Robert Conquest, and Frederick Barghoorn. A copious-bellied, ivory-colored Buddha proclaimed from a high shelf that life was good.

When not in her kitchen or sewing room, Dolly played Mozart in the living room. Ivory bibelots decorated the shimmering lid of the Yamaha alongside a photo of her from Kunming in which she is coquettishly peeking from behind a splayed fan. The piano was set off by a lacquer screen, also from Cathay. Some windows opened to what was once a Roman encampment, and beyond were the flying buttresses of centuries-old St. Stephen's Cathedral, miraculously undamaged by war. Cobblestones below were worn smooth by the likes of Mozart, Beethoven, Schubert, and Mahler, who perhaps cast covetous eyes on the same caryatids.

Austria, the birthplace of Adolf Hitler and Adolf Eichmann, produced even more Nazis in proportion to its population than Germany did. Like Germany, Austria (and Vienna itself) was split into zones of occupation (American, Soviet, British, and French) after the war. After a 1955 treaty guaranteeing independence and neutrality, the foreign troops left, and the city, only a few score miles from Hungary, Poland, and Czechoslovakia, morphed into an Iron Curtain listening post and news center, where Dad shopped his eyes and ears. His void in German was filled as pleasantly as possible—with German-language papers and a dictionary—at his favorite coffeehouse.

The Schottenring Café was off the busy Ringstrasse, ten minutes from the apartment, with newspapers in its racks and a waiter who, at the flick of an eyelid, refilled coffee cups as well as glasses of water. His name was Karl; he was a fleet fellow, as intrigued by Dad's linguistic labors as Dad was by Karl's myriad tasks as a waiter. Also intrigued was Harry Brainin, a new friend and a reporter for the Austrian Press Agency, who, citing Philip IV of Spain, declaimed over coffee, "I speak Spanish to God, Italian to women, French to men, [and] German to my dog," which Dad appropriated and cited shamelessly for years.

Within six months Dad had acquired the basics of German. Dolly, who took Brainin on in master-class chess, steered his pronunciation into something halfway understandable. With linguistic and other preliminaries out of the way, Dad launched a start-up. Through a newly revived old-boy network, he learned that Shanghai crony Don Starr was now the foreign editor of the *Chicago Tribune*; he wrote him, offering him help in Vienna, and was immediately signed on as a stringer.

Dad asked me years later if I knew the origins of the term *stringer*. I did not. He explained that newspapers once calculated the pay of their freelancers by pasting the column inches of their output end to end and measuring against a length of string. In Ohio, stringers filed stories on two-headed calves, barn fires, and unusual plant life. Dad overheard one editor in Lima shouting into the phone, "Keep 'em coming, Jack. Last one on the aspidistra [a type of houseplant] made page one!" Aspidistra-type stories now flowered everywhere: in the evolution and economics of coffeehouses, the antics of the brilliant but scandalous Herbert von Karajan of the Vienna State Opera, the perennial commemorations of the Mayerling Incident's tragedy of an impossible royal love affair, the torte wars between Viennese bakeries, and the Hapsburg bones uncovered in excavations for new buildings.

Salted away with the lighter fare were more serious social, economic, and political stories, usually about frictions inside the Soviet bloc. Two years earlier, in 1956, the Soviets had suppressed uprisings in Poznan (Poland) and Budapest. The *Trib*'s staffer for Eastern Europe, Larry Rue, led that coverage. Now reporting from Bonn, Rue welcomed Dad's help from the east. A decade older, Rue was slowing down, and I marveled at yet another part of the old network: they had worked together on the 1951–1952 collapse of the monarchy in Egypt. Rue had had a *Trib* byline since the 1920s, when he was hired by publisher Robert R. McCormick because of a shared love of flying. McCormick flew his own plane. Rue trained with the Lafayette Escadrille, American volunteer fliers of World War I and the template for the Flying Tigers.

Thanks to Starr, the *Trib* continued as his main client, but as knowledge of his rebirth spread, so too did a client base, which came to include *Time Magazine*, NBC, and the *New York Times*. For *Time* he covered Soviet party chief Nikita Khrushchev's visit to Austria in the summer of 1959. In October 1960 Khrushchev startled the world in a UN shoe-pounding incident. But in that earlier visit, as Dad reported, he appeared perfectly rational, spouting homespun, country humor in an almost charming way, making those later outbursts seem like, as Dad put it, "a geopolitical stunt."

Time's go-betweens were Bonn Bureau Chiefs John Mecklin and Jim Bell. Mecklin, formerly with UP, joined the Kennedy administration and worked with the press in Saigon in the Vietnam War buildup. Bell, a colleague from Dad's Beirut days, was known for the trench coat he wore everywhere—even, some suspected, to bed. Dad also filed for *Medical World News*, a journal for doctors. He more than satisfied his editors with pieces on the rebuilding of Vienna's five-hundred-year-old general hospital and on the daily routine of a Hungarian collective farm doctor.

With such infinite variety, he picked up the skills of editorial repackaging. An abrasive von Karajan made a zesty brief news item for NBC but was adapted for a more ruminative piece on the music scene for the *Trib*. An article for *Time* on an Austrian contract to build oxygen steelmaking facilities for Russia became a display on industrial innovations for the *Trib*'s business section.

NBC used Dad for radio spots, but thousands of words rolled out of Hohenstaufengasse for *Time*—for example, on the life of Adolf Eichmann, whom Mossad kidnapped in Argentina and brought to trial in 1961. A former SS officer, recalling that Eichmann "loved animals," led Dad to Simon Wiesenthal.

Dad's profile of Wiesenthal for the *New York Times* Sunday magazine, published February 2, 1964, headlined "Sleuth with 6 Million Clients," was the first mainstream profile of this death-camp survivor, who spent the rest of his life hunting Nazi war criminals. Wiesenthal himself was a frequent visitor to the apartment, where, while helping himself to Dolly's apple strudel, he listened to her survival story.

I met him myself. It was late 1969, and by that time I too was a foreign correspondent, then filing on East-West trade from a desk appropriated at Vienna's press center. Wiesenthal sidled over and introduced himself; he was a tall fellow in a crumpled three-piece suit and was a little paunchy, but he had eyes and ears like a bloodhound's. I was a fresh face, but he had the scent.

"I know your father," he said, extending a warm hand of welcome.

The start-up cried for cheap transport. Jussi Anthal, who covered central Europe for Stockholm's *Expressen*, sold Dad a ratty Opel, which transported him to his first story outside Vienna, the backwater crossroads village of Chikago near the Czech border. There wasn't much doing there, but the contrast with its namesake, though corny, made a well-received *Trib* squib.

The car was a lemon, but the aspidistras bloomed, such as a series on a Benedictine monastery overlooking Melk, on the Danube River west of Vienna. While waiting for a new carburetor, Dad visited the monastery and was shown around by the abbot himself, then invited to dinner in the refectory. Instead of monastic gruel, the meal included a superb goulash and fresh bread from the in-house bakery. Even more intriguing was his discovery that the place was a repository for thousands of works of art, books, coins, and medals that had been confiscated from Jews during the war. Dad broke the story. The trove was catalogued by the Committee for Jewish Claims on Austria, and the treasures were returned to their rightful owners.

Among the countless invaders of Vienna throughout history were the Turks, who retreating in 1683, left precious coffee beans. The enterprising Viennese ground the beans to make a watery brew that seemed to give a lift. By the early twentieth century there were twelve hundred coffeehouses in the city, many of them marble palaces with soft bentwood furniture and high vaulted ceilings, offering varieties of coffee as well as pastries. With a faster tempo of life, only about forty remained in Dad's day.

To stay in business, the Schottenring Café, near Vienna University, made major compromises, importing jukeboxes and the latest popular discs. Marble and bentwood yielded to cheaper plastic. Lights became institutionalized neon. Yet even as his German improved, Dad still patronized the place. He loved its convenience and hummed its pop tunes on his walks to and fro. (One favorite—"I Never Promised You a Rose Garden," the Lynn Anderson Ole Opry hit—was at one point hummed almost constantly, perhaps for Dolly's benefit.) The shadowless neon he didn't mind, either. Though harsh, it made studying easier. And Karl, the waiter, was happy because of a lot of new business Dad brought in.

Ever gregarious, Dad turned that café into an adjunct press club. Among those I saw there were Mike Handler, Paul Underwood, and David Binder from the *New York Times*; Osgood Caruthers of the *Los Angeles Times*; Colin Lawson of the London *Daily Express*; and George Vine of London's *Daily Mail*, who had been rescued in Shanghai. Not old-Vienna enough for some, the Schottenring was sometimes abandoned for more atmospheric places, such as Café Leopold Hawelka, by the state opera house. It was in a building of wooden beams and Thonet chairs, where celebrities held forth, such as painters Friedensreich Hundertwasser and Ernst Fuchs, filmmaker Peter Kubelka, and his sister, the romance writer Susanna Kubelka.

Another magnet was the Red Bar and café of the Hotel Sacher, across from the opera house. A larger-than-life portrait of Frau Anna Sacher, a butcher's daughter who married the hotel's founder and transformed it into a pricey haunt for self-indulgent aristocrats, looked down rapaciously on the boozers.

The Sachers endowed not only a great café and hotel but also a renowned fudge-covered chocolate cake. Three blocks away, another café, Demel's, offered a cake not all that different, and for a while it was war between the partisans of Demel torte and those who thought it plagiarized Sacher torte—and from which more aspidistras bloomed. At peak intensity, Dad hosted David Brinkley for an NBC Special. Brinkley wanted to know which of dozens of Viennese cakes were properly accompanied by *schlag* (whipped cream). Coming to Guglhupf, a yeast-risen coffeecake of the same name, one expert advised, "*Guglhupf mit* [with] *schlag.*" But coffeecake is rarely served with whipped cream in Vienna, or anywhere. That such a misstatement was made on American television and that *guglhupf* in Viennese slang also means "crazy house" gave cartoonists a field day. Long after Brinkley's departure, the term *guglhupf* was slang for nutty American.

Only a pulse away from such zaniness was Vienna's melancholia, evoked by the plangent tones of Anton Karas's "The Third Man Theme" and leading to one of the highest youth suicide rates in the world. A favorite site for the suicides was the Vienna Woods, north of the city, where kids bundled up, drank or sniffed themselves silly, then blew out their brains or downed lethal doses of pills.

Dad and I both knew Ken Ames, a writer for the *Economist*. He was no kid, but he too was driven to a similar despair. More than most Westerners, he laid bare the twists and turns of the East European economies, and he did it with deftness and wit. Yet on one of those long winter nights, Ken chose not a hike in the woods but a long hot bath, in which he downed two bottles of gin and slashed his wrist. A contemplative fellow, he did not confide in anyone, and in the postmortem investigation no one could say what he was thinking.

His death occurred on a Saturday night in 1975 in an apartment near the cabaret district. Ken didn't shut off the bathwater completely, so warm water, blush pink, seeped into the ceiling of the apartment below and dripped away all Sunday and into Monday, when the residents finally came home and called the police.

Edgar E. and Katharine J. Clark rented a big house on the approach to the Vienna Woods. As stringers for NBC and *Time*, they gave elegant dinner parties to coax news from a variety of informed sources. In 1959, upon their reassignment to the United States, they introduced Dad as their replacement.

Ed, formerly of UP, had been in Iran with Dad. Kathy, formerly of AP and INS, achieved prominence in Belgrade during the 1954 break between

Tito and his chief lieutenant Milovan Djilas, whom Tito incarcerated. A seminal Djilas work, *The New Class*, blew the whistle on communism decades before its collapse.

The Djilas story helped make Kathy's career, and in that era it would have been hard to find a better connected couple in Vienna than Kathy and Ed Clark. When they entertained, a string ensemble played from a podium in their oversized reception room, and couples waltzed as they might have under the Hapsburgs. Besides Dad and Dolly, the regulars included Fritz Molden, an anti-Nazi Austrian publisher married at the time to Joan Dulles, the daughter of CIA Director Allen Dulles; Hans Benedict, an Austrian AP man and later a broadcaster; Bruno Pitterman, the Socialist Party leader and eventual vice chancellor of Austria; Mike Handler of the *New York Times*; and John Mecklin of *Time*.

Kathy had a warm spot for Dad ever since he helped her out of a crisis over a planned Thanksgiving dinner with "all the fixin's"—that is, except dessert. Kathy found it impossible to find pumpkins for pumpkin pie. Austrian farmers, she learned, grew pumpkins for bovine, not human, consumption. Dad heard out her sad tale and suggested a substitute that just might work: roasted chestnut puree. After extracting the innards, he said, you mash them; add spices; add color with turmeric; mix with eggs, milk, and honey; and presto—you've got an almost perfect pie filling. Kathy and he were the only ones to know, and when dessert came, everyone sang the praises of that "incredible pie!"

Late one evening the doorbell rang. Dad leaned out from the sixth story to see a man in an oversized overcoat pacing on the ground below. He said he was from Warsaw and needed to see Mr. Farnsworth urgently. He'd been sent by Sydney Gruson, who had run the *New York Times* bureau in Warsaw and with whom I'd worked in London. Dad clopped downstairs (the elevator still only took people up), but in case there was trouble he brought a heavy-handled walking stick. Night visitors could be let in only by unlocking a hulking oak door with an oversized iron key. As Dad pushed on the door, the man outside was dwarfed by a coat sinking to his shoes. Another man stood in the shadows across the street beside a big black suitcase.

Fiery-eyed, with hollow cheeks and sallow complexion, the man at the door said his name was Tommy Atkins. Although they'd never met, Dad had heard of Tommy, who was a legend among East Europeans. He had fought in the Jewish underground, helped Jews out of Poland and into

Palestine, and then chosen to become one of the few to return; he was rumored to be working for Mossad. He had joined the bureau under Gruson's predecessor, Abe Rosenthal. Tommy, it turns out, was a "fixer," a guy who knew his way around. He was born in Lodz, which had once boasted the largest Jewish population in Poland after Warsaw. No one seemed to know his real name. Tommy—generic for British soldier—it certainly wasn't. Tommies built the empire, but more recently they had fought against Israel's statehood.

His story was incredible. He had just married. Bride and groom were to exit separately, join up in Vienna, and emigrate to Israel. Tommy slipped across the frontiers concealed in a diplomatic vehicle. His new wife never left; apparently she had cold feet. The story was that he had to return to convince her to leave, but he needed exit stamps to reenter.

Somehow Tommy knew about a trip Dad had recently taken to Poland. Invited into the apartment, he asked to see Dad's passport, and upon viewing the Polish exit stamps, seemed relieved. The man in the shadows was now invited up as well, and his suitcase contained all the tools of the forger's art. What they really wanted was a place to doctor passports for those fleeing to Israel from the gulag of Eastern Europe. Dolly offered goulash, apple strudel, and access, for as long as they needed, to the ample work space of her sewing room.

22

A Son's Story

DAD'S LIFE WAS a bit too exciting, and the work was more than enough for one person. Like Charlie Chaplin in *Modern Times*, Dad couldn't keep up, and in mid-1963 he offered me a job. I'd been at UP for five years, at the *New York Herald Tribune* for three years, and at the *New York Times* for a year, which had just given me a coveted posting to London. But instead of cheering me on about that, Dad put me off with a warning that the *Times* was in severe trouble and that my best chances lay in joining forces with him. The litany was familiar: unions threatening strikes over labor-saving equipment, and revenues undermined by TV and suburban papers. Stringer operations such as his, which saved news organizations a ton of money, were the wave of the future. I could help myself and his new venture prosper.

I demurred. Perhaps he was right, but I thought I still needed the security of a large organization. I was blessed with a young family: my first wife, Barbara Ann Blaha, a budding writer I'd met while at UP, and two stellar sons, Andrew and Alexander. Andrew was born in Bronxville, New York, and Alex was born in London, at 27 Welbeck Street, three months after our arrival in England. Having just settled in, neither Barbara nor I had any desire to move again, no matter what lay over the rainbow.

What might have been—who knows? His thinking was right on. The *Times* and other papers were and still are endangered, and the *Times* was in trouble for all the reasons just cited. What saved the day then was its total makeover by two artful editors, Abe Rosenthal and Artie Gelb, who, by introducing smart sections—Bizday, Arts and Leisure, Science—converted the paper into a daily magazine, broadening the readership nationally and globally. My rejection displeased Dad yet proved to be sound. It's hard to imagine anything for me in Vienna rivaling what fell into my lap at the *Times*, including almost four decades circling the globe myself—plus getting paid for what I loved, which was writing news. Also, thanks to *Times* grants and Newspaper Guild scholarships, Andrew and Alex had a fine education and productive careers.

What a year already! Most of it I had spent investigating one of the all-time great swindlers, Billie Sol Estes of Pecos, Texas, who made millions selling fictitious fertilizer tanks to farmers and scamming finance companies. A lay preacher in the Church of Christ, who believed that even dancing was a sin, he ended up behind bars for ten years, and then, like John Dillinger or Billy the Kid, he metamorphosed into a folk hero about whom songs get written. "Stand tall, Billie Sol, we don't know you at all," goes a Phil Ochs ballad.

The scandal, in the summer of 1962, touched the office of Vice President Lyndon Baines Johnson. Lady Bird, it developed, was a Billie Sol Estes friend and supporter, and there were those all too now familiar questions about what she and her husband knew and when they knew it. I coordinated with Harrison Salisbury, who ran the national news desk after returning from fabulously productive tours of Russia and China.

A source was Attorney General Robert F. Kennedy, already a master of the familiar Washington game of using the press against political foes. It was my second dealing with Bobby. My first was in 1960, while he was the chief counsel to a Senate rackets subcommittee and I was at the *New York Herald Tribune*; he helped on a series I prepared on racketeering in the Teamsters Pension Fund. Bobby and his chief investigator, Carmen Bellino, a certified public accountant, pointed up discrepancies in the union pension accounts that showed boss Jimmy Hoffa stealing from the members. That reportage, of which I am duly proud, laid out a lot of the unsavory dealings. (After winning a pardon from his thirteen-year prison term from President Nixon in 1971, but apparently having swindled less forgiving Mafia bosses, Hoffa disappeared in 1975, and he was last sighted in the parking lot of a restaurant in Bloomfield Township, Michigan.)

My second encounter with Bobby came early in his brother John F. Kennedy's tragically aborted presidential term. It was well-known that Bobby—and the president—sought some excuse to dump Johnson as vice president on JFK's 1964 reelection ticket. Billie Sol Estes's relationship with Lady Bird stuck out. I followed a money trail on mortgages and other recorded contracts. I keep thinking I didn't look hard enough. I lived weeks on end in Texas, building on earlier pieces by Tom Wicker and Gladwin Hill and also by Oscar Griffin Jr., the editor of the weekly *Pecos*

Independent and Enterprise, who won a Pulitzer Prize. In Pecos I borrowed a desk in the *Enterprise* office, and once I picked up the phone to hear a male voice that sounded like nails scratching glass. "Careful crossing the street, fuckin' northern rat scum." It wasn't my first hate call, but it was my scariest. I told Griffin about it. "Get used to it!" he said.

My weightiest contribution was a piece appearing on May 3, 1962, about the death of an agricultural adjustment agent named Henry H. Marshall, who sniffed the fraud early on. His body lay near his pickup truck about eight miles from Franklin, in east Texas—he'd been shot five times in the stomach, the bullets traced to his own bolt-action 22-caliber rifle nearby. The sheriff and a local justice of the peace ruled it suicide, incredible even for the tall tales of Texas. Each time that rifle was fired it had to be pumped to allow another cartridge into the chamber. Sybil Marshall, Henry's widow, who lived with their son in a white frame house, told me, "There's a very definite question in my mind whether it was suicide." Robertson County Sheriff Howard Steagal belittled any suspicion. "Anybody who kills himself is a little crazy anyway," he stated (ignoring the obvious impossibility of a suicide victim shooting himself five times), "and you can't expect logic to prevail." But after a court-ordered exhumation, bludgeoning was apparent, and the ruling was changed to homicide.

All that came out weeks later. On the night of May 2, 1962, after tramping around Franklin, I took a room at the only hotel, a kind of *Psycho* Bates Motel. There were no other guests. The clerk even looked like Anthony Perkins. But having driven from Austin, I didn't relish sleeping in the backseat of the rental car. If there was anyplace to eat dinner, I didn't find it, but I did grab a sandwich at a corner eatery and made no attempt to hide my affiliation. People stared as if I were a Martian. Inside the room the first thing I did, recalling noir films, was wedge my wooden desk chair against the doorknob. I did sleep for an hour or two, but around 2:00 a.m. the clicking sound of a slowly turning lock gave me a hell of a fright.

"Who's there?" I shouted, my chair fortunately holding. There was no answer, so I'll never know. But someone *did* turn that knob! It could have been someone going to the wrong room by mistake. But investigators later tied six deaths to the Billie Sol Estes scandal. Although none involved reporters, that incident in Franklin might have been a first.

23

Dance of the Apprentices

MY REJECTION OF Dad's offer was good for him as well as for me. Exceptional proxies turned up, and he thrived as a mentor. The first was Charles E. Johnson, born on the South Side of Chicago to a Pullman porter and an office charwoman. Already a father and going for a doctorate at the University of Vienna, this tall, imposing African American arrived courtesy of the US Army.

Johnson supported a family by taking bit parts in a local theater group. Dad was gathering background for a *Time* file. They met and hit it off. Some years later Johnson searched me out in the Washington bureau of the *New York Times* expressly to tell me how much he admired and respected my father.

He attended Chicago schools, and like practically all South Side kids, strayed into the street gangs that seemed to be the only outlet for supercharged adolescents. He ran with the pack every day except Saturday, his day of escape at the movies with even cooler dudes: Errol Flynn, George Raft, and Humphrey Bogart. Once at Dad's Vienna apartment, he said, "I don't think you realize, Mr. Farnsworth, what it's like for a black kid in America to discover all his heroes are white."

Yet much of what he achieved may also have been simply to prove a high school counselor, who was white, wrong. He recalled the counselor's cutting words: "Young man, you're not cut out for college." Johnson was stubborn, and from that moment he was determined to both get away and get an education. He enlisted in the army chiefly for the further education it offered bright recruits.

After acing intelligence tests, he found he had a gift for languages and qualified for the Defense Language Institute at Monterey, California. He was offered Spanish or German for six months or Russian or Chinese for a year. He opted for Russian, spent a "blissful" year in California, and then drew "spook work" in Frankfurt, where he also picked up German, practicing on anyone he met, including the fraulein he married. Ever since he had spent all those Saturdays with the Hollywood dudes, his ambition had been acting. After military service, he, his wife, and their baby moved to Vienna. He had heard there might be work at the Austrian National Theater, or Burgtheater, and he won a part in a Peter Handke play.

Dad not only hired him on the spot but profiled him for the *Chicago Tribune*'s Sunday magazine, an article that was later reprinted in *Ebony* magazine. Unfortunately for Dad, all the publicity drew Johnson back to the United States, where he found his way into academia and taught, among other places, at the Harvard Business School.

Like Charles Dickens's character Wilkins Micawber, Ken Donoghue, the successor to Charles Johnson, expected something to turn up, and it usually did. He and Dad met as both tried to enter a revolving door at the American Express office near the Ringstrasse. Ken was in a fit of despair because a large check he was expecting had failed to arrive. During that Alphonse-et-Gaston moment, as each man's bow deepened, CBS colleague Ernie Reed happened by and introduced them.

Ken had an unruly beard that was a darker shade of red than his carrot hair. Hair and beard, he liked to say, reduced the aggression he felt toward the human race. He was a friend of the writer J. P. Donleavy and one of the acknowledged models for Donleavy's 1955 classic novel *The Ginger Man*, about sex-obsessed student life at Dublin's Trinity College. Both men had attended under the GI Bill. Ken started as a medical student. Donleavy took up painting and seemed pretty good at it, but according to Ken he couldn't get local galleries to display his works, so he took up writing instead.

Since those early days in Dublin, Ken had traveled east, somehow surviving despite a talent for avoiding work. Dad offered him the apprenticeship. If nothing else, Ken made him laugh. The two places Ken frequented most were American Express, eternally hoping for that fantasized check, and his shrink's studio on Porzellangasse practically next door to where Sigmund Freud lived for almost half a century. Ken described long couch sessions on "the phantasmagoria of the cosmos."

I met Ken myself, and I heard him invent madcap worlds where miniaturized humans lived in the bureau drawers of mad scientists, where monsters were fey, and where princesses refused to be rescued from towers. Despite his gift for invention, it took him forever to write a news story.

Searching for perfection, he was forever reworking the first sentence. When Ken eventually produced a subject and a predicate, they were too ponderous for any newspaper, perhaps too much influenced by Carl Jung, a translation of whose work he was preparing for a Swiss journal. Dad laboriously shaped Ken's style for the *Chicago Tribune*.

The working day started with the *International Herald Tribune*. Before going to school in Dublin, Ken had studied Greek and Latin at Harvard, and he was faster than Dad on the daily puzzles, despite a severe handicap. As a kid in Boston, he had lost his right eye while playing with a wire hoop, which meant that he could never drive a car; he was vulnerable even on a bike. Though bookish, he found talking easier. When covered with dark glasses, both eyes seemed normal. When he was asked which eye was false, he sometimes removed the glasses to let the artificial eye drop, telling shocked onlookers it "gleamed with the milk of human kindness."

Like Charles Johnson, Ken Donoghue finally returned to the United States; his destination was Salt Lake City. "Why there?" Dad asked him. "To find a cheap room," Ken replied. And so Ken exited Dad's life as enigmatically as he entered.

The music was familiar, and Dolly strayed toward the Boesendorfer piano. She and Dad were at the Concordia Press Club, a stone's throw from the Burgtheater. The dark-haired young man bent over the keyboard drew on a George Gershwin medley, including "The Man I Love." When he stopped playing, he and Dolly discovered that each of them spoke Serbo-Croatian.

Dusko Doder, the stringer for the Sarajevo daily *Oslobobjene*, was also at the Concordia that night. The pay from *Oslobobjene* was a pittance, and that evening he was thin and hungry. Dad and Dolly invited him home for a decent meal. They found out that he was nineteen, an unenthusiastic medical student at Vienna University, an ex-member of the Yugoslav national table tennis team, a chess player, and a Bosnian Serb who wanted to defect to America and be a reporter. He became yet another apprentice, and later, thanks to Dad's counseling and introductions, he became a reporter for AP, UPI, and eventually the *Washington Post*. "I owe your father much more than you can ever imagine," he told me years later in Washington.

Dusko was born in Sarajevo, where an assassination had triggered World War I, and his parents were still there. His dad, a pharmacist, wanted Dusko to be a pharmacist, too. An infant during World War II, he recalled being tethered to his mother as the Nazis mobilized her among others to dig ditches and perform other labor for "the improvement of public works." After the war he learned Russian and became mediocre at chess but better at table tennis—so good, in fact, that he made the national team and earned minor celebrity status and privileges, including a coveted exit visa and the *Oslobobjene* stringership.

Dusko lived in something little bigger than a closet at a rooming house, where he did no more than sleep. Offered the sewing room by Dolly and Dad at Hohenstaufengasse, he eagerly accepted, cautioning that if the Yugoslavs ever found him now, it would mean the gulag. Over weeks and months, as Dusko dug into this new life, his English-writing skills improved, and Dad trained him as a journalist. His copy always needed *the, a,* or *an*; articles don't exist in either Serbo-Croatian or Russian. He was a quick learner. Taking a parental as well as professional interest, Dad worked with him for several months, then urged him to go to college in the United States and hook up with a wire service. Dusko fulfilled no normal entrance requirements, but his breadth of knowledge and experience won him a place at Washington University in St. Louis, where in four years he exhausted just about every grant and scholarship. He took advantage of the introductions Dad set up for him in New York with Roger Tatarian of UPI and Keith Fuller of AP. AP made him an offer as its number two reporter in its Concord, New Hampshire bureau, but not before he picked up more grants and earned a master's degree from the Columbia University School of Journalism.

With that Hohenstaufengasse experience and American academic training, he swam like a dolphin. New Hampshire politics proved as Byzantine as Sarajevo politics. Later the AP transferred him to Albany. But after two and a half years, he was homesick for Europe. UPI offered Moscow as number two to long-time resident correspondent Henry Shapiro, yet another offer he couldn't refuse. Then *the Washington Post* grabbed him, and he became a US citizen.

My brother Frank was yet another graduate of that Hohenstaufengasse School of Journalism. Having finished college but unsure of a career path, he was awaiting the draft. So he too met all the entrance requirements. Thanks to a desire to be independent of the old man, he later took up computers, worked for New York City in human resources, then joined Aramco to help computerize mapping of reserves in the Rub-al-Khali, or Empty Quarter, of Saudi Arabia.

Yet the months Frank had spent in Vienna made such an impression that upon his retirement in 1993 and move to a small community—Fort Plains, New York, between Albany and Syracuse—he refurbished a commercial property to open a coffeehouse uncannily similar to the Schottenring Café. He brewed varieties of coffee, ordered scrumptious fresh pastries delivered daily, and offered the latest newspapers—the latter stored, as in Vienna cafés, on wooden racks. At the opening, which was attended by a felicitously surprised citizenry, I brought out my violin to offer music worthy of a grand opening, including a *gemütlich* (pleasant and cheerful) Mozart "Eine Kleine Nachtmusik."

24

England A-Go-Go

MY POSTING TO London inevitably brought me and my father together more frequently. No oceans now—just a channel and half a dozen storied rivers. On one trip my two sons were in tow. But to both Dad's and Dolly's angst, they ran wild on new hardwood floors, spawning complaints about noise and damage and driving home a lesson about the awkwardness of mixing generations at close quarters.

By this time we were settled in London, and I had no regrets about my choice to stick with the *New York Times* instead of working with Dad. Barbara and I made new friends right and left. The office was by Fleet Street, looking across the Thames at Printing House Square. The rubble still being cleared suggested the intensity of Hitler's Blitz.

My colleagues couldn't have been warmer: Jim Feron, the night rewrite veteran of the Metro Desk; Larry Fellows, a former US diplomat, whose German wife, Ruth, was once a principal ballerina in Cologne; and Sydney Gruson, the bureau chief, who took me under his wing, perhaps in recognition of Dad's services for Tommy Atkins. Two years later Sydney ran the international edition. His successor was two-time Pulitzer winner Anthony Lewis.

One afternoon during Tony's reign, I needed to consult him. I knew he was in because the door to his office had just closed softly from the inside. As I approached, Marion Underhill, his gatekeeper, smiled and gently shook her head. "Nap time," she said. Tony was the only reporter I've ever met who was self-assured enough to organize snoozes on office time. No doubt it contributed to his brilliance and longevity. He died two days short of eighty-six, not only having won those coveted Pulitzers but also having written a classic on the Supreme Court, *Gideon's Trumpet*, about the right of indigent defendants to be represented by counsel.

One contribution at the bureau was his superb organization of coverage of Winston Churchill's state funeral on January 30, 1965. No doubt assured of a hallowed place in history, Churchill, who died at eighty, left precise instructions on the choreography, and Tony deployed us to record the big picture and the nuances.

The last days were at Churchill's West End house near Hyde Park Gate, where doctors, newsmen, and a constabulary kept the vigil. Sometimes he came to the window, his fingers shaping the trademark *V* for victory for well-wishers. I'd seen him only once before, in the pit of the House of Commons, where he'd steeled the courage of a beleaguered nation. A sudden hush signaled a presence at one of the portals. Assisted by aides, the awe palpable, he painstakingly made his way to the Tory benches and took a seat on the aisle behind the first row of ministers. Puffy in his dark suit, he really did look like the A. A. Milne character Winnie the Pooh, the nickname chosen for him by the press years ago. His eyes lifted toward the galleries, the wisp of a smile and that famous *V*. He rose, apparently tired, and the aides magically reappeared to assist his departure.

I happened to be on duty at the West End house that early Sunday morning, January 24, 1965 BCP (before cell phones), when he breathed his last. I rushed to a corner pay phone, having made sure I had the right coinage—big heavy coppers that dug holes in your pocket. The obit was already in type. For the presses to roll, only a confirmation of the death was necessary. Thanks to the time difference and my fleet feet, we made the bulk of the readership that day.

The body lay in state for three days during preparations for the state funeral. A gun carriage bearing the lead-lined coffin rolled through central London at dirge speed, drawing hundreds of thousands of silent mourners. At Tower Hill I saw the coffin taken aboard a launch for passage up the Thames River to Festival Pier. The East End docks and their gantry-mounted cranes were in full view. As the launch pulled away, the jibs on those cranes tipped in silent genuflection, as if even inanimate objects were paying their last respects—a contribution to the majesty of the occasion by the dockworkers of London.

Such solemnity was a break from the pop and swizzle of swinging London with its edgy Beatles music, mod Carnaby Street look, and flashy discotheques. A seamier side emerged from revelations about a government war minister named John Profumo, who lied to the House of Commons about an affair with a call girl named Christine Keeler, who happened also to be sleeping with the Russian military attaché.

Besides Cold War intrigue, the bureau was fully caught up in the troubles Britain was having in paying its way in the world. We had to show why the United States should care, which wasn't all that apparent. Economic interdependence hadn't yet made the charts. Later, during monetary reorganizations in which Asian Tigers pawed the turf, the landscapes of Gary (Indiana), Buffalo, and Detroit began looking like Leeds, Manchester, and Sheffield.

The *Times* gave the stories good play, signaling a passionate interest in the Sceptred Isle. As paramours, we reporters had to know everything about the object of our affection. Items as minor as titles for nobility were ignored at our peril. Lords and ladies, dukes and duchesses, viscounts and viscountesses also made news; failure to refer to them properly meant rockets from Managing Editor Clifton Daniel or wordsmith in chief Theodore M. Bernstein.

Daniel was one of the editors who fell in love with London while stationed there during the Blitz. But when I joined the paper he was seen as a rather starchy boss, and I kept my distance. I warmed to him a lot when I had to show him around the newly evolving city. High mucky mucks were usually taken in tow by the bureau chief, but since it was vacation time with little notice of this drop-in, such duties suddenly fell on me.

I picked him up at Heathrow Airport in a low-profile car because that's all I had—a Renault Dauphine with a gear stick that broke off in your hand. I offered to take him for a home-cooked meal that Barbara, despite our young'uns, was ready for, bless her—but he confessed an urge to visit one of the gaming clubs, which certainly weren't around during the war.

I couldn't afford Crockford's, the Rolls Royce of clubs, but I had already joined a Chevy-at-the-levee sort of place called the Victoria Sporting Club at Marble Arch. Daniel had no English currency and asked if I'd lend him some money. Of course I would, for the managing editor of the *New York Times*, but I had only a five-pound note. So we ended up at my apartment anyway, and he met the kids and Barbara, who found a twenty-pound note in the cookie jar. Before ATMs, that was the only way to get after-hours spending money, barring a little night thievery. Barbara declined his invitation to join us—there was no time to arrange for a sitter—but wished us well.

We then had the greatest string of luck I've ever experienced before or since, except perhaps for not getting killed in Korea or Franklin, Texas. At least four times we hit winning numbers or pay zones on the roulette wheel. After about half an hour of play, we netted two hundred pounds, and by mutual consent we sank that ill-gotten gain on dinner with a fine claret at the club's renowned restaurant. Daniel said that neither of us would ever earn money at a faster rate in our lives, and at least in my case he was right. Rather than the stiff despot I expected, this soft-spoken, courtly, whip-smart Anglophile from Zebulon, North Carolina, proved to be a delight. He reminisced about growing up in a town where his was one of the few white families and where his dad ran the drugstore. After an initial rejection by the *Times*, he joined the AP and was yet another cable desk crony. Later picked up by the *Times*, he served in Europe and then Washington, where he met Harry Truman's daughter, Margaret, whom he married.

We didn't talk about that because he was a very private man, but he did politely ask about Dad, who by then was stringing for the *Times*. I said he was probably writing yet another draft of a profile of Nazi hunter Simon Wiesenthal for the Sunday magazine. Daniel smiled. Everyone knew the ordeal writers went through under the irascible but gifted Sunday editor, Lester Markel.

Since his luggage was still in my Renault, I gave him a lift to his hotel, the Savoy, on the Strand. He had worked there in the war, knew the best pubs, and tried all those dishes with funny names, like bubble-and-squeak or toad-in-the-hole, and he wasn't opposed to a pint or two. In other words, off duty he was a right regular bloke.

Throughout the evening neither of us mentioned Dad's articles from the Far East, many of which had been critical of Truman's policies. Truman didn't take criticism easily, and his son-in-law bridled when the old man was attacked. So a gulf existed that was probably better not to cross. Daniel headed into the lobby but then turned back to the open window of the Renault and offered a final comment of the evening: "A good reporter writes what he understands to be true and lets the chips fall where they may, and we're all the better for it." I thought of the chips that had fallen into our laps before supper. But he was right in the other sense as well: news freely gathered was freedom itself.

I often worked outside London. One assignment was to report progress on the *Queen Elizabeth 2*, a ship then simply known as Hull 736 at John Brown Shipbuilders in Glasgow. The keel was laid on July 1, 1965, and I was shown around a few weeks later. "She's the last of her kind, but the best of her kind," one hard hat told me. Yet even as the cranes were adding superstructure, she looked like a Tinkertoy. Years later I thrilled at seeing her vibrant and glittering vastness overwhelm a pier in northern France.

I also visited Sunderland in the northeast of England. From there I took a helicopter halfway to Norway to one of the new North Sea oil rigs. My story in the spring of 1965 conjectured that the North Sea would transform global oil markets, which it did. That rig in the middle of nowhere was a lonely place, and I was glad no gales blew that day. The chow, by the way, was damned good. I recalled days in Korea when food quality also seemed linked to proximity to danger. Two days after Christmas in 1965, a neighboring rig collapsed in a vicious North Sea gale, killing thirteen.

One of the biggest running stories was the closing down of unprofitable coal mines and the impact on small communities, especially in the Midlands, where plentiful coal had spawned the Industrial Revolution. A center of unrest was a town, appropriately enough named Coalville, one hundred miles north of London, where several mines were about to close, and everyone was mad as hell. It was a painful story. You understood the wrenching economic changes that miners faced, and you couldn't help but sympathize. But you also realized that here was a way of life that maybe should end because of lung disease and other ailments from hours underground. It made no sense that miners should fight for a shorter life span.

Or maybe it did, as an issue of respect. Britain wasn't as mobile as the United States. People were reluctant to move. What they wanted was a sense of dignity. Successive Labour governments had failed to win improvement for the miners, and the Tories were returned to power with a vengeance. Yet jobs still weren't there decades later. No matter how great that British pluck, the answer maybe rings out in a cockney dirge: "It's the sime the whole world over / It's the rich wot gits the graivy / It's the poor wot gits the blaime / Ain't it all a bloomin shime?"

One morning in late 1963 at our apartment in Dolphin Square, I opened a special delivery letter inviting me to the War Office to meet a Mr. Elwell on a matter of national security. I was to inform no one and to bring the letter to gain access. Mr. Elwell was not further identified. I had no idea what was up, but I made the appointment, offering to drop by that morning on my way to work.

In those days, Barbara and I enjoyed new miniwheeled Moulton bicycles, which were all the rage, along with thigh-high miniskirts, tie-dyed shirts, and the yellow flag with three red stripes of North Vietnam. The small wheels made the bikes identifiable and stowable. I'd been to the treasury numerous times, usually biking along the embankment, but I had yet to enter its big-domed Whitehall neighbor. Remodeled in the last century, the huge building was where the wars of empire were mostly won, except one involving a chunk of North America.

I secured wheels beyond the Cenotaph, a memorial to the British and Commonwealth soldiers killed in two world wars. A guard took the letter, which I never saw again, and after numerous elevators and corridors—presumably leading to places where the sun never sets—escorted me toward Elwell's office. I was struck by the absence of people. A search-and-rescue operation would have taken days to find me. The building boasted two and a half miles of corridors, which set a record until the Pentagon. I sat in a utilitarian office overlooking a dim courtyard, expecting to encounter headless images of Anne Boleyn and Thomas More. The room had a desk, a couple of hard straight-back chairs, and a picture of dour Queen Elizabeth II (with her head). The loudest noise was a wall clock: it was just after 10:00 a.m.

Elwell, if indeed that was his name, finally arrived, joined by a second man whose name I never got. Elwell took a corner of the desk. The other man perched on a second chair, and for minutes we made small talk about life in London. The two Britons were amazingly well-informed about me and most of my colleagues. "You're wondering what all this is about," Elwell finally said, clicking his tongue. I couldn't have put it better myself. It turned out that MI-5 had been eyeing me. I'd read spy stories all my life, but here, just a bike ride away, was that all-too-real yet unreal world of John Buchan or John le Carré. They were on my trail, not for any suspected skulduggery, they smilingly reassured me, but rather for the occasional luncheons I'd been having with a Soviet news source—someone I knew as an economics officer by the name of Igor Petroff, whom they identified as "dangerous," from the KGB, now filching NATO secrets.

I had no particular feelings about him. We'd had lunch together several times, and apart from small talk about Russian chess masters whom he apparently knew personally, we talked about the dollar and the pound sterling. Innocent enough. Yet my new friends were working toward his persona non grata expulsion. They urged me to continue seeing him, get chummier, invite him to dinner, uncover as much as possible on him and his contacts, and keep them informed. No money was offered, although they said I'd be reimbursed for expenses. They were asking me to perform as a "gesture of patriotism through the Atlantic partnership that binds our two nations against a ruthless enemy," as Elwell put it.

It was incredible, so incredible that I remember every detail. As a working journalist, I was being asked to serve two masters, and one wasn't even my own country. Of course, I couldn't do it, and I said so in no uncertain terms. It would have been a firing offense at the *Times*. I left the War Office soon afterward, never to hear from these men again. Extraordinary as it was for them to have asked me, those were extraordinary times.

Spies were all the rage, and Britain, despite all the new gaming establishments, was down on its luck. Key figures of another establishment had been fingered as Soviet spies—with names like Donald Maclean, Guy Burgess, Anthony Blunt, John Cairncross, and, most notorious of all, Kim Philby, who later appeared on a commemorative stamp as a "hero of the Soviet Union."

Philby's cover was the *Times* of London, for which he covered the Spanish Civil War. After a period with British intelligence in World War II and the immediate postwar era, he again hooked up with the *Times* of London as a Mideast correspondent. My meeting in Whitehall occurred a few weeks after Philby's defection to Moscow. He married Eleanor Brewer, the ex-wife of *New York Times* diplomatic correspondent Sam Pope Brewer. So perhaps in MI-5's view, the *New York Times* was already complicit. The attempted recruitment showed one thing for certain: the extent to which MI-5—and, by implication, the CIA—was flailing. Because of the intimacy of these two spy organizations, it's unlikely that Washington hadn't been informed of the attempt to suborn me; maybe it had even initiated the attempt.

The Philby story itself was also full of ironies. In the late 1940s, he was the British intelligence representative in Washington and a weekly luncheon companion of James Jesus Angleton, the storied head of counterintelligence for the then new CIA. Angleton apparently had his own suspicions about Philby, but the two still regularly met a few blocks from the White House. I referred to those lunches in a 1985 story about spy haunts in the capital. A source told me the eatery was Harvey's, which no longer exists. The morning of November 14, when the article appeared, I took a call from a gravelly voice identifying itself as "Jim Angleton." He "enjoyed" the article, but had to correct "a little misinformation." The site was not Harvey's but a restaurant of the Hotel Statler two blocks away. The head of counterintelligence found it incumbent to set the record straight for the *New York Times*.

Not long after my arrival in London, I invited Dad for a visit. Although he knew the farthest reaches of the British Empire, he'd never before seen where it all started. Thanks to the apprenticeship of Charles Johnson, my rejection of his job offer was no longer an issue, and he was only too happy to play tourist. As was her wont, Dolly tagged along. I prepared to unfurl such wondrous attractions as Buckingham Palace, the Tower, London Bridge, and Westminster Abbey. Yet as I reeled off an itinerary, I discovered that what Dad most wanted to see wasn't even on my list. He asked if I'd ever heard of Speakers' Corner.

I had, but barely. The few months of settling in—with a new baby—hadn't afforded much time for sightseeing. I knew roughly where it was—at the northeast corner of Hyde Park, a short walk from the Victoria Sporting Club and Claridge's Hotel—and that it was a place where some people said "mostly weirdos" sounded off on Sunday mornings. He sat me down and made me pay attention. He'd first heard of it from his grandfather, Lank, who with Grandma Lydia had once visited London. "My grandfather said it was the eternal flame of English freedom, where a man steps on a soapbox, damns the king or queen, preaches blasphemy, revolution, [or] free love, and no one can lay a hand on him," Dad explained.

The tradition started around the time of the American Civil War, evolving into as open a forum of democracy as exists anywhere, identified with Karl Marx, George Orwell, and anyone else with a bee in his bonnet. In other words, it was part of the freedom journalists depend on, often take for granted. Dad and Dolly arrived on a Saturday. That Sunday Dad and I (Dolly was still making her toilette) piled into the same Renault that ferried Clifton Daniel around.

There were only a handful of people at the site, which was the former Tyburn Gallows for public executions, and most were walking their dogs. A wide-eyed soul said he'd come out for "a wee bit of argumentation." People drifted in and out of earshot of those on various soapboxes. A man with white hair and a leathery face spoke about exploitation of the workers "who work all day and get hardly a shilling for a wee bit o' bread." Dad moseyed toward that soapbox, and while the bloke took a nip "to refresh" himself, Dad asked whether it was all workers who were being exploited or just some. "All, brother!" the man replied hotly. "From the machinations of the capitalists, no worker is spared." We moseyed off. Since we'd been his only audience, the speaker shouted after us, a bit deflated, "Where you going?" Dad turned, smiling broadly, and replied, "To the barricades, brother!"

One October evening in Cambridge in 1965 James Baldwin, the African American essayist and novelist (e.g., *Go Tell It on the Mountain, The Fire Next Time*) debated William F. Buckley Jr., the conservative polemicist, publisher, author and longtime host of the TV show *Firing Line*. Organized by students at the Cambridge Union, the debate was a much anticipated event of verbal pugilism, covered by the BBC and other media as if cued by a George Bellows painting. The proposition was that progress in America since 1776 had been at the expense of African Americans: Baldwin for, Buckley against. Students decided who was the victor by their applause.

Buckley, who had attended prep school in England, arrived with a take-no-prisoners reputation as a debater. Many had heard of and even read Baldwin, but no one knew how this short, wiry fellow with big eyes and a soft voice would fare against a champ who ate his rivals for breakfast.

Baldwin demolished Buckley. In retrospect, there was probably no way Buckley could have won over such a zealously anti-American audience, especially with the US military escalation in Vietnam at the time. Buckley's barbs and sesquipedalian satire fell flat. Baldwin knew a thing or two himself about debate. Though born and raised in Harlem, he'd been schooled in the South, and he spoke, for example, of the miles he had to walk every day while white students jeered from their convertibles, their whitewall tires layering him in swirls of road dust.

There was no doubt that Buckley lost the debate. Yet he seemed truly taken aback by the student reaction. Maybe he didn't expect it, in England, of all places. My story said that his arguments seemed less cogent than usual and that as he stalked around the amphitheater airily jabbing at his opponent, he resembled a "tired panther." Some weeks later I got a postcard from him with words in Spanish that said, "Not like the panther he knew of old."

It was a quotation from Pedro Calderon de la Barca, the seventeenth-century Spanish playwright who is perhaps most famous for saying, "Life is a dream, and dreams themselves are only dreams." Buckley, in whose Spanish-language class I had found myself as a Yale freshman, was having fun. We'd known each other but not well, and that postcard was just like him: provocative, erudite, and trenchant.

The son of an oilman, he grew up in Mexico, so Spanish was his first language. He served in the army near the end of World War II; in 1946 he entered Yale and taught Spanish. He also wrote three dozen books, founded the magazine *National Review*, and was a passionate sailor and a devotee of the harpsichord.

25

Mission Impossible

SOONER THAN EXPECTED, I was again a war reporter. I barely knew where Cyprus was, but in the summer of 1964 much news focused on the long-term ethnic strife between its Greek and Turkish population and the threat posed for the Atlantic alliance. The third largest Mediterranean island, after Sicily and Sardinia, and supposedly the birthplace of the goddess of love, Aphrodite, was the home of two peoples consumed by mutual hate.

For the gathering storm, the *New York Times* deployed a correspondent in Israel, Bill Blair, and as backup, my London colleague Larry Fellows, who knew the island from his own days in Tel Aviv, which was a short hop away. Then on the morning of Friday, August 7, 1964, war erupted about as real as it gets. Enraged by attacks against the Turkish minority, Turkey deployed its air force to bomb and napalm villages used by Greek irregulars to attack the Turkish community. Making it an even bigger story, Turkey used American-built Phantom jets, part of its NATO force, and these were being used to attack a NATO ally.

People were on vacation, and I was holding down the fort. Mission impossible: Go to Nicosia and file a story in time for Saturday's editions. Cyprus was six hours ahead of New York and one hour ahead of London. I picked up my passport, money, toiletries, and a Hermes typewriter (incredibly like Dad's years ago at Penn Station), and I was off. After three hours in the air, I checked into the marble and stucco Ledra Palace Hotel in the Greek sector of Nicosia.

Moments after entering my second-floor room, I heard the close firing of machine guns and instinctively dropped. Peeking out a window, I saw only a deserted swimming pool and weaving palms. The firing continued sporadically. As far as I knew, the hotel was undamaged. During a lull I rushed downstairs to try to find out what the hell was going on.

No one was agitated. I found the bar, crowded with mostly British and American journalists and Finnish UN personnel, and introduced myself.

Joe Alex Morris Jr., of the *Los Angeles Times*, filled me in on the gunfire. "Routine," he said, putting me only slightly at ease. "Turkish irregulars clearing weapons. But the ammo's live." The Turks were dug in near a post office about five hundred yards up Ledra Street—a demarcation known as the Green Line, where the United Nations maintained a buffer. Joe warned that filing was risky. Copy had to be hand delivered to the post office. "Don't let them think you're Greek!" Laughter at the bar. "Tip big and hope they're sober." More laughter. "Long phone delays to the States."

As we talked, I learned again how small and coincidental the world of journalism is. Although this was a first encounter, Joe had also worked for both the *New York Herald Tribune* and UPI, and his dad had risen to foreign editor of both organizations. As UP's offical historian (before the merger that created UPI), Joe Sr. authored *Deadline Every Minute*, a bestseller about that wire service's first fifty years. Joe Jr., who never shrank from bullets, went on to cover crisis after crisis in the Middle East until tragedy struck in 1979. He was in Tehran during the events that led to the fall of the shah. I happened to be there myself three months earlier at the beginning of the same revolution, and it was a crazy, chaotic situation even then. On February 10, Joe was at an Iranian airfield when a firefight broke out between supporters of the Shah and those backing Ayatollah Ruholla Khomeini. Joe was killed by a single stray bullet in the chest. The world lost a dedicated newsman and a much needed sleuth for the eternal mysteries of the Middle East.

At that bar I also met George De Carvalho of *Time* magazine; he was looking for someone to ride shotgun with him on a tour of the island he was about to undertake. His purpose was "hunting jets." It seemed like a good opportunity to pick up material. He promised to return by sundown, which would still allow time to file the story that day. In accepting, I discovered another extraordinary reporter. George had won a Pulitzer with the *San Francisco Chronicle* before jumping into the Middle East for *Time*. In World War II he fought as a paratrooper with the Eighty-Second Airborne Division, made two combat jumps, and was wounded four times.

Departing in a tawny Avis Ford, we left stray dogs and chickens in our wake. Emblazoned on the windshield was PRESS—USA. At Greek and Turkish checkpoints, he shouted with fiery urgency, "*Time* magazine—*New York Times*," which usually got us through. But at one Greek checkpoint at a hairpin turn, teenage irregulars, their tommy guns oscillating, made us open the trunk, revealing a couple of cartons of Marlboros. One of the gunman swiped a handful of packs. Amid the departing swirls of dust, George shot him a Sicilian salute.

As we headed north toward Turkish villages, Greek-Cypriot Radio, which we were monitoring, reported more bombing. George later said that all he really wanted that day was a swim in the sea, which we finally saw through a break in the hills. Also toward the north coast, we spotted the Phantoms at about ten thousand feet. George slammed the brakes, and we dashed across fields of grass for a better view. The two planes circled each other almost playfully, then, as if suddenly aware of unwanted attention, vanished into cottony clouds.

It reminded George of his adventures as a kid. He grew up in Shanghai. In 1937 he and his chums from Gonzaga College, a Jesuit school, watched Japanese planes on bombing runs. The kids chased after shrapnel, never realizing that the hot metal could tear them apart. He later exited to Hong Kong. I mentioned Dad's years in China. George said he was well aware of the other Clyde Farnsworth and was happy to see a chip off the old block.

While returning, we picked up from the radio that those Phantoms had napalmed several more villages and that Greek gunners had downed one of the planes, whose pilot ejected and was captured. It was more than enough for any story. I wrote quickly and tried phoning the story in, but the wait to New York was at least six hours (as Joe Morris had warned), which meant I had to find that crazy post office. There were no taxis (as Joe had also noted), and if I hoofed it I'd get shot. But every hour a Finnish UN officer, trying to enforce a shattered truce, left the hotel to inspect the Green Line buffer. A jeep with a UN banner was parked in the driveway.

I hung around until catching the Finn, in flak vest and helmet, walking toward his jeep. He handed me a spare vest and helmet, and I was back in Korea. There was more machine-gun chatter as we bounded toward the checkpoint. Our headlights approached walls of sandbags and razor wire. He urged a wave, a smile, and a shout of *New York Times*. These Turks, also teenagers, were strutting, grunting, smoking, and playing soldier with real guns. As they lifted the barrier, the Finn said he'd wait—but not long. He seemed to know his young Turks, and everyone bantered in broken English. Barrels of fun!

The post office was in a building walled by sandbags. I passed more clusters of youths, awaiting their turn at the barricades, and also many black-shawled women. People ate fruits and dates and drank Orangina. They stared. I waved, trying, despite a sea of sweat, to seem casual. Inside the post office I said I had an important story to send to America. It would take six hours before anyone would even look at my copy. I offered to punch the tape myself, which didn't sit well. An official who seemed to run the place took my baksheesh of five pounds and promised to see what he could do. He didn't advise waiting.

Back at the Ledra Palace bar, I bought vodkas for myself and my new Finnish friend. Just before midnight a call came through from the Foreign Desk. None of my brilliant prose handed in at that infernal post office ever made it, and the foreign desk insisted that I immediately dictate my story to the recording room so that it could be jammed into the paper. A weak connection meant spelling out every word. My story led the paper. God knows what the phone bill was!

I learned that Archbishop Makarios III, the Greek religious leader, would be taking a busload of Western correspondents on a tour of the napalmed villages. The bus was leaving at 4:00 a.m., which was rapidly approaching. I signed on as a legitimate way to discover what those Phantoms had wrought. I rolled myself into a back seat of the press bus, too roiled to sleep. At each stop, women in long black dresses wailed and ululated what had to be curses at the Turks. Even if partly staged for our benefit, they were effective. Everything visible on that infernally hot and dusty ride showed that the Turks had played for keeps. Charred canisters were laid out on which the name Dow Chemical appeared. From one stop to the next, I saw medical workers administering to the bedridden. Long rooms and corridors held dozens of the more severely wounded. The air smelled of bad eggs and rotting meat.

After I had spent three days in Cyprus, Foreign Editor Emanuel (Manny) Freedman, whose stoop-shouldered, unsmiling mien suggested a burden of woes, asked me to follow the story from Ankara. The pilot who had parachuted from the Phantom was dead. It was unclear how he died: homicide was not a bad guess. In an effort to cool passions, the United Nations took charge of his body and flew it to Ankara. The Turkish authorities declared their intention to give him a state funeral, which Manny insisted I cover.

As I arrived, the whole of Kemal Ataturk's capital with its broad boulevards, floral parks, and monument-crested mosques seemed in mourning. A military band slow-marched to the adagio of the *Eroica* symphony as six white horses drew an ebony and gold coffin mounted on a caisson. The *Times* played the full ceremonial story I filed later that day also on page one, but to show even more even-handedness, Freedman pressed for more stories now from Turkey. The following day an urbane, English-speaking assistant secretary greeted me in his map-strewn office at the Ankara Foreign Ministry. While we were sipping orange juice and making polite small talk, he suddenly asked where I was from in the States. Barbara and I had lived in Ossining, New York, before the transfer to London.

"How far is Ossining from New York City?" he asked.

"I don't know—thirty or so miles," I said. He rolled down a wall map showing Cyprus across the Mediterranean from the southern coast of Turkey.

"Do you realize that from there, Cyprus is little farther than Ossining is from New York City?" With a marker, he traced the short stretch of blue-green, then pointed west to Greece. "A world away," he said. "But for hundreds of years, Turks commuted to Cyprus. Those Turkish people who live there are our Turkish people. We can never abandon them. Turkey will never tolerate the mistreatment of its people on the island of Cyprus."

Did that justify napalming Cypriot villages, I asked. He knew nothing of napalm. I said I had seen the canisters in Cyprus. "Beware of Greek propaganda," he said. There was no way to square that circle inside the Turkish Foreign Ministry.

In 1974 Turkey invaded Cyprus and set up the Turkish Federated State of Cyprus in the north of the island. Only Turkey recognized it. That resolution, together with the renewal of tourist income, quieted things down into the twenty-first century.

26

A Death on the Rhine

ON A SULTRY July morning in 1965, Larry Rue didn't answer his usual call for breakfast, and the chambermaid, a Serbian *gastarbeiter* (guest worker) in a starched white pinafore, hesitantly knocked to rouse him. She figured he had overslept, as he sometimes did. She knocked again, a little louder. "Herr Rue, Herr Rue." She unlocked the door with her passkey. He lay under the feather quilt, motionless. She approached and called out again. No response. Authorities later established that the *Chicago Tribune* correspondent for central Europe had died in his sleep. He was sixty-nine and had been working on a story on the West German Social Democratic Party. It was still in his typewriter.

Outside the place was idyllic. The Schaumburger Hof hotel was a timbered mosaic, with graystone terraces and gardens, overlooking a broad sweep of the Rhine at Bad Godesburg. Queen Victoria slept there during one of her infrequent excursions to the Continent, accompanied by Albert, her consort. Rue, a bachelor, was alone. Several miles southeast of Bonn, the West German capital, Bad Godesburg was a peaceful place where people came for baths and mineral waters and the new wine. Beyond neat rows of linden trees, boats of all descriptions chuffed due south toward Basel and the Alps or northwest toward Rotterdam and the sea.

Across the Rhine, a little upriver, were the ghostly shapes of the Siebengebirge, or Seven Hills. On one of these, Drachenfels, Siegfried triumphed over the dragon Fafnir, gaining the ring of the Nibelung and the hand of Brunnhilde—the plot of Richard Wagner's *Ring Cycle*. Now Drachenfels drew picnickers to a stone fortress covered by the graffiti of thousands of lovers' hearts.

Two months after Rue's death, Don Maxwell, the *Trib*'s managing editor, visited Vienna and was given a five-star tour, including the Schottenring and Sacher's, and an open house at Hohenstaufengasse. Although he and Dad had exchanged cables, this was their first face-to-face meeting. They took to each other immediately. Maxwell's big friendly features, contagious smile, and resonant voice reminded Dad of Granddad Lank. They discovered a common evangelical upbringing as they harmonized "Amazing Grace." Maxwell's father had been a Methodist gospel singer and a friend of Billy Sunday, and Lank had been an elder and chief dunker at the Disciples Church. Maxwell had also worked as a reporter in Depression-era Cleveland (the *Press*). He commended Dad for recent pieces in the *Trib*, pointedly remarking that he hadn't "gone native" but rather wrote for the general reader. Dad said that all his life he wrote as if explaining things to his son. Maxwell said that's the way it should be. "Too many reporters forget," he stated.

What came next was beyond Dad's wildest dreams. Maxwell said he wanted to make an honest man of Dad by putting him on the staff of the *Chicago Tribune* as Rue's successor. Dad was fifty-seven, when it's hard to embed anywhere, let alone at a competitive news organization where the emphasis is on eternal youth. Because he could not now serve more than one master, he had to jettison the stringer operation he had so painstakingly built up in the past decade. The enlarged paycheck made it easier.

His beat included both Bonn and Vienna, as well as the territoriy north to the Baltic, east to the Urals, and south to the Mediterranean—in fact, the old empire of Charlemagne. And with it came an emperor's chariot: a five-speed, black Mercedes 280 S sedan. There were downsides: spending a lot more time in Bonn—dullsville versus the effervescence of Vienna—and enduring separations from Dolly. He worked out a return to Vienna every second week. He too settled at the Schaumburger, where he made a friend: a corpulent German shepherd that spent much time on a mat outside the room of his master, the hotel owner, Herr Mundorf.

Bonn was different from Vienna: more institutional, driven by process, yet not without drama. It was the end of the era of Konrad Adenauer, the first postwar leader of West Germany, known almost reverently as *der alte* (the old man), and the country was soul-searching over the survival prospects of its new democracy. This former mayor of Cologne, condemned to a Nazi concentration camp for his liberal ideas, had already won four successive elections as chancellor. The big question was what would happen when *der alte* was no longer around.

Ludwig Erhard, the architect of the postwar economic recovery, replaced Adenauer, and my father reported that the institutions survived in fine shape, with the legislative, judicial, and executive branches checking and balancing one another. Political parties were robust. Anti-Semitic incidents were usually followed by denunciations in Parliament and the press. The legacy of Nazism had been death and appalling destruction. The last thing Germans wanted was to start down that road again—that same phenomenon that Douglas MacArthur cited with Japan a decade earlier.

The other big issue was the division of Germany between the Soviet-dominated East and the democratic West. Although it was never stated openly, the Russians, covertly backed by the French, saw a divided Germany as a weak Germany. That might be good for them, but was it good for Europe? Dad believed that a united Germany anchored to the West by economic and defense treaties posed no threat. If others thought differently, at least there was a point on which all Westerners now agreed: the cruelty of that division in human terms.

Larry Rue's assistant in Bonn, a feisty blonde named Alice Siegert, had relatives in East Germany on whom she showered gifts during visits. I met her in Bonn and engaged her in a discussion on her divided country. "How would you feel," she asked, "if you needed papers each time you crossed from Washington into Virginia?"

East Berlin extended 110 miles inside East Germany. On assignments, Rue often drove through West Germany into the western sector of Berlin, traversing numerous checkpoints. There was no turnpike-type E-Z pass. Gray-uniformed VoPos, Volkspolizei, ordered the passengers out of their cars and made them declare their assets. One of Dad's declarations underestimated his change by sixteen pfennigs. The arbitrary search held him—and others behind—for hours!

Stops took place in a no-man's land of clawlike fences and coiled barbed wire. Searchlights skewered the night from skeletal towers bristling with machine guns. Land mines spiked adjacent fields. VoPos, toting Pushka tommy guns, rolled underneath each vehicle what looked like a garage jack with a broad slanted mirror to reveal who or what might be hiding away in the chassis.

VoPos figured in my own wildest caper. I'd flown into East Berlin's Schoenfeld Airport from Algiers on the way back to Brussels. I could have shuttled to West Berlin and returned via Tempelhof. But the next bus didn't leave for hours. So why not cross Checkpoint Charlie on foot? If lucky, I would convince the guards to let me hike and, once in West Berlin, taxi to Tempelhof for one of its more frequent flights to Brussels. It could save time. It might even make a story.

The *Times* traditionally gave latitude to its correspondents, who knew better than any deskbound functionaries where to be at any given time. It was wise, of course, to keep the desk informed. I hadn't preplanned this enterprise. The idea came suddenly, and I acted. The story received an imaginative full-length display in the Paris *International Herald Tribune*—then a collaborative effort of the *New York Times, Los Angeles Times,* and *Washington Post*—but the *New York Times* editors spiked it. I never understood why. James L. Greenfield, then the foreign editor, who manned a desk at the State Department for years, was a stickler for protocol, and perhaps he didn't like being surprised. The Paris *International Herald Tribune*'s editor Buddy Weiss was an old friend and a solid newsman. The more surprised he was by a story, the better.

Buddy and I cooperated at the *New York Herald Tribune*, where he'd been the city editor. We worked the Jimmy Hoffa and other page one stories together. When the *New York Herald Tribune* folded, Buddy moved to the Paris *International Herald Tribune,* then thriving largely because of him and his savvy wife, Peggy Sunday, also a second-generation journalist. Cronyism worked for Dad on any number of occasions, and maybe it then worked for me. Or maybe this really was a strong piece.

At any rate the cabbie dropped me in the shadow of the Berlin Wall, but well away from the VoPo hut. He couldn't take me across and probably had no desire to be observed anywhere near his nutty passenger. On the way, while still on a backstreet below broken glass, spikes, and concertina wire, he delivered a poignant lament. Way above us was the tower of the newsweekly *Der Spiegel,* its searchlights illuminating the entire city. He half turned to tell me in German almost tearfully, "Someday my daughter may see the other side of this wall, but for me, never in my lifetime." The comment captured the despair of the period. It was January 1969, two decades before that hated wall came down.

Carrying my suitcase and a minitypewriter, I approached two unsmiling VoPos, their tommy guns aimed at my chest. I identified myself as a correspondent with the *New York Times,* presented my passport and press credentials, and said in German that I wanted to walk to West Berlin. The junior man looked at me uncomprehendingly, asked me to repeat, went to a back office, and didn't return for a long time; he was probably making calls to the Central Committee. Finally he returned with a judgment: If I was crazy enough to walk, I could walk. The VoPo let a vaporous smile evaporate, warning in no-nonsense German that I had no trouble understanding: "Walk slowly, because the men in the towers get very nervous."

I picked up my things and started out, wondering why I hadn't waited for the damn bus. I was very much alone, sweating profusely, even on this cool night. As shadows swallowed the hut, the only sounds were sizzles and zaps of electrified barbed wire. Searchlights played chiaroscuro near my sweating torso.

I tried not to look at the machine guns, pointed down from the high platforms. Just keep walking, I told myself. At the first V-shaped tank trap, where monstrous iron impediments rose and razor wire bristled, I zigged sharply right and went on, walking slowly, eyes glued to the road. At the next trap I zagged left. Searchlights now seemed more distant. Eventually something made me lift my eyes, and I feasted on the cacophonous glitter of West Berlin. Those guards also looked at me oddly but waved me through. One shook his head as if this were a tale for the *kinder*. The walk took forty minutes but seemed a lifetime. The sudden glow of a *weinstube* (tavern) drew me toward a double vodka.

By the late 1960s I was living in Brussels, the seat of both the European Community and NATO. Charles de Gaulle had booted the headquarters of NATO out of Paris, but soon a new base was found near the airport in the municipality of Zaventem, a twenty-five minute taxi ride from downtown Brussels. Assigned to cover both institutions, I resettled the family and tried to refresh my French. I was desperate to use the language, until it became perfectly clear that everyone I met spoke English better than I spoke French. This situation reversed itself when I reached France a few years later. Unlike Belgians, the French are not multilingual or even bilingual.

I worked from a sixth-floor office on the Avenue des Arts along the Brussels ring road. From my windows I could make out the silvery spheres of the Atomium of the 1958 World's Fair at the other end of the city. The theme—well before Three Mile Island and Chernobyl—was the marvelous world opening for peacetime nuclear power. During those heady days, when people spoke in almost reverential tones of a United States of Europe and Atoms for Peace, the European Community was a crucible for integration and nuclear pooling. At twenty stories, the Atomium, denoting a molecule of iron magnified 165 billion times, gave shape to the era. The exhibits, linked by soaring escalators, were exciting enough to bring the kids to.

But optimism soon gave way to practical considerations of safety and sovereignty. Charles de Gaulle's nationalism and the growth of what came to be called Euroskepticism killed Atoms for Peace and nearly the dream of unification. During interminable meetings in Brussels, the six founding members of the European Community—France, West Germany, Italy, Belgium, the Netherlands, and Luxembourg—seemed forever at one another's throats. After countless walkouts and all-night marathons, they found it more convenient to stick together.

The biggest spat was over de Gaulle's veto of Britain. France's partners had no choice but to wait out de Gaulle, a strategy that paid off in the 1970s. Not by accident, the English Channel tunnel, or Chunnel, moved forward, too, providing that long-dreamed-of physical link.

Minus the quarrels, it wasn't the most dazzling of beats. Conflict enlivens. No victory, no suspense, no story. I was watching grass grow—in this case, the standardization of rules for agriculture, energy, and so on in preparation for a United States of Europe. But who cared about a common price for fats and oils, or regulations for flaxseed and wool? Hardly anyone in Europe cared. A colleague from the *Financial Times*, Ian Davidson, confided that he was writing for no more than a dozen civil servants in the British Treasury.

Seymour Topping, replacing Jimmy Greenfield as foreign editor at the *New York Times*, cautioned, "Don't tell us how the sausage is made, just give us the taste and smell." Topping was too smart to define news. By definition it needs an element of surprise. Then, as Grandma noted years ago, it should shake up things a little.

I opened my travel guide to find that Brussels wasn't all that far from sleepy Bad Godesburg: two and a half hours by autobahn. So reunions with Dad were easy, via Aachen, the capital of Charlemagne's Europe. Occasionally Dolly joined. Dad sent Mom money and wished her well, but the split was irrevocable. We got to know the Schaumburger Hof, a few bends upriver from Bonn. My sons, Andrew and Alex, loved the place: quaint rooms, squeaking doors, spouted ewers, linden-shaded walks, barges day and night, and Herr Mundorf's tired old dog.

Dad took us on day trips, such as the ruins atop Drachenfels, a few winemaking establishments, and even the American embassy snack bar for milk shakes and malts. He seemed to enjoy being a grandfather. He told stories, made gorilla faces (as he used to do before my sister, my brother and me), and Andrew and Alex squealed with delight. While he got to know his grandchildren, I developed a certain ease with Dolly.

One hot afternoon I took advantage of the pool around the corner from the embassy snack bar. Dolly was there too, doing laps. We were the only patrons. She progressed slowly and methodically, seemingly oblivious to everything but the pulsing of arms, feet, and head, as if traversing the English Channel. I dove into a distant lane and, like the hare, did five laps quickly, exited winded, and saw Dolly still at her tortoise pace. It was unclear whether she saw me. Her arms and legs unhurriedly propelled her, and she seemed oblivious to everything except the rhythmic smack of her hands and the mechanical roll of her mouth gulping air. I watched for a minute or two and waved. Still no recognition sign. I dressed and rejoined Dad, who was playing games with the kids in the snack bar. An hour later, as we prepared to leave, Dolly still hadn't joined us. Dad went to fetch her. We trailed along. She was still doing laps. Slap! Slap! Slap! He smiled. "She'd stay here all night if we let her."

It was remarkable. Never had I thought of her having such stamina. Indeed, I hadn't thought much about her, except in hostile ways, for splitting up my parents. Suddenly I came to see that stamina as the key to her personality and history. It got her out of Hitler's Europe and made her a survivor.

Dad used to swim, but exercise was no longer his cup of tea. What he seemed to love most those weekends was to snug up on a corner bench on the Rhine excursion boats, look out at the ever changing riverscapes, and talk about his memories. Stories sizzled. Occasionally I joined in; I now had stories, too. We had both covered wars: China and Korea for him, Korea and Cyprus for me.

Even before those boat rides, we had started covering the same stories together: in West Berlin, the games the Soviets were playing to punish the city as an outpost of freedom; in Brussels, the games de Gaulle was playing to diminish NATO and the United States. At one NATO ministerial meeting, after Dad had filed to Chicago on my office telex, he offered to punch my longer copy to the *Times*. He did some well-justified tightening and fixing of errant spelling, and then we treated ourselves to mussels and fries at a downtown brasserie halfway to the Atomium. Like the words on the signs we saw on some of the Brussels shop windows, we were *pere et fils*.

27

One Prague Summer

IN THE SPRING of 1968 Alexander Dubcek assumed power in Czechoslovakia. Reversing years of hard-line rule, the new communist leader ended censorship, opened borders, ousted Soviet advisers, and allowed opposition parties to flourish. "Socialism with a human face," he called it. Moscow wasn't pleased, and intervention seemed likely. Yet for reporters hanging around into late summer, it was like waiting for Godot. Many went on vacation. By a fluke I arrived August 20, just hours before half a million troops breached the frontiers.

I flew in from Belgrade, where the head of a worker management council spoke like a Harvard Business School graduate. "Profits" assured the future of "enterprises," and the worker-owners were entitled to "dividends." In prepping for Prague, I arranged to interview Dr. Ota Sik, the deputy premier, who was on leave from teaching business economics at Charles University and was negotiating a loan from West Germany to support the Dubcek reforms. I never saw Sik. A German economic sphere so near Russia's border was a bridge too far. The professor, threatened by imprisonment or worse, fled to Switzerland to join the economics department of St. Gallen University.

Prague seemed even hotter than Belgrade. Despite the exodus of reporters, tourists still packed the gemlike city with its medieval castle, clock towers, cobblestone streets, statues, galleries, and breweries. Among the visitors were four hundred geologists at an international convention and a film crew shooting *The Bridge at Remagen*, with George Segal and Robert Vaughn, about the push by US forces into Germany. By the dispensation of Soviet Premier Leonid Brezhnev, or someone, the movie making continued—the defeat of the Nazis was presumably a favorite subject of the Kremlin. In place of the Rhine, however, the film used the Vltava River, which twists like a corkscrew through Czechoslovakia. "The Rhine is too busy and too wide," Vaughn said.

My immediate goal was real enough: find Tad Szulc, another *New York Times* correspondent. He had covered revolutions and Cold War intrigue for decades and was now the Prague bureau chief. For years I'd marveled at his exploits. He scooped everyone on the April 1961 Bay of Pigs invasion. I'd met him once, at a correspondents' reunion on a drizzly evening in Paris in 1967. He arrived fashionably late, in a black cape with a scarlet pimpernel, recalling that signature of noblemen in the French Revolution. Always impeccably attired, he was an impressive, prodigious, omnivorous, and intimidating newsman.

He had checked into the Hotel Alcron, on Stepanska, off Wenceslas Square, Prague's Times Square. Discharging a Russian Fiat taxi from the airport, I checked in there, too. The décor was communist kitsch—dark wood, etched glass, cascading chandeliers, and conspiratorial drapes—and like much else under the Reds had been allowed to get shabby. This was the hotel my father, Szulc, and other regulars had chosen while covering the Prague Spring in 1968. Because of the hotel's popularity with the media, it had been used as a base by many in a new wave of Czech writers and filmmakers—Milos Forman, Arnost Lustig, Milan Kundera, and Vaclav Havel—along with such foreign notables as Jean-Paul Sartre and Simone de Beauvoir. Through clouds of unfiltered Gauloises Brunes cigarette smoke, Jean-Paul, wearing his trademark corrective shades, chatted at the bar with Simone. They told everyone the achievements of humanized communism pleased them. When the tanks rolled in, Jean-Paul announced from Paris that he felt "personally betrayed."

Szulc was registered at the hotel but was out. He couldn't be far, the clerk said; his car was still in front. I took note of the burgundy Chevrolet with white walls and chrome hubcaps in the reserved parking area off the driveway. Szulc, with his majestic capes and impressive vehicles, was part of a grand tradition of American reporters cutting a swath bigger than life: Richard Harding Davis, in Rough Rider hat and boots, giving pointers to Teddy Roosevelt; the *Times*'s own Scotty Reston, advising John F. Kennedy; and TV newscasters from Ed Murrow and Walter Cronkite to Diane Sawyer and Rachel Maddow.

The porter showed me to my fourth-floor room, smiling as he pointed to the poster of Dubcek in the elevator. The room was small and musty. I pulled the heavy red velveteen drapes open to raise a dusty window. I had work to do—reading notes, trying phone numbers, telexing my arrival to the desk—but I suddenly decided all could wait. I had to get beyond these walls.

Wenceslas Square opened up grandly a couple hundred yards from the lobby. It was big, bigger even than Times Square, but people didn't have the driven look of New Yorkers. Even when going somewhere, they weren't in much of a hurry. Fair-haired women in flowered dresses carried baskets of fruit. Men on benches slowly turned pages of *Rudé Právo*, the local newspaper. As police officers blew whistles to direct traffic, people talked quietly among themselves. Everything seemed as it should. I peered down an alley. Two boys kicked a soccer ball between a well-stocked shoe store and a restaurant. I thought of my own boys and kept an eye out for toys as well as the renowned crystal goblets for gifts for others at home.

Moseying up toward the National Museum, I checked out the equestrian statue of Good King Wenceslas, who brought Christianity to Bohemia and was still going strong after his thousand-year-old martyrdom. I noticed crowds at the ice cream and sausage vendors, and I joined a sausage line. The aroma was irresistible. My sausage, dribbling hot fat and cooled by mustard and relish, was a delight, and I didn't care how it was made. Having forgotten how hungry I was, I stood in line again, washing it all down with a golden brew everyone called Pils.

From the National Museum I went down toward the Old Town Square, which a guidebook indicated was little more than a quarter mile away. As if borne by a slow current, I bobbed along with the crowds, past the Gunpowder Tower, the gilded astronomical clock and the Hebrew clock, the house where Franz Kafka was born, and the Old-New Synagogue, eventually ending up at a wide footbridge across a real enough river, the fifteenth-century Charles Bridge spanning the Vltava, which divides the city. This was the turf of Holy Roman emperors, saints, and rabbis—to say nothing of the classical composers Smetana, Janacek, Dvorak, and even Mozart, whose carriage from Vienna traversed that same Charles Bridge to the premiere of his final opera, *La Clemenza di Tito*. Prague was one of the few great cities in Europe left relatively intact after two world wars. But years of bureaucratic indifference had taken another kind of toll. Effluents from coal, oil, and gas left it worse off than Paris before Charles de Gaulle's great minister of culture André Malraux started Operation Scrub. Prague needed a Malraux.

Back on Stepanska, I spotted a barbershop. Barbers were great sources of information. A lean fellow with white smock, chin hair, and a Dubcek pin stood in the doorway of the otherwise empty shop. I asked in English if he was open for business. He nodded. From the rear a fan wheezed.

"American?" he inquired.

There was no point in denying it.

"Russians tomorrow!" he volunteered, looking glum.

I was unable to take the threat seriously, especially with so many tourists and the semblance of normality. But here was that "man in the street" that newspaper reporters always seek. I pulled out a notebook and said I was an American correspondent. "Tell America we love freedom," he exclaimed. He told me more than I wanted to know about his cousin in Chicago. It cost me 3 crowns (about 42 cents), and I left a 2-crown tip. Later I learned that the barber of Stepanska had slipped away, as had thousands of other Czechs—perhaps to Chicago, or maybe Seville.

Back at the Alcron I found Szulc in a chandeliered suite off the second-floor landing. Two other people, a man and a woman, were with him, and they were all hunched over a Grundig Oceanic shortwave radio, listening to what sounded like Radio Moscow's English-language service. I tapped on the open door. They motioned to enter but shushed me.

In a dull monotone, the Moscow reader reported solidarity with the Soviet Union by a Czech workers' committee from a Ceteka factory in the outskirts, which I knew as an arms exporter to North Vietnam. The reader praised the committee for courage in its struggle against "bourgeois parasitism." After the broadcast I introduced myself. Szulc nodded coolly. The man beside him wore a canny Good Soldier Schweik smile on his bony face and turned out to be the AP's Czech-born correspondent Peter Rehak. The other person was the *Times*'s straw-haired Czech interpreter Kitty Pavel.

Szulc said that other *Times* reporters, such as Henry Kamm and Tom Hamilton, had been in and out, and he wondered whether I'd find enough to keep me busy. His voice was deep, resonant, and nicotine-lubricated, and his face was a fusion of land masses. He didn't smile or appear welcoming, which made me uncomfortable. I filled him in on my plans for economic stories and indicated I wouldn't be in the city long. He crushed a cigarette, strode to his desk, and returned with a press release. A smile flashed across that continental divide. "Remember the Good Ship Lollipop?" he asked.

I was befuddled.

It turned out that the International Federation of Multiple Sclerosis Societies had put out something about trying to recruit Czechoslovakia as a member. Such efforts were under way at this very hotel, probably as we spoke, Szulc said. The smile broadened. The person in charge was Shirley

Temple Black, the former child star, now married, active in Republican politics and serving as the new federation secretary.

"Mrs. Black is floating around here somewhere if you want to interview her." He tried to sound helpful.

It wasn't a bad story, and both of us later saw Shirley Temple Black in the context of Americans caught by the invasion. But she was then of little interest. I said I had no desire to move in on movie columnist Louella Parsons's turf. Szulc and I later became good friends, but the subtext then was that he didn't relish my presence on his story and maybe his Pulitzer, and I needed to give him space—which was fine by me.

I excused myself, sent an arrival telex to the Foreign Desk, and tried firming up some appointments, but after more frustration I found the bar. Jean-Paul and Simone had long bid adieu, but it was filled with others of interest, including Alan Tillier of *Newsweek*, Friedl Ungerhauer of *Time*, Ken Ames of the *Economist*, who, as mentioned, later took his own life in Vienna. Everyone was at loose ends. Was that barber right? In the dining room, where Szulc found us, a chanteuse in stunning décolletage chanted from the Beatles. When she sang "Yellow Submarine," the more schnockered of us joined in, "We all live in a yellow submarine."

Later that night, back in our rooms, after the interminable invasion debate, there was an almost ethereal buzz, interrupted by the roar of a low-flying jet. The sounds emanated from the western outskirts of the city around Ruzyne Airport, where I'd landed not so many hours ago. It was the sound of Tupolev and Antonov troop transports. At 1:30 a.m. on Wednesday, August 21, Prague Radio made it official, with an announcement that detachments from the Soviet Union, East Germany, Bulgaria, Hungary, and Poland had crossed the frontier at several points. Planes, tanks, and half a million troops marked the end of the Prague Spring.

Szulc raced to his Chevy. A little earlier I'd gone to sleep—a terrible confession to make, given that this was one of the biggest stories of a lifetime. I had popped off, absolutely. To me that ethereal buzz was sleep-inducing, and Szulc had never tried to rouse me. With the AP's Rehak riding shotgun, he had driven across the Vltava to the Mala Strana district and the American embassy at 15 Trziste Street. Thanks to briefings from Ambassador Jake Beam and other diplomats, and their willingness to open communications facilities, Szulc and Rehak filed timely bulletins and stories. And the world woke up on August 21 to another outrage.

Washington was probably not too unhappy, however. The more details about this one, the better. The story took the heat away from Vietnam, where the Johnson administration was still trying to recover from the shock of the unanticipated Tet offensive. I took no part in any news activities that night. Szulc had all the space he needed.

There was one thing no one foresaw: the Soviets bisected the city, and not even Szulc's Chevy made it back to the levee. T-54 tanks and slightly newer T-55s, in use since World War II, blockaded the bridges. Since he couldn't return to Wenceslas, the city's vibrant heart, where Czechs had demonstrated for centuries, it fell upon me to do the reaction the following day. That disconcerting fit of sleep had, ironically, worked to my journalistic advantage.

And what a story! It had nothing to do with economics, but a lot to do with shoe leather—and the Czech people. Many moons later, I still see my life from the perspective of that longtime warp. My father shared part of it. I ended up staying days, then weeks, and finally almost three months. I learned Czech and fell in love with the country. Clifton Daniel told me later that the paper had made a joint Pulitzer submission of the work of Szulc, Kamm, and myself. We were runners-up that year to Bill Tuohy of the *Los Angeles Times*, whose file on Tet was the apple of the judges' eye. Kamm won a Pulitzer in 1978 on refugees from Indochina.

I woke early on August 21 and knew something was up when I ventured into the hallway to feel a deathly stillness, as if locked into a space-time discontinuity. I rushed to Szulc's suite, but no one was there. From the hallway, a distant female voice yelled, "Tanks outside!" Downstairs, a front-desk man, wearing a Dubcek pin, was in tears. Outside, on Wenceslas, near the sausage vendor (who was, incredibly, still doing a booming business), three tanks with red stars formed a perimeter behind sandbags. Other tanks rattled up and down the broad square along with armored personnel carriers and two-and-a-half-ton military trucks.

People stared in disbelief and anger. Graffiti demanded IVAN GO HOME. I walked up beyond the equestrian statue toward the National Museum, where youths had dug up cobblestones and were pelting the armored vehicles with the stones and flaming canisters of gasoline. More alarming was that the armored vehicles pelted back. There were hundreds of casualties, but no one ever counted how many. Watching televised accounts years later in Cairo's Tahrir Square and Kiev's Maidan Square brought it all back.

In the smaller side streets, Czech youths ran with the tanks. One tank did wheelies while a kid stuffed a pole with the Czech red, white, and blue tricolor flag into the cannon's mouth. By now I was with the crowd up from the square, around the Prague radio building on Vinohradska Street, just behind the National Museum. The Soviets were trying to take down the pro-Dubcek station. Dubcek masses defended the entrance with rocks, sticks, and their own bodies.

During the stalemate a T-55 rampaged on what was left of the street, its fenders smoking from gasoline-soaked rags, burning boxes, and other flammable debris. The wounded behemoth halted, blocked by the smoldering wreckage of an overturned trolley. A black-hooded tanker, a young scared Asian, lifted himself above the hatch and angrily swept off the debris. Youths shouted curses, and flung rocks and flaming bottles of gasoline. The tanker retreated inside and bolted the hatch. Suddenly his cannon fired off a round, pulverizing the flank of a building at point-blank range. The casualties were impossible to see beyond the rising plumes of smoke.

From one chewed-up side street a panel truck appeared, the only other moving vehicle. The tank's 50-caliber gun crackled. Glass shattered. The air was dense with smoke and diesel fumes. Some people tried to help the wounded men in the truck. Had I been closer, I might have applied a combat medic's experience. But two decades had passed, and at this point I could be doing more harm than good. Younger specialists saved me from hard choices. An ambulance shrieked into this war zone, and other hands lifted the bloody humans to care for them.

Layered with soot and grit, I found myself in the lee of a doorway near another American, A. R. McBirney, a geologist from the University of Oregon. "The last time I was here was 1946," he said. "I return to see this!" A student from Holland shook his head and declared, "The Russians can never win this." Maybe not. But their action in August 1968 further clamped the lid on an amazingly creative country for another two decades. That crackdown followed similar ruthlessness in Budapest in 1956 and East Berlin in 1953. No doubt, too, the Russians were lucky. Any organized resistance would have been their nightmare. The West's de facto recognition of Soviet hegemony ruled out a NATO response but not necessarily a low-intensity conflict.

Another green light for the invasion was the Vietnam War and the range of domestic US preoccupations, including antiwar and civil rights protests, the assassinations of Martin Luther King Jr. and Bobby Kennedy, and a presidential election in which the incumbent Lyndon Johnson chose not to run. The Russians might have expected trade or other embargoes, like the one that would be incurred after the Soviet Union invaded Afghanistan in December 1979. But here too they were lucky. Within a year Richard Nixon flew to Moscow to boost détente.

It may be foolhardy to compare Europe half a century ago with anything in today's world. Like fingerprints or snowflakes, times differ. Issues do, too. Islamic fascism is not communism. Yet regimes then and now use similar harsh measures to stay in power and subdue populations seeking freedom and opportunity. Extremism is not the answer; neither is the crushing of freedom.

The first day of the Soviet invasion of Prague I filed three stories, all telephoned to New York from *Times* bureaus in Europe. Because telex was undependable and the Internet was not yet invented, my copy moved by phone relays to New York. Foreign Editor Seymour Topping had all European bureaus call us periodically to relay copy. Warsaw had no trouble getting through. So most copy went through Warsaw Bureau Chief Jonathan Randal. I also took advantage of the magic fingers of David Binder, the bureau chief in Bonn. Slowly the phone connections improved, and the bureaus in London and Paris took over. Joe Frayman, Joe Collins, Jules Arbose, and Lou Spear facilitated from London, and Andreas Freund and Dennis Powell worked from Paris.

Late on day one, while I was writing my third story, my phone rang. The call was not from Warsaw or Bonn or even Paris or London: it was Szulc's voice from across the still-blockaded Vltava bridges. "Somebody here, who knows you well, desires a word!" he said. I blanked out, until hearing a familiar, nicotine-lubricated voice: "Hello, son! I hear you're doing economic stories!"

I must admit I hadn't even thought of *him*. But of course—Dubcekism and the Prague Spring were Dad's beat. I said that it was great to hear him and that I looked forward to seeing him and hearing of his adventures as soon as time permitted. Hesitantly, I added that I was still under intense filing pressure. He said he understood only too well, then asked if I could do him just one big favor.

"Of course." I swallowed hard. He had driven into town, had been at the wheel since 4:00 a.m. from Munich, where he was reporting Bavaria's economic revival, and was under filing pressure, too. The *Chicago Tribune* had nothing like the institutional support of the *New York Times*. He had material, and the embassy telex was backed up. Could I take his dictation and punch it through on the Alcron telex to Chicago? "Do this for the old man," he pleaded, "and he's in your debt forever."

The inability to communicate when you have something to say is classic horror for a news reporter. There was no question I had to do what I could. He dictated a piece about racing Russian tanks to Prague. I rushed downstairs to the telex and found it free. As I punched, I thought back to my youthful visits with Dad to the AP office at Rockefeller Center, and the magic of news on teleprinters, and I hoped that someone at the *Trib* would see his magic. Unfortunately, the line was severed three-quarters of the way through—yet enough got through to later earn him a "hero-gram." The story was played on page one with a route map, the final sentence broken off with an ellipsis. "At this point," an editor in Chicago wrote, "this dispatch was cut off."

The next day the bridges were still blocked, and the crowds were even larger but less truculent. Despite continued but more isolated violence, there was growing fatalism. In Wenceslas Square, the equestrian statue was now a resistance shrine, with beds of flowers and votive candles memorializing the many killed. Hundreds milled about. Red-starred jeeps and armored cars dispersed crowds elsewhere but left the people near the statue alone. The invasion was already going smoothly enough. Prague was not Stalingrad.

I wandered off, notebook in hand. Attracted by a gathering around an elderly woman and a Soviet officer, I stopped to listen. They seemed to be arguing, and the language was Russian, but the feel was Speakers' Corner. The older woman shook her finger at the officer, a major, evidently giving him a piece of her mind. As my Russian skills left much to be desired, a young woman beside me offered to interpret.

The older woman said, "We are Slavic people like you. Never have we taken any hostile acts against you. What possible justification can you have for treating our people in this manner?" The major said he was from Novgorod: "We are not invaders. We were invited by members of your central committee who felt they were no longer in a country of socialism. Our country was invaded a generation ago because we did not pay attention to the enemies of socialism. Never again will that be permitted to happen."

My interpreter, whose name was Helen, drew me aside to confirm that Vasil Bilak, Miroslav Kilder, and other conservatives on the central committee had sought the Russian intervention. "These men are traitors," she whispered. "They will do anything to improve their standing with the Russians. They don't care about Czechoslovakia."

A student at Charles University, she was seeking to brush up on English and interpreted for me the whole day. As we walked toward the river, she spoke of the passive resistance that was coming into play. "Czechs fight with their heads," she said. She described how youths had altered road signs to confuse the Russians and pointed to the proliferation of flyers and graffiti. One representation was a red serpent around a sausage-shaped Czechoslovakia.

We passed a Gypsy fiddler dressed in black who wandered around the Old Town Square playing within earshot of the Soviet tankers. He went from one mournful melody to the next yet never acknowledged his audience. People listened and left money. Dubcek was sympathetic to the Gypsies. For the first time they had recognition as a national identity. Hard-liners showed little sympathy for minorities. Against the chilling background of tanks and armored cars, that soulful music made my interpreter weep. One day later the fiddler vanished.

Helen also told me of the new clandestine station called Radio Free Czechoslovakia (RFC), with its mobile transmitters, that encourage passive resistance. Instead of using call letters, it identified itself with strains from Smetana's *Moldau*. At its suggestion, women seated at outdoor tables made red, white, and blue Czech lapel flags. RFC also encouraged the spray painting of red serpents with the logo IVAN GO HOME. Such messages proved so contagious that anyone seen just listening to a portable radio was subject to arrest.

Helen came from a family of liberal activists. Her father was a member of a group of political freethinkers seeking alternatives to the Communist Party. Her uncle fled after the 1948 coup that ended the Czech Republic and was shot and killed by border guards, like Alec Leamas in John le Carré's *The Spy Who Came In from the Cold*. That incident led to the family being blacklisted from decent jobs or an education. Her father, a physics professor at Charles University, worked as a janitor. She was a sales clerk; even though she more than met the entrance requirements, the university wouldn't accept her. Only after that spring did she matriculate.

I saw Helen on other occasions. Too young to know any other life but communism, she still had a great knowledge about the West and an even greater curiosity. She asked about President Johnson and the assassination of President Kennedy and his brother Bobby. She said she wanted to help me because "it is important for Americans to know what is really happening in our country."

She once asked if I was curious about more than Prague's downtown, and when I said yes, she invited me to her grandmother's house on the northern fringe of the city. It was at the end of three trolley lines and then a fifteen-minute walk. The street looked out across potato fields. As we approached the house, a neighbor's black police dog sniffed me, then snapped at my trouser leg. "Good communist dog," she said laughing. Luckily for me, its teeth tore only fabric. Helen shouted at the dog in a language it must have understood, because it fled. Grandma didn't seem any more pleased to see me than that dog. She was frightened. This was not a place that strangers visited, especially strangers from America. Neighbors might talk. She asked Helen whether anyone had seen us. As we sat in the small sitting room, she made painful small talk and did not even serve us tea. Helen said later that her grandmother thought I was a spy.

Sadly, I lost touch with Helen, except for one unforgettable moment two months later. I caught sight of her near the clock tower. Anxious to know how she and her family were doing, I rushed to her. She refused to recognize me. "How is your grandmother?" I asked, as we continued walking.

"Not very good," she replied.

I invited her for coffee.

She shook her head firmly. "I should not be seen with you," she said. "The writing is on the wall."

I owe her an enormous debt. In those frenetic days she interpreted not just words but events, and she tried to show me—and through me our readers—what life under communism was really like.

Within four days the tanks were withdrawn from the bridges, and Szulc and Rehak and Dad, after soup-kitchen meals and nights spent with blankets on the embassy floor, were back at the Alcron. But the Russians now imposed a curfew; anyone outside at night could be shot, and from what we knew it was no idle threat. The need to tap embassy sources meant that the *Times* had to be there full-time and sleep on the floor. I didn't mind. I was so gung ho I would have slept on Wenceslas's horse.

Soon after that switch, the embassy itself, a seventeenth-century Hapsburg palace with grand rooms on lush grounds, became the story. It was day five. Three Soviet soldiers with automatic weapons climbed a fence into a hilltop section of the compound five hundred meters (just under a mile) from the chancery, attracted by apple trees. They lounged on the grass, eating apples. Two unarmed Marine guards, one bearing the American flag, challenged the intruders, who refused to move. The better part of valor was to disengage. The Marines alerted political officer Mark Garrison. Unarmed as well, he marched uphill to warn the soldiers in Russian that they were not only trespassing on American property but "eating American apples." Within minutes, reluctantly yet peacefully, the soldiers left. The State Department later delivered a protest to the Soviet ambassador in Washington.

Other developments seemed more ominous. Two armored scout cars and a military truck posted a watch just outside the entrance to the embassy. A mounted 50-caliber machine gun pointed at the oversized oaken door. This time Ambassador Beam himself, also a Russian speaker and later the ambassador to Moscow, challenged them. They told Beam that their mission was to "maintain order." They stayed until dawn the next day. Beam later described the harassment as "haphazard and not part of any organized plan."

But the next incident seemed to take everything to a new level. It was early morning on August 26, and the night sky had been ablaze with luminous tracers. Suddenly the embassy roof caught fire. It developed during exchanges between Soviet tank machine gunners on the east bank of the Vltava and snipers from loose bands of Czech resisters west of the river in the hillside woods below Hradčany Castle, the presidential residence. The embassy officers were close-mouthed, but I was sure the Soviet gunners had precipitated the fire. The curfew kept Czech firemen from responding, and for all I knew it could have been the start of World War III. Using extinguishers, hoses, and axes, the Marines, embassy staff, and a handful of others in residence, myself included, brought the fire under control. Centuries-old timbers had burned through, leaving the attic a charred waste, and the floor beneath, with its top-secret communications sphere, was badly damaged. The acoustically sealed Plexiglas bubble was mounted on cinder blocks to foreclose eavesdropping. Inside were a desk, chairs, and telephones for supersecret palaver.

World War III it was not, but rather a result of the nonstop burning of secret papers—a normal precaution in emergencies. The furnace had simply overheated. The damage was substantial, and a Red Army chopper gaped and gawked next morning from every conceivable angle, Ivan and Leonid presumably enjoying a good laugh.

My father reinstalled himself in the Alcron with the tools of his trade, including his own Grundig Oceanic shortwave radio for keeping up with events and a telex keyboard used as a typewriter. On competitive stories he punched the tape himself, and when possible he fed it into a post office telex, saving time and fees.

Other Prague-beat regulars filtered back as well, and the return was like a class reunion. Some were old friends from their days in Bonn, Vienna, and even the Far East. They included Osgood Caruthers, the urbane *Los Angeles Times* central European correspondent, formerly with the *New York Times*, AP, and the United Nations; Russ Jones of NBC, formerly of UP, who had won a Pulitzer for his reports on the Hungarian uprising in 1956; Russ Braley, a wartime naval officer and longtime foreign correspondent of the *New York Daily News*; and George Vine of London's *Daily Mail*, whom Dad had rescued in Shanghai in 1949. They all knew the Schottenring Café and Dolly and had shared the *gemutlichkeit* (cordiality) of Hohenstaufengasse. Vine, square-jawed and doughty, pulled me aside over a Pils one evening to tell me what a great man my father was. "So many newsmen these days are merely technocrats, but Clyde—he's a humanist. You can tell a man by his friends, and your Dad has friends who adore him."

It was from Vine that I first heard about the life-saving intervention in Shanghai. "You surely know the story?" he asked. I shook my head. It was the first I'd heard of it. Vine gave me a quick summary of how he and Graham Jenkins had been snatched to safety from the murderous Colonel Yeh. "Ask your Dad about it sometime," Vine said. Later I did. Dad guessed the reason he hadn't told me was that I'd never asked, and he was happy to relate it amid dramatic flourishes, such as dropping to his knees to describe his kowtow to the dreaded Colonel Yeh.

Dad left Prague in mid-September 1968. I stayed until mid-November, when my visa was pulled. I next saw him in West Berlin on the way back to Brussels, catching him at the Zellermayer, a boutique hotel near the Kurfuerstendam, and he bought me dinner at what was then the city's best eatery, known simply as the French Club, part of the French diplomatic complex.

This time I needed his advice, not about anything professional but about a wrenching problem of the heart. I'd developed an attachment to an American a freelance journalist, whom I will call Susan, who worked in Prague., who worked in Prague as a film writer. After the Prague Spring, the *Times* hired her to answer the phone and write occasional cultural stories. Because of intimate working conditions and not a little chemistry, the professional relationship, especially after the invasion, turned emotional. She had taken a room some blocks from the Alcron. Since we worked late, frequently past midnight, Szulc insisted someone walk her home, a task that usually fell to me and to which I had no objections. But the curfew made it dicey. The Russians were shooting violators, which obliged us to watch for the ever circulating armored vehicles. At first it was wildly exciting, keeping to the shadows and pretending to be spies, in the cold, in German-occupied Paris. Eventually it made sense to stop the games. Instead of dashing to her rented room blocks away, we slunk up a flight of stairs in the Alcon to mine.

I learned that she was an army brat from New Orleans, the daughter of a retired colonel in the engineers, and that she was traveling on a generous grant from her grandmother. But her world tour was different from most. Rather than traveling like a whirlwind through a lot of places, she spent a long time in a few places that she got to know well. Before Prague she was in Florence. She traveled with a steamer trunk packed with clothes and the memorabilia of a girlhood in the Philippines and Frankfurt.

That Susan and I seemed to be together much of the time was accepted as part of the environment. No one questioned it or made any comments. I may be deluding myself, but I believe that the only people who suspected the emotional link were Dad, with his bountiful personal experience, and Szulc's perceptive wife, Marianne, who had also joined the bureau from Vienna. I couldn't help thinking of the parallels. Prague seemed to be the other side of the moon from Brussels, just as China must have seemed distant from Mount Vernon. Because of the intensity of the moment, Susan and I rarely discussed the future. I'm sure that Dad and Dolly, at least initially, never did, either.

Susan took me to the airport, and we had a tearful farewell. She stayed a little longer in Prague and later returned to the United States. Upon my arrival in Berlin, I was in knots; I had to confide in someone, and Dad heard me out. The wheel had turned full circle. A son who had reviled his father for an extramarital affair was now confessing his own—and seeking that dad's advice. While Mom was still alive, such infidelity would have been impossible. But eight months had elapsed since her death from colon cancer, and the world was different, or at least I was.

Our dinner brought us close. While acknowledging that he'd guessed about Susan and me, Dad seemed truly moved by my story. When I described tears streaming down Susan's cheeks, he observed knowingly, "It's the woman who always suffers most." He had no particular advice, only a warning to be aware of possible adverse career implications. For the first time, he told me of Kent Cooper's interference in his private life in Delhi.

As for my own life, I decided on the path of least resistance, which meant returning to Brussels and resuming life as a correspondent of the *Times*. Although Dad was my role model, the Prague circumstances weren't the same as China's. This was not wartime. Susan was not dependent on me the way Dolly was on him. After some conventional reporting—for example, on the ways Berliners were dealing economically with their divided city—I returned to Brussels and found I was happy to be back. The kids and Barbara welcomed me. So did my acquaintances, who extended a hero's welcome. I was an honored guest at any number of parties. People I hardly knew told me what a great job the *Times* had done in Prague. Many times the joke was replayed about my good Kremlin sources. It was heady.

As for Barbara, she was, as always, cheerful and good-natured. She pressed me on nothing and professed to be happy with the gift of crystal, and we resumed where we left off. Both Andrew and Alex had grown and were now bilingual in English and French, even spouting Flemish (old Dutch), which half of Belgium spoke. If nothing else, the boys could always find jobs as concierges.

28

Is Paris Worth a Jag?

SOON AFTER I was in Prague, the *New York Times* played musical chairs with its European bureaus. Drew Middleton, who had covered D-Day and early postwar Britain, landed a position in Brussels as the military correspondent focusing on NATO. I drew Paris. Like 90 percent of the reporters I knew, I'd always dreamed of working there. My only one regret was the loss of a magnificent *New York Times* car: not the shabby Ford Zodiac I inherited from my predecessor Ed Cowan, but a new beige 2.8-liter Jaguar that publisher Arthur Ochs Sulzberger had authorized, which would have put even the Szulc Chevy to shame. I broached the subject with Drew, offering to take the car off his hands. Drew reminisced about visiting a Jaguar plant while he was bureau chief in London, and I knew I'd never get that car back.

Sulzberger, nicknamed Punch after a puppet character (as in Punch and Judy), believed it was important for bureaus to burnish their image. In the late 1960s, the *Times* was seeing better days, and Punch, though sensitive to bottom lines, saw penny-pinching as false economy. It was during a visit by Punch and his wife, Carol, that the car issue had come up. I had used that old Zodiac to chauffeur them around. Carol, a refreshingly direct person, drew me aside. "Punch wants you to buy a new car," she confided, "and he wants it to be a good car."

Since this was an order from Olympus, I had happily chosen a Jaguar Mark II powered by the workhorse XK twincam six engine. Why not? It was a "good" car, and not all that expensive. Belgium, it turned out, was *the* place to buy new cars because of all sorts of tax advantages. I submitted the paperwork to New York, ready to quote Carol Fox Sulzberger if challenged. Extras included whitewall tires and a fabulous radio. The only flak was over reclining seats, which the accounting department refused to approve. I didn't quibble.

Now I was unhappy to give that car up, but I didn't cry too much. If Paris was worth a Mass to Henry IV, it was probably worth the loss of a Jag. Although I had often commuted to Paris, the idea of living in the City of Light was a Powerball jackpot. A decade earlier, in 1959, still with UPI, I had tried to wangle Paris. Barbara and I took a holiday there. My ulterior purpose was to see if UPI might be hunting a French-speaking hand. I would have swept floors or emptied trash.

I wandered the boulevards hunting the UPI office, which I discovered was down a cul-de-sac and up steep Jean Valjean stone steps. There was no receptionist. The fellow there, Arthur Higbee, seemed hungry and looked lean as a stick as he rattled short bursts from his Underwood typewriter. He looked up but didn't smile. He just nodded in response to my query—sure, we'd stay in touch.

France triggered memories about my mother and stories about her family. In 1916, at Verdun in eastern France, there were nearly three quarters of a million French and German dead and wounded. Mom's two brothers, Henri and Paul Herailh, were survivors of chlorine gas attacks. In the 1930s, when I was two or three, I walked with my mother down the same boulevards as she dropped coins into the tin cup of a one-legged veteran of Verdun selling pencils. In the late 1940s, I was again with my mother as well as Frank and Sue; we were dining out with my cousin Françoise and her husband, Paul, in a restaurant called La Grenouille (the Frog). Paul, after having too much to drink, made doughy pellets from leftover bread, which he tossed at fellow diners. They reciprocated the volleys, amid peals of laughter.

Now, in 1969, I was part of the *Times* bureau on Rue Caumartin, not far from the opera house. (We later moved a few blocks to Rue Scribe, and later still to Avenue Charles de Gaulle, Neuilly, now the seat of the paper's global edition.) The office, I discovered, was a home away from home for the luminaries of the day. James Jones was still trying to match the phenomenonal success of *From Here to Eternity*. A stout fellow with a Captain Marvel chin, he seemed sad, or maybe just pensive. He was between books, discussing a project for the *New York Times* magazine with Josette Lazar, the Rumanian-born representative of the Sunday Department. James Baldwin, Mary McCarthy, Janet Flanner, Henri Cartier-Bresson and his wife, a photographer in her own right, Martine Franck, were also in and out. Martine and I worked together. As I interviewed farmers about common agricultural prices, she caught their gestures, such as scratching a bulbous nose, in edgy news shots.

I reminded Baldwin that we had met a few years ago during his celebrated victory over Bill Buckley. Baldwin said he had never forgotten, and we smiled at wisps of memory. *Times* luminaries Harrison Salisbury, James Reston, A. M. Rosenthal, Max Frankel, and Arthur Gelb were also in and out. Often the visits corresponded with the pilgrimage of publisher Sulzberger, whose arrival usually signaled a party at the Meurice, to which all of Paris was invited. At one gathering I introduced Salisbury to Mary McCarthy, the satirical novelist who was married to Jim West, an American diplomat. Harrison and Mary stuck together that evening like Siamese twins, or a heavenly ganache.

Once the publisher's mother, Iphigene Ochs Sulzberger, a sprightly octogenarian, stopped off on her return from China and took everyone in the bureau to lunch at Le Verre Galant (the Valiant Nip) overlooking Île Saint-Louis. We were all amused by the affection she expressed for Chou En-lai, the Chinese premier and longtime foreign minister, who had been her guide through much of the trip. She'd been "swept off her feet" by Chou, she said, adding, "What an adorable man!" Had Dad been there, I'm sure he would have murmured something like, "Ah, crafty Chou, up again to his old tricks!" I told her about Chou buttering up American journalists in wartime Chungking and cited Dad's description of him as a propagandist who had done more than anyone for the cause abroad. She seemed bemused and amused.

Barbara and the kids and I rented an apartment near the Bois de Boulogne as I took up the métier of European economics correspondent, replacing the grizzled and gently sardonic Dick Mooney, who returned to New York to become deputy foreign editor. The late 1960s and early 1970s were tumultuous, not unlike the earlier years of the current century that culminated in the crash of 2008. Because of the war in Vietnam, the monetary system of fixed exchange rates was disintegrating. The war was so unpopular that taxes couldn't be raised to pay for it. As deficits and inflation ballooned, the resulting piles of surplus dollars forced the United States to stop swapping them for gold in Fort Knox, which had been a key element of the former fixed-rate system.

Even more disconcerting were increases in the price of oil, which doubled, then doubled again, caused by turmoil in the Middle East and an Arab oil embargo in the early 1970s. With fuel shortages and people whacking each other in gas lines, things didn't look good anywhere. Yet from that disarray a new system was emerging. The world moved from a fixed to a floating exchange rate: the dollar would fluctuate like other currencies, and gold, no longer at the center of the system, was left to find its own price level. The new rules meant fewer rules, managed loosely by such bodies as the International Monetary Fund and the Organization for Economic Cooperation and Development (OECD).

We lived on rue Eugene Labiche, named after a nineteenth-century master of farce whose plays are still popular. We were around the corner from headquarters of the OECD, which, while helping to manage the new order, sometimes saw ribaldry develop at its meetings that would have done the old master proud. There was Dutch Foreign Minister Jo Luns, six foot six, shoeless in fire-engine red socks, spreading alarms about the latest financial crisis; international staff official Harry Travers, a Briton we nicknamed "Harry the Leak," feeding journalists secret memoranda expressly to embarrass France; and an aide to French Finance Minister Francois-Xavier Ortoli, retaliating with other documents pointing to the perfidy of *les Amerloques* ("Yanks"). Talking heads had mouths to feed, spurring a periodic exodus to the many fine local eateries, but our sources were only as good as the escargots or flan. As Labiche himself had once said, "To write a sprightly play you must have good digestion. Sprightliness resides in the stomach."

The main issue we dealt with was the price of gold. The French wanted it well above the then official $35 an ounce. They accused Americans of using cheap gold to gain unfair economic and commercial advantages, especially in acquiring European business. At a meeting in Copenhagen in June 1969, nerves got so frayed that then Treasury Under Secretary Paul A. Volcker, later the chairman of the Federal Reserve, had to let off steam. Several reporters tagged along as he rushed from a contentious high-level meeting that had just ended into the adjacent Tivoli Gardens. A towering inferno, as tall as Jo Luns, he strode past the Himmelskibet carousel, the Daemonen roller coaster, and the Valhalla Borgen swing. His eyes were focused on a concession at the far end of that park, where he finally let off steam by tossing hard wooden balls at crockery.

The dollar continued weakening, depressed by what seemed then like an unquenchable demand for gold. Yet to average people, it all seemed so unreal, so far removed from their everyday lives, and we reporters were challenged to report it in more meaningful ways. "Monetary shmonetary," snapped Dennis Duggan, a columnist for *Newsday*, as we sat in the Lion's Head in Greenwich Village during my home leave in 1972. We had worked together at the *New York Herald Tribune*. I tried to explain how the turbulence affected everyone, but I couldn't do so concretely enough to satisfy him. I used a lot of big words to try to convince him of the importance of a smoothly functioning monetary system.

He heard me out before we switched to more comely subjects. He introduced me to Shirley MacLaine, who dropped by with Pete Hamill, a columnist for the *New York Post*. From the dollar's gyrations, talk turned to the more provocative whirls and whorls of Linda Lovelace, whose film *Deep Throat* was a Main Street sensation. Shirley found the "love button" gist of the film "amusing."

We had a lot of laughs that evening, even as we returned to the eight-hundred-pound gorilla. I warned that a broken monetary system with accompanying spikes in gold and oil squeezed pocketbooks, threatening greater unemployment and greater misery. Shirley listened more closely than the others, perhaps finding confirmation of her own views that all was not great in Nixon's America and that his Democratic rival George McGovern should have won.

In this new century, the situation seems eerily familiar. Again we have been fighting wars we were loath to pay for, with politicians making promises they couldn't keep. Discourse has been iniquitous, stinging, and mean. With greater ease in communications and financial transactions, a sneeze anywhere could lead to pneumonia—demonstrated, for instance, by precarious mortgage meltdowns or rogue trading at banks. Yet having lived through the Depression, two world wars, and a lot of smaller ones, I still tend to see the sunny side up.

To convey economic news authentically, you needed more than telephone interviews or superficial rewrites of the wire stories. Nothing substituted for face-to-face interviews and the real feel for wherever the news was made. One day, emulating Harry Houdini, I touched down in three cities on the same day to file three separate stories: Frankfurt, on the hard line being taken by the Germans against the dollar; Turin, for a rare interview with Gianni Agnelli, the imperial head of Fiat, then Europe's biggest automaker; and Vienna, for an analytical piece on East-West trade. All made the paper the same day, a kind of three-card monte.

Basel, Zurich, and Geneva were among my other ports of call. I knew train and flight schedules by heart, or I rented a car to zoom the few hours by road to most cities. Basel, where the storied Rhine begins its four-hundred-mile trek to the North Sea, was the site of monthly gatherings of central bankers at the Bank for International Settlements (BIS), another one of the alphabet soup of agencies fostering cooperation while assuring high-on-the-hog living for a privileged staff.

Besides the pressure on gold and the dollar, there was rampant speculation over the French franc and the German mark. The Germans had taken pride in policies that curbed inflation, with the mark reacting by bumping the upper limits of its fixed parities. The French were less successful on the inflation front, and so the franc flipped below. During the late 1960s France and Germany argued viscerally over currencies, and it was precisely to avoid such increasingly serious spats that by the turn of the century the Europeans finally agreed on a single currency, the euro, eventually adopted by nineteen of the twenty-eight countries of the European Community.

The collapse of a conference in Bonn in November 1968, which triggered explosive national rivalries, did more than anything to hasten the euro's birth. Germany agreed to increase the value of the mark, and France agreed to devalue the franc. Bernard Clappier, the deputy governor of the Banque de France, disclosed to the press the precise amounts. But no one had given much thought to the elderly president of France; after seeing the devaluation reported in the press, including in early editions of the *New York Times*, Charles de Gaulle countermanded, telling the French people by radio and TV that the franc would hold.

Soon afterward he resigned. He staked his reputation on a referendum that he lost, and his political strength had been undermined by social unrest, sparked by the student riots of May and June 1968. Yet a devaluation had been necessary and was finally carried out by his successor, Georges Pompidou, in August 1969. Within two months, Bonn increased the value of the mark.

As I tried to make sense of it all, my worst moments were at that Bonn conference of November 1968. De Gaulle's functionaries had worked out the numbers but had not explained them well enough to the aging leader, who then saw a breathtaking undercutting of *la gloire* (glory). If de Gaulle was challenged by the developments, so too was yours truly, who had to explain to Managing Editor Abe Rosenthal why our readers were misled.

Abe came up through the ranks of the *Times*; he worshipped the institution. In his view it never made mistakes, at least not lightly. My explanation about the overriding of functionaries by the president of France sounded lame. We shouldn't write as facts what we don't know, he lectured. My story had precise numbers on a devaluation that hadn't materialized. I said the whole press corps erred, which didn't sit well. He insisted that

I explain, in gory detail for later editions, why I erred—in other words, chapter and verse of premature devaluation and official recantation—and opine for our readers what it all meant. It was not a bad idea for recovery, but it gave me my roughest moments on the paper. I expected banishment to a barren St. Helena—such as shipping news, to record maritime arrivals and departures. As it happened, I must have done something right. I stuck around Paris another decade.

The seemingly endless market turmoil led almost everyone to realize the imperatives of a less rigid system of exchange rates. But more time was needed for a consensus to solidify. Then on November 9, 1970, everything stopped in France, comparable to the day of the Churchill funeral in Britain five years earlier. DeGaulle died thirteen days before his eightieth birthday. Though fiercely proud in life, he, unlike Churchill, said he wanted no state funeral—which then his spirit may have been happy to see honored in the breach. The main ceremony was a Mass at Notre Dame Cathedral. Bach's *Magnificat* closed the service, just as it had after de Gaulle's triumphal return to Paris in 1945.

Yet even more dramatic was the sudden transformation of the Champs Elysees: all vehicular traffic was banned. I watched as thousands of men and women, old comrades from the war, younger Gaullists, from all walks of life, in funereal black, assembled at the Franklin D. Roosevelt metro station along the full width of the Champs. As they emerged, most wore the Cross of Lorraine, the heraldic symbol of old France that he had infused with new life as the wartime sign of a free France. Human waves rolled along the Champs to the Tomb of the Unknown Soldier, and all that could be heard was the rhythmic shuffling of shoes on cobblestones. After the mourners laid wreaths at the tomb, they quietly dispersed toward the bistros and cafés of what is now Avenue Charles de Gaulle. As during the tolling of Big Ben, when jibs of those gantry cranes over the Thames bowed in silent genuflection to Churchill, it was impossible not to shed a tear as the entire Champs mourned a hero of France.

I had met him three years earlier at a tenth birthday party in Rome for the Treaty of Rome, which created the European Community. He was in a receiving line of dignitaries. Barbara was with me, and we eagerly waited to shake his hand. Though surely exhausted, he wore a practiced diplomatic smile. I then stood six foot one, and it struck me as I drew closer that I stood taller than this storied general, whose height was legendary. But de Gaulle had shrunk in old age, as, sad to say, we all do.

29

Shivaree

MY FIRST INKLING that mismatched exchange rates could blow up the European Community came on a tranquil Sunday in mid-November 1968, the week before the botched Bonn conference. I was with other economic reporters, including George Williamson of *Business Week* and Paul Lewis of the *Financial Times* (and later the *New York Times*), outside a private dining room of the Hotel Euler by the railroad station in Basel. Central bank governors were inside at their regular monthly luncheon meeting.

Karl Blessing, the rotund, usually jovial president of the Bundesbank, was the first out. It had gone badly, we knew, because he was a raging bull. "I have absolutely nothing to say," he said hotly. Under his breath he muttered, "We risk bad markets tomorrow." Others scurried away mum, one central banker so anxious to avoid the media that he almost got run over by a trolley.

I called a source at home: Paul Erdman, an American banker in Switzerland, who prided himself on always being in the know. I hit pay dirt. He told of acrimonious exchanges between the French and German bank governors. "People are trying to keep the cat in the bag," said Erdman, who knew the Swiss bankers in the room, and upon my call he had every intention of letting that cat out.

The unusual blow-up started when the sedate, demure governor of the Banque de France, Jacques Brunet, stepped out of character by lecturing Blessing on what the Frenchman called the "unfortunate consequences" of German monetary policy. Bonn's insistence on maintaining an undervalued currency was damaging the economies of its partners in Europe, the usually placid Frenchman said, and the Germans had the obligation to correct "fundamental disequilibrium." Blessing shot back that the franc, not the mark, was behind the monetary disorder and that France had the obligation to correct the fundamental disequilibrium by devaluing the franc. Both men were dutiful civil servants and had known each other for years.

For them to speak out so contentiously was unheard of, at least in the recent past. No territorial disputes unleashed armies, as at Verdun or Ypres. Yet those clashing currencies riled up passions in ways unseen in decades.

Erdman turned out to be an interesting fellow in his own right. He later gained fame as the author of such financial thrillers as *The Billion Dollar Sure Thing* and *The Silver Bears*, the latter made into a film starring Michael Caine. But up to then his main achievement was starting a Swiss private bank, no mean achievement for an American. His doctorate in economics from Basel University, marriage to a Basel native, and mastery of Switzerdeutsch (a Swiss-German dialect), gave him a leg up. His Salik Bank, named with the Arabic word for embarkation on a spiritual journey, operated from a three-story chalet a short walk from the rail station. His top-floor aerie, up a spiral staircase, was usually the first port of call in my regular rounds.

Erdman, an intelligent, highly opinionated fellow, spoke freely and glibly on practically any subject. He also cut a dashing figure, always dressed in a modish three-piece suit; yet I recall wondering why someone so well-read and not at all financially deprived seemed so wary of orthodontists. His lips coiled in a permanent smirk, the result of a condition known as delacerated incisors. Subliminally, perhaps I feared a Draculan lunge at the neck. When I first met him, I thought that if he weren't a vampire, he would be my favorite gnome. His contacts ran deep in government economic and monetary bureaucracies and the financial levels of large corporations. "If anything is happening anywhere involving money," he said, "we're first to know." I learned of him through Erich Heinemann, the *Times* banking reporter and later a much-cited economist and critic of the Federal Reserve. Erich told me that Erdman made bundles betting against the British pound, which positioned him to buy the bank.

Erdman was an unreconstructed gold bug. "Gold keeps politicians honest," he told me. "Otherwise governments do only what they do best, which is lie, feather their bureaucratic nests, and devalue our money." American officials seemed determined to hold the official price at $35 an ounce. I told him what a senior Treasury Department official had just told me: gold, used for things like filling teeth and making jewelry, was worth no more than $22. "The more they talk like that, the more I buy," Erdman said, flashing those incisors. Today gold is worth more than $1,000 an ounce.

Erdman was in the tradition of John Maynard Keynes, whose speculation in early twentieth-century Britain supported a life of leisure—and time to write elegantly constructed economic theories. But Erdman shared another tradition, marked more by Jim Fisk and Jay Gould, manipulators of markets in nineteenth-century America. Emboldened by his success with the pound and gold, he tried to make a killing in cocoa. Not even traders for Nestlé make killings in cocoa.

For its own account and the accounts of its clients, Salik bought enough futures contracts to try to corner the cocoa market. If Erdman could squeeze shorts by forcing them to pay what he chose to close contracts, he'd reap billions. Yet for such an undertaking he had to borrow heavily. He counted on repaying from the profits he seemed sure to make. According to the postmortems, Salik at one point controlled 40 percent of the global supplies of cocoa.

Then, as happens so often with sure things, came the unpredictable. Ghana had an unanticipated bumper crop. There was a run on both cocoa and the bank. Erdman was left holding the bag. The losses were made up by the United Bank of California, which had made an offer to acquire Salik before the scandal broke, and it stuck by it. But because of a stain on the escutcheon of Swiss banking, the authorities came down hard on Erdman, who was summarily jailed. The Swiss hewed to a Napoleonic code: guilt is presumed until innocence is proved.

Swiss jails weren't the worst: the food not at all bad, and those with money can hustle vintage wine. Instead of sneaking in a file to bust out with, a buddy brought him an Olivetti, and he started writing. A claret, shared with an inmate who was a French safecracker, yielded professional expertise, which was incorporated into *The Billion Dollar Sure Thing*. After eight months Erdman posted bail of $133,000 and promptly fled. In 1973 a Swiss court sentenced him to eight years. But those eight years—and the rest of his life—were spent in California, near Sonoma, writing a series of popular thrillers, pontificating on the global economy, or holding forth on pro football, after making, as he once put it, a "successful career change."

Other prestidigitation gave Switzerland more unwanted headlines with the fall of a mutual fund empire run by Bernie Cornfeld, a gremlin-eyed extrovert with a wispy beard. Similarities existed with another Bernie: Madoff. Both started off legitimately, then diversified into Ponzi schemes that landed them behind bars after their clients lost pots of money. Eleven years older than Madoff, Cornfeld grew up in Istanbul and Brooklyn. His father, a Romanian Jewish actor, died soon after settling the family in America. The young Cornfeld, a Coney Island pitchman, later hawked mutual funds, broadening to tap into the steady paychecks of American soldiers in Europe. Moving to Paris, he started Investors Overseas Services (IOS) to promote GI capitalism.

Cornfeld mastered the legalities of holding his assets beyond the reach of national tax collectors. The main business was always somewhere else. Good market picks and a zero take by governments turned IOS vehicles into big winners, and the client list grew. Payoffs guaranteed that probes came to naught. To make things even more tax-proof, he moved to Geneva, the birthplace of John Calvin, who preached that riches are a sign of God's favor. Placating France for lost jobs, he built special offices in Ferney-Voltaire, in Geneva's French suburbs, and hired French citizens. But the key planning remained in Geneva.

Selling mutual funds to GIs was good business, but not great. Financial security wasn't high among their wants or needs. Few knew or cared what the funds were, and the sums were small. But with a new vehicle, effusively named the Fund of Funds, Cornfeld diversified into the far more lucrative domain of flight capital from the many countries around the world that were mismanaging their economies. Not just Europe, but the world, was his oyster. IOS salespeople, as many as 25,000 at the peak, found enthusiastic customers in cattle barons in Argentina, drug lords in Mexico, and dictators in Africa—anyone with money, legally or illegally obtained. He worked best wherever controls kept people from expatriating their wealth. Governments didn't much like it, but though huffing and puffing, did little to stop it. Besides greasing palms, he knew a thousand and one other ways to get funds out of even the most restrictive environment, always playing on the impulse of greed.

As money poured into Geneva, Cornfeld became an emperor of world finance, written up in *Fortune* and *Business Week,* pandered to for the business he brought to Wall Street. As so much flight capital was going into dollar securities, the crimson-spangled banner of IOS was even credited with redressing deficits in the US balance of payments and bringing discipline to world finance. If governments didn't shape up, it was said, IOS would ship out their capital.

The story followed the lines of classical hubris and fall. As the principal believer in his own myth, Cornfeld cultivated an imperial lifestyle. His assets included two private jets, a town house in London, an apartment in Manhattan, a villa in Geneva, a chateau in France, and chalet in Gstaad (Switzerland). He ate lunch with Tony Curtis and Hugh Hefner, surrounded himself with starlets, hosted lavish parties, and even retained an "orgy master" when things got dull. Although he lived in several places, it all seemed to come together in Geneva, where the scent of gold was not only in musty vaults but also in opulent restaurants, sumptuous hotels, lakeside villas, in the Guccis and Puccis and dazzling displays of jewels, and in Ferraris and Aston Martins. Everything was protected by the police, who cracked down hard on petty crime but looked away from multimillion-dollar swindles.

And a multimillion-dollar swindle is exactly what IOS became. Everything was fine while the markets were rising, because cracks could be patched over. But in the summer of 1970 the markets tanked, and for the first time, the redemptions of the Fund of Funds and other IOS mutual funds outpaced new sales. As IOS sank, reporters were all over the place trying to figure out what happened to all that money.

Many of those associated with Cornfeld had sticky fingers, which raised another problem: IOS lacked the internal controls to police itself. But thanks to Cornfeld's mastery of public relations, it was a while before any of this became apparent. He shamelessly seduced members of the press and other notables. He retained, as consultants, Clay Felker, a former editor of the *New York Herald Tribune* Sunday magazine and the founder of *New York* magazine; Harold Kaplan, a former deputy assistant secretary of state for public affairs and one of the defenders of the United States in Vietnam; Sir Eric Wyndham White, a harrumphing Briton who had headed the organization that oversees the General Agreement on Tariffs and Trade, which manages the global trading system; and James Roosevelt, the oldest son of Franklin and Eleanor Roosevelt, who left the American delegation to the United Nations to join IOS as a troubleshooter. Even Adlai Stevenson, the twice-defeated presidential candidate, thought of linking up. Roosevelt said that Cornfeld showed him a letter from Stevenson expressing readiness to join the board. Other consultants sought out by Cornfeld were Erich Mende, a former vice chancellor of West Germany, and Sweden's Count Carl Johan Bernadotte, the great-grandson of Queen Victoria.

Reporters, as usual, were on the outside looking in, but despite all those prestigious names, it didn't smell good to a bunch of us, including Bill Ellington of AP-Dow Jones, George Williamson of *Business Week*, and Frank Vogl, a Frankfurt-based correspondent for the *Times* of London. A common refrain was "the numbers don't add up." But in the absence of hard facts, we were wary; we had to think about the jobs that could be lost if this leviathan sank—and also about getting sued.

One evening I chanced a personal call to Cornfeld himself. He'd been impossible to reach during the day, but like the Phantom of the Opera, he loved the music of the night, and I got through to his villa. I said I was with the three above-mentioned journalists and we had questions about his operation. I expected an imperial brush-off. Instead he amiably invited us over to chat.

His lakeside chateau, the Villa Elma, was built by the great Napoleon himself for Josephine. Cornfeld acquired it from the Colgate family. Our taxi deposited us before the imperial front door, and a liveried servant brought us into the salon, where Cornfeld stood behind a bar and took orders for drinks. He wore a saffron robe secured with a yellow sash, suggestive of Buddhist leanings.

A teetotaler, he occupied himself licking a giant lollipop shaped like the Eiffel Tower. After each lick, he reinserted the lollipop into its cellophane wrapper. Perhaps a trope from Andy Warhol, it added a surreal quality to the music of the night. Guests that evening included a couple at the bar whom no one introduced: a striking blonde and an older fellow, both in Guccis and Puccis. We learned that he was a portfolio manager from New York and that she was "a friend." Other women came and went, not necessarily talking of Michelangelo, and it soon became clear that we were invited not to be handed any scoops but to be sounded out ourselves on what we knew. Cornfeld had made us the subjects of our own interview. We asked him to reconcile the inconsistencies in the IOS numbers. But Cornfeld absolutely refused to be drawn out. Every question met a question. "And what do you think?" he'd ask, or "If that were the case, what would it mean?"

We tried to be polite. We were enjoying his hospitality, drinking his whiskey, and eyeing the gorgeous women. Bill said later he felt like accusing Cornfeld of being one of the world's great swindlers, in the same league as Jim Fisk, Jay Gould, and even Charles Ponzi himself. But staying within the bounds of cordial discourse, we decided that unless we wanted an orgy, it was best to leave.

When the books of IOS were finally audited in the postcollapse official investigation, a lot of other people's money could not be accounted for. Although Cornfeld maintained that he stole nothing, he, like Erdman, served time in a Swiss jail and later also settled in California. The real villain was Robert Vesco, a New Jersey financier whom Cornfeld brought in to rescue the company but who looted it instead. Vesco socked away $200 million into untraceable offshore accounts. Fleeing the United States, he turned up in, among other places, Costa Rica and Cuba. After decades on the lam, he died in Cuba in 2007.

* * * * *

As the press plumbed the skulduggery in Geneva, incredible developments made other news in Vienna. It was 1975. Besides an Iron Curtain listening post, the city of the Hapsburgs was now the European capital of the Organization of the Petroleum Exporting Countries (OPEC) and the site of negotiations on future levels of world oil prices.

Four days before Christmas and all through the house, all creatures were relaxed, including reporters and cops. As we waited to pump sources, half a dozen men entered the lobby and made their way around brightly decorated trees. Wearing overcoats and toting sports bags, they were readily assumed to be part of the oil countries' delegations.

A tall, baby-faced fellow with a Hispanic accent politely asked where the meeting was. A colleague said "upstairs," pointing to a fire-door staircase to the second floor. The party swiftly made its way up. Seconds later we heard gunfire, and the world woke up to what, before 9/11, was perhaps the most brazen of all terrorist capers: the kidnapping of the world's oil ministers. The terrorist leader was Venezuela-born Carlos the Jackal, who was wanted for terrorist strikes all over Europe and was later romanticized in films. In the ensuing firefight, an Iraqi security official, an Austrian police detective, and a member of the Libyan OPEC delegation were killed.

To avoid the threatened execution of one hostage every fifteen minutes, the Austrian government agreed to broadcast a statement on state television every two hours about the justice of the Palestinian cause and offered transport so that Team Carlos and his forty-two hostages from a dozen countries could exit from Schwechat Airport, destination Tripoli. After large sums changed hands, all hostages were freed, unharmed. Some capers later, Carlos was caught and locked away in eastern France. Needless to say, OPEC beefed up its security.

30

When the Music Stops

IF VIENNA OFFERED journalistic fodder, it was also a chance to see Dad, who badly needed shoring up. While my fortunes were rising, his were in the dumps. The *Chicago Tribune* had terminated him. His only compensation was the title to that now worn yet still beloved Mercedes Benz.

The story behind the story was new management. Don Maxwell had retired and was replaced by Clayton Kirkpatrick, who rose from copyeditor to editor in chief. He decreed cutbacks, especially in foreign news. Bonn-based stringer Alice Siegert stayed on, and her responsibilities were broadened to include forays Dad had once made to the east. Not even new management could ignore second-generation Poles, Czechs, and others, who were still a large part of the readership.

Kirkpatrick moved the paper to the political center, a wrenching change after decades of conservativism, and boosted the coverage of Washington and local news. Foreign news was expendable. No one pleaded for a merciful severance. Don Starr had died. Don Maxwell was ailing. Bottom line: the human story was disastrous.

Since John Peter Zenger, whose acquittal in a 1735 libel suit established the first important victory for freedom of the press in the English colonies of North America, newspapers in the United States have undergone cycles of creative destruction: trimming fat, hiring the lean and hungry, and rethinking technology and finances. My father packed his own teletype for faster and cheaper transmission. While cutting costs, he won hero-grams. On the insensitivity meter, what happened next was off the charts. *Tribune* editors invited him to their capacious executive suite on North Michigan Avenue, all expenses paid, and gave him lunch. In what galaxy are a trip, a car, and a lunch (no matter how dry the martinis) adequate for nearly two decades of service?

Dad visited us in Paris just before his flight to Chicago. He was sixty-seven and knew that something was up, but didn't seem too worried. He made a pancake breakfast, performed coin and card tricks for the boys, and told silly jokes. ("Why is six afraid of seven? Because seven ate nine.") We went out to dinner the night before, and he made gorilla faces behind the waiter's back. It was just like old times. In the morning, after promising to call on his return to let us know how the trip went, he drove to Orly Airport and dropped the car at long-term parking.

He didn't call when he returned. He drove nonstop from the airport five hundred miles to Vienna without talking to a soul. I learned later that he had picked up hives, a burning and itching skin eruption, caused by severe tension. Never had he thought his beloved *Trib* would kiss him off quite so contemptuously.

Financial security, in fact, never figured in his life. He lived for the present. Having faced earlier career reversals and the monster of financial ruin, he always emerged stronger than before. Why should it be different now? He wasn't a reporter to get rich. If you wanted money, rob a bank. You're a reporter because of exhilaration, glamour, passion for getting a story, thrill of the unpredictable, love of stringing words together, and desire to inform the public. He'd been raised by grandparents whose pioneer stock inspired the need to do your duty, to leave something better for a new generation. There was no complaining, no surrender, even when the odds were against you.

So he tried again to pick himself up. He revived earlier stringer connections, such as the old faithful *Medical World News*. He undertook brave efforts to produce short stories and screenplays, which he tried to market through the loyal Bertha Klausner agency. He was also of considerable help to me. For *Times Books*, an imprint of the *New York Times*, I was completing a history of postwar Europe, a subject he knew much better than I. I had long shelved any sensitivity to his editor's scalpel. He not only crunched the manuscript but also offered evocative chapter headings and a super title, *Out of This Nettle*, from the call to action by Hotspur in *Henry IV*, part 1—"Out of this nettle, danger, we pluck this flower, safety"—which Dad's high school English teacher had made students memorize.

Although Dad was an excellent reporter, automatically committing to memory salient quotes and pertinent descriptions from any scene he ever witnessed, I now fully appreciated his gifts as an editor. When he challenged, there was cause. His bête noire was the passive tense. Whenever it was feasible, he turned every passive verb in the manuscript to an active verb. Thanks to him, I finished *Nettle* in good time and published it to good reviews. It even became a classroom text.

Dad retained all his old enthusiasm. Every time I saw him he had a new project under way, each with a capacity to lift all boats. He started a thriller about an old spook called back into service for a mission in mainland China; a comedy about chocolate cake wars in Vienna; and an "unauthorized" biography of Mao Tse-tung. Each had potential. But he lacked the drive and soon got discouraged.

Most hours were spent on Mao. He unearthed material to support a thesis that the Chinese leader was one of history's great killers. These days the point is undisputed. But in the late 1960s and early 1970s, the "great helmsman" was much venerated, especially on college campuses, and Mao's *Little Red Book* ranked, along with the King James Bible and the Koran, as one of the most studied tomes. Dad titled one chapter "Kill, Killing, Killed," and it began, "The sum of Mao-inspired suffering and death hides behind its vast dimensions a half-century of ill-kept, secretive or half-forgotten history." Here was the story of a megalomaniac who was clever as a fox, in the tradition of despots from time immemorial. Dad also pieced together a portrait of Mao's daily life and came up with interesting tidbits—for example, that the residence in Peking, once known as the Palace of the Fragrant Concubine, had been a villa among compounds occupied by favorites in the imperial court. The palace itself was a walled H-form of tile roofs covering about ten ground-floor rooms, identifiable from the air by a garden swimming pool.

"We may visualize Mao in his later 70s, still swimming, but say only 15 or 20 minutes at a crack, in his Peking villa pool, breathing heavily for a rationed number of breaststrokes, then puffing and laddering up to a toweling by the bodyguard, who also helps him on with his robe," Dad wrote.

Another element in the late-age vignette: "Mao ate five small meals a day, being satisfied to sit with a tray at his tea table if guests were not present. For any food that was dull, there was a doll's dish of chili sauce never to be confused with tomato ketchup. Pepper was a fetish of Mao's. He associated it with his own hot temper, with Hunanese choler in general, and seriocomically broached the thesis that pepper-loving peoples were more revolutionary than others."

Dad expounded on the baggy attire imposed on hundreds of millions of Chinese. Mao's jackets, "overlong in the sleeves—a trait of long standing—seemed to flap on him like yardage of a becalmed yacht."

It was interesting, but not enough to put sauerbraten on the table. He needed real income. One backup was Social Security. But having worked most of his adult life outside the United States and therefore not having contributed much to the system, he got little from it. Another backup: Yours Truly. Confucian, filial, or whatever loyalty required that I lend a helping hand. Like a Mexican immigrant gardener sending money orders to Nuevo León, I set up support for Hohenstaufengasse.

Dad was still working on Mao in August 1975, when he had a heart attack. Fearing the worst, I rushed to his bedside at the Allgemeines Krankenhaus, or general hospital, the subject of an early story for *Medical World News*, and found him in an airy room with other cardiac patients. Though attached to tubes and looking uncomfortable, he was surprisingly buoyant and talkative.

The hospital was a complex of small, low buildings on a hillside a couple of miles from the apartment. I learned that the taxi had delivered him to the wrong entrance and driven off. It was the middle of the night. So with a shivered heart under a slivered moon, he sat on a hard wooden bench while Dolly frantically hunted for the right entrance and finally rounded up orderlies and a stretcher. "I thought I was a dead man," he told me with a wan smile. Despite that adventure, he seemed buoyed by my arrival. He was even candid about the circumstances, informing me, though I hadn't inquired, that he'd been stricken after a bout of intense lovemaking with Dolly: "It was the first time we'd made love in weeks. I was suddenly dizzy and short of breath. I got up to go to the window to get some air and then felt sharp, throbbing pains around my arms and shoulders." He cracked a manly grin and crunched my arm. "And let that be a warning." It was typical of our relationship then that we kept little back.

He was stricken at the start of my vacation. Since Barbara and the kids were already in a rented house in central France, I decided to hang out in Vienna while he was recovering, both to help with his affairs and to improve my German. I knew he was bogged down by the Mao book. On his desk in the apartment were thousands of words on Mao's life in neatly piled pages and loose-leaf folders. Although much was interesting, much was also turgid, stilted, and muddled, needing the same doctoring offered for *Out of This Nettle*, so I devised a plan of blitz rewriting to jump-start a publisher's advance. Dolly said she also had trouble with the manuscript. Although English wasn't her forte and she lacked credentials as a critic, she knew what she liked, calling herself the average reader. She said repeatedly, "He must tell a story." On this we agreed. We also agreed to say nothing until he got out of the hospital, hoping to pleasantly surprise him.

Although I knew little about China and even less about Mao, years of newspaper reporting had made me a ninety-minute whiz on practically any subject. Thus, I'd blitzed on disasters, radio astronomy, nonproliferaton treaties, and whither goest the global economy. A book on Mao, I told Dolly with perhaps an excess of bravado, was "just another assignment." I boned up on Edgar Snow, Han Suyin, Herbert Feis, Ross Terrill, and others on his bookshelves and expounded on Mao's birth in Shaoshan in central China, disputes with his rich peasant father whom he couldn't stand, and the long walk to Changsha, where he registered in middle school, read his first newspaper, and snipped the pigtails of his fellow students, in often vehement acts of defiance of the Manchu imperial order.

From my point of view, it was exciting. Dad's years in China and plans that had almost materialized for Mom to bring the family had instilled a deep curiosity. I could imagine it, but until those weeks in Vienna, I'd never studied China. Now I could both learn and make a contribution to his well-being. I created an early narrative flow he could supplement. The results were a hundred typed pages.

Upon his return, I deposited the manuscript on his desk with a note on what I'd done, then I went for a walk. It was my last day in Vienna, and I girded myself for troubles in Paris. Monetary storm clouds had gathered yet again, and Barbara was none too happy over my prolonged absence. Upon my return, Dad was at his desk. Sour-faced, he barely greeted me. "Did you write this stuff?" He tossed the clump of pages at me. They fell on the floor. I bent down to pick them up, thinking it was a practical joke.

"I asked if you're responsible." His voice rose.

"Yes. I left you a note." I awaited the punch line.

"What is it supposed to represent?"

"It's a narrative of Mao's early years."

"What makes you think I want or need this? What's more, it's in *New York Times* style. Why should that be the model for the English language?"

It was like being back on Heartbreak Ridge.

"You write like the *New York Times*," he reiterated, "but why should that be the model for me and *my* book?" I protested that I was just trying to write the skeleton of a story, which he could transform in any way he saw fit. But he asserted with some heat, "I need no favors from the *New York*

Times." It got no better for a long time, and it was probably my fault. I had gone off hell-bent on a show-offy, presumptuous plan, failing completely to consider psychology.

I was dealing with an infirm yet still fiercely proud and independent-thinking man, who had fallen on hard times, but who sought no writing lessons from a son, no matter how well-intentioned. His attitude probably also signaled deep resentment toward my rather comfortable circumstances while he struggled with no job at all and, apart from me, diminishing means of support. I never again raised the subject, never again even glimpsed my own work. His own jottings I didn't see again until I was rummaging through his papers after his death.

The memory of that raw encounter filled me with apprehension as we started working on this book in the fall of 1978. Yet that collaboration went smoothly. The difference was that he faced no fait accompli; he participated in all but the penultimate stages. He also accepted that his own powers were failing and that if his own story was ever to get out, he needed me.

Falling on hard times is not a new affliction for old reporters. Among the more celebrated was that formidable Middle Eastern hand of the *New York Times,* Dana Adams Schmidt, who was injured in a jeep collision while covering a civil war in north Yemen in 1965 and was best known for bringing attention to the plight of 35 million Kurds in eastern Turkey, Soviet Armenia, northeast Iraq, and northwest Iran—the region known as Kurdistan. For centuries the Kurds had struggled for autonomy and had partly achieved it in Iraqi Kurdistan in 1991. In 1963 Schmidt put Kurds on the map almost as comprehensively as T. E. Lawrence had the Arabs.

That year Schmidt borrowed a mule and disappeared for a couple of weeks. Not his wife, his Middle East colleagues, or even the *Times* editors knew his whereabouts, and anxiety rose. Reporters were being bumped off then as now. But he returned with one of the biggest stories of the year: a firsthand account of the Kurdish rebellion and an in-depth interview with its leader, Mustafa Barzani, with whom he'd played chess during long hours in the wilds of Kurdistan.

Any rebukes from New York were drowned by kudos. He won the George Polk award of the Overseas Press Club and turned the enterprise into a book, *Journey among Brave Men,* which scholars compared to Lawrence's *Seven Pillars of Wisdom.* Schmidt continued reporting from the Middle East and later transferred to London and Washington. After a falling out, he quit the *Times*, where he had worked for twenty-eight years, in 1972. We worked together in London, and I saw him occasionally in Washington, once over a dinner table, after my own reassignment to the capital in 1977.

We were at the house of the poet (later to be my second wife) Elisavietta Ritchie, whom Schmidt had once befriended in Beirut. Imagine my surprise when during dessert he asked me for a loan of $500. Later I realized he wasn't joking. He said he could hardly afford groceries, let alone the rent. After leaving the *Times* he took several lesser-paying jobs, including with the *Christian Science Monitor*. He described the depletion of savings and the inadequacy of his small *Times* pension and Social Security. It was the winter of 1988, and he was seventy-two. Watching this venerable newsman beg for a handout was painful.

In his doleful face I saw my father, so I wrote the check. I later contacted Sydney Gruson, then the number two man at the *Times* (behind Punch Sulzberger) to see what could be done institutionally. Gruson told me of a fund for impecunious correspondents—the first I'd ever heard of it. He mailed Schmidt $14,000, apparently from this mysterious fund, which nobody had ever heard of before or has heard of since.

Several months later Schmidt visited the *Times*'s Washington bureau, then on the fifth floor of 1701 K Street. From the desk where I was banging away, I saw him through the glass partition in the reception area. He was waving, urging me to come out. He hadn't called, and the receptionist didn't offer easy access. She later told me he had come to see Johnny Apple, then the chief Washington correspondent, whom Schmidt had also worked with, but Apple wasn't in.

I could not *not* go, and once again, as at that dinner on Macomb Street, he asked for money. It was for rent and heating bills this time. I asked about the $14,000. "Gone," he said, shaking his head vigorously. I said no matter how much I respected him, I couldn't keep doing this. Schmidt said that he understood and that this would be the last time because he was writing something that would make him whole. It was so much like what I'd heard from Dad that I wrote another check.

There were more visits, more sworn testimony, and more checks. Then the visits stopped. I like to think that another Gruson fund kicked in. Johnny Apple also wrote checks, and possibly other colleagues did as well, or perhaps foundations. Johnny's ample jowls rocked and rolled when we discussed it. "Our tithe," he said, almost cheerily.

31

Back to the Future

THE *QUEEN ELIZABETH 2* (*QE-2*) is late. Darkness envelops Cherbourg's pier as passengers watch and wait beside hawsers thick as pythons. Rain pelts the inky sea. Foghorns herald a distant glow. *"Elle arrive, Elle arrive"* (she arrives). There are millions of points of light. Chains clang, carts clank, and spume showers the dock. It's far from the Tinkertoy I saw building in Glasgow.

The hawsers are secured and the gangplanks made fast. Megaphones bark in French and English. More blasts of the horn are accompanied by whistles and shouts. Loudspeakers announce a new sitting for dinner. From the recesses come the sounds of Jimi Hendrix. Gates clang shut. As fast as the dock was transformed, it untransforms, and the world of lights, music, and laughter slips off again on cradles of foam.

It is February 1975. I had driven Dolly and Dad from Paris, to bid them bon voyage. The Mercedes, Dad's severance from the *Trib*, had already been shipped ahead. "California dreamin'," they had decided to drive from New York to Los Angeles, where Dad's brother Guy and his Shanghai crony Peppi Paunzen, both in California, would assist in their resettlement. Peppi, now running a restaurant in Encino, had married Gladys Buroker, an executive of an LA hospital management company. For as long as they needed, Dad and Dolly had free lodgings in Peppi and Gladys's garden cottage in Sherman Oaks.

Guy and his wife, Marge, lived in Fresno, where he handled community relations for a radio station. Guy and Dad would visit their two other siblings: Harry, a retired merchant seaman and the survivor of a 1942 Liberty ship sinking in the North Atlantic, who now lived near Fort Sill, Oklahoma; and Olive, a dental technician who had recently married a certified public accountant named George W. Brock and lived in Ashland. My own sister, Sue, married with two children, Nicole and Warren Hammond, would welcome Dad and Dolly in Rhinebeck, New York.

Though available for emergencies, I returned to Paris relieved that at least for now, some of my obligations had departed, too, on the *QE-2*. Having spent so much time on Dad's problems, I'd neglected my own. The quadrupling of oil prices riled up financial storms. And the publisher was about to descend for his annual visit. I thought of army inspections. Though never so stated, orderliness in the Paris bureau was in order.

Arthur Ochs Sulzberger, a Marine officer in World II and Korea and my angel for that all-too-fleeting Jaguar, was a "clean-desk man." My work space was a no-man's land of clippings, scraps of notes, and scattered press releases. I got things in order, much as Grigory Potemkin must have done with those villages on the Dnieper for Catherine the Great.

Bureau tensions were abating after a flap between Flora Lewis and John Hess—Lewis was from the University of California at Los Angeles and the AP, and Hess was from the University of Utah and the *Bisbee* (Arizona) *Daily Review*. The flap had elements of slapstick. Hess had once locked Lewis out of an office in the *Times*'s Paris bureau. Years later she ran the bureau.

They didn't see eye to eye on much of anything, but this fracas centered less on contrarian judgment than on the way the *Times* was run. To Hess, Lewis had appalling privileges because of her marriage to Sydney Gruson, Dad's former pal in Warsaw and later a senior *Times* executive. Lewis never denied the nepotism. But whatever advantages she had she believed were well earned after years as a loyal camp follower. Like working wives everywhere, she balanced family and career. Following Gruson on his postings, she raised three children and wrote four well-received books and a number of news articles for the *Washington Post*, *Newsday*, the *New York Times* Sunday magazine, and other outlets.

Yet for years she couldn't even aspire to the *Times* staff. *Times* policy, now long scrapped, barred a married couple from working on the paper together. Gruson later divorced Lewis and remarried. Only then, as a wife no longer, did Lewis win the appointment as bureau chief.

Hess labeled the appointment "alimony," and it was like the birther controversy—those who believe that President Barack Obama was born in Kenya will never be convinced otherwise, no matter how many times his birth certificate is produced. Similarly, nothing could convince Hess that Lewis deserved the job on her own merit. For years Lewis had kept her own career in check. As Gruson hopscotched around the globe, she trailed with the kids and a typewriter, quietly building freelance relationships.

Their kids were all born abroad: Kerry in Ireland, Sheila in Israel, and Lindsey in Mexico. Parallels exist with Hillary Clinton. Both women played second fiddle to famous husbands. Bill Clinton did what he could to help Hillary. But who says she wouldn't have had the right stuff all on her own?

Though promoting democracy, news organizations are perhaps the most despotic of all institutions. One powerful individual, or a clique of the like-minded, runs things. Yet without a unified command, deadlines wouldn't be met. Publishers and editors also decide key personnel issues, including bureau chief appointments. Punch and Gruson weren't about to cede that to John Hess.

Yet even under autocracies, rivalries and fiefdoms are inevitable. The Clydesworth era felt storms between such towering figures as scrappy Abe Rosenthal in New York and ruminative Washington Editor Scotty Reston. Reston, the pipe-smoking, Scottish-born former diplomatic correspondent, emphasized national and international news. Rosenthal believed the world ended at the Hudson River. Sometimes Reston won, and sometimes Rosenthal did; the paper prospered from their dialectic.

The Hess-Lewis confict was meaner and more personal. A crabby conspiracy theorist, Hess once wrote a book damning Julia Child and *Times* food writer Craig Claiborne. Craig, a generous figure, was both a personal friend of mine and almost everyone's favorite on the staff. Although I did not dislike Hess, he reminded me of a dachshund nipping at one's ankles.

I knew that Lewis was good. Even with the ever present Scotch dangerously tilting, she cut to the quick in the Vietnam peace talks—they were going nowhere, and she wrote that. She also kept tuned to the politics of money. Well before Washington's think tanks caught on, she looked beyond a collapsing dollar to the big picture of the way it was ushering in a new multipolar world.

Hess was already part of the Paris bureau when I joined in 1968. A dwarfish man with a Grumpy beard, he was studious, was hard- and late-working, and spoke passable French. Upon my arrival I couldn't help but hear about Hess having locked Lewis out of the office, which had happened in the summer of 1967. Henry Tanner was then the bureau chief. A gentle soul, born in Bern, Switzerland, he was mortified.

That summer Gruson and Lewis moved from London to Paris—he was head of the Paris edition of the *Times* (which later folded but is now resurrected under the masthead of the *International New York Times*), and she was stringing for *Newsday*. Rumors circulated that the *Times* ban against a married couple working together might be lifted and Lewis would take over the bureau. At any rate, she felt free to make use of *Times* facilities as she had in London, where as a stringer for the *Washington Post* she had regularly popped in to swap gossip.

But that summer, the breeze, gentle off the Thames, was chill off the Seine. In London Lewis had used her husband's office, especially when he was out of town. In Paris she made herself at home, too. Bureau Chief Tanner was on holiday, so she appropriated his office and sometimes the office chauffeur, a fellow from Tunis named Jean Mohammed, who, in his black Citroen DS, raced through Paris like Hermes on his fiery chariot. But with Tanner away, Hermes sat in the office reading *L'Equipe*. I suspected that Hermes was the breaking point: Hess, or perhaps his wife, Karen, had competing needs for the chariot. Osgood Caruthers spoke of frictions in Moscow between him and Bureau Chief Max Frankel that also reflected rival claims on the office chauffeur. So sharp were those knives that when Max rose to executive editor, Osgood accepted an offer from the *Los Angeles Times*.

On the day of the locked door, Natasha Chassagne, the bureau secretary, told a perplexed Lewis that Hess was custodian of the key. Lewis guessed what was up and quietly retreated. The deed, she figured out, was expressly to embarrass her, and it did, after the story made the gossip columns thanks to tips by Hess.

Hess liked neither Gruson nor Lewis and would do anything to yank their chain. He claimed they were bringing the paper to ruin. I never saw it that way, and, after recounting this story I hope the readers will conclude that Hess—and maybe others opposed to Lewis—simply didn't realize how good she was. L'Affaire Hess probably delayed her appointment. Punch wanted no scandal, and so even after Tanner's retirement he kept Lewis on the hook by promoting another seasoned reporter to the post, fellow Marine Henry Giniger, a veteran of Iwo Jima.

In 1972, with Hess still at the bureau, Lewis got the coveted appointment, and for a while the differences were papered over. She was not confrontational or vindictive. Her goal was a smooth-running operation, especially with the Vietnam peace talks underway. But after some months it was clear peace was not in store in either Vietnam or Paris, and Hess was reassigned to New York.

The following spring Aristotle Onassis, now the husband of Jacqueline Kennedy, mixed Bloody Marys for Flora Lewis and me at a corner table at

Maxim's overlooking the Rue de la Paix. Oil prices had exploded. Onassis owned a fleet of oil tankers as well as Olympic Airways, whose costs were directly affected by higher-priced fuel. Olympic's office was practically next door on rue Scribe. I passed it every day, and on a whim I decided to invite Onassis to lunch. It was one of those routine things reporters do—"covering bases," as we used to say.

When his secretary called back, she said archly that Mr. Onassis didn't accept invitations to lunch but that he'd be happy to invite *me* to lunch at Maxim's, which was then recognized by Michelin as one of the four or five best restaurants in the world. The secretary added that Mr. Onassis would be especially honored if my colleague Flora Lewis would join. A condition was that everything be off the record, which meant a promise not to write specifically about it. When I filled Flora in, she was amused. "Sure, why not? Maybe we'll learn something."

Reporters and their sources often meet informally, mostly for lunch. Usually the reporters pick up the check and get reimbursed by the office. It encourages the buttering up of sources and a guarded disclosure of information. In Washington, breakfasts too are popular. In Paris, however, breakfasts never caught on.

Nothing rose of any news interest with Onassis. Olympic Airways's costs had mushroomed from the oil crisis, but we knew that. The subject wasn't oil, anyway, except in the most peripheral of ways; it was Onassis, a newsmaker of the period, his life and his loves. He had no inhibitions about talking about himself, perhaps sensing that this forum might someday help him be better understood.

I'd been with Flora on other interviews. She usually did most of the talking. This time she was quiet, except when coaxing him on. His coquetry was a subtext; he had probably planned it that way. It would have looked odd, especially to the gossipy patrons of Maxim's, for him to be sitting with Flora Lewis, especially without Jacqueline present, to whom he'd already been wed five years.

He was a short, muscular man almost twenty years older than Flora. "My dear Flora," he called her, as she fetchingly smiled. He told of his life as a youthful tobacco importer while clerking at a telephone exchange in Buenos Aires. He winked and occasionally peered over our heads at the décolletage of a hatcheck girl. "I was on a floor just below the bank of operators," he told us. "As they reached up to plug the wires, I could see all the way up their legs!"

He laughed, not at all self-consciously, macho proud of his earthy achievements, including his marriage to Jackie and an indestructible relationship with superdiva Maria Callas. He was also proud of his rivalry with his erstwhile brother-in-law Stavros Niarchos, who claimed to have the world's biggest fleet of tankers. When I asked Onasis whose fleet was bigger, without hesitation he shot back, "Mine!" On our walk back to the office, Flora called him "authentic."

In often unconventional ways, Flora was, too. She moved from bureau chief to an even more prestigious post as the *Times*'s foreign affairs columnist. She won honorary degrees and lifetime achievement awards, but all she ever wanted was to write, loving that even more than talking, smoking, or drinking. She was among the first to break the AP's glass ceiling. Later she reported from Washington. So many men were called to the war that Flora, like Rosie the Riveter and my own mother, did the heavy lifting at home.

Flora never stopped lifting. In six decades she wrote thousands of columns. She called herself a dabbler, but she "dabbled" like Georgia O'Keeffe or Mary Cassatt. In the *Times* obit, former London, Paris, and Washington Bureau Chief Craig Whitney observed that Flora tried to "outthink and outwrite the competition on the job, and she could outdrink and outsmoke it off the job."

I add a resounding "Cheers!"

32

Home Again

REASSIGNED TO THE Washington bureau of the *New York Times*, I returned to the United States in January 1977. My poor mother! That I'd followed so much in Dad's footsteps would have horrified her. Not only was I gallivanting like him, but I had broken up a family. Absence from the hearth did my marriage little good. Barbara, a strong and admirable woman, would agree. We were divorced in the spring of 1977.

Ray Vicker of the *Wall Street Journal* traveled everywhere with his wife, but that was an unusual arrangement that few could afford. And the Vickers had no children. My *Times* colleague Malcolm Brown, himself divorced, took an informal survey of *Times* correspondents of the 1970s: half were divorced or separated. Shocking, it then seemed; a half-century later it's the norm.

Barbara stayed in Paris to finish up schooling for the boys—and also to say goodbye more gently to a city that at first she despised for its chill hauteur, then came to appreciate for its transcendent charms. Andrew achieved distinction in the equivalent of high school in Paris and then took an advanced course at the Lycée Emile Janson to enter one of France's top learning institutes. He had his eye on Hautes Etudes Commerciales, a top business school, and he even got accepted, which was an unusual feat for an American. But he hedged with a bid to Harvard, which, it turned out, wanted him, too. In the end he joined Harvard's class of 1981, a decision I was happy with, except for the tab.

Alexander continued classes in his fourth year at Ecole Active Bilingue. In September he and Barbara moved to West Cornwall, Connecticut, where Barbara, with proceeds from our divorce settlement, bought a used bookstore uphill from a much celebrated covered bridge and started a business as an antiquarian book dealer. Alexander finished his final year at Housatonic Valley High School. Guild scholarships eased the cost of both boys' higher education.

But since the boys had spent so much of their youth in Europe, it wasn't surprising that in time they both chose to live and raise families there: Andrew in France and Switzerland, and Alex in Sweden. Andrew got a master's degree in business administration at Dartmouth College in New Hampshire and worked in human resources. His wife, Tessa, joined the prestigious Paris Institute of Political Studies, otherwise known as Sciences Po. Alex, after a year at Middlebury College in Vermont, Barbara's alma mater, studied at St. John's College in Santa Fe, and like Dad's apprentice Dusko Doder, earned a master's from the Columbia University School of Journalism. He and a Swedish classmate, Carolina Johansson, set themselves up as news professionals in Stockholm. Alex zeroed in on photo journalism, and Carolina focused on business news. Andrew and Alex each have two boys: Dylan and Philip, and Adrian and Dennis, respectively.

I visited Dad and Dolly during a stopover in Los Angeles in March 1977 on the way to Eugene, Oregon, where I lectured at the University of Oregon. By this time, they were in a two-bedroom garden apartment on Dickens Street in Sherman Oaks, about ten minutes from Peppi and Gladys Paunzen.

At an open house at the Paunzens, I met Peppi and Gladys for the first time. Peppi was bony with a long narrow face, flashing eyes, and a penchant for suits a size too big. Gladys was well put together in a *zaftig* sort of way. Peppi said she looked like his mother. Peppi's younger brother was there as well, a dapper fellow who had also spent the war years in China. Unlike Peppi, he didn't talk much, and he had a passion for the stock market, apparently unrequited. I also remet Dad's old *Los Angeles Times* colleague Osgood Caruthers, by now retired from journalism. A widower, Caruthers had just remarried. His bride, Virginia, acted on TV, and they were the souls of sporty elegance in a hot red MG.

It was a merry, lighthearted afternoon of nostalgia and ribaldry. Peppi riffed on another Yamaha piano: "Kiss me once, charge me twice, and cheat me once again, it's been a long, long time." Later he drew me aside. "Your father's a friend in the deepest and truest sense of the word," he said. "How can I ever forget what he did for me and my whole family?" Heartened by that day in LA, I was unprepared for the next events, which occurred in rapid succession: Peppi died. Dad's brother Guy died. Dad's health worsened. Dad and Dolly, together for twenty-five years, split up, and he came to live with me.

The twin blows of Peppi's and Guy's deaths added to his own precarious health, which included an enlarged and neglected prostate. Dolly and he drove together to Guy's funeral in Fresno. Just before the obsequies, while they were still at their motel, he broke down, sobbing loudly in his grief. Dolly said it was "unnecessary" to make such a vocal demonstration—that grief privately expressed could be equally "effective." In his overwrought state, he blew up.

She later related that he accused her of insensitivity, of never caring for his brother, and of not having an ounce of feeling in her. He said that she was not wanted at the funeral, and he ordered her to leave Fresno forthwith. Bitterly angry and emotionally bruised, she packed up her few belongings, left their motel, and returned to LA by bus. Dad drove himself back to LA, and for a long period they didn't converse. When I called once from DC, Dolly told me, "Your father is a different man. He is not the same man I once knew and loved."

Dolly took her revenge by opening a flirtation with Peppi's younger brother, Harry, who drove a Buick LeSabre convertible and dressed like a racetrack tout. They went for rides or to the movies, and he helped her with shopping. "She says Harry knows how to treat a lady," my father told me later, jealousy exploding. But instead of leaving things alone, he reescalated. He returned to Vienna and did to Dolly what perhaps was most unforgivable of all. They had sublet their apartment. After the tenants left, he moved back in and sold everything at fire-sale prices, including the apartment itself. He ended up with a pittance that barely covered his return airfare. When he returned to LA and informed Dolly, she was absolutely, irremediably, unquenchably aghast. In retaliation she handed him a list of items in the Vienna apartment that she said were hers personally and demanded an immediate $3,000 payment. That list, which I found in his papers after his death, I reproduce because of the light it sheds on the elegance of a former life lost now in the swelter of recriminations:

> MY BEDROOM—Chippendale set (1 round table, 2 armchairs, 1 settee for two); 4 Persian carpets (1 Kerman, 1 Isfahan, 1 small Bucchara, 1 small Tabriz); in front of my bed 1 Rumanian Kelim; 1 two-candle crystal lamp (above my bed); my bedroom curtains.
>
> LIVING ROOM—1 gilded Rococo table (Sienna marble top with gilded kidney-shaped mirror above); 1 rose porcelain standing lamp; 1 Turkish

copper tray set in Damascus mosaic folding table; 1 Monet print, gilded frame; 1 Chinese lady's scroll and framed picture (Chinese musician, Taipei); 1 brass-copper combined Japanese lamp (Shanghai); 1 figurine Mongolian dancers; 1 Samovar with brass tray.

SALON—1 Indian god, small figurine ivory; 1 set of ivory elephants; 1 Japanese bowl; 2 small Chinese porcelain dishes (Kunming); 1 mother of pearl box (Jerusalem '45); 1 small incense bowl, brass; 4 Chinese fans.

STORED AWAY—2 porcelain vases, 1 flower, 1 round, matching round plate (Rome '53); 1 Venetian clock (Rome '52); 1 crystal ashtray (Prague '68); 1 wood-cut filigree picture (Jimmy Wei's present to me); 1 small crystal sugar bowl (Innsbruck '50).

Of course, Dad didn't have $3,000, but in a moment of excruciating repentance he vowed to give it to her. A little after that incident, I found him on my doorstep in Washington, DC. At the time I was living at 1830 24th Street, a group house owned by John and Svala Ritch, he a key Democratic staffer on the Senate Foreign Relations Committee, and she an Icelandic artist of striking beauty and talent who kept a plum-headed parakeet. She once asked if I'd ever had a relationship with a bird. I laughed, explaining that "bird" in Cockney meant any female.

The well-connected Ritches hosted soirees. Among their guests were John's patron, the effervescent Senator Joe Biden from Delaware, and the spritely George McGovern, the 1972 Democratic presidential candidate, who flew Liberator bombers in World War II. In shaking hands with McGovern, I said mine was the hand that shook the hand of General de Gaulle. "Vive la France!" McGovern said. He and de Gaulle saw eye to eye on the folly of the war in Vietnam.

Another housemate was Tom Bethel, an English transplant and conservative polemicist. He and John often took genteel and not-quite-so genteel pokes at each other. I stayed on the sidelines. I then thought (and still do think) that political argument rarely changes a mind, and besides, as a journalist I was paid to see both sides. We put Dad in a spare room. After I related the news of his breakup, John, Svala, Tom, and another housemate, Tatty Gresham, and I all agreed to stage a welcoming party to cheer him up. He was all for it and volunteered as chef, offering a signature dish from Vienna, choucroute garni, which contains plenty of sauerkraut and grilled bratwurst.

The party was a rousing success. But even after such a cordial embrace, Dad was not crazy about group living. He relayed an offer from two cronies in Vienna who were among the invitees: Ed and Katharine Clark, who remembered chestnuts pulled from a fire with inspired faux pumpkin puree. They owned a house at 4354 Q Place and offered to rent it for much less than my tab at 24th Street.

We eagerly accepted, and soon Dad and I began our collaboration on this book, often working in the backyard until we were drowned out by airplane noise. We were just below a National Airport flight path, which after 9/11 was adjusted to follow the course of the Potomac. When the Clarks wanted their house back, we moved again, this time to the airy Palazzo apartments at 5353 Columbia Pike in Arlington, Virginia. He loved our new sixth-floor digs even more than the Clarks' place. He had his own bedroom and bathroom and a good-size balcony for ruminative pipe smoking, and he socialized with our multicultural neighbors, including a Korean named Kim from Taejon who cut his hair twice a week and swapped war stories.

Andrew and Alex joined for extended periods, making the Palazzo a homestead. Dad, majestic in a flowing silver and crimson abaya acquired in Cairo, made pancakes or grits while recalling the Arabian Nights splendor of the long-ago razed Shepheard Hotel or a French soldier who lost an arm at Bir Hakheim and was kissed by five generals. Alex took up pipe smoking. After meals it was touching to watch Alex and his grandfather share pipe cleaners and a pouch of Captain Black tobacco as they settled before the TV for *Gunsmoke*.

There were other good moments. We went out to dinner a lot. Dad favored a Szechuan restaurant called Hsiang Fong on Wilson Boulevard, where he loved the hot-and-sour soup and crispy fish and bantered with the young Chinese waitress. Her parents, he discovered, were born in Chengdu, where peasants smote rocks for B-29 runways in 1944. He even recalled some of the Chengdu dialect, which greatly amused her and was more than she knew herself.

He attracted attention by the way he ate. Noting that Western utensils were for lesser mortals, he gestured grandly that the knives and forks be replaced by chopsticks. As the waitress brought out bowls of steamed rice followed by crispy whole fish, moo shu pork, or twice-cooked duck, he shoveled everything first into a rice bowl, then into his gaping mouth. He told his grandsons he ate like a Chinese coolie, and they loved it. He also managed to see old friends. George Vine, retired and living on a farm in

Somerset, England, called on his way through Washington. We saw a lot of Gerry McAllister, Dad's fellow arsonist at Kweilin in 1944. McAllister had settled in Washington as an official of the Aircraft Industries Association.

Anna Chennault, the widow of the general, was also in Washington, where she pulled strings as a Republican committeewoman and the chairwoman of the National Republican Asian Assembly. Dad and she met at the Georgetown home of author William J. Gill (*The Ordeal of Otto Otepka*). But Dad and Anna never really hit it off, and the reunion was strained and truncated. He later told me that she had always felt uncomfortable around him. He was a reminder of the days before her marriage, when she was just another woman in the Chennault harem.

Though deeply wounded by Dolly's treatment of him, Dad never lost touch with her and always harbored the desire to reunite. He wrote her and even called her. She answered his letters and spoke with him on the phone, but she never offered any encouragement about ending their separation. She did inform him, however, of her own health problems. She had breast cancer and had had her left breast surgically removed. One day in October 1981, after we had lived together for three years, Dad made a unilateral decision to return to Los Angeles. "It's necessary to rescue Dolly," he summarily informed me. "Time to reclaim my manhood."

Despite her cancer, it turned out that Dolly little needed rescue. She was being looked after by both Gladys and Harry. She drew Dad's Social Security check and supplemented this income both by old reliable seamstress work and renting out a room in the apartment. Sensing that Dad was in even worse physical and financial shape, Dolly wanted no part of him. He persisted. He called her after her operation. "I want to come and take care of you," I heard him say. I could not hear her reply, but it must have been an earful. He didn't speak for several minutes, and then as he tried to utter something more, she hung up.

"That poor woman," he said. "She is dying. I must go to her!"

He was in no condition to leave. Earlier in the year he'd had a long hospital siege with a defective gall bladder and was still in a weakened state. He said he would not rest until arrangements had been made. I offered a round-trip air ticket so that he would have the option of returning. He insisted it was a permanent move to resume his life with Dolly and that he could drive. But a year earlier he had almost cracked up a car, and by this time I was doing all the driving. I said he couldn't take the wheel of any car, and he accused me of imprisoning him.

Again a son was father of the man. Not only was I totally supporting him, I was also telling him what he should or should not do for his own good. When he came to live with me, I thought his presence would be both stimulating and fun. It was a little of both. But that was only one side of it. The other side was a nightmare. I never anticipated the hospital vigils, arranging for nurses, the pitiful shouts at 3:00 a.m. to help find the bathroom, the tremendous amount of work just keeping him clean and fed, which I managed while banging out stories for the *Times*.

I resolved the immediate crisis by finding a driver for the Mercedes, a former merchant seaman living at the Old Sailors' Home in northeast Washington. Recommended by a friend of a friend, Roland Brown was a few years younger than Dad but fit as a fiddle and seemingly reliable. The trip was a release for him from dullness at the home. I offered a stipend in addition to expenses, and he accepted. With his salty humor and infectious laugh, he was ideal. He knew most of the world's port cities and reminisced about Yokohama, the Bund, and Soochow Creek. He was an easy conversationalist, and from what I knew, honest. I had the Mercedes checked out so that it was in excellent running condition, and we set a date of departure. During the planning Dad's mood changed dramatically. Crankiness turned into solicitousness and an eagerness to please. He attacked stove, fridge, and linoleum grunge, and made lentils, meat loaf, and a couple of apple pies.

While I was at work he spent exhilarating moments over maps planning the route, anticipating the fields of grain, silos, and water towers; the remote hills lacerated by heat lightning and/or real lightning; the whoosh and whistle of far-off trains; and the cheery din of truck stops with their gobsmacking bowls of chili twenty-four hours a day. Though anxious to see Dolly, he perhaps valued even more the act of going there. Having traveled all his adult years and now ailing, he may well have figured this was his last big trip and that he'd better enjoy it.

Roland Brown spent the last night before the appointed day with us, partaking of lentils and apple pie, and after a 7:00 a.m. breakfast of grits and juice, he and Dad set off in the well-packed Mercedes, Roland behind the wheel and Dad settled in as copilot. Destination: Route 66. Apparently the ride was pleasant. Roland fulfilled his part, except for jumping ship on the approaches to Los Angeles "to visit a friend." Dad boasted he knew the way so well that he could merely put himself on automatic pilot. He reached Sherman Oaks without killing anyone.

When he got to the apartment, there was no welcome mat. How dare he come back! Dolly shouted. According to his subsequent account, she verbally flayed him. He had squandered their joint assets and made her life miserable. Now he was going to diminish her even more. To give him a room to sleep in, she had to get rid of a paying tenant. It was money she needed. She had no money, and he had no money. How would they live? He replied that he had come to take care of her with love in his heart. He reached out his hands to her.

"What a joke!" she laughed. She lifted her blouse to show the bandage and plastic prosthetic cup over the cavity at her left breast. "What can you do about this?" she howled. "How can you help me? You are ridiculous! I want nothing to do with you!" Henceforth, she said, the apartment was divided in half. With the index finger of her right hand, she drew an imaginary line in the living room, which she forebade him to cross. He would have his quarters, and she hers. Never was he to step into hers. Never did she even want to see him. When she was in the living room, would he please have the courtesy to leave?

It was devastating. He spent a week under such conditions. He thought she might relent, but she did not. He had to leave, but extrication presented problems. He was physically incapable of driving back, and was out of money unless he disposed of his beloved Mercedes. He was so desperate he took the first offer. The $800 barely the value of the shortwave radio, but it more than covered a Greyhound bus ticket from Los Angeles to Washington, DC. He left the balance in an envelope for her with a note apologizing for being unable to care for her properly and swearing his eternal love. He quit LA forever on the 10:00 p.m. Scenicruiser bound for Phoenix, the first leg of his return to DC.

The first I knew that he was on his way back was when I got a message from Jo Tate, the telephone operator in the *Times*'s Washington bureau. Dad's wretched condition had drawn the attention of the Greyhound office in Chicago, which called the *Times* with the information that he would be reaching the Washington Greyhound terminal on the bus from Pittsburgh the following evening at seven o'clock. I called the apartment in Los Angeles. Dolly confirmed the arrival time. I asked her what happened, but she declined to discuss it further. "Ask your father," she said sullenly.

I saw him inside the bus as it slid into its dock at the 11th Street terminal, and he managed a gracious smile of recognition. Helping him out, I saw that he was pale, hollow, and drawn, the shell of the man I'd waved adios to almost three weeks earlier. He'd been riding buses for two and a half days. Though absolutely exhausted, he was also hungry, so I took him to an Italian restaurant named Gino's on Columbia Pike. It had red-checkered tablecloths, Chianti, and good, tasty Italian-American spaghetti and meatballs, which we both loved. He said it reminded him of an eatery he patronized on Mayfield Road in gangland Cleveland.

"Son," he said, negotiating tomato-sauce drenched spools of spaghetti, "let me tell you what a sight for tired old eyes you were at that bus station." He didn't know I'd be there. "I'm glad to be back," he said, close to tears. I told him I was happy that he was back, that everything in the apartment was just as he had left it, and that we would resume normal life. "Thank you, son," he said, squeezing my hand.

I couldn't help harboring resentment toward Dolly. After all they'd been through and all they had once meant to each other, she showed herself to be without much generosity, charity, or humaneness. Not the treatment of her at Guy's funeral, the unilateral sale of their property in Vienna, or even Dad's failure to be able to provide for her in her old age seemed to justify such abject cruelty. When I mentioned my thoughts to Dad, he said only, "She has been the great love of my life." I asked whether he still loved her, and he replied, "Yes." Later, reporting Dad's arrival, I spoke to Gladys Paunzen, who was looking after Dolly. She expressed relief about the news of his safe return.

"I like your father and Dolly very much," she said. "It hurts me to see this happen. But it is perhaps for the best. Your father cannot do anything for Dolly now, and she cannot do anything for him."

Although Dad and I were very close in those early days of his return, the pressure of work on my part and his tendency to brood endlessly about his broken life with Dolly pulled us in different directions. We continued to collaborate on the book, but the sessions became strained and abrasive, filled with his explosive complaints and tantrums about the extent of detail I was demanding from years past and threats to call the project off. Several weeks later, when he again entered the hospital, now from complications from an enlarged and cancerous prostate, I realized that ill health was behind his bad humor.

My son Andrew was living with us. Since I had to be away on short reporting trips, it was Andrew who attended to the emergencies of his grandfather, who suddenly found that he couldn't urinate. Andrew took him to Dr. Josef Dvorak, a general practitioner on Old Dominion Road, several blocks from Columbia Pike, and from there Dad was admitted to

Arlington Hospital for one of the half a dozen monthlong stays as his condition worsened over the next three years.

After a series of X-rays, both Dr. Dvorak and Dr. Joseph Finerty, a urologist on nearby Lee Highway, recommended against surgery to remove a cancerous tumor obstructing the urinary duct. Because of its unfortunate position, surgery, I was told, could exacerbate the condition.

The two physicians recommended that Dad be equipped with a Foley catheter, a tube that fits through the penis and urethra into the bladder. A small rubber device secures it against an inner abdominal membrane, and at the other end is a bag that automatically fills with urine and must be frequently emptied. For patients who can walk, the bag is strapped around a leg. Dr. Finerty pointed to old medical cartoons displayed in his office that showed senior gentlemen with Foley bags secured to their top hats. Laughing, he made a circular motion with his hands, supposedly illustrating the rising rings of urine-filled tubing.

I bristled. For me there was nothing funny, and it certainly wasn't funny for my father. Either the catheter or a life-threatening operation! Both doctors said he'd get used to the catheter, and with reluctance I went along. He wore the bag on his leg for the next two and a half years of his life, but he never got used to it. I often think it would have been better for him to have undergone the operation, regardless of the risks, rather than submit to such indignities.

Although doctors and nurses tried to explain why he had to wear the catheter, he hated it, and often, in his own bed at night, he simply yanked all that tubing out, enduring the pain. Several times I found him in bed with the catheter out and the sheets bloody. Of course, then he couldn't urinate, and I'd rush him to some red-eyed, bored intern at Arlington Hospital, who would break open a sterile kit, lubricate the catheter tip, seize the penis and laboriously reinsert the catheter.

I cannot count the number of times I made that trip in the early hours of the morning down Columbia Pike, Carlin Spring Road, and George Mason Boulevard with Dad bundled into my Ford Pinto, a look on his face of utter shock and pain. Yet even in that period he maintained a sense of humor. His boyhood friend, Filson Roberts, visited. Once Filson asked if Dad knew which highways and byways all that tubing went down. Dad cracked a rare smile: "Down memory lane!"

The catheter forced huge changes in our routine. He couldn't be left alone when I went to work. So I retained nurses in morning and afternoon shifts to attend to some tasks, including draining and changing the bag. At night I'd make dinner and get him ready for bed by removing the leg bag and inserting a larger night bag, which for drainage lay on the floor beside his bed. Invariably, he got up in the night. Impeded by the bag, he couldn't walk. So he crawled, the tubing dragging like the tail of some impaired field animal. When I first saw him in this state, I cried. Helping him up and into clothes, I bundled him into the Pinto for the ride to the emergency room. What abject misery in the name of Foley's catheter!

We lived like that for nearly two years. Weakened by several extended hospital stays, he became less and less able to do anything for himself. I faced the choice of nurses, or even home health aides, twenty-four hours a day, which I could hardly afford on a reporter's salary, or a nursing home. Dr. Dvorak recommended the latter course, and I reluctantly agreed. We looked at places in the District of Columbia and in northern Virginia, but even then it was hard finding a bed. In early 1983 Dr. Dvorak told me of an opening at Camelot Hall, a red-brick complex across Lee Highway from a Safeway supermarket in Arlington, not a quarter mile from the start of Route 66. I made the arrangements. During the drive Dad was sullen and uncommunicative. I tried to explain why we were doing it, emphasizing that it was for his own good because neither I nor home nurses could cope. I promised to visit often. It was awful!

As nursing homes go, Camelot Hall was as good as you could expect: relatively clean with mediocre food and erratic care. Certain nurses were sensitive to his needs, but others were woefully negligent. Dad did not make friends there, but he did have good talks with one of the night nurses, telling her about his life in wartime China. She approached me once to say, "Your father is a terribly interesting man!"

I tried to live up to a promise by taking him out frequently to one of the Asian or Italian restaurants in the area. Sometimes we were with either or both of my sons, and sometimes it was just the two of us. There was always great sadness upon our return to the nursing home. In the early days he made aborted attempts to escape. Once after a dinner outing, as I left to speak to a nurse, he drew Andrew aside. "Your father doesn't give a damn about me, but can't you do something to get me out of this jail?" Andrew told me about it later. "One of my worst moments ever!" he exclaimed.

Dad shared a room on the fifth floor with a retired metalworker from the Washington Navy Yard named Michael Guiliani, who was a few years older but in sounder physical shape. While Dad brooded most of his time, Mr. Guiliani romanced the ladies. Mr. Giuliani's favorite belle lived down the hall. She fancied a pink-flowered housecoat and yellow barrettes in tousled milkweed curls. He wore polyester slacks and floral shirts that never quite met across the belly. For hours they sat silently slumped in their wheelchairs, holding hands. On one occasion, Mr. Guiliani did more than hold hands. She didn't seem to mind, but for some ungodly reason the staff did, and Mr. Guiliani, incredibly, was banished to another floor.

Some part of Dad just wanted to die. Against my wishes, he spent longer and longer periods in bed. I asked that he be dressed and walked every day, but increasingly the staff forgot or was too short-handed, or he refused to rise. One evening when I questioned why he wasn't dressed, the nurse in charge said that he was too tired to get out of bed. Tired he was, probably from not eating or drinking. This was the part that wanted to die. Sometimes I think I should have hastened the end. I see this now, but then I was conditioned to let life take its natural course, no matter how miserable, and so I tried to make the circumstances tolerable.

The end was horrible. Basically, I took every day as it came, dealing with all the little problems to make him comfortable. Whenever I visited, I tried to get custard or orange juice inside him, but he was more difficult to feed than a six-month-old. He got so dehydrated that Dr. Dvorak had to hospitalize him to get liquid and food into him through tubes. He made a recovery and returned to the nursing home relatively lucid, but the improvement in his condition was soon cut short by renewed demoralization and another downward spiral into even greater physical weakness. He now refused food. The nurses tried feeding him but gave up. I had better luck spoon-feeding him thimble-size cups of ice cream and yogurt, but this was hardly enough. He was wasting away.

Dad required more personal attention than either I or Camelot Hall could provide, and I tried to get him into a hospice to live out his final days. Here too the news was bad. Because he didn't have a fatal illness and there was only limited space in the area hospices, he was ineligible. I retained an outside agency to give him the special attention he needed. At this stage, he could do little for himself. The agency sent a young Filipino named André, who was training to be an agronomist, which helped a little. Dad was fond of Filipinos and reminisced about a quick trip to Manila in the early 1950s. He commented that Filipinos are the world's best dancers, which made André laugh.

But this improvement proved even more short-lived. Long periods of inactivity created bed sores. An air mattress was ordered to better cushion his body. He often pulled the sheets off, and I sometimes found him lying naked against the bare blue plastic cover. Incontinence aggravated infections. One evening after work, toward the end of April 1984, as I was helping to turn him, I suddenly became aware of the extent of the sores. They were horrible—ugly, pustulant gashes the size of a man's fist—and I cried bloody murder. He was not being cleaned frequently enough to prevent the acid of his feces from rotting the flesh of his buttocks and hips. The dressings around the wounds were contaminated, and, as if he were aware of this, he would try to rip the dressings off.

The chief nurse said that they were doing the best they could, but because of his inactivity the problems were beyond their capacity. His general boycott of food meant that he was not getting the proteins necessary to fight the sepsis. Dr. Dvorak ordered him back to Arlington Hospital to at least deal with those sores. As this was being done, he underwent more urological testing, which, perhaps blessedly, found that the cancer had spread to his liver.

His chances for recovery were slight, Dr. Dvorak said. He asked whether I wanted "heroic" measures that might extend Dad's life for a brief period. Dad had once told me that if he ever got into a state where he was completely out of it, I was to "pull the goddamned plug." I recounted that conversation, noting that instead of a Dr. Dvorak, he needed a Dr. Kevorkian. He never returned to Camelot Hall. He lay in a special room at Arlington Hospital for almost three weeks, clad only in a blue-flowered hospital gown. They shaved his beard. He had lost maybe fifty pounds. When I visited, I spoon-fed him yogurt and ice cream. The bed sores persisted, but the bandages now were maintained with at least some degree of sanitation.

On the door was posted a sign: Infectious Wound—No Visitors. I was allowed in, but I had to don a special yellow gown and scrub my hands upon entering or leaving. The inflammatory response by the immune system was sepsis microbes in the blood. Like those lepers rescuing a downed pilot in his wartime story for *Liberty*, Dad was a pariah. Yet it wasn't necessarily a bad thing. The room was *his* personal hospice; he was finally getting intensive twenty-four-hour care.

The third week of May, 1984: As usual I was working long hours, but I was still visiting most evenings. I held his hand, rubbed his moist forehead, and read aloud long sections from his life as told to me. Although he was in a trancelike state from drugs that now, thank God, were keeping the pain out of his wracked body, he showed flickers of sentience when names like Dolly, Amelia Earhart, Chennault, Lank, or Grandma tumbled out. And there were moments when he tried to smile, such as when I read to him how Frankie Cancellare chopped down that banana tree in Chungking or how Viennese pastry rivals warred over chocolate cake.

I sat beside him holding his hand, but he did not look at me. When his eyes were open, they looked only at the wall opposite where one of the nurses had taped his favorite photo of Dolly. She stood, posed in her tight brocade kimono, flowers in her bobbed black hair, coquettishly peeking from behind a delicately wrought fan. On May 23, 1984, I read to him until close to midnight, then I drove home exhausted. Less than two hours later the phone roused me. The duty nurse said he had breathed his last.

Andrew and I drove to Ohio. We buried him beside his grandfather Lank on a prominent knoll of Ashland County Memorial Park, less than five miles from his birthplace. Though numb, I knew death was a blessing. The night before, in front of relatives who barely knew him, I delivered a eulogy about his life as a correspondent, concentrating on his days in China. I retold the story of the rescue of those two English reporters from the clutches of the murderous Colonel Yeh, which, I must admit, seemed remote indeed in Ashland. The following morning, as he was interred amidst grassy slopes, budding trees, and other graves in various states of repair or disrepair, I smiled wanly at Andrew.

In January 1987, almost three years after his death, I had lunch in Washington with George Vine, just in from Los Angeles after visiting Dolly. She was in the terminal stages of metastasized breast cancer and died a month later. We spoke of Dad and Dolly and the broken dreams of their later years. When I told him about this book, he remarked that the collapse of their lives was a story that needed to be told. "I loved them both," he said. "It's the stuff of tragedy, and the film waits to be made!"

33

Trade Winds

AFTER DAD'S DEATH in May 1984, I took a week off. Bureau Chief Bill Kovach, a Tennessean recruited by the *New York Times* after covering civil rights for Southern newspapers, offered more time, but a voice in the wings, raspy and grinding, shouted, "Stop goofing off!"

Congress had just passed the Caribbean Basin Initiative to give seventeen countries duty-free access to US markets. Americans bought Caribbean baseballs, shirts, skirts, and underwear, and they were a natural market for a lot more. I proposed to look at the implications for jobs in Haiti, the poorest country in the hemisphere. Kovach and Business Editor John Lee, a whip-smart, mannerly Virginian, okayed the idea. "At times like this, work is often the best cure," Kovach said.

The two weeks I spent in Haiti were both exciting and ghastly. The country was engrossing, spellbinding, and all-consuming, the most screwed-up place I'd ever visited—and a fantastic assignment! The first sign that I was somewhere different, by order of magnitude, was on the flight from Las Americas International Airport in Santo Domingo, Dominican Republic. Over those central highlands of the shared island of Hispaniola, deforestation was unmistakable. On the Dominican side were healthy trees; on the Haitian side, only stumps, after thousands of cuts of machetes. The poverty that drove people to such desperation was further evident in the metronomic taps I heard one morning from my hotel in the northern town of Cap-Haïtien. A young man in an adjacent field was hacking at a stout pine. The work seemed senseless—it took hours to sever one limb. But after that earlier sight from the air, I knew firewood was a kind of currency: this was how people survived.

Not since wartime Korea had I witnessed hardship on such a dystopic scale. How could you not want to help such an individual—or nation? Two-thirds of the workforce was unemployed and had to catch as catch can for daily bread. Begging was endemic. An American taking out small change sparked a riot.

While driving to Cap-Haïtien from Port-au-Prince, I saw several hundred people shouting and shoving at the locked gates of a grain storage warehouse in the port of Gonaïves. Tempers flared. Managers reneged on a promise to give food away, and people got roughed up. The police never came—and luckily, too, because they would have made the situation worse. I also met upper-class Haitians, who could afford Paris or the posh restaurants of Pétionville, a breezy suburb above Cité Soleil, the slums of Port-au-Prince. Such extremes summed up the country. Haiti had no middle class.

Institutions that functioned elsewhere and caused things to work because of a social compact were less apparent here. There was no way to check bribes and payoffs.

Everyone, from officials at the airport to public service workers, had a hand out. When I arrived, the country was at the tail end of thirty years under the authoritarian Duvaliers: first "Papa Doc" and then his son, president-for-life "Baby Doc." The Tonton Macoutes, the notorious Duvalier police force, were renamed National Security Volunteers, but they were hardly less toxic. Driving in Gonaïves, I got lost, so I asked a policeman for directions. Big mistake! Making himself at home in my Avis Ford, he unholstered a sidearm, rested it on his lap, and directed me to the middle of nowhere for a shakedown.

The new American policy was giving some enterprises and a few Haitian workers a new lease on life, and American executives and their Haitian counterparts spoke of it glowingly. Yet the amount of assistance for the country as a whole, everyone agreed, was a droplet. The prevailing Haitian wage was $2.65 a day, about as low as anywhere on the globe.

Since those days, Haiti, except for the catastrophic earthquake in 2010 and Hurricane Matthew in 2016, has remained under the radar. Washington's focus has long shifted from the Caribbean Basin Initiative to the spread of Islamic terrorism, Russian expansionism, the challenges of new technology, and the ascendancy of China.

Sometime around the turn of this century, Japan was replaced by China as the second-richest power in the world. But China, now a regular supplier of Walmart and Costco, never made the waves in the American psyche that Japan did. In the 1980s, with international trade as my beat, we as a country suddenly discovered that our vanquished enemy was eating our lunch.

The reaction was swift. The rising number of Japanese vehicles on US roads, a sign of consumer preferences in price and quality, led union stalwarts in Detroit to smash any Japanese cars they saw. Other protests, spurred by a richly valued yen, encouraged the Japanese to buy out such all-American entities as Universal Studios, Columbia Records, and even Rockefeller Center itself. For a time the AP's rent was collected by Mitsubishi Estate. Would we soon be calling Rockefeller Center Mitsubishi Center or even Hirohito Center?

Professor Ezra F. Vogel of Harvard University rubbed salt in the wound with a popular book, *Japan as Number One,* showing the apparent superiority of Japanese ways of doing business. He pointed to strike-free labor-management relations and an education system yielding superproductive workers. Everyone in Japan worshipped corporate efficiency, and all the freshest thinking about productivity came from the Land of the Rising Sun.

Yet at the same time the Japanese were accused of unfair trade practices. Tempers flared. American negotiators threatened and cajoled in steel, machine tools, autos, and semiconductors. The Japanese said the problem was less unfair trade than the failure of Americans to live within their means. Japanese goods were so entrenched at times that we were fighting ourselves—consumer against producer. To both the supporters and the bashers, I, and colleagues such as Stu Auerbach of the *Washington Post* and Ken Bacon of the *Wall Street Journal,* protested "a plague on both your houses," and we felt the heat from both sides. "Once that happens," Auerbach noted after a White House briefing, "you've got the story about right."

Lobbyists were everywhere and nowhere. In Japanese, the term for *lobby* literally means "action behind the curtains," not unlike *kabuki,* the stylized Japanese drama, which was also in play. Tokyo had just accepted "voluntary" quotas on auto exports, for example, even though there was nothing at all voluntary about them.

Then everything suddenly changed. Sometime in the mid-1990s, we learned that Japan's amazing growth had been bolstered by huge corporate borrowing and speculative excesses. Instead of winning kudos, Japanese workers got the ax. Businesses and banks collapsed. Overextended positions were unwound into the next century. Joblessness spread, and conditions failed to improve for a decade and a half. That debacle was accompanied by an incredible 80 percent drop in Japan's stock market index. Although we had a sampler in 2008, our own Dow Jones had suffered nothing like it since the 1930s.

I visited the Far East in 1985 for the first time since my GI days to report how things looked from there. Conclusion: not all that bad for the United States. You could argue that our manufacturing base had been ravaged by unfairly low-priced imports. Yet consumers benefited from better goods and services and wider choices. Concurrently, Japan and South Korea were on their own feet, easing reconstruction burdens. And both made goods that their people, and our people, wanted—a lesson for US manufacturers, who seemed to take consumers for granted. Although our options as a nation were fewer, militarily we were still number one, integrated into widening structures of interdependence.

The trips I made dramatically showed how things had changed on the ground, which was most dramatic in Seoul, a city transformed from rubble: No more ragamuffin refugees, kids lined up for food by GI garbage cans. No more concertina wire, charred tanks, or odors of death. Now there were only well-dressed people, flashy cars, and silvery buildings rivaling Manhattan's. At Sajik Park, near building sites for new hotels, I met students from Yonsei University who were willing to practice their English.

When I said I'd been in the Korean War, they expressed polite interest. I broached the issue of life with North Korea, and they became more animated. "It's a prison," a red-cheeked female interjected. "I am sorry for the people." Her male companion added, "It will change someday, but only from the inside."

I arranged with the Foreign Ministry Press Office to return to Heartbreak Ridge, in what was called the Demilitarized Zone, or DMZ, dividing North and South, under control of South Korea's Twelfth Division. Getting there was a five-hour drive northeast from Seoul. A Foreign Ministry minder drove me in a navy blue government Kia, sharing the relatively new highway with other fast-moving Kias, Hyundais, and Daewoos.

My last time in South Korea had been in a GI truck, passing old men with huge loads on wooden A-frames, calling to mind the reflection of Archimedes that with a lever and the right place to stand he could move the world. There were no old men now. Except for the fact that there were no Japanese cars, these roads could have been interstate highways. Japan and South Korea refused to import each other's cars, but both joyfully sold to us.

The road seemed unusually wide. The reason was that in case of an attack by the North, the South could easily land troop transports to repel the invader. Somewhere in the north-central part of the peninsula, we entered a heavily forested upland of crude dirt roads. There were no more street lamps or signs, no improvements at all. The reason made strategic sense: to deny ease of access to any invader from the North.

These uplands were cold, as I remembered. We'd given up our sedan for an open army jeep, and now for the first time since my arrival, I felt tossed back in time. A South Korean military driver took over the driving. Peaks and ridgelines loomed, but I recognized nothing. Still there was the same freezing drizzle, and I tugged at a light jacket. We passed a squad of South Korean soldiers double-timing on a muddy sideroad, rifles forward at the ready. My heart went out to them.

At the crest of the last hill, we negotiated a high plateau. "Heartbreak Ridge!" the driver announced. I took his word for it; I saw no memorable landmarks—nothing, that is, except those ubiquitous roving searchlights. We stopped at a command post made of logs, sandbags, and engineering stakes. And suddenly, again as in the past, there was the scent of burning soft coal, and I had a sudden urge to palaver with buddies and spoon C-rations around a potbellied stove. Stepping out of the shadows, Colonel R. S. Moon of the Sixty-Fifth Artillery Battalion of the South Korean Army welcomed me. He was squat and solidly built with vigilant eyes. He invited me in from the cold, and toward a potbellied stove, its lid red hot, open burlap sacks of soft coal to one side.

Colonel Moon had apparently been dispatched as my greeter. He read a little speech prepared in English, expressing the "deep thanks" of the Korean people for the sacrifices of the United States. "We will never forget," he said. I acknowledged his thanks and explained my own insignificant role as a medic.

Outside again, we approached the wire and mesh fence along the edge of the ridge, interspersed with barbed wire, guard posts, flood lamps and more searchlights. Here was no man's land, but then I suddenly realized why so little was familiar. After so many years, vegetation had returned to a once scarred landscape that was now a fresh upland forest.

Private Soon Chul Aum, a draftee from Chunchon, the nearest big town twenty or so miles south, joined us. He'd been on patrol in one of those valleys of the shadow of death. The DMZ stretched two kilometers (one and a quarter miles) north and south of the line, and both sides regularly sent out patrols, the colonel explained.

"And what did you see?" I asked Private Soon.

"Rabbits," he replied.

34

Merry-Go-Round

IF YOU'RE A Washington reporter too preoccupied to travel to the ends of the earth, the ends of the earth usually come to you. Other countries' leaders visit often, trying to cajole money, weaponry, and other favors. Sometimes they hold press conferences and even sit down exclusively with the *New York Times.*

I saw two such leaders, President Mobutu Sese Seko of Zaire, now the Republic of the Congo, Africa's second-largest country after Algeria, and President Nursultan A. Nazarbaev of Kazakhstan, the largest and richest country of Central Asia. Mobutu came in December 1986, and Nazarbaev in July 1990. Both angled for US political support and economic aid and seemed to quite enjoy the capital's three-ring circus.

Mobutu had already ruled the former Belgian Congo for two decades, and he would hold on to power for another eleven years. When rebels took Kinshasa in May 1997, he went into exile in Morocco and died of prostate cancer four months later in Rabat. At the time of this writing, Nazarbaev remains in power in Kazakhstan, having already begun his fourth presidential term and his third decade in office.

The site of the Mobutu interview was the newly renovated Willard Hotel, a couple of blocks from the White House, where Zaire's leader had just seen President Reagan. They hit it off. Mobutu, a stout anticommunist, channeled covert American aid to Jonas Savimbi's rebels in Angola, who were fighting a left-wing regime. But Zaire's economy, despite hundreds of millions of dollars from the International Monetary Fund and the World Bank and $70 million a year from the United States, was still a shambles after years of mismanagement and corruption. Upon Mobutu's arrival in Washington, one dissident, Serge Mukendi, charged that Mobutu had amassed a fortune of as much as $5 billion, more than the country's total foreign debt. Besides being charged with looting the country, Mobutu stood accused of human rights abuses.

We were in the Willard's grand ballroom. Wearing his signature leopard-skin toque, glasses, and ceremonial robes, Mobutu sat at the center of a row of gilt chairs. At least a dozen members of his cabinet, similarly dressed, were on either side. I sat opposite. These days such a show would make YouTube or Twitter. I addressed him as "Mr. President," lacking breath deep enough for his full name: Mobutu Sese Seko Nkuku Ngbandu Wa Za Banga, which translates into "the powerful warrior who, because of his endurance and inflexible will to win, goes from conquest to conquest, leaving fire in his wake."

My first question dealt with charges of corruption and personal aggrandizement. He was reputed to own chateaus in Europe and to charter Concordes from Kinshasa to Paris for shopping expeditions. I cited reports that he might be the world's richest man and that he personally could repay Zaire's total foreign debt. "Is your wealth greater than Zaire's total debt?" I asked.

He looked hostilely at me, as if he were weighing feeding me to the lions, but then, turning first to the right and then to the left, began to laugh, as if what he'd just heard were the funniest thing in the world. Every lackey in every chair laughed, too, and some of them even clapped and stomped their feet. The hilarity continued for a couple of minutes, then he gave a long-winded answer about his "penury." He said he was not allowed to live beyond a budget that is published every year and known "down to the last centime." He added, "I know that we disturb people in some ways and make them unhappy, and so they do everything they can to bring me down. The person that you call Mobutu and his country are victims of disinformation. I rule only through popular support."

Mobutu maintained warm relations with the United States until the collapse of communism at the end of the 1980s. Washington pressured him to democratize, but he never did. Eventually, in 1993, he planned another visit to Washington, to ask for help once again. But a new president, Bill Clinton, and a new secretary of state, Warren Christopher, refused a visa. Mobutu clung to power for four more years.

Nursultan Nazarbaev, the son of a shepherd, had risen in the ranks of the Communist Party as a Kazakh smelter worker. He received me more modestly at the Madison Hotel, across the street from the *Washington Post*. He'd met with George H. W. Bush administration officials, members of Congress, and the American business community, trying to drum up interest in investing in the vast untapped oil, mineral, and food sectors of Kazakhstan. "We want a large number of American companies to work with us, and we understand that it has to be profitable for US businesses," he said, trying to showcase fresh capitalist credentials.

A totally unrelated matter put me off: he was chain-smoking. I had recently given up smoking, and now in the line of duty I was parting dense clouds just to see him. If only I could open a window! But the hotel's centralized temperature controls left the windows firmly shut. I weighed a walkout similar to my father's with Averell Harriman in 1951 in Tehran, but I decided that this was probably excessive and might even trigger an incident. I'd lived with cigarette smoke for years—since getting hooked by free packs in Korea. I was intensely curious about Nazarbaev's country and was already scheduled on the bureau list for a story. So I took an easier way out: like Bill Clinton, I didn't inhale.

The interview was in July 1990, only months before the dissolution of the Soviet Union, and the Soviets were behind on an estimated $2 billion to $4 billion of payments to foreign suppliers. US Treasury Secretary Nicholas F. Brady, a Yale classmate, told me that the timing of this mission, in which Nazarbaev was seeking business partnerships, couldn't have been worse. "Under today's conditions in the Soviet Union," Brady said, "it is difficult to make a profit, and US citizens are reluctant to go there."

But by the end of 1991, less than two years later, much of the earlier uncertainty had cleared. Nazarbaev won a presidential election in a country that had at least partly broken free from the Soviet Union. During the next three decades, as he clung to power, he built solid relationships with international companies on a number of joint ventures, mainly minerals extraction.

Critics accused him of corruption, nepotism, and suppression of political opposition. Yet unlike the Congo, Kazakhstan has shown an improving living standard and greater longevity. I gather, from those who have seen Nazarbaev more recently, that now he too has given up tobacco. Maybe he is even thanking me for not smoking.

35

O Canada!

SOON AFTER THE Nazarbaev interview, Foreign Editor Bernie Gwertzman gauged my interest in another posting. "No oceans this time," he said, "just puddles of fresh water."

"'O Canada'?" I asked.

"'O Canada'," he confirmed.

I had worked in Washington for fifteen years. Though absorbing a lot about the often nearly mindless way our government works, I burned myself out. Canadian news seemed more relaxed, and perhaps there would be cooler climes. I could report more of the stories I loved to write, about the way people live and work.

By this time, the spring of 1991, I had remarried. My wife, Elisavietta, was not unhappy about moving to Canada. Soon we were absorbed by the northern literary community, sipping Chablis with Margaret Atwood, basking in the clutter of Farley Mowat's digs by Lake Ontario, and agreeing that Robertson Davies's snowy beard, from the ivory tower of Massey College, made him look like God.

Although we barely knew Canada, it was a pretty civilized place, and its denizens had long ago learned to manage the cold. Large segments of its great cities were cozy underground. You could spend the winter in Montreal without galoshes or overcoat simply by ducking into the heated *ville souterraine* of shopping centers, restaurants, theaters, museums, and banks, all linked by gaily caparisoned corridors to metros and bus depots. Toronto and Edmonton offered similar refuges. Winnipeg added a paradise of skywalks.

Canadian cities tackled snow with ingenuity, mobilizing brigades to rid the streets of the unseemly piles of plowed snow that would otherwise clog things up till spring. In Toronto, from my new twelve-speed Raleigh bicycle, I marveled at the workers with their special melt machines under nocturnal floodlights, smoothly hosing tons of grubby snow and ice into the sewer system. We stayed in Canada five and a half years. In such an apparently docile, well-tempered place, there were no Pulitzers or *New York Times* Publisher's Awards. Yet what I found were people like ourselves, who, for some mysterious reason, we tended to ignore. I can think of no stories that I did not find compelling, or at times harrowing.

Ken Ward, a thirty-seven-year-old Enoch Cree from Alberta, tested positive for AIDS and decided that his mission was to tell his fellow braves about his condition and about the precautions they should be taking, which he himself had failed to take. At one point, after addressing a small group at the Whitecap Reservation near Saskatoon, he was in tears. "I do the best I can." He fingered a necklace of bear claws over a striking beadwork vest. "I try to show there is hope!"

Russel D. Ogden, a Simon Fraser University researcher, conducted a rare study on assisted suicide and found cases of bungled back-alley euthanasia, especially among those with AIDS. In one case, a victim's wrists were slit; in another, the victim was shot and killed. Two others were injected with pure heroin, and it was hours before they died.

Nine-year-old Christine Jessup disappeared after buying bubble gum in a shop in Queensville, Ontario. Three months later her body turned up with stab wounds and signs of sexual molestation. A neighbor, Guy Paul Morin, who kept bees and played the clarinet, was convicted of the murder and spent eighteen months in prison before DNA evidence cleared him. What triggered his prosecution was that he seemed odd, he was a loner, and he didn't talk the way other people talk. How many cases are there in the United States where incrimination results from a mere innocent divergence from the norm?! Yet for Canada, that case was so unusual that it haunted law enforcement for years.

Until living in Canada, I'd never appreciated its immensity. The largest country after Russia, it extended almost as many miles north to south as east to west. As a kid, I devoured polar adventures, such as *Hell on Ice* by Commander Edward Ellsberg, about a vessel trapped in pack ice in the Bering Strait. So I wasn't averse to acting out juvenile fantasies when in March 1992 I found myself in Grise Fiord, on the southern tip of Ellesmere Island, nine hundred miles from the North Pole, where I had an igloo-building lesson from Mayor Jaypatee Akeeagot. His Siberian Huskies were resting after running miles across the corrugated sea ice.

Despite my thermal parka, boots, socks, and gloves, I'd never been so cold. Akeeagot found matches he was never without, and from under layers of seal skin he produced a Coleman stove and tin cups. Out of that melt of pristine snow and ice, he made hot, strong, celestial tea. We were on Lady Ann Strait, where he hunted seal. Luckily for me, there were no seals that day—and no storms requiring refuge. If the latter had occurred, he said, he would have marked out a rough circle and used a daggerlike knife to carve ice and snow blocks. For the roof, he would have shaped a dome and punched out ventilation holes in case we wanted a cozy fire.

During that period of polar exploration, I ran into some hard news. A peripatetic island of freshwater ice, as large as Larchmont, New York, had just taken an unexpected turn south. Polar scientists named it Ice Island. In 1982 it had broken off from a glacier at the north of Ellesmere and had subsequently been used for studies on seafloor temperatures, ice dynamics, seismic refraction, and deep-earth structures, as well as for tracking US and Russian subs playing hide- and-seek around the North Pole. Integrated into the Polar Continental Shelf Project, Ice Island was expected to circumnavigate the pole for decades, yielding all sorts of precious data.

But during a long night in March 1992, ten years after its formation, Ice Island cracked into three segments. It was loaded with equipment from the National Research Council, an Ottawa scientific agency, and suddenly everything had to be removed: not just scientific instruments, but barracks, labs, a mess hall, an administration building, a weather station, and a minipower plant. Briefed at Resolute, 250 miles south, I hopped on a Twin Otter, Canada's twin-propeller workhorse of the North, to report for the *Times*. On the return, we picked up a few odds and ends. A bigger helicopter, a Sikorsky S-61, did heavier lifting.

The flight from Resolute took us over Cornwallis Island, a Mars-scape of bald, undulating hills streaked with silvery grays, greens, and blues. Light rippled from a remote, unfriendly sun. Less than an hour across the gelid sea, the Otter descended toward hellish pressure ridges. In the Arctic dusk, I made out a cluster of huts and a well-iced Maple Leaf. We hit the ground hard and taxied to a forklift.

Global warming was the culprit, despite the fact that the weather that day was pretty damn cold. Men, their faces barely visible in hooded jackets and balaclavas, stood by to load the Otter. Claude Brunet, a forty-two-year-old mechanic from Quebec and the manager of the recovery effort, said it would take two months to clear everything. Asked what would be last thing removed, he said, "The Maple Leaf." Complaints were few, reflecting the men's good pay and camaraderie. Their major worry was polar bears, the largest living land carnivore. The half-dozen men in the crew put all food away securely and kept their rifles close.

Although the men feared *Ursus maritimus*, it probably had a lot more to fear from them. Churchill, my later destination, on the western shore of Hudson's Bay, was a prime feeding zone and near the denning areas where the females give birth. Fresh water, flowing from the Churchill River, freezes by November, and winds push ice islets into open water where seals are plentiful. Famished bears, waking from hibernation, crowd the ice floes to reach the seals.

"By instinct, the bears know it's freeze-up time when they can gorge," Charles Jonkel, a bear biologist visiting from the University of Montana, told me. But, he noted, years of warming had reduced the sea ice, which meant that more bears now drowned in the open water. The US Geological Survey, which studies such things, projects that climate change will wipe out two-thirds of the polar bear population by 2050.

Humans and bears lived in unusually close proximity. In Churchill I met the keeper of the bear jail, a Manitoba Natural Resources deputy named Laury Brouzes, and accompanied him as he inspected the traps around the Churchill dump. Beefy, with Ray-Ban sunglasses and a sidearm, Brouzes told me, "My job is to protect people from the bears, and bears from the people." The melting of sea ice keeps bears foraging longer around inhabited zones, especially the local dumps.

From Brouzes I heard about one seven-hundred-pound male breaking into Lorraine Allen's kitchen while she was baking cupcakes. Ripping out a window frame in her double-wide modular home, it lumbered into the walk-in kitchen to gorge on delights on the cooling table. Summoned by radio phone, her husband ended the party with his shotgun.

The "jailhouse" was a twenty-pen Quonset in "downtown" Churchill. Any ursine loiterers were darted, individually tagged, and locked up for later transport. Nets borne by heavy-duty choppers returned them to the wild. But Brouzes warned that the encroachers got only one chance. Caught near the dump a second time, they are considered "recidivists" and are killed. I witnessed one return-to-the-wild operation. After a male was darted and put to sleep, cables lifted his ruglike mass of yellowish-white fur into the chopper's net. My photo in the *Times* possibly even reached Ursa Major.

I ran into yet another bear specialist, Malcolm A. Ramsay, a professor of vertebrate ecology at the University of Saskatchewan, with a group of graduate students who were studying contaminants, such as polychlorinated biphenyls (PCBs), in the food chain. PCBs, once used in coolant fluids, were later banned in most countries because of their toxicity. Polar bears sit atop the food chain, eating the seals that eat the cod that eat the plankton that eat the algae that eat the PCBs from old fridges and the like that have been dumped into rivers and lakes. As Ramsay put it, "Biology makes polar bears the blotter for all our environmental stresses."

Although the far north was not in the least boring, I had carte blanche to go where the stories were, and a couple of developments on Canada's Pacific coast seemed, as the French say, *vaut le voyage,* or worth the trip. One concerned changes in Vancouver as the result of an influx of tens of thousands of Asians in the past decade, including many from Hong Kong who were fleeing the Crown colony ahead of its scheduled return to China in 1997.

Vancouver, which counted 15 percent of its population as ethnic Chinese, was already a bustling Pacific Rim trading center. Gleaming towers, silvery hills, and crisscrossing ferries imparted the look of Hong Kong. More than 90 percent of the students at some schools were Chinese, and bilingual signs and Chinese newspapers seemed everywhere. Terms such as *feng shui,* harmony with spiritual forces, which Dad once tried to explain to me, were common.

Clashes broke out between these immigrants and older Canadians over such isues as competition for jobs, housing, and services; the violence of ethnic street gangs; clannishness; and even new patterns of residential building. Richer émigrés replaced traditional houses with "monster" houses: extra guest rooms, bathrooms, hot-tub rooms, and rec rooms, leaving no space for hedges and gardens.

Tung Chan, a Chinese member of the city council, accused critics of a double standard. "When a European has a large house," he said, "it's called a mansion—if a Chinese family, it's a 'monster house'." Yet it was important to avoid backlash. He cited a Chinese proverb: "Coming upon a river, follow the flow."

Windsor, Canada's southernmost city, between Lake St. Clair and Lake Erie and across the Detroit River from Detroit, is a tourist gateway and a manufacturing hub. Before the Civil War, word trickled out on Canada's enlightenment about slavery and made it a destination on the Underground Railroad.

Scarred by shackles and bullwhips, hunted by hounds and bounty hunters, escapees from Southern plantations made their way mostly at night. So great was the influx that just before the war, a quarter of Windsor's fifteen thousand inhabitants were former slaves, generating a storehouse of black history, with museums, Baptist churches, and mostly black settlements.

North Buxton, a village with two churches and tidy gardens, held the record, with more than one thousand black families. "For those researching roots, this is where they come," said Joyce Middleton, the head of the museum. Additional displays were at the North American Black Historical Museum at Amherstburg, along a narrow point of the Detroit River, which fugitives swam at night. During their walk north, the fugitives had only the Big Dipper and moss on the tree trunks as guides. The museum displayed artifacts from those who made it to Canada, including Elijah McCoy, the inventor of railroad lubrication systems, and Mary Ann Shadd, the first black woman publisher in North America, and one of the rare women ever, to edit a newspaper, the *Provincial Freeman* of Windsor.

As a boy growing up with a French mother in World War II, I'd heard about the islands of St. Pierre and Miquelon as symbols of France against the jackboots. Mom never visited there, but half a century later I did. After a French official in a blue military shirt stamped my passport "Port de St. Pierre," I downed a *grand crème* (coffee with cream) at a waterfront café in her memory.

Paris it wasn't. Yet St. Pierre looked and sounded like a French village. The streets were cobbled, the brasseries served mussels and skate-fish wings, and the language had a quick Parisian clip, or at times the clumpiness of Brittany or the Loire. Still, St. Pierre wasn't much bigger than that waterfront, and tiny French-made cars, with nowhere to go, went around and around until almost turning into butter.

The economic and population center of this place would fit inside Manhattan. Larger neighbors, Grande and Petite Miquelon, linked by sandy causeways across a windswept archipelago of lichen-carpeted rocks and gnarled junipers, were even more sparsely settled. The ferry from St. John's churned waters not far from where the *Titanic* sank. It was spring. There were no icebergs, but swells from prior storms swallowed us into those depths, then spewed us to high heaven.

I may well have been the last US reporter to set foot on St. Pierre, a place that doesn't exactly generate news. Yet beside that bow to my mother, I had other reasons for going. It was April 1994, and by then I was covering what seemed to be the likely secession of Quebec from Canada. Separatists, believing that Quebec got a raw deal in the federation, were again pressing for independence after their failure in 1980, and this time the polls said they'd win.

Ottawa had already agreed to a second referendum, and so besides taking the pulse of Quebec, I was testing the sentiment for or against independence in other francophone parts of North America. French was still spoken in pockets of Nova Scotia and New Brunswick and also as far west as Manitoba and Alberta. How committed were other French-speakers to supporting independence? Not very much, it turned out.

The deeper I delved, the more I found people who believed that independence was a distraction from bread-and-butter issues: lagging economic growth, the ravage of imports from Japan with déjà vu all over again from China, and the still rising oil prices. The boom years of the second half of the 1990s hadn't yet kicked in. The Quebec story, outside Quebec, was an old movie.

Another discovery was that despite St. Pierre's proximity to Quebec, two hundred miles across the Gulf of St. Lawrence, these islanders marched to a more distant drum. France, maintaining its toehold, paid the bills and kept the islanders on a generous allowance. St. Pierre was less worried about whether Canada would break up than whether France might turn off the spigot.

When President Charles de Gaulle visited in 1967, he pointed to the islanders as the symbol of France's past glories. Yet a few decades earlier it would have been hard to find any French influence at all, except perhaps in the Prohibition-era warehouses of Napoleon brandy. St. Pierre was the hub of Al Capone's bootleg empire as he weighed routes to the speakeasies of the United States.

French civil servants, who made up half the population, had now replaced the gangsters. To maintain its colony, Paris financed electricity, medical services, and sports facilities; flew in popular performers; and bankrolled frothy boulevard comedies. So with my eyes wide shut, I imagined myself in some chilly French resort and ordered another *grand crème*.

Yet inside Quebec, the buzz was frenetic, and it finally and totally dominated my routine. A referendum in 1980 had found 60 percent of eligible Quebec voters opposed to "sovereignty association." This time the question was simpler: Should Quebec "become sovereign"? Yes or no. Only Quebecers were allowed to vote, and all polls placed the yeas far ahead.

Secession was serious business. The last time it had occurred in North America was 1861. As October 30, 1995, approached, the framework of the new republic had been laid out, and people in high places panicked. In the end, the nays carried, but only by the narrowest of margins: 50.58 percent to 49.42 percent. Out of 5 million ballots cast, that was a margin of twenty-five thousand votes.

What a difference it would have made now turns into one of those great unanswered questions. Quebec is one-sixth of Canada's land mass, contains a quarter of the country's population, and rises practically to the North Pole. A new nation in that space might not have triggered civil war, but there was the probability of extensive low-level conflict—not a Bosnia or a Syria as much as a Northern Ireland. The English-speaking minority of Montreal and the eastern townships was already rebelling against draconian language laws, such as French-only street signs. An ugly term, Quebec Nazis, was coined, as English-speaking diehards swore to take up arms rather than submit. In case of secession, they might have found allies, with unpredictable consequences: A Boston brigade for Montreal? Albany contingents in Chicoutimi? In addition to dealing with surges in Iraq and Afghanistan, we could have faced incendiary tensions in Quebec.

Economically, the stakes also were high. Even minimum border formalities will slow down commerce. It took the European Community nearly four decades, from its founding in 1957 until 1993, to finally abolish all internal restrictions. With new internal restraints, Canada would have been headed in the opposite direction. Congress might have faced statehood negotiations with several Canadian provinces: the Maritimes, to offset intra-Canadian losses with greater access to the United States, or an underdeveloped Newfoundland, which would feel that loss in spades. Indeed, while still a British colony in the late 1940s, Newfoundland weighed joining the United States. Then British Columbia, Alberta, and Manitoba might also have checked out the Lower 48.

It took a while for the stakes to be realized. Although the polls favored the separatists, most observers figured that common sense would prevail, but it almost didn't. The single most decisive event was a mammoth demonstration in Montreal on Friday, October 27, 1995, three days before the scheduled vote. Approximately 150,000 souls poured into the city from across Canada in support of unity.

What started as a grassroots call for solidarity mushroomed into a dramatic national event that drew people from as far away as the Yukon, many of whom took advantage of cut-rate "unity fares" from trains, buses, and airlines. On top of the flag waving—never before had there been such forests of Maple Leafs—unity marchers spontaneously burst forth with the national anthem, "O Canada," loudly chanting, "Our home and native land. True patriot love in all thy sons' command." Banal words, perhaps, but poignant against the imminent prospects of dismemberment.

Barbara Williams, a writer from Toronto who was born in England but had been a Canadian all her adult life, was totally revved up among the thousands who shouted, waved, and sang. She hadn't slept, in anticipation of catching a 4:30 a.m. bus to Montreal. "I love this country," she said. "The best country in the world, and I had to do something to keep it together."

36

Oz

IN 1997 I had the distinction of being the first *New York Times* resident correspondent in Australia since Robert Trumbull, who wrote a World War II bestseller, *The Raft,* about downed airmen in the Pacific. Other notables had passed through, such as Sydney-born Jane Perlez, or South East Asia correspondent Seth Mydans. Jane and I worked together in Washington before she went off as a *Times* hotspot correspondent. Seth I met in Sydney.

It was January 1977 when Seth, Elisavietta, and I closed a restaurant one night swapping tales of paternal derring-do. Carl Mydans, Seth's father, was the *Life* photographer whose photos shaped impressions of the Depression and World War II. Carl and his wife, Seth's mother and *Life* reporter Shelly Smith, were prisoners of the Japanese in the Philippines for two years. That night in Sydney, Seth and I were sure our fathers had also known each other. They could have met around Number One Shimbun Alley. Carl Mydans headed *Time*'s Tokyo bureau while Dad was reporting on Angus Ward and Douglas MacArthur.

For Seth, newspaper reporting went back even farther. His maternal grandfather, Everett Wallace Smith, reported from New York and San Francisco before starting the journalism program at Stanford University. We found other overlaps. His grandparents, David and Leah Mydans, emigrated from Russia and settled near Boston, where Carl was born. Elisavietta's father, George L. Artamonoff, also emigrated from Russia.

George and his older brother, Ivan, the sons of General Leonid Artamonoff, served in the Red Army, then the White, and Ivan was killed. George was wounded and was rescued by an American medical team in the Crimea, and then, thanks to his early mastery of English, interpreted for US Navy doctors, first in a field hospital and later on a ship off Sebastopol. A recommendation of those doctors led George to Yale. While shoveling coal for room and board, he earned an engineering degree. After the attack on Pearl Harbor, he returned to military service, rose to colonel, and later headed the Marshall Plan's Tokyo office, where he too could have met Carl Mydans.

I worked a year in Australia, more or less as I had the previous six in Canada, visiting every region and staying long enough to report on what seemed fit to print. Yet life was closer to the edge. I was on a measly stringer's retainer, supplemented only if what I reported saw the printed page. No publication, no "pineapple," as our Aussie pals might have put it. Yet here too was another uncanny parallel with my father: both of us ended careers as low-paid stringers for the *Times*.

The arrangements took time to unravel, which meant long waits for pineapple. I maxed out my Visa card. After filing from Woomera, a town named for a device that adds thrust to the Aborigines' spears, I thought my next dateline might be debtors' prison. The Woomera story was about the closing of a satellite ground station called Nurrungar and the beefing up of a communications intercept site at Pine Gap, six hundred miles north, jointly operated by the Australian National Reconnaissance Office and the US National Security Agency—in other words, secret eavesdropping, surreptitiously reinforced. Even back then it was News Fit to Print!

Woomerians, close-lipped defense types, weren't authorized to comment on any of this, which gave me trouble. Luckily, everyone was hoopla about a *Star Wars* film opening at the local theater, loosening their lips enough to shake out a story line. As Darth Vader's Death Star blew up, Aussie and American personnel and squadrons of their kids whooped their delight, yielding the lead.

Help calls were eventually answered by a rush of backed-up funds, but we'd already gotten used to living low on the hog. In meeting what Elisavietta called "real" people and focusing on the more fascinating things about that overlooked continent, I shoehorned thirty-nine features into the paper that year from such places as Monkey Mia, Kangaroo Island, Kalgoorlie, Cardwell, and Alice Springs—easily a *Times* record from Down Under.

Our means of transport was a rented blue Toyota Corolla, which we learned to drive on the left side of the road. It took us across deserts, mountains, and coastal plains—via bed-and-breakfasts, which were cheaper than hotels and better for sources. We were tempted to sleep outdoors, but we were wary of spiders, snakes, and crocodiles with prior claims,

Nevertheless, we found campgrounds and fed on barbecued crocodile (which tastes like fishy chicken).

Invariably, when I produced a business card, we met incredulity—variations on the theme "What can *the New York Times* possibly find of interest here?" But when I explained a particular story idea, people generally warmed up and seemed flattered that a news outlet as grand as the *Times* cared. I thought what a wonderful profession it is that allows someone basically as shy as I am to go up to strangers in distant lands and get them to open up.

Since Elisavietta and I lived as vagabonds, the car transported not only us but our worldly chattels, including blankets, tablecloths, eating utensils, and spare clothes. Also somewhere was a Guardian double violin case with two nineteenth-century German violins. I'd played as a kid and had tried to keep up in Washington and Canada, joining occasional quartets and community orchestras.

I'd brought along Paganini's *24 Caprices* for solo violin, impossibly difficult yet transcendent works, and considered practicing in my spare time in the Outback. In my head was a tale, perhaps apocryphal, of the Bulgarian-Israeli pianist Alexis Weissenberg, who honed a concert career practicing many hours a day, months on end, in the Negev. I had nothing like that in mind, but I liked to play.

I found more-than-competent chamber musicians in Sydney, Adelaide, Coober Pedy, and Hobart; took lessons in Hobart from Constantine Lavroff, the concertmaster of the Tasmanian Symphony Orchestra; and eventually wrote an account of it all, entitled "Paganini in the Outback," for my former Washington violin teacher, Melissa Graybeal Ruof. She said she was "amused." Her rendition of one of the caprices during a home recital was my inspiration.

You can't report on Australia without a nod to its animal life. Thanks to separate evolution, 80 percent of its fauna is unique, such as the kangaroo, the koala, and the echidna (spiny anteater). Although Kangaroo Island, off the south coast near Adelaide, was not without its kangaroos, what drew us was a conflict over furry, big-eared koalas.

Koalas were—and still are—reproducing faster than their food supply. They eat only the mildly toxic leaves of eucalyptus trees. But the leaves had been overeaten and the trees were dying, threatening not only famine but also erosion. Koalas had been introduced decades earlier, along with platypuses, brush turkeys and wombats, as a shield from the rampant economic development on the mainland. Then, with no natural enemy, koalas duly flourished and reproduced like rabbits.

The conflict was over the local authorities' introduction of a koala sterilization program. "Sheer lunacy," said John Ayliffe, a farmer, adding that "sterilized koalas still eat, and that's the problem." According to David Bell, a retired airport supervisor, "Guns are cheaper. Sterilize five, and a randy sixth waits in the trees."

The authorities rejected killing, however. Drew Laslett, the wildlife officer in charge of sterilization, gave the official argument: "Our national icon falling dead from trees is hardly good for tourism." We toured the island with Laslett and several volunteers as they tried to put the new sterilization program into effect.

In the high branches of a eucalyptus tree known as manna gum, also called the "ice cream tree," two koalas, a male and a female, warily peered down through chewed leaves. I took Laslett's word about the sex. Volunteers with poles and gloves encouraged descent, but the usually gentle critters, terrified out of their wits, bit and clawed.

One of the volunteers, Tim Lashmar, who was planning a career in forestry, was bitten in the hand. Greg Johnson, the local veterinarian, who had converted a recreational vehicle into a mobile surgery unit, anesthetized the critter. "I'd hate to think how often I've done this on dogs and rams," said Johnsson. "But koalas!" The photo of koalic laparoscopy was the first, and probably the last, in the paper of record.

Other images emerged from the cameras on an Akela crane on Hill 210 in a Queensland rain forest. Far below that hill, near cycads, ferns, and orchids bordering a winding stream, signs in yellow and red warned of crocodiles in the billabongs (stagnant pools of backwater). Hours earlier I'd landed at Port Douglas, aka Hollywood West, a center for jungle filmmaking. Director Terrence Malick and an all-male cast, including Sean Penn, Nick Nolte, Woody Harrelson, and John Cusack, along with scores of technicians and extras, were re-creating Guadalcanal, the main island of the Solomons and the site of one of the bloodiest battles of World War II, in *The Thin Red Line* (1998).

The extras, sweaty in fatigues, pendant dog tags, and jauntily cocked helmets, huddled along the slopes, gripping their M1 rifles and preparing for an assault on the Japanese redoubt. Malick, commanding the extras, was reimagining the James Jones novel about Guadalcanal, where Jones himself was wounded. Wearing a cowboy hat against the rising sun,

Malick stood at the edge of a platform built out over the valley. Beside him, the crane, with remote-controlled lenses at its tip, was primed to record the assault. Malick's gray-black General Ulysses S. Grant beard glinted like gunmetal.

"Keep low and keep firing back." Malick used a megaphone to shout. But the voice itself seemed surprisingly soft, with a smooth Huck Finn kind of drawl. He was born in Ottawa, Illinois, the son of an oilman. "If one of you stumbles," he continued, "the others go on. Don't stop. Don't help a comrade. Think of waterskiing. Keep up with the boat." He went back to the monitor, leaving the controls to his Oscar-winning cinematographer John Toll.

Dash Mihok, an American actor, played a Charlie Company grunt. The character is outwardly sure of himself but deep down scared shitless. During the assault Dash lost his footing, which was not called for in the script. Malik cut, and Dash, now at the crest, berated himself, convinced he'd screwed up. "Dash wants to be Rambo," Malik cracked, and the actor cooled off. This movie was not about larger-than-life heroes who never falter, but average Joes who do. And that stumble didn't end up on the cutting-room floor.

The Thin Red Line figures on almost all lists of best war movies. Financially it didn't do badly either, grossing twice its budget of $52 million, and nominated for seven Academy Awards. But it runs nearly three hours. *Times* critic Janet Maslin sniped, "The heart-piercing moments that punctuate its rambling are glimpses of what a tighter film might have been."

Malick was trying to do too much, which was not necessarily bad. I saw both action and an almost poetic meditation on war, the kind of dissonant companionship you find, for instance, in John Milton's poems "L'Allegro" and "Il Penseroso," which got me thinking again of patrols and attempts to ease the pain of others, the beauty of breaking dawn over snow-capped Korean hills, and rabbits on Heartbreak Ridge.

In that rented Corolla, we maundered toward Darwin, then Broome to the northwest. I loved those mostly empty highways. The car was fleet as a solar wind. Storms, quakes, meteors, and the sun itself rounded those laterite hills. Over the serpentine Great Northern Highway, heat waves spired into cities, ever fading, ever re-forming, and at times we were surrounded by megaliths of sand and stone and rainbow fantasies of Sturt's desert rose, amaranthus, and agapanthus on walks to nowhere.

When heading into the sun, as we were when we approached Broome, we were forced into its blinding rays, and the going was rougher, with the realization that this was a shared road and that some vehicles were in your face. Especially at dusk, before the swift cut to night, it was possible for those unaccustomed to driving on the left to get mixed up.

This must be what happened on that road two years later. Robert Hughes, the Australian author of *The Fatal Shore*, living mostly in America but making periodic trips back home, was headed into the setting sun when he collided with a car coming east. I paid attention because I knew those highways and also because he was yet another hero of mine. His bestseller about the former penal colony was my main reason for asking for Australia, and he was among the sources I tapped while there. So I was anxious to find out exactly what happened. D. T. Max, in an essay in the *Times* Sunday magazine, concluded that after living so long in the United States (and driving on the right side of the road), Hughes got confused.

Another reason for paying attention was that having driven the same northern desert, we ourselves were nearly history. We'd been alone on two lanes for many miles before a distant rumble transmuted to thunder. Through swirls of dust, the headlights bore down on us of one three-trailer roadtrain inching ahead of another, their horns blasting in the night. I swerved onto a patch of desert. The roar passed, and we were back again to the buzz of flies.

An Aboriginal boy came into view, pedaling a rusty bike. As he approached, we waved and he waved back. And so in one of the least peopled parts of the earth, I started thinking about renewal, and it was in that brief interlude, after four decades in the business, that I decided maybe it really was time to retire. I thought about my own son Alex, already on his way to becoming a globe-trotting photojournalist (among his credits a magical *Newsweek* cover of Stockholm in transformative evening glow), who, after his grandfather's death, bicycled through most of the North American continent.

He started from Barbara Farnsworth Books, his mother's classy premises in the foothills of the Berkshires in West Cornwall, Connecticut. Both Alex and Andrew shared the chi of adventure and romance, but Alex, in keeping with what was already his chosen profession, expressed himself both on radio and in print. He arranged with a friend at radio station KBUT in Crested Butte, Colorado, to phone in his impressions every week. Here is one early entry, as recorded by KBUT:

This is Alex Farnsworth, reporting from Chardon, Ashtabula County, Ohio. I am traveling five times faster than the pioneers, and a fifth as fast as the modern automobile. I am traveling on the edge of what is old and what is new. I am riding my mountain bike from Connecticut to Crested Butte. I average 11–12 miles an hour. I have 15 pounds of gear. I am and have been on the road for a week. This first week was an eye-opening slice of the American pie.

I rode east to west across southern New York State. This was a grueling encounter with long six-mile ascents. I rode in and out of endless valleys on country roads, passing farms, huge, sparkling, sprawling reservoirs and rivers. I rode over the Catskills and the Alleghenies, and I think in New York State alone I've climbed enough feet to get me on the top of Mount Everest. I have had no flats and I don't expect to. A slightly modified mountain bike is a safer touring bike than any other bike I've seen. I travel dirt roads when I can. I ride over potholes, rocks, pebbles, grass, fearless of any damage. Sometimes this is necessary to avoid collisions with 18-wheelers. I have learned to take that deep breath before, rather than after, being passed by a truck.

In the past week I have been parched, hungry, burned, exhausted, drenched, cold and hot and robbed. I left my wallet at a pay phone in Corrie, Pennsylvania, for five minutes, only to come back to it $60 poorer. It is indeed a sad comment about America that in a poor industrial town where most people are on unemployment, some basic human values like honesty are compromised.

On the road, I see garbage, dead animals, but I also see lots of working farms. I am often alone for hours on some roads. I am alone on a big bike ride. In the towns where I stop to socialize I am often the talk of the town. People are amazed at my undertaking. As a result, people treat me to beers, food, and, on one occasion, I was offered a place to sleep. I have been included in dozens of prayers.

Many places I travel through surprisingly remind me of foreign countries, where people, when asked, have no knowledge of how far the next town is. Poverty does exist here, but people love and respect these bikes, especially kids for whom, presumably, I embody their dream of freedom. Right now I have nothing but flatlands ahead of me as I ride for the next three weeks on the old floors of an ancient inland sea.

I was impressed. West from Chardon, Ohio, Alex touched Lima, where his granddad was a police reporter, and later Cincinnati, where the old man did broadcast news for four years. So as Alex churned blue highways as a young radio correspondent, I thought, as someone said, history rhymes.

Yet again the industry finds itself in one of its periodic danders. Traditional organizations have long folded, and those remaining, including the AP and the *New York Times*, have seen better days. Most people don't even read newspapers, at least the tactile variety, instead getting sound bites from TV and online. Alex was probably influenced by some of the doomsaying when early on he put his eggs into the digital basket. He was handy, with his grandfather's knack for making things work. Photography and videos were in demand, thanks to the ubiquity of smart phones, Wi-Fi, YouTube, and other magic. And his impressions of the world were easily relayed by tablets and cell phones to proliferating outlets.

Years earlier I'd given Dad a tour of our Washington bureau. We were ditching typewriters for newfangled "black boxes" with their supposed "DNA of the future." He had respect for any new technology, which he probably inherited from Lank, who was among the first in Ashland with a Model T, telephone, and radio. Dad himself was handy splicing wires and repairing motors.

But while he, Lank, and my sons tended to see the good emerging from technology, I saw the bad—especially when, to groans in our Washington newsroom, all operating systems crashed, and I lost what I had just created on a screen—vaporized, poof!—forcing me, on deadline, into agonizing moments of reconstruction. "Save!" our technology guru Earl Smith bellowed. Many of us had, and it still did no good. Around that time I, for one, boned up on the Luddites and looked for looms to smash.

Change *is* painful. I should have gone lighter on the bashing and heavier on convincing myself of the benefits of change. Everyday a new app gives us news or information to save money and time, or to see the world in new ways. The changes are faster than ever, but the world adjusts, constantly upgrading the delivery system. In the 1730s, when John Peter Zenger's *New York Weekly Journal* accused the governor of New York of rigging elections, he set the type by hand in a clanking flatbed press. Those broadsheets sought to explicate the world around him, including the governor's corruption.

Apart from click-swift delivery systems, news today has similar contours, crying out for Zengers to take up the next case of rigged elections, warrantless wiretapping, Abu Ghraib, Watergate, or any monkey business by the high and mighty—or to give the background of a new movie, book, celebrity bash, earthquake, tidal wave, or murder. News and features are what we humans do.

Bibliography

Barber, Noel. *The Fall of Shanghai*. New York: Coward, McCann & Geoghegan, 1979.
Chang, Pang-Mei Natasha. *Bound Feet and Western Dress: A Memoir*. New York: Doubleday, 1997.
Forster, E. M. *A Passage to India*. London: Edward Arnold, 1924.
Hecht, Ben, and Charles MacArthur. *The Front Page*. New York: Samuel French, 1928.
Herken, Gregg. *The Georgetown Set: Friends and Rivals in Cold War Washington*. New York: Alfred A. Knopf, 2015.
Johnson, Paul. *Modern Times: The World from the Twenties to the Eighties*. New York: Harper, 1983.
Kennedy, Ed. *Ed Kennedy's War: Censorship and the Associated Press*. Baton Rouge, LA: Louisiana State University Press, 2012.
King, Steven C. *Flying the Hump to China*. Bloomington, IN: Author House, 2004.
Lelyveld, Joseph. *Great Soul: Mahatma Gandhi and His Struggle with India*. New York: Alfred A. Knopf, 2011.
Lynch, Michael. *The Chinese Civil War, 1945–49*. Oxford, UK: Osprey, 2010.
Matowitz, Thomas G. Jr. *Cleveland's National Air Race*. Charleston, SC: Arcadia, 2006.
McCullough, David. *Truman*. New York: Simon and Schuster, 1992.
Rooney, Andy. *My War*. New York: Public Affairs, 1995.
Serres, Alain. *And Picasso Painted Guernica*. Crows Nest, New South Wales: Allen & Unwin, 2010.
Tuchman, Barbara W. *Stilwell and the American Experience in China*. New York: Macmillan, 1970.
White, Theodore H., and Anna Lee Jacoby. *Thunder Out of China*. New York: William Sloane Associates, 1946.

Index

Abdullah I (king of Jordan), 51–54, 55
Abdullah II (king of Jordan), 54
Acheson, Dean, 130, 135, 142
Adenauer, Konrad, 198
Agence France Presse, 42
Agence Havas, 42
Agnelli, Gianni, 223
AIDS, stories on, 270
Alam, Chalfont, 13–16
Alexanderson, George, 73, 105
Allyson, June, 141
Alsop, Joe, 73, 74, 92–93
American Volunteer Group, 108
Ames, Ken, 171, 208
Ames, Rachel, 171–72
Anders, Irena, 57–58
Anders, Vladislaw, 56–58
Andrica, Ted, 19
Angleton, James Jesus, 188–89
AP: and Chinese civil war, 121; in Columbus, father's work for, xi, 5, 29, 30–32; correction in Lindbergh baby case, 33–34; father's forced resignation from, 103–4; and German surrender, 49–50; history of, 43; in India, father's work for, 62–66; rivals of, 42–43
AP in China, Chungking press hostel, 69–73
AP in Manhattan: author's visits to as child, 37, 38–39, 40–41, 43–45; Cable Desk, 41–42; commute to, 39; father's work for, 32–34, 36, 41–42; offices, described, 40–42
Apple, Johnny, 239

AP war correspondent, father as: departure for Russia, 45, 46–47; honorary rank, 47. *See also* China, father as war correspondent in
Arab Legion, 50–51
Arbose, Jules, 211
Argentina: father in, 147–48, 153; father's dumping of gun before entering, 39–40
Arnold, Henry (Hap), 84
Artamonoff, George L., 278–79
Ashland, Ohio: father's burial in, 259; father's early life in, xi, 3, 5, 7–8, 9, 11, 151
Ashland College, father at, 5, 12
Ashland Times Gazette, 12
assisted suicide, stories on, 270
Atcherley, David, 26
Atkins, Tommy, 182
Atkinson, Brooks, 71–72, 74, 75
Atoms for Peace, 201–2
Atwood, Margaret, 269
Auerbach, Stu, 262
Australia: animal life in, 280–81; author in, 278–83; filming of *The Thin Red Line* in, 281–82
Austria: and Cold War, 167. *See also* Vienna

B-29 Superfortresses: at Chengdu airfields, 83–84; father's ride-along in, 84–87
Bacon, Ken, 262
Bad Godesburg, Germany, 197, 198, 202–3
Baker, Newton D., 20–21
Baldwin, James, 190, 220–21

289

Bank for International Settlements (BIS), 223–24
Barber, Noel, 124
Barzani, Mustafa, 238
Beam, Jake, 208
Beardsley, Tony, x
Beatty, Morgan, 29, 32–33
Beauvoir, Simone de, 205
Beirut, father and Dolly in, 147, 148
Bell, Jim, 168
Bellino, Carmen, 175
Benedict, Hans, 172
Bergener, Al E. M., 17–22, 25, 28–29
Beria, Lavrenti, 145
Berlin, West: author and father in, 216–18; author's pedestrian crossing from East Berlin into, 199–201; drive through East Germany to, 199
Bernstein, Joe, 20
Bernstein, Theodore M., 184–85
Bethel, Tom, 249
Bethlehem, father in, 8
Biden, Joe, 249
Bilak, Vasil, 212–13
Binder, David, 170, 211
Black, Shirley Temple, 207–8
Blackstone, Harry, 13, 16
Blaha, Barbara Ann (author's first wife): divorce, 246; life after divorce, 246–47; married life, 174, 182, 184, 186, 196, 218, 236, 237; in Paris, 220
Blair, Bill, 192
Blessing, Karl, 226–27
Blumenthal, W. Michael, 107
Blunt, Anthony, 188
Bonn, father in, 198
Bouvier, Leon, 48
Brady, Nicholas F., 268
Brainin, Harry, 167
Braley, Russ, 216
Brewer, Eleanor, 188
Brewer, Sam Pope, 188
Brezhnev, Leonid, 204
The Bridge at Remagen (film), 204
Brinkley, David, 171
Brock, George W., 240

Broun, Heywood, 15, 41
Brouzes, Laury, 272
Brown, Malcolm, 246
Brunet, Claude, 271–72
Brunet, Jacques, 226–27
Brussels: author in, 201–2, 219–20; author's return to, after Prague invasion, 218
Buckley, William F., Jr., 190–91
Burgess, Guy, 188
Burma: Allied field clinic in, 81–82; allied operations along Burma Road, 65–66; Chinese offensive in, 79–82

Cairncross, John, 188
California: father and Dolly in, 240, 247–49; father's return to, to reconcile with Dolly, 251–54
Canada: arctic regions of, 270–73; author in, 269–77; management of cold and snow in, 269–70; and Quebec secession, 274–76; and Underground Railroad, 274
Cancellare, Frankie, 71, 77, 105, 138, 139
Canton Repository, 12, 13
Caribbean Basin Initiative, 260, 261
Carlos the Jackal, 232
Carswell, Horace S., Jr., 90–91
Carter, Jimmy, 116, 146
Cartier-Bresson, Henri, 220
Caruthers, Osgood, 170, 216, 243, 247
Cassidy, Henry J., 45, 47
CAT. *See* Civil Air Transport
Cauvet, Charles, *160*
censorship: in Chinese Civil War, 122–23; in World War II, 49–50, 70–71, 84–85, 88–89, 91
Chan, Anna, 93, 109–10
Chan, Tung, 273
Chassagne, Natasha, *160*, 243
Chennault, Anna, 93, 109–10, 251
Chennault, Claire Lee, *158*; and building of Chinese air force, 92, 108; on Chinese civil war, 116; Chinese fondness for, 111; and Civil Air Transport, 104, 107, 108, 110–11, 132; as commander of Fourteenth Air Force, xii, 87, 92, 108; described, 92–96; divorce from first

INDEX 291

wife, 93, 110; friendship with father, 104, 109–10, 114, 121; marriage to Anna Chan, 93, 109–10; and National Air Races, 25, 26
Chiang Ching-kuo, 128–29
Chiang Kai-shek: challenges faced by, 95–96; and flight to Taiwan, 128; and Maoist forces, 79, 99; relations with American generals, 94, 95, 97–98; US supporters of Mao and, 97; and World War II, 79, 80, 92
Chiang Kai-shek, Madam, 77, 92, 94
Chicago Tribune: father's work for, 99, 167–68, 169, 178, 198, 211–12; release of father, 233–34
China, communist: Cultural Revolution, 117–18, 129; holding of US diplomat, 129–32; and US intelligence, 132
China, father as war correspondent in, *158*; air bases, Japanese overrunning of, 87–88; American generals in, 92–98; arrival in, 67; assignment to, 64–65; career and, 126; Carswell's B-24 crash, 90–91; and censorship, 70–71, 84–85; and Changsha banquet, 76–77; and Changteh press junket, 74–76; at Chengdu airfields, 83–91; and Chinese Salween offensive, 79–82; in Chungking, 69–74, 97; and Colonel accused of mercy killing of US airman, 88–89; corruption in, 96; on death of friends, 84; under fire from Japanese, 75, 81; food and, 68, 69, 74, 81; and foot binding, 67; and "friend business," 70; graft among Chinese servants, 70; Japanese dropping of plague-infected food and clothing, 76; and journalists' misbehavior, 71, 73; in Kunming, 67–69, 102–3, *157*; and Kweilin airfields, demolition of, 87–88; and "mosquito press," 72–73; rats in, 69–70; rickshaws and sedan chairs in, 73, 74, 76, 77–78; ride-along for B-29 bombing raid, 84–87; ride-along for P-40 strafing run, 89–90; Teng-chung, Chinese attack on, 80–82; travel to, 66; US airmen in, before World War II, 92,

108; vice president Wallace in, 77–78. *See also* Chiang Kai-shek; Mao Tse-tung
China, postwar Shanghai: described, 104–5, 106; father and Dolly in, 104–7, 113–14, 120, 121, 124–26; Foreign Correspondents Club, ix, 99, 105, 120, 124–25; Jewish refugees in, 106–7, 120
Chindits, 65–66
Chinese air force, Chennault and, 92
Chinese civil war, xii; communist approach to Shanghai, 119, 121, 124–25; evacuation of Shanghai, 124–26; and failed US China policy, 113–17, 129–30, 132, 134; fall of Peking, 120; father's freeing of detained journalists, ix, 121, 122–24, 216; father's reporting on, 114–15, 116, 118–19; flight of foreign nationals, 121–22; and hyperinflation, 121; Nationalist flight to Taiwan, 128. *See also* Mao Tse-tung
Chou En-Lai, 96–97, 221
Chow, Mrs. Tommy, 74
Christian, Shirley, 116
Christopher, Warren, 267
Churchill, Winston, 65–66, 115, 182–83
Chu Teh, 96
CIA: and communist China, 132; and Shah of Iran, 146
Cincinnati, Ohio, father in, 162–65
Civil Air Transport (CAT): CIA and, 132; and fall of Shanghai, 125; father as PR man for, 104, 105–6, 107, 108–9, 110, 113, 114; fund-raising banquet for, 110; and Korean War, 132; origin and growth of, 108
Claiborne, Craig, 242
Clappier, Bernard, 224
Clark, Edgar E., 145, 172, 250
Clark, Katherine J., 172, 250
Cleveland News, father at, 5, 17–29
Cleveland Press, 19–20
Clinton, Bill, 267
Cochran, Jackie, 25
Collier, Joe, 15
Collins, Joe, 211

The Colony of Forever Peaceful Hill (C. A. Farnsworth), 72, 153
Columbus, father in, xi, 5, 29, 30–32, *155*
Coogan, Jackie, 66
Cooper, Kent, 47, 103, 217–18
Cornfield, Bernie, 228–31
Coslick, George M., 4
Cowan, Ed, 219
Cragg, Perry, 20, 22, 23–24, 105
Cromwell, John, 142
Cronin, Ray, Jr., 29
Cyprus conflict (1964), author's coverage of, 192–96
Czechoslovakia, Soviet invasion of: author's coverage of, 204–16; West's tolerance of, 210–11. *See also* Prague
Czolgosz, Leon, 18

Dali, Salvador, 143
Daniel, Clifton, 184–85, 209
Davidson, Ian, 202
Davies, John Paton, 97
Davies, Joseph E., *156*
Davies, Robertson, 269
Davis, Elmer, 91
Davis, Richard Harding, 205
Dean, William F., 136
death penalty: father's coverage of Pierpont execution, 31–32; father's views on, 32
De Carvalho, George, 193–94
Deep Throat (film), 223
de Gaulle, Charles, 201, 202, 206, 224, 225, 275
Dillinger, John, 30
Djilas, Milovan, 172
Doder, Dusko, 179–80, 247
Domei Tsushinsha, 42
Donleavy, J. P., 178
Donoghue, Ken, 178–79
Doolittle, Jimmy, 25
Dork, Eddie, 20
Dorn, Frank, 79–80
Downhold Club, 42
DPA (Deutsche Press Agentur), 42
drug legalization, author's views on, 44
Dubcek, Alexander, 204

Duggan, Dennis, 222–23
Dulles, Joan, 172
Dunning, John A., 88–90
Dvorak, Josef, 254–55

Earhart, Amelia, 25, 26–27
Ebony magazine, father's work for, 178
Eckstein, Burt, 149
Egypt: AP Cairo Bureau chief, 49–50; father in, 46–47, 48, 144; overthrow of King Farouk, 144
Eichmann, Adolf, 169
Eisenhower, Dwight D., 49, 68, 132
Eisenhower, Milton, 151
Eisenhower jackets, 68–69
Electric Auto Lite Company (Toledo), labor unrest (1934), 27–28
Ellington, Bill, 230–31
Ellsberg, Edward, 270
Ely, Charlie, 11–12
England, author in, 182–91
English Channel Tunnel, 202
environmental contaminants, 273
Epstein, Israel, 75, 77, 117–18
Erdman, Paul, 226–28
Erhard, Ludwig, 198–99
Estes, Billie Sol, 175–76
eugenics, 32
euro, introduction of, 224
Europe, US aid after World War II, 115
European Community: and euro, adoption of, 224; and hope for united Europe, 201–2
European currency disputes, 224–25, 226–27

Faisal II (king of Iraq), 54, 55–56
Fall of Shanghai (Barber), 124
Farnsworth, Alexander (son of author): adult life of, 247, 283; bike trip across US, 283–85; birth of, 174; early life of, 218; education, 175, 246–47; time with grandfather, 202–3, 234, 250
Farnsworth, Andrew (son of author): adult life of, 247, 283; birth of, 174; early life of, 218; education, 175, 246–47; and

grandfather's illness and death, 254–55, 256, 259; time with grandfather, 202–3, 234, 250

Farnsworth, Clyde A. (father), *155*, *156*, *157*, *158*; as absentee father, xi; advice to son on extramarital affair, 216–18; appearance of, 35; author's visit to in Vienna, 182; burial of, 259; death of, 100, 259; as editor for author, 152–53, 234–35; failing heath of, 248, 251, 253–59; fiction writing efforts, 72, 153–54, 234, 235–38; fitness routine of, 36; as frequently confused with son, ix–x; heart attack of, 236–37; late-life financial problems, 234, 236; late-life residence with author, 249–52, 254–56; as painter, 7; politics of, 28; reunion with family, 142; reunion with son, 141–42; visits with grandchildren, 182, 202–3, 234; visit to author in London, 189–90; work with author, 203; on World War II entry, 38; and writing of *Tangled Bylines*, xii–xiii, 238, 250, 254. *See also* Farnsworth, Marthe Herailh (author's mother); Prcic-Dittrich, Paula "Dolly" (father's second wife); *other specific topics*

Farnsworth, Clyde H. (author), *155*, *159*, *160*, *161*; childhood of, 33, 35–41, 43–45, 142; economic support for father, 236; education, 141; enlistment, 148; father's job offer to, 174; father's news-writing advice to, 152–53; as frequently confused with father, ix–x; marital problems, xi; Pulitzer submission for, 209; work with father, 203. *See also* Blaha, Barbara Ann (author's first wife); Ritchie, Elisavietta (author's second wife); *other specific topics*

Farnsworth, Frank (author's brother), 4, 100, 148, 180–81

Farnsworth, Guy (father's brother), 7, 240, 247–48

Farnsworth, Harry (father's brother), 7, 240

Farnsworth, Howard and Nancy (father's great-grandparents), 9

Farnsworth, "Lank" (father's grandfather), 3–5, 7–8, 9, 11, 12, 189

Farnsworth, Lydia (father's grandmother), 3–5, 7–8, 9, 11, 12, 189

Farnsworth, Marthe Herailh (author's mother): accent of, 36; appearance of, 35; children's financial support of, 36, 143; courtship, 5; death of, 217; divorce, x–xi, 142, 143; family's death in World War II, 103; as French speaker, 35–36; husband's affair with Dolly and, 99–100, 103, 111–12, 142; life after divorce, 143; and marital tensions, 29; married life, 21–22, 29, 33, 36, 37, 38, 45, 142; politics of, 28; on rejected suitors, 143; visits to France with children, 220; on World War II, 37–38

Farnsworth, Myrta McFrederick (author's grandmother), 7

Farnsworth, Olive (father's sister), 7, 240

Farnsworth, Oliver Frank (author's grandfather), 5, 7

Farnsworth, Suzanne Madeleine (author's sister), 33, 38, 100, 143, 148, 163, 240

Farouk (king of Egypt), 144

Faultless Rubber Works (Ashland, Ohio), 11–12

Felker, Clay, 230

Fellows, Larry, 182, 192

Ferguson, C. Vaughan, *156*

Feron, Jim, 182

fiction writing, father's efforts at, 72, 153–54, 234, 235–38

film industry in wartime China, 74

Finerty, Joseph, 255

Fisher, Violet, 73

Fisk, Jim, 228

Flanner, Janet, 220

Flying Tigers, 26, 90, 92, 108, 111

Fogarty, Jack, 163–65

Foote, Michael, 50, 52–53

Foreign Correspondents Club of Hong Kong, ix, 99, 127

Foreign Correspondents Club of Shanghai, ix, 99, 105, 120, 124–25

Forman, Harrison, 75, 76, 77

Forman, Milos, 205
Fornacca, Peter, 142
France: author's visit with mother to, 220. *See also* Paris
Franck, Martine, 220
Franco, Francisco, 42
Frank, Gerold, 18
Frankel, Max, 221, 243
Frayman, Joe, 211
Freedman, Emanuel, x, 195
Freund, Andreas, 211
Fuchs, Ernst, 170
Fuller, Keith, 180

Gainham, Sarah, 171
Gallombardo, Tony, 142
Gandhi, Mohandas K., 63–64
Garrison, Mark, 215
Gelb, Arthur, 174, 221
Gelder, Stuart, 73
Germany: father in, 198; post-war political status of, 198–99; reunification, father on, 199; Wittenberg, father in, 8–9. *See also* Berlin, West
Gideon's Trumpet (Lewis), 182
Gill, William J., 251
Gilmour, Eddie, 45
Giniger, Henry, 243
Glenn, Edgar E., *158*
global warming, 271–72
Glubb, John Bagot, 50–51
gold exchange standard, abandonment of, 221–22, 225
Gould, Jay, 228
Great Britain, and European Community, 202
Greenfield, James L., 200, 202
Gresham, Tatty, 249
Griffin, Oscar, Jr., 175–76
Grover, Preston, 63, 64–65, 103–4
Gruson, Sydney, 172, 182, 239, 241–43
Guatemala, father in, 151–52
Guernica, bombing of, 42
guns owned by father, 39–40
Guth, Oscar, *156*
Gwertzman, Bernie, 269

Haiti, author in, 260–61
Haizlip, Jim, *155*
Hamill, Pete, 223
Hamilton, Tom, 207
Hammond, Nicole, 240
Hammond, Warren, 163–64, 240
Handler, Mike, 170, 172
Hanna, Dan, 19–20, 28
Hanna, Mark, 19, 28
Harriman, W. Averell, 144–46
Harrison, Rex, 138
Hauptmann, Bruno Richard, 33–34
Havas, Charles-Louis, 42
Havel, Vaclav, 205
Hegener, Bill, 142
Heinemann, Erich, 227
Hemmerling, Larry, 142
Henry, O., 22
Henson, Henry, 18
Hershey, Robert D., Jr., *161*
Hess, John, *160*, 241–43
Higbee, Arthur, 220
Hill, Ernie, 144
Hill, Gladwin, 175
Hitler, Adolf, 37–38, 42, 56
Hoffa, Jimmy, 175, 200
Holley, Lillian, 30
Hong Kong, father in, xi, 99, 127–28
Hoover, J. Edgar, 13
Houdini, Harry, 16
Howard, Jack, 162
Ho Ying-chen, 68
Huang, J. L., 77–78
Huggins, Miller, 4
Hughes, Howard, 25
Hughes, Robert, 283
Hump, the, 66, 83
Humphrey, Charlie, 18
Hundertwasser, Friedensreich, 170
Hussein (king of Jordan), 54
Hussein, Faisal, 52
Hussein, Saddam, 56
Hussein ibn Ali (Sharif of Mecca), 52

India: father in, 62–66, 103; independence movement in, 63–64; and sexuality in Hinduism, 62

International Herald Tribune, 200
International Monetary Fund (IMF), 222, 266
International News Service (INS), 42, 43
Investors Overseas Service (IOS), 229–31
Iran: author in, 193; father in, 58–61, 101–2, 144–46, *156*; Islamic revolution in, 146; nationalization of oil industry, 144–45; postwar communist influence in, 145–46; poverty in, 61; US embassy hostage crisis in, 146
Iraq, father in, 54–58
Isaacs, Harold R., *158*
Israel: Abdullah I of Jordan and, 53–54; Eastern Europeans' flight to, 173

Jacoby, Anna Lee, *158*
Japan: economic decline of mid-1990s, 262–63; father in, 134–35; post-war success of, 134–35, 261–62
Jenkins, Graham, ix, 122–24, 216
Jessup, Christine, 270
Johansson, Carolina, 247
Johnson, Charles E., 177–78
Johnson, Lady Bird, 175
Johnson, Lyndon B., 175
Johnson, Paul, 117
Jones, James, 220
Jones, Russ, 216
Jonkel, Charles, 272
Jordan. *See* Transjordan
Journey Among Brave Men (Schmidt), 238

Kamm, Henry, 207, 209
Kaplan, Harold, 230
Kazakhstan, and US businesses, 267, 268–69
Keeler, Christine, 183
Kendrick, Marion, 33
Kennedy, Ed, 49–50
Kennedy, Jacqueline, 243, 245
Kennedy, John F., 175
Kennedy, Robert F., 175
Khomeini, Ruhollah, 146
Khrushchev, Nikita, 168
Kilder, Miroslav, 212–13
Kim Il-Sung, 135

Kingsbury, Bill, 85–86
Kirkpatrick, Clayton, 233
Klausner, Bertha, 154
Korean War: author as newspaper editor in, 149–50, 152–53; author in, 43, 132–33, 149–50, *159*, 282; Chinese intervention in, 136, 137; Civil Air Transport and, 132; communist takeover in China and, 117; early North Korean successes, 136; father's reporting on, 136–37; start of, 130, 135; Truman-MacArthur dispute on, 140; United Nations and, 135
Kovach, Bill, 260
Kubelka, Peter, 170
Kubelka, Susanna, 170
Kundera, Milan, 205
Kyodo news service, 42

Latin America, father in, 147–48, 151–52, 153
Lavroff, Constantine, 280
Lawrence, T. E., 52
Lawson, Colin, 170
Lazar, Josette, 220
Lee, Paul, 50
LeMay, Curtis, 83–84, 133
Lewis, Anthony, 182–83
Lewis, Flora, 41, 241–45
Lewis, Paul, 226
Liberty magazine, father's novelette in, 72, 153
Li Lihua, 74
Lillge, Richard, 149
Lim, Robert, 76
Lima, Ohio, father in, xi, 13–16, 17, 168
Lima Morning Star and Republican Gazette, father at, 5, 13–16, 17
Lindbergh, Anne Morrow, 33
Lindbergh, Charles, 13, 25, 33–34, 37
Lin Piao, 96, 116, 118
Liu Po-cheng, 118–19
Lochner, Louis, 41
London: author in, 174–75, 182–85, 186–88, 189–91; Speakers' Corner, 189–90; sporting clubs in, 184–85
Luns, Jo, 222
Lustig, Arnost, 205

Luther, Martin, 9
Lyons, Leonard "Kid," 19

MacArthur, Douglas: described, 134, 138; father's interview with, 134–35; and Korean War, 137, 140; meeting with Truman on Wake Island, 138–39; in occupied Japan, 134–35; support for Taiwan, 139–40
MacLaine, Shirley, 223
Maclean, Donald, 188
Makarios III (Archbishop of Cyprus), 195
Makley, Charles, 30–31
Malick, Terrence, 281–82
Malraux, André, 206
Manchuria, Soviet occupation of, 115–16, 135
Mao Sen, 123
Mao Tse-tung: early life of, 75; efforts to expel Japanese and, 79, 95, 96; exposure of real agenda, 113, 117; father's unfinished biography of, 235–38; and holding of US diplomat, 129–30; Soviet backing of, 113, 115–16, 128; takeover of China, ix, 99; and tension with Soviets, 128; US elements sympathetic to, 95, 96–97, 117–18; wooing of US journalists, 97
Markel, Lester, 185
Markley, Sarah Jane (grandfather's first wife), 8
Marshall, Henry H., 176
Maslin, Janet, 282
Matheny, Ralph, 3
Maxwell, Don, 197–98, 233
McAllister, Gerry, 87–88, 111, 251
McBirney, A. R., 210
McCarthy, Mary, 220, 221
McClintock, Red, 4
McCormick, Robert R., 168
McCoy, Elijah, 274
McDermott, William F., 143
McDonald, J. Clifford, 4, 5
McGovern, George, 249
McKay, Geo. J. J., 19
McKinley, William, 18–19

Mecklin, John, 168, 172
Medical World News, father's work for, 168, 234, 236
Melanchthon, Philipp, 8–9
Mencken, H. L., 33
Mende, Erich, 230
MI-5: recruiting of author, 187–88; and Shah of Iran, 146
Middleton, Drew, 219
Middleton, Joyce, 274
Mihok, Dash, 282
Miner, Harold B., *156*
mines: English closing of, 186; in Lallaing, France, author at, *160*; mine explosion (Millfield, Ohio. 1930), 24–25
Mintz, Jake, 24–25
Miquelon, Grande and Petite, 274
Molden, Fritz, 172
Molotov, Vyacheslav, 145
Molotsky, Irv, x
Monte Cassino, battle of, 56
Montgomery, Bernard, 47, 49
Moody, James, 121–22
Moody, Jimmy, 122
Mooney, Richard E., *161*, 221
Moosa, Nina, 72, 74
Moosa, Spencer, ix, 72–73, 74, 121
Morin, Guy Paul, 270
Morris, Joe Alex, Jr., 192–93
Morris, Joe Alex, Sr., 193
Mossadegh, Mohammad, 144, 145–46
Mount Vernon Daily Argus, 48
Moutbatten, Lord, 146–47
Mowat, Farley, 269
Mukendi, Serge, 266
Mydans, Carl, 278, 279
Mydans, Seth, 278
My War (Rooney), 69

Nahas, Mustafa, 144
National Air Races (Cleveland), 25–26, *155*
NATO, de Gaulle and, 201
Nazarbaev, Nursultan A., 266, 267–68
NBC, father's work for, 99, 168, 169
New Life Movement, 77

news organizations: current state of, 285; despotic rule in, 242
Newspaper Guild: formation of, 15–16; and news reading time, pay for, 41; scholarships from, 174, 246
News World Communications, 42
Newton, Bill, 105, 113, 114
New York Herald Tribune, author at, ix, x, 174, 175, 200, 222
New York Times: author at, x, *161*, 174–75, 182, 184; and family-friendly language, 71–72; father's work for, x, 99, 168, 169, 185; financial troubles of, 174; London Bureau staff, 182. *See also* Paris Bureau of *New York Times*
Niarchos, Stavros, 245
Night Falls on the City (Gainham), 171
Nixon, Richard M., 175, 211
Noonan, Frederick J., 27
North Korea: creation of, 135; Soviet support for, 135, 137. *See also* Korean War
North Sea oil rigs, author's coverage of, 186

Ogden, Russel D., 270
Ohio State Penitentiary: deadly fire at (1930), 22–24; execution of Pierpont at, 31–32
Onassis, Aristotle, 243–45
O'Neill, Bill, 127
OPEC (Organization of the Petroleum Exporting Countries), terrorist kidnapping of oil ministers (Vienna, 1975), 232
Operation Ajax, 146
Operation Matterhorn, 83–84
Oppenheimer, Joe, 42
Organization for Economic Cooperation and Development (OECD), 222
Ortoli, Francois-Xavier, 222
O'Sullivan, J. Reilly, 64–65, 68
O'Toole, Ed, *161*
Out of This Nettle (C. H. Farnsworth), 234–35

Pahlevi, Mohammed Reza, 58
Pahlevi, Reza Khan, 58
Palaski, Alphonse, 60

Palestine, father in, 50
Palestinian Liberation Organization, 54
Palmer, Lili, 138
Pan-American Exposition (Buffalo, 1901), 18–19
Paris: author's family apartment in, 221; author's visits to, 220
Paris Bureau of *New York Times*, 160; author's assignment to, 219–20; author's reporting error at, 224–25; author's reporting on economic issues from, 221–24, 226, 230–31; Lewis-Hess struggles at, 241–43; location of, 220; luminaries frequenting, 220–21; Sulzberger's visits to, 219, 221, 241
Pauley, Edwin W., 115–16
Paunzen, Gladys Buroker, 240, 247
Paunzen, Harry, 248
Paunzen, Peppi, 107, 114, 120, 240, 247
Pavel, Kitty, 207
Pearl Harbor attack, 37
Perlez, Jane, 278
Perón, Juan Domingo, 147
Persian Gulf Service Command, 59–60
Petroff, Igor, 187–88
Philby, Kim, 188–89
Pierpont, Harry, 30–32
Pitterman, Bruno, 172
Poland, in World War II, 56
polar bears, 272–73
police, and reporters, relationship between, 4, 39
Polish Army of the East, 56–57
polychloride biphenyls (PCBs), 273
Pompidou, Georges, 224
Powell, Dennis, 211
Prague: described, 206; Prague Spring, 204–5
Prague, during Soviet invasion: author in, 204–18; author's affair in, 216–18; author's use of local student interpreter, 212–14; father in, 211–12, 214, 215–16; resistance in, 209–10, 212, 213; and US embassy, 214–15
Prcic-Dittrich, Paula "Dolly" (father's second wife), 101, *159*; author's views

on, 100; background of, xi, 100–101; breast cancer of, 251; in California, 240, 247–49; character of, 203; in Cincinatti, 162–64; and collapse of father's first marriage, 111–12; death of, 259; described, 99; emotional breakdown of, 148; evacuation from Shanghai, 125; father's attraction to, 99; and father's career at Scripps Howard, 113; father's failed efforts to reconcile with, 251–54; and father's friends, 216; father's heart attack and, 236; and father's Mao biography, 236–37; and father's resignation from AP, 103–4; father's separations from, 148, 164–65, 198, 247–49; father's travels in Mideast and, 147; in Germany, 202–3; in Kunming, China, 102–3; length of father's relationship with, 100; in London, 189; marital problems, xi; marriage to author's father, 143; on Mossadegh, 145; origin of romance with father, 101–2; in Rome, 143–44; in Shanghai, 104–7, 113–14, 120; as translator, 146–47; in Uruguay, 148; in Vienna, 148, 153–54, 164, 166–67, 172–73, 179–80, 182
Profumo, John, 183
Prohibition, 44
Putnam, George P., 26

Quebec, secession movement in, 274–76
Queen Elizabeth 2, 185–86, 240

Radakrishnan, 63
Radio Free Czechoslovakia (RFC), 213
radio newscaster, father as, 162–65
Ramsay, Malcolm A., 273
Randal, Jonathan, 211
Randolph, Jack, 91
Rasputin, Maria, 21
Ravenholt, Albert, 79, *157*, *158*
Reagan, Ronald W., 266
Reed, Ernie, 178
Rehak, Peter, 207, 208, 214
religion, father on, 5

reporters: in Cleveland, badges worn by, 25, 29; late-life financial problems of, 238–39; marriage and, 246; and rules, obligation to break, 44
Reston, James (Scotty), 205, 221, 242
Reuter, Paul, 42
Reuters: and bombing of Guernica, 42; history of, 42–43
Rita (club singer), 132–33
Ritch, John and Svala, 249
Ritchie, Elisavietta (author's second wife), 99, 122, 239, 269, 278, 279–80, 282
Roberts, Filson, 12–13, 255
Roberts, Rankin, 75
Rockefeller Plaza (New York City), 38, 43–45, 262
Rogoff, Vladimir, ix, 121
Rome: author and wife in, 225; father and Dolly in, 143–44, 147
Rommel, Erwin, 46, 47
Rooney, Andy, 68–69
Roosevelt, Franklin D.: and Chinese civil war, 114, 115; death of, 115; and New Deal, 37; and World War II, 47, 58, 85, 91, 92, 97
Roosevelt, James, 230
Roosevelt, Kermit, Jr. "Kim," 146
Roosevelt, Theodore "Teddy," 18
Rosen, Art, 142
Rosenthal, Abe, 173, 174, 221, 224–25, 242
Ross, Charlie, 138, 139
Rousselot, Bob, 109
Rue, Larry, 168, 197, 199
Ruof, Melissa Graybeal, 280
Russell, Specks, 23–24
Russia: father denied entry to, 47; father's travel to, 45, 46–47

Sacco and Vanzetti case, 11–12
Sadler, Jerry, 60, 156
St. Petersburg Tourist News, father's work for, 3–5, 6
St Pierre Island, 274–75
Salik Bank, 227–28

INDEX

Salisbury, Harrison, 175, 221
Sanders, Harry, 137
Sarber, Jess, 30
Sartre, Jean-Paul, 205
Schmidt, Dana Adams, 238–39
Scripps Howard: father as reporter for, 5, 39, 99, 113, 141, 143; father's resignation from, 153. *See also* Chinese civil war
Seko, Mobutu Sese, 266–67
Service, John Stewart, 97
Shadd, Mary Ann, 274
Shah of Iran, installation of, 146
Shanghai Massacre, 79
Shapiro, Henry, 180
Shenkel, William T., 84
Sheppard, Sam, 22–23
Siegert, Alice, 199, 233
Sik, Ota, 204
Silberman, Pete, 107
Sinelnikov, Vadim, 75
Singlaub, John K., 116
Smedley, Alice, 96–97
Smith, Earl, 285
Smith, Everett Wallace, 278
Smith, Shelly, 278
Snow, Edgar, 96–97
Social Security, overseas correspondents and, 236
Sorge, Richard, 97
Souder, Ed, Jr., 114
sources, importance of buttering up, 4, 244
South Korea, author's visit to (1985), 263–65
Soviet Union: backing of Mao Tse-tung, 113, 115–16, 128; in Iran, 145; and North Korea, establishment of, 135; occupation of Manchuria, 115–16, 135; occupation of Poland, 56; secret agreement for landing of crippled US planes in, 85; spies in Great Britain, 187–88; and Yalta Conference, 115
Spanish Civil War, 42
Spear, Lou, 211
Stalin, Joseph, 47–48, 56, 83, 85, 115, 128, 135, 145

Starr, Don, 120, 167, 233
Starr, Mathilde, 120
Steagal, Howard, 176
Stein, Guenther, 75, 77
Stevens, Ted, 66
Stevenson, Adlai, 230
Stilwell, Joseph W., 79–80, 93–97
Stone, Walker, 113, 143, 153
stringers: author as, 279; financial troubles of, 174; newspaper financial troubles and, 174; as term, 167–68. *See also* Vienna, father's stringer service in
Sulzberger, Arthur Ochs, 219, 221, 241
Sulzberger, Carol Fox, 219
Sulzberger, Iphigene Ochs, 221
Sunday, Peggy, 200
Sunday Creek Coal Company mine explosion, 24–25
Sun Yat-sen, 95, 117, 129
Swiss banking scandals, 227–31
Szulc, Marianne, 217
Szulc, Tad, 205, 207–9, 211, 214

Taiwan: and Korean War, 140; Nationalist flight to, 128; prospering of, 129; Truman's refusal to support, 139–40
Talal (king of Jordan), 54
Tanner, Henry, 242, 243
Tatarian, Roger, 180
Teamsters Pension Fund, author's investigation of, 175
technology, and news business, 285
teletype technology, 43
Tenth Air Force, US, father with, 47
Thin Red Line, The (film), 281–82
Thomas, Norman, 28
Thomas, Preston, 24, 31, 32
Thomson, Milo, 32
Thomson Reuters, 43
Tillier, Alan, 208
Time magazine, father's work for, 99, 168, 169
Tito, Josef Broz, 146–47, 172
Tokyo, author in, 133
Toledo News-Bee, father at, 12

Toll, John, 282
Tong, Hollington K., 69, 71
Topping, Seymour, 202, 211
Transjordan, father in, 49–54
Travers, Harry, 222
Truman, Harry S.: and Chinese civil war, 113–14, 114–15, 116–17, 129, 132, 134; described, 134, 138; father's coverage of, 138–40, 185; and Iranian nationalization of oil industry, 144; and Korean War, 135, 140; low approval ratings of, 140; meeting with MacArthur on Wake Island, 138–39; press conference (October 1950), 139–40; and Taiwan, 139–40
Truman, Margaret, 185
Trumbull, Robert, 278
Tucker, George, 46–47
Tudeh (Iranian Communist) Party, 146
Tully, Andy, 139
Tuohy, Bill, 209
Turkey: author in, 195–96; and Cyprus conflict (1964), 192–96

Udet, Ernst, 26
Ulery, Charles A., 90
Underwood, Paul, x, 170
Ungerhauer, Friedl, 208
United Nations: father's reporting on, 137–38; and Korean War, 135
United Press (UP): author at, 174; history of, 42, 43
United Press International (UPI), history of, 42
Uruguay, father and Dolly in, 148

Vancouver, Asian migrants in, 273
Vesco, Robert, 231
Vicker, Ray, 246
Vienna: author's move to, 153–54; author's visit to father in, 182; cafés in, 167, 170–71, 181; Dolly in, 149, 153–54, 166–67, 172, 179–80, 182; father and Dolly's apartment in, 154, 162, 166–67, 248–49; father in, 166–73, 169, 179–80, 197–98; high suicide rate in, 171; terrorist kidnapping of OPEC oil ministers, 232
Vienna, father's stringer service in, 167–70; apprentices in, 177–81; closing of, 198; offer of work to author, 174
Vietnam War, 117, 190, 221
Vincent, Casey, 87
Vine, Ellen, 123, 124
Vine, George, ix, 122–24, 170, 216, 250–51, 259
Vogel, Ezra F., 262
Vogl, Frank, 230–31
Volcker, Paul A., 222
von Karajan, Herbert, 168, 169

Wallace, Henry, 77–78
Walzer, Elmer, 42
Ward, Angus, 129–32
Ward, Ken, 270
Washington, DC: author's assignment to, 245; author's residences in, 249–50; author's time in, 269
Waters, P. A., 16, 17
Watters, Mort, 163, 164
Wedemeyer, Albert C., 97–98, 117
Wedemeyer Report, 117
Wei, Jimmy, 70–71
Weiner, Tim, 128
Weiss, Buddy, 200
Weissenberg, Alexis, 280
West, Jim, 221
White, George, 27
White, Theodore H., *158*
White, Wyndham, 230
Whitney, Craig, 245
Wicker, Tom, 175
Wiesenthal, Simon, 169, 185
Willauer, Whiting, 108, 132
Williams, Barbara, 277
Williams, Jesse, 85
Williamson, George, 226, 230–31
Wingate, Orde, 65–66
Wingate's Raiders, 65–66
Wolf, Kurt, 120, 124
Wolff, Bernhard, 42
Wolff Agency, 42

Wong, Harvey, 128
World Bank, 266
World War I, deaths in, 37
World War II: debate on US entry, 37–38; father's unwillingness to return to US after, 103–4; Iran and, 58–61; Pearl Harbor attack, 37. *See also* Burma; China, father as war correspondent in; *other specific topics*

Wu, Butterfly, 74

Yalta Conference, 115
Yuan, Bennett, 125–26
Yueh, Hsueh, 76–77
Yugoslavia, Tito and, 146–47

Zaire, and US aid, 266–67
Zenger, John Peter, 233, 285